To
Barbara
Hepworth
with warm personal
regards and best
wishes

Pat Morse
8/18/95

AMERICA
TWICE BETRAYED

AMERICA
TWICE BETRAYED

Reversing Fifty Years
of Government Security Failure

George P. Morse

**With a Foreword by
John A. Walker, Jr.**

Bartleby Press
Silver Spring, Maryland

Printed in the United States of America

Published and Distributed by:

Bartleby Press
11141 Georgia Avenue
Silver Spring, Maryland 20902

Library of Congress Cataloging-in-Publication Data

Morse, George P., 1917-
    America twice betrayed : reversing fifty years of government security failure / George P. Morse ; with a foreword by John A. Walker.
        p.   cm.
    Includes index.
    ISBN 0-910155-32-1
    1. Official secrets—United States—History. 2. Espionage—United States—History. 3. National security—United States—History. I. Title.
    JK468.S4M64   1995
    327.12'0973—dc20   95-14067
                                                                      CIP

We gratefully acknowledge permission to use excerpts from the following:

From *The Glory and the Dream* by William Manchester. Copyright © 1973, 1974 by William Manchester. By permission of Little, Brown and Company.

From *Merchants of Treason* by Thomas B. Allen and Norman Polmar. Copyright © 1988 by Thomas B. Allen and Norman Polmar. Used by permission of Delacorte Press, a division of Bantam Doubleday Dell Publishing Group, Inc.

From *Without Precedent* by John G. Adams, with the permission of W.W. Norton & Company, Inc. Copyright © 1983 by John G. Adams.

From *Witness* by Whittaker Chambers. Copyright © 1952 by Whittaker Chambers. Reprinted by permission of Random House, Inc.

Contents

Acknowledgments

It is with very special pride and pleasure that I acknowledge, first and foremost, the invaluable contributions made to this publication by my son, Robert Morse. Without his careful, talented and persistent efforts, I would not have been able to complete this book and I thank him most affectionately.

I am grateful for the constant and patient assistance of my wife, Margaret. She has spent countless hours meticulously improving my work. Always calm and cheerful, she has made a joyful adventure from what otherwise would have been a burden.

Over a long period of time, I have relied on the wise and expert advice of my friend, Ward Warren and express my thanks for his selfless and experienced concern about the many areas and issues addressed in this book. This knowledge and sensitivity to the political and intelligence scene has been of great help in avoiding many pitfalls.

I owe so much to my dear friend, Dr. Malachi Martin for his wise counsel. A distinguished and bestselling author, he has been very patient in his guidance, yet firm and unswerving in his insistence on excellence.

Finally, two men, from afar, have represented for me what is the ideal American. Their service, courage, dedication and sacrifice for our country helped form, and reinforced, my conviction concerning the values and character a great nation requires of its citizens.

General Douglas MacArthur, whom I never met, was an authentic and fearless American hero. His military genius preserved the lives of countless American soldiers in the Pacific.

William J. Donovan was equally fearless and without superior as a patriot. Our association was not intimate and all too brief. Donovan's determination and dedication made possible an incomparable intelligence system, conceived by him alone and brought to fruition against great odds and opposition within his own government. It was a system that stood unmatched for years after his death.

We shall not see either of their like again.

Foreword

The most obvious person to evaluate a book about national security is one who has successfully penetrated that system. I should know. For a period of nearly eighteen years, I spied against the U.S. for the Soviet Union. By experience, I know the fatal weaknesses of the defenses designed by the government to protect its secrets.

As *America Twice Betrayed* so eloquently portrays, the list of spies is long, devastating and continuing, right up to the present day. And the American security system is failing to stem that frightening parade of spies.*

The reader may well ask: "Why is John Walker, a convicted spy, concerned about protecting America's secrets after all he has done to steal them?" I am guilty of stealing her secrets and I did this country great harm. I am eternally thankful that the long conflict with the Soviet Union did not develop into war. I thank God that, because of our strength, no other nation dared attack America. I willingly accept the penalty for my crimes and I take every opportunity, to the best of my ability, to make amends for the wrong I have done.

To that end, I have cooperated, while in both the maximum security prison in Marion, Illinois, and here in Atlanta, with the FBI, Naval Intelligence and National Security Agency, answering questions and providing detailed information on the successful techniques I used to compromise our security systems. I gladly assisted the author, George P. Morse, in his efforts to make the security system better and stronger to achieve his purpose of defeating those who would harm this country. I did this, not for any reward or benefit—none has been offered—but for the benefit of my country, hoping that it may dissuade others similarly tempted and, also, to provide guidance which will help America strengthen her defenses against future spies.

---

*I disagree with Mr. Morse when he refers to espionage as treason, an entirely different crime.

First and foremost, it is necessary to understand the answer to the question: "Why?" Why does an American commit espionage against his country? There are a number of answers to the question, and for some persons several answers may apply:

1. *Money.* The simplest of all reasons and one not requiring much explanation. What is not so simple, however, is to overcome the negligence on the part of security managers who fail to recognize the telltale signs of employee financial troubles or unaccountable assets.
2. *Venom.* In the hearts and minds of a significant number of persons, feelings of resentment, hatred, envy and vindictiveness make them susceptible to overtures from clever foreign agents who know how to exploit such weaknesses.
3. *Ideology.* Historically, as Mr. Morse clearly describes, it was far more typical for the person committing espionage to do so for ideological reasons. In this connection, the Soviet Union was by far the most benefited nation because of the wide appeal of Communism. Now largely discredited with the collapse of the Soviet Union, the philosophical influence was great among a wide range of classes, including intellectuals, academics, and religious and social reformers.

   Today, ideology is much less likely to be a motive for spying, but one's commitment to another nation and its needs and objectives is still a powerful influence. Other nations exert a similar pull on the emotions of Americans with ethnic ties to those nations. It is essential therefore that our intelligence and security managers be alert to these basic feelings which, perhaps unbidden, arise in people with great love for their nation of origin.
4. *Ego.* One may view a security system as an intellectual challenge which can be defeated by guile and skill. It is a massively complex project to accumulate information, remove it from a security area, contact a foreign agent, transport the material to the agent, all while concealing one's extra assets and avoiding the suspicion of friends and family. Still, one may consider espionage as the ultimate game of one man against myriad security officers.

While the above elements are the principal reasons that may induce one to spy, there are subtle influences as well. At this point, I could take the opportunity to describe the emotions and rationales that led to my involvement, but it would serve no useful purpose. What I did correctly evaluate was that our security systems were rife with problems and could be penetrated easily. In fact, the counter-espionage and security managers were so ineffective that I was never detected or suspected of criminal activity.

Mr. Morse clearly understands these problems, however. This book reflects an exceptional depth and intimacy of knowledge based upon scores of years as a practitioner and a student of "security." He has designed a unique, bold plan that is positive and effective.

—John A. Walker, Jr.
United States Penitentiary
Atlanta, Georgia

Introduction

For eighteen years—both in and out of military service—he assiduously pursued his chosen craft of espionage, blatantly stealing working papers of the Navy and the Defense Department. Not a single one of his supervisors seems to have ever suspected him; certainly no one ever tried to verify or disprove suspicions that may have been aroused. Not a single associate or co-worker ever indicated concern as documents vital to U.S. security were stolen and sold to America's deadliest enemy. When he retired from active service in the Navy, he successfully recruited his family and friends to carry on his traitorous "work."

Later we shall describe just how damaging John A. Walker, Jr.'s particular "work" of espionage was to America's vital interests and to America's position in the world—literally, to our very survival during the Cold War. What is almost impossible to believe is how easily Walker was able to obtain vital U.S. security information and how badly the U.S. security system, supposedly in place to protect America's vital secrets, actually functioned. This case poses a crucial question: did the United States have any real security system at all? It was assumed that we did. But that assumption was incorrect; the U.S. security system does not work, as the John A. Walker, Jr., case—just one of the more spectacular cases to come to light—proved.

I do not exaggerate; it is the system that does not work. The Walker case was in no way an exception. We sometimes heard during the Walker case, that "it was really not as harmful as all that; surely the damage any single spy could ever do is quite limited." In the Walker case it was even supposed by some that the FBI or the Office of Naval Intelligence had really known about Walker all along and had just let him go on feeding "disinformation" to the enemy. Forget it. These are self-serving justifications for the disasters of failed systems, and they are themselves deserving of severe punishment. Other cases have resulted from similar derelictions, and often it has been in wartime and not just during the "Cold War." Neither the FBI nor the Office of Naval Intelligence ever knew, or bothered to find out, anything about Walker's treasonable activities. Nor was it either our government's investigative arm or our government intelligence functions that ever found out about Walker and were thus eventually able to trap him. No, it was his wife. A traitor was only finally caught because of problems that arose in his personal and family life. And even then his wife had trouble convincing those responsible for our security shield of his espionage activities.

Nor was this the first time such an event had occurred. The great majority of spies and enemy agents have actually been uncovered by accident, or through exposure by the subject's relatives or defectors from the intelligence services of other nations. They have *not* generally been uncovered by our official government security, investigative, or intelligence systems.

In those instances when our government security services or agencies *have* identified a traitor, more often than not it has been because the suspect had some contact with the embassy of the foreign power involved. Embassies of enemy or unfriendly nations are normally put under surveillance for precisely this purpose (one commonly employed security measure that *has* worked, at least some of the time).

In truth, the Walker case was a major embarrassment for our investigative and intelligence systems. Unfortunately, it was one of many such embarrassments that occurred during the eighties and nineties, and had been occurring for some decades before that. After Walker was tried and convicted in August 1985, Secretary of Defense Caspar Weinberger issued the standard dose of phony medicine to the American public, saying that the Pentagon was "tightening security provisions for military officers with access to secrets and closing any possible loopholes . . . to minimize that kind of thing happening in the future." Nothing was "tightened." Nothing was done. Nothing was changed, as evidenced by the continuing "parade of traitors."

Meaningless words. Anyone knowledgeable about how the U.S. security system actually works, and how it has always worked since it was put in place after World War II, is necessarily highly skeptical of such claims by officials trying to reduce the amount of public embarrassment they must endure when a similar case is made public.

The fact is that we have no assurance at all that the Walker case is not being re-enacted today, over and over again, for the benefit of any number of our potential adversaries. Both in and out of the Department of Defense, it is likely that American secrets are still being compromised in ways similar to those which John Walker found so easy and effective to employ, for there is really no *effective* U.S. government security system in place to stem the hemorrhaging.

There is an *official* government security system in place, all right, but as the Walker case was only one of many cases to show, it is not and never has been an effective system. Now, as this book is being written, comes the case of CIA traitor Aldrich H. Ames, who began his career just as Walker was being arrested. Ames was directly responsible for the identification and execution of at least ten undercover agents working for the United States. Again, the litany of outrage and promised improvements has begun.

And if our U.S. government security system is in a bad way, our defense industries and defense suppliers are even worse, more sieve-like in their security than even the government agencies. For example:

- Our stealth bomber capability was sold to the Russians for a tiny fraction of its multi-billion-dollar costs.
- Classified documents on radar systems, missiles, and air defense were all sold by an employee of the Hughes Aircraft Corporation for a pittance.
- Secret, critical, and expensive American technology enabling submarines to evade sonar detection was illegally sold to the Soviet Union by a subsidiary of a major Japanese Company.

That a relatively low-level enlisted man such as John Walker could organize and carry on a "family business" of stealing, conveying, and selling highly classified documents for eighteen years, using colleagues and relatives in the Navy and the defense contractor system, speaks volumes about the quality of U.S. government security. Compounding the tragedy has been the abysmal failure of the government's counter-intelligence and surveillance capability, both that of the Navy and that of the FBI, to function in this and in other similar cases.

The truth is that the history of detection and apprehension of Americans working as spies for the Russians, and others, is far from a glorious record of skill, persistence and accomplishment on the part of our government intelligence and security "experts." The awesome efficiency and technical capability characterizing our security agencies assumed in spy thrillers is far from the reality.

America's security failure is not a recent phenomenon. During World War II, journalist Whittaker Chambers, a repentant Communist agent, identified high government official Alger Hiss as a fellow Soviet spy and supplied documentary proof of what he had revealed. Nevertheless, despite his urgent and persistent efforts, exerted at great personal cost, to supply the proof for what he was saying, he was not believed by American officials. His story came to be accepted only after heroic perseverance on his part in the face of rejection at nearly every level of the government, including the Roosevelt White House, and especially by the media. The truth only came out, years later, as a result of dramatic Congressional hearings in the course of which he was mercilessly pilloried. A man less willing to subject himself and his family to the unremitting vilification which Chambers suffered would never have persevered in making his story finally believed and tolerated such personal abuse for the sake of his country. Alger Hiss was finally indicted, tried, and convicted for his treason but then only on a lesser charge of perjury.

A history of more than a half century of our country demonstrates a general failure of the security system of the U.S. government, along with a marked inability of our intelligence and investigative agencies to detect espionage and other treasonable activity. This inability has been compounded by the relatively recent phenomenon of the greater willingness of people today to betray their country for money, often for less value, comparatively speaking, than Judas received in the thirty pieces of silver that was paid then. The combination of such factors has brought about a situation where vital American secrets are too often being traded in the international marketplace like commodities, or stocks and bonds.

Meanwhile, there are those who downgrade the importance of the whole issue, and who, especially today, argue that the changing times now make the protection of American secrets unnecessary. There are those who apparently believe that the whole idea of government security has become nothing but an anachronism of the Cold War.

Just a few short years after the Walker case was filling the headlines, America is now providing food and other aid to our new friends, the successor states of the now-dismantled Soviet Union. The Clinton Administration is giving hundreds of millions of dollars in aid to Russia, and one of President Clinton's close advisors, George Stephanopoulos, recently declared: "We spent $4 trillion defending this country against past threats, largely from the former Soviet Union. We can certainly invest a few hundred million in promoting reforms that will make us more secure in the future." President Bush's last ambassador to Moscow, Robert Strauss, made statements of a similar kind. Interestingly enough, the foodstuffs shipped to Russia in December 1990, included staples stored since 1948 in anticipation of another Soviet blockade of West Berlin!

On March 30, 1994, the Clinton Administration lifted export investigations on most computer and telecommunications equipment to Russia, Eastern Europe and China. In addition, the international Coordinating Committee for Multilateral Export Control was disbanded. Exporting nations were unable to reach agreement concerning a successor committee to control weapons-related exports to "countries of concern"— North Korea, Libya, Iran and Iraq, as well as nuclear and chemical weapons and missile technology. They will continue negotiating.

Concern has shifted away from security threats. In January 1992, for example, the FBI re-assigned 350 of its agents from counterespionage duties to the investigation of gangland crime in America's cities. While nobody will argue that domestic crime is not also a major problem, the fact remains that this country's end-of-the-Cold-War euphoria has already been proven to be highly illusory.

It was not love of liberty, but a failed economic system, that forced the old Soviet Union to give up its satellites and begin its desperate struggle to create a Western-style economic system. Even as Mikhail Gorbachev was talking about freedom in early 1991, Lithuanian and Latvian citizens were being murdered by Red Army troops as they tried to defend their democratically elected parliament and government. Even as Boris Yeltsin tried to concentrate the power he won after the failure of the anti-democratic coup of August 1991, and held through the violent confrontations with the Russian Parliament in October 1993, conflicts involving Russia raged on in Armenia, Azerbaijan, Georgia, and parts of Central Asia—not to speak of the continuing instability within Russia itself, and the very problematic nature of Boris Yeltsin's continued ability to go on ruling "democratically."

Reasonable claims were made by both former Soviet President Gorbachev and Georgian President Edward Shevardnadze, that the Yeltsin government was behind the violence seeking to overthrow Georgia's democratically elected government. Actions in Chechnya prove that Russian brutality still exists.

Potential conflicts have arisen out of the separation of Ukraine from Russia, where questions of nuclear disarmament appear to be far from resolved. Enormous problems threaten the whole area of the former Soviet Union because of the large number of ethnic Russians now settled in most of the ex-Soviet countries. The Russian government will certainly always feel obliged to protect these ethnic Russians should unrest occur in any of the countries where they are living and if her influence is reestablished in the process, so much the better for her always aggressive and voracious appetite.

Democracy has always had a particularly hard time in the land of the Czars. History *can* repeat itself. Following the February Revolution of March 12, 1917 (Russia still used the old Julian calendar before the 1917 revolution; that is why an event named for February actually occurred in March), Russia remained a democracy just nine months until the October Revolution of November 7, 1917. This latter event, the real "revolution," was a take-over of power by the Communists engineered by the Bolsheviks under the leadership of Lenin. There is still no assurance that the "democratic" revolution in the Russia of our own day is a permanent feature on the world scene.

Early in 1993, no less a personage than Alexander Solzhenitzyn was warning about what he called the "crazy idea" of a possible resurgence of Communism. "If, God forbid, Communism returns," Solzhenitzyn declared, "it will only unnecessarily prolong our torment for years, suppress all that is living, and anyhow will itself collapse in convulsions in the course of several years. But it immediately would bring back the coercion of the universal lie, and, above all, the Gulag."

As if to fulfill Solzhenitzyn's prophecy in a very ironic way, the elections of December 1993, brought to the fore Europe's most recent unabashed Fascist, Vladimir Zhirinovsky. Frankly aspiring to Stalin's old imperial mantle and dreaming of world conquest, Zhirinovsky saw his mis-named Liberal Democratic Party garner the largest single bloc of votes in these parliamentary elections. This kind of response registered by average Russian voters clearly reveals dangers ahead for those who would ignore that country's history. The December 1993, election results indicate widespread desire among Russian militants and the Russian military to see the Russian empire, and what they regard as Russia's greatness, restored. Mr. Zhirinovsky has surely given a wake-up call to any who may still be in a euphoric slumber about this ambition with his travels through Europe in late 1993 calling for such things as "the return of 300,000 Russian troops to East Germany," demanding "stifling war reparations from Bonn," threatening "to destroy Germany in World War III" should he come to power, and proposing "not to complete the Russian pull-out of 60,000 Russian soldiers stationed in Eastern Germany." Two years earlier Zhirinovsky had threatened to drop nuclear bombs on Germany if it interfered in any way in Russian affairs.

Zhirinovsky, of course, is an extremist, more than an extremist, a fanatic. Already, since his election he has alienated many of those who voted for him. But his election demonstrates the frustration felt by many Russians over attempts to move to a market economy. An extremist promising to return to Soviet power and respect but without the ridiculous threats of Zhirinovsky would have had more staying power. We have actually seen such extremists in power in Russia and in Eastern Europe. They do not pose an imaginary danger; they once converted the whole region into a wasteland and condemned millions of human beings to living deaths in prisons while they proceeded with plans to try to subjugate the entire world. Extremism and a spirit of aggression are thus alive and well and fighting for supremacy in the lands of the former Soviet Union, and there is no reason to believe that espionage and treason will not continue to be among the weapons they will employ.

The violence which followed Yeltsin's decrees attempting to define the terms of the country's "free" elections and, especially, his decree dissolving the Russian Parliament in October 1993, raises serious questions about whether Russia can really manage a true democratic system. Moreover, the results of the elections in December 1993 were hardly reassuring. Although Boris Yeltsin did get the new constitution he wanted providing for a strong executive, the extreme ultra-nationalist parties and the ex-Communist groups together outpolled the two largest parties favoring democratic reforms. Continued conflict between the president and parliament—with all the resultant instability that flows from that situation alone, to say nothing of the economic difficulties stemming from the dismantling of the former collectivist economy—would appear to be part of Russia's foreseeable future.

Throughout its history, beginning long before the Soviet Union and even before the Czars, Russia has been an expansionist, imperialistic power. Even the great Russian champion of democracy, Alexander Solzhenitzyn, has made statements claiming parts of other ex-Soviet republics as Russian soil.

On February 24, 1994, Russian President Boris Yeltsin, in a major Kremlin address, called for more Russian assertiveness in dealing with other nations and a slower approach to economic reform. According to *The Washington Post*, Yeltsin called Russia a "guarantor of stability" throughout the former Soviet Union and said the state of ethnic Russians living in neighboring countries is "our national affair." He warned East European countries not to join NATO without Russia and stated that Russia's foreign policy will be based upon "the promotion of Russia's national interests." While emphasizing "openness and cooperation," he said that "Russia has the right to act firmly and toughly when necessary." These plain words should make it easy for us to understand that Russia will remain our adversary in world affairs, at least on some critical issues. Their support of the Yugoslavian Serbs provides tangible evidence that

Yeltsin's words were not empty. Russia, as a minimum, will still remain a major nuclear power, possibly at the head of some type of alliance of some of the former Soviet republics. Such a new combination may not be as frightening as the old Soviet Union, but it would still be a major power center and a formidable future adversary if it should so choose.

In other words, there appears to be very little evidence that the end of the Cold War has eliminated the need for American government security, and for continued vigilance against the harm that can be done to America by her present and future enemies (and even by her friends!). There are still those who wish to secure and capitalize on vital American secrets, including valuable technical information, and they are willing to pay for these secrets.

The skilled and experienced espionage arm of the former Soviet Union remains in place, not only in Russia but in some of the other former Communist countries. These espionage arms have not been dismantled, and the available evidence indicates they will remain in operation, although there may be some shift in emphasis away from military intelligence over to commercial, scientific, and technological intelligence.

At his confirmation hearings in 1993, the new Clinton Administration CIA director, R. James Woolsey, noted that "economic intelligence is the hottest current topic in intelligence policy."

Following great conflicts the "victors" are too often almost willfully blind to further crises and dangers. This has been amply demonstrated in the periods following World War I, World War II, and the Cold War. The nations of America and Europe have been all too often reluctant to face yet *another* crisis. To demonstrate this at the present time we need look no farther than the inaction of the nations which did not stand up to the Soviet Union when faced with the bloody consequences of the break-up of the former Yugoslavia; all the "allies" seem to be vying with one another in looking the other way. Perhaps the high-water mark of post-Cold War cooperation has already come and gone in the marshaling of so many countries under the U.S. banner in the Gulf War to contain Iraq's Saddam Hussein.

We cannot take freedom and democracy for granted; they are fragile concepts everywhere, but especially as one moves farther east from Western Europe. This is especially true in countries which have already had a long history of harsh authoritarian rule. Ethnic and other hatreds seem to lurk not far below the surface, and bigotry, discrimination, and prejudice can break out at any time.

And what of other enemies of freedom around the world? Almost by definition some countries must remain enemies, or potential enemies, of the United States, which remains the world's great beacon of freedom as well as the world's chief protector against aggression. Does this not betoken a pattern of continued espionage directed against us, almost by definition? In the spring of 1990, for example, an American serviceman, Army Specialist Albert Sombolay, was convicted of spying for Iraq and Jordan during the summer of 1990, having passed deployment data, samples of chemical-weapon protection equipment, and identification documents to a Jordanian intelligence officer. As we all know, it was not long after that on January 16, 1991, that the Gulf War against Iraq began— espionage had thus been successfully carried out against America by agents of a country with which we would soon be engaged in a hot war.

Other countries, including Iran, Syria, Libya, and their allied terrorist organizations, have also stolen secrets from us and have used them against us. The remnants of the former East German secret police, the *Stasi*, as well as ousted members of the Russian KGB remain, not to speak of other Eastern European intelligence services. To whom might such specialists offer their skills and knowledge now? There is evidence that some of them are being employed by various radical nations and terrorist organizations hostile to the United States, some of which are currently attempting to acquire both nuclear arms and the ability to use them. The rigid Communist regime of North Korea, with its dangerous nuclear ambitions, immediately comes to mind.

Then there is Communist China, still committed to its own style of monolithic suppression of freedom and still focused on the United States as a major target of espionage. As recently as December 1993, Chinese intelligence agents were evidently engaged in stealing classified CIA documents from a Beijing hotel room that were carelessly left by a Pentagon official. A headline incident such as this demonstrates a number of things:

1) America continues to be a priority espionage target for foreign powers;
2) foreign intelligence agents will readily resort to illegal acts (such as, in this case, hotel room searches) as a matter of normal procedure in order to acquire the information they want;
3) some American officials apparently regard security as a matter of such small importance that they are capable of leaving CIA documents unguarded in a hotel room in a Communist country.

The truth is, as one intelligence official was quoted: "If you go to one of these places, unless you sleep with it under your pillow or bring it with you to dinner, it will be photographed. You should conduct yourself as if it is being routinely done—bugging rooms, searching rooms." The official commented that the Chinese, knowing very well who the Pentagon official was, no doubt made sure his room was accessible to searches. One U.S. press account of the incident concluded: "The Chinese intelligence services have a reputation for being aggressive spies against U.S. targets, according to security experts." The current post-Cold War era is perhaps not as benign as some people assume.

What about friendly nations? We are certainly not aggressive towards them. But we are not very vigilant either. And so they, too, steal our secrets from us. The Jonathan Pollard case, which we will review later, as well as the "accidental" 1967 sinking of the United States spy ship, *Liberty*, have certainly demonstrated the extent to which Israel, for example—not only a friend but virtually an ally—has been willing to go when it considered its interests to be in jeopardy.

More recently, with respect to Israel, there came to light in late 1993 the existence of an extensive information-gathering network conducted by the Anti-Defamation League of B'nai B'rith which regularly gathered and traded information with police departments and federal law officials, some of which was described as "legally confidential" material acquired through "official friends," and some of which, apparently, also found its way to the governments of Israel and South Africa. This, of course, is espionage in the classic sense, that is, the acquisition of desired security-type information through "agents."

Similarly, there have been major Japanese and European companies not only willing to acquire pirated American technology, but even to sell it to the former Soviet Union. There are no doubt elements in these and other countries even more willing to steal American secrets for their own competitive or military benefit. As time passes and circumstances change, other nations and organizations will have greater and greater desire and need for America's secrets. Unless our security capability is vastly improved, they will find it even easier to steal our secrets and compromise our programs than Communists and others have found it in the past.

This book has been written in order to call attention to the basic failure of U.S. government security programs to protect vital U.S. secrets. Indeed, it is my contention that the way security has traditionally been conceived and organized by the U.S. government makes it virtually *impossible* to protect our secrets. As I have already remarked, the system is fundamentally flawed. Americans generally have no idea how poorly our U.S. government security systems really function. The reality is that they do not work at all. An official security system in place which officials can point to, simply provides a false sense of security for many, even those inside the system.

In this book, I propose and present a new system of U.S. government security and new techniques which not only could make possible the successful performance of our security mission, and remedy many of the failures of the past, but could at the same time substantially reduce both the monetary and human costs associated with security. This should be attractive in these times in which budget-cutting is imperative. Yes, it could be done. In the final chapter of this book I outline a government security system that really would work—in contrast to the one we have now.

I have not taken on either lightly or light-heartedly the double task of criticizing our present government security arrangements and of laying out a plan for a new alternative security system which really would work, and which really would succeed in protecting America's vital secrets. As I indicated, I have been involved in the security business for over fifty years, for the greater part of that time in government security. I personally lived through, witnessed and was involved in some of the major developments in the U.S. security system during and following World War II. This book is the fruit of much that I have seen and reflected upon over those years.

The early portions of the book describe the history of the *futility*—it is impossible to forgo the use of this particular word, as will be abundantly seen in what follows—of so many of America's official efforts to protect its secrets. In order to demonstrate our long history of failure in preventing espionage, Chapter One surveys and catalogues some of the cases where the United States has been betrayed over the past half century and more. Further, it describes how various traitors were able to commit their crimes in spite of all our security efforts, how they finally did come to be identified and brought to justice (when they were!), and presents some of the consequences of their treasonable actions. I call this first chapter "Parade of Traitors," for that is what it represents. (We must never forget that the cases of the actions of the traitors we review are only a portion of the ones which were in fact brought to light, to say nothing of the treasonable acts which, though discovered, are never publicized, and thus, like much crime, are unknown.)

Chapter Two describes the growth and evolution of the official United States government security programs, including the exaggerated impact which the political climate in each important era had on these programs, and which, not incidentally, contributed so much to repetitions of the same old failures, as well as to the same old responses to these failures, year after year and decade after decade. Both the Truman and the Eisenhower Administrations are most strongly implicated in the failure to put a really effective security system in place, and subsequent administrations have done little or nothing to improve the situation.

Chapter Three describes the nation's current security program. Some Americans may be quite surprised to learn of what it actually consists and how it operates. They may be surprised, but they will not be reassured.

Chapter Four explains why the present U.S. government security system does not work and cannot work. It examines the primary assumptions upon which American government security programs have traditionally been based and analyzes how effective these programs really are. Certain security and investigative techniques are described which do not work and have never worked. It is necessary to consider the current moral climate in American society, so characterized, as it is, by a marked deterioration of standards, which only makes the security task harder.

Chapter Five discusses some of the moral and psychological factors which, especially today, are involved in such decisions as whether to yield to the temptation of easy money and to the excitement of betrayal of the official secrets to which one has been given access. We also address the methods through which Security Management entities can respond to these factors.

Chapter Six explores the continued relevancy of security in the era following the end of the Cold War, when, as we shall see, effective security continues to be essential.

Finally, Chapter Seven, presents a viable and practical solution to what by then should be seen by all as the persistent United States security debacle. My recommendations for better security management involve a whole new approach to the overall question of U.S. government security, an approach which can not only provide for greater protection for our national secrets, but also provide for enormous cost savings as well, savings of hundreds of millions of dollars for operations alone. This latter factor is surely not negligible in an era when the question of the federal deficit dominates our national debate. More than that, simply in terms of the recovery costs for compromised secrets and systems alone, the benefits of the new security management program will likely run into the billions of dollars!

But the driving force must be the preservation of our nation and the protection of our secrets. This we can—we must—do.

ONE

A Parade of Traitors

People today generally do not like to speak of "traitors" and of "treason." They are uncomfortable with these terms. These charged words may seem unnecessarily harsh. But unless we are willing to call things by their real names, the tendency to trivialize the subject of security will only be encouraged. The fact is that treason has been a dismayingly regular feature of our history, especially over the past two generations. Traitors have been uncovered with almost monotonous routine. By covering up with euphemisms what really takes place when a trust—or a country—is betrayed, we are well on the way to excusing conduct which is inexcusable.

Here are some of the damaging and often shocking instances over the past half century where persons have used their official positions and their access to sensitive or critical information to betray the United States.[1] "Betray" is the precise word which describes their behavior. We have chosen to include only those cases in which American traitors are involved, i.e., native born or naturalized, with all the rights, privileges and duties entailed. "The Report of the Royal Commission" of the Canadian Government, published on June 27, 1946, dramatically re-

---

[1]The information in this chapter comes from a wide variety of sources, including articles in *Time, Newsweek, The New York Times, The Washington Post, The Washington Star,* and *The Washington Times*; from numerous books such as *Family of Spies* by Peter Early; *Fifteen Years of Espionage* by Paul M. Joyal; *Friendly Spies* by Peter Schweizer; *Merchants of Treason* by Thomas Allen and Norman Polmar; *Moscow Station* by Ronald Kessler; *Who's Who in Espionage* by Ronald Payne and Christopher Dobson; *Spy/Counterspy: An Encyclopedia of Espionage* by Vincent and Nan Buranelli; and recent espionage cases by the Department of Defense Security Institute.

vealed that the Soviets were able to recruit a remarkably large number of Canadian citizens, particularly as the Report states (page 57) ". . . persons with an unusually high degree of education, and many were well regarded by those who worked with them in agencies and departments of the public service, as persons of marked ability and intelligence."

Moreover, we must not forget that virtually every treasonous act was made possible by a security neglect or failure at the management level of our government; these failures themselves constitute dereliction of duty, bordering on criminal negligence. Instances in which spies from other countries breached our security unaided are not included, although these instances were also permitted by our security management and performance failures.

Whenever possible, the impact and cost of each traitor's act has been included. Lives have been lost, our national treasure squandered, and our nation placed in peril. In fact, had a major war occurred between the United States and the Soviet Union, some of the information sold to the Soviets, such as plans for the defense of West Germany and cryptographic communications lists, would have cost thousands of lives and might, in some theaters, even have tipped the military balance in favor of the Soviets.

1936
John Farnsworth

John Farnsworth was a Navy lieutenant commander who was discharged in 1927 for borrowing money from an enlisted man. Later he began spying for the Japanese. He managed to do this by renewing contacts with his old Navy friends, discussing their new equipment and capabilities with them, and then reporting his findings to the Japanese. In 1934, however, Naval Intelligence discovered that he had a classified document in his possession, and he was placed under surveillance. Arrested in 1936, he was imprisoned in 1937.

1930's and 1941 - 1945
Soviet "Cells"

The Soviet Union began spying in the United States in 1927. With America's entry into World War II, the improved relations between the two countries, the abundance of material and the expanding Russian trading opportunities in the United States ushered in a golden age of espionage for the Soviet Union in America. The United States was reluctant to make a public issue of Soviet espionage and the Soviets knew that, at least during the war years, this was an opportunity to gather industrial, political and military-technical intelligence.

The Soviets had recruited many of their American traitors through "Study Circles" of Washington government employees during the 1930's, and these persons had continued their career ascents over the intervening years. It has been discovered that, by the time of the war years, the Soviets had, as a minimum, agents in the following agencies.

- Office of Strategic Services (Duncan Lee, Leonard Mins, Helen Tenney, J. Julius Joseph)
- Counter-Intelligence of the War Department (Donald Niven Wheeler)
- War Department (and, indirectly, the FBI) (William Ludwig Ullmann)
- Air Force (Abraham George Silverman)
- State Department (with access to the secret cable room of OSS) (Alger Hiss, Maurice Halperin, Robert T. Miller, Donald Hiss)
- Coordinator of Inter-American Affairs (Joseph Gregg, Bernard Redmont, William Z. Park)
- Justice Department (Norman Burster)
- Treasury Department (Harry Dexter White, Nathan Gregory Silvermaster, Harold Glasser, Solomon Adler, William Taylor, Sonia Gold)
- Foreign Economic Administration (Frank Coe, Allan Rosenberg, Lauchlin Currie, Philip Keeney, Michael Greenberg, Bela Gold)
- War Production Board (Irving Kaplan, Victor Perlo, John Abt, Edward Fitzgerald, Harry Magdoff)
- Department of Agriculture (Harold Ware, John Abt, Nathan Witt, Lee Pressman, Henry H. Collins, Bela Gold)
- Office of Price Administration (Charles Kramer, Victor Perlo)
- UNRRA (Solomon Leshinsky)
- Department of Commerce (William Remington, Nathan Witt)

These represent only those three cells which were revealed by defectors such as Elizabeth Bentley and Whittiker Chambers. It is believed that at least four other cells operated in Washington without ever being compromised. In fact, in 1943, the Soviets discontinued the use of cells and had all of its traitors deal directly with its formal espionage apparatus in order to minimize the exposure of other agents and traitors by additional defectors.

By the end of World War II, because of exposure by defecting Communists, denunciations by the House Un-American Activities Committee, the Senate Internal Security Committee, and revelations by individual Members of Congress and newspaper reporters, most of these infiltrators had resigned their government positions and quietly "faded away." As for the FBI, it was apparently unable to provide the evidence needed to prosecute them. Members of undetected cells have never been identified in a coordinated and coherent manner. This truly monumental scandal was never detailed in all its shocking magnitude and never will be.

1945
Amerasia

The magazine *Amerasia*, which pursued an editorial policy favorable to the Communist Chinese over the Nationalist Chinese, published a secret British report which appeared to have come from the OSS. As a consequence, both the OSS and the FBI separately searched the magazine's premises and located a substantial array of classified material which had indeed been removed from various government agencies without authorization.

The editor pleaded guilty to possession of classified documents, and a contributing writer Department of State employee, Emmanuel Larson, pleaded "nolo contendere;" both were fired. Other contributors, however, were cleared by a grand jury.

1946 - 1953
The Rosenbergs and Their Spy Ring

Julius and Ethel Rosenberg were born and raised in New York, children of Jewish immigrants. Both were involved in left wing and Communist causes during the 1930s, and both supported Stalin's 1939 pact with Hitler, American neutrality at the beginning of World War II in Europe (during the time Germany and the Soviet Union were allies), and immediate American intervention on the side of Russia after Hitler's attack on Russia—a pattern of opinions considered by experienced American security investigators to be strongly indicative of pro-Soviet and pro-Communist views—following the "party line," in other words.

The Rosenbergs were key members of a Soviet spy network which included some names which became quite well-known to newspaper readers of the day. They included:
- Klaus Fuchs, a German scientist, who worked on the wartime Manhattan Project organized to develop the atomic bomb. He came to work as a naturalized British citizen and supplied secret data to the ring's courier. The information supplied by Fuchs was by far the most valuable, resulting in a time savings for the Soviets of at least eighteen months in the development of their own nuclear weapons.
- Henry Gold, who had immigrated to the United States as a child with his Swiss-Jewish parents and had been spying for the Soviets since 1935. He was the ring's courier.

- David Greenglass, brother of Ethel Rosenberg, who enlisted in the United States Army and was eventually assigned to Los Alamos, where he served as a machinist.

Greenglass was drawn into the ring by his sister and brother-in-law. He reported to them on research performed and devices developed in the course of the Manhattan Project. He later stated that he could casually question the Los Alamos scientists about virtually any aspect of the Manhattan Project and receive complete explanations from them. His most important contribution was a description of the triggering mechanism for the atomic bomb. The network broke up in 1946 when Fuchs returned to England and Greenglass to civilian life.

The belated identification and capture of the members of the Rosenberg spy ring came about in the same serendipitous manner as in too many other successful acts of espionage against the United States.

In 1945, a Russian code clerk, Igor Gouzenko, defected to Canada and implicated the British scientist Dr. Allan Nunn May as having provided samples of U-233 and U-235 to the Soviets. May had also been associated with the research effort at the University of Chicago which had successfully brought about the first self-sustaining atomic chain reaction, and he had reported on all this to the Soviets as well. In one of his notebooks there was also a hand-written notation which read simply: "Fuchs." Even with this lead, it was not until 1950 that Klaus Fuchs was finally arrested in Great Britain. The confession of Fuchs led to the other members of the Rosenberg ring, as well as to Soviet spymaster Anatoly Yakovlev and to Morton Sobell, who had provided Yakovlev with data on U.S. rocket research from the laboratories of General Electric.

For their treason, the Rosenbergs were executed in the electric chair in 1953. David Greenglass was sentenced to 15 years in prison, Sobell to 30, Gold to 30, and Fuchs, in Great Britain, to 14.

For many years after the execution of the Rosenbergs, leftist and Communist apologists in America continued to claim they were innocent. In 1989, however, audio tapes recorded by none other than Russian leader Nikita S. Khrushchev were acquired and published in this country by *Time* magazine; what these tapes revealed should put the matter to rest once and for all. Khrushchev said: "I'll share a secret with you; we got assistance from some good people who helped us master the production of nuclear energy faster than we would have otherwise, and who helped us produce our first atom bomb." It is worth quoting these Khrushchev tapes at greater length because it is important to realize that the Rosenbergs really were guilty of the crime of treason for which they were executed:

These people suffered for what they believed in. They were committed to ideas. They were neither agents nor spies for the Soviet Union. Rather they were people sympathetic to our ideals. They acted on their progressive views, without seeking any payment. I say "progressive" because I don't think they were Communists. They did what they could to help the Soviet Union acquire the atomic bomb so that it could stand up to the United States of America. That was the issue of the times.

I don't mean to diminish the merits and accomplishments of our own scientists, but one must not discount the help that was provided to us by our friends. Those friends suffered; they were punished. But their names are known, and thanks to their help we were able to build the atom bomb. We did that to achieve equality.

I was part of Stalin's circle when he mentioned the Rosenbergs with warmth. I cannot specifically say what kind of help they gave us, but I heard from both Stalin and Molotov, then Minister of Foreign Affairs, that the Rosenbergs provided very significant help in accelerating the production of our atom bomb.

This remarkable testimony by Nikita S. Khrushchev should close the debate about whether or not the Rosenbergs were guilty of treason against the United States. If it hasn't, it may be because many people, for ideological and other reasons, do not care to scrutinize the acts too carefully and are unwilling to face up to the truth that too many of our citizens have proved to be traitors, whether for gold, for ideology, or both.

1948
Alger Hiss

Alger Hiss was a New Dealer of impeccable reputation, having graduated from Harvard Law School and having worked for the Agricultural Adjustment Administration, the Justice Department, and the State Department, as well as having been a staff member of the American delegation at the Yalta Conference between Roosevelt, Churchill, and Stalin in 1945. Hiss had served as secretary general at the United Nations Charter Convention in San Francisco, also in 1945—all in all, he appeared to be the quintessential American "establishment" figure, comfortably functioning at the highest levels of government, having been elevated by powerful supporters.

In 1939, however, Whittaker Chambers, a journalist and former Communist, had denounced Hiss as a Communist actively engaged in espionage; Chambers reported Hiss to then Assistant Secretary of State

Adolf A. Berle. Berle listened, and took notes on what Chambers was telling him, but otherwise did not act. Apparently, this high government official, to give his conduct the most favorable interpretation, was simply unable to credit either the idea or the fact of Communist subversion at high levels within the U.S. government or to take the allegations of Chambers seriously. In this he was to prove typical of many high government officials during the wartime and immediate postwar periods.

In 1945, Igor Gouzenko defected to Canada from the Soviet Embassy in Ottawa. He reported that there was an assistant to the U.S. Secretary of State who was a Communist agent, although Gouzenko did not know the agent's name.

When Whittaker Chambers re-emerged and repeated his charges concerning Hiss, this time publicly before the House Un-American Activities Committee, Hiss flatly denied the charge in testimony before the Committee and stated that he had never even met Chambers. Nevertheless, in continuing testimony, Chambers credibly claimed to have actually lived with the Hisses during a period of time in the 1930s, and he demonstrated a detailed familiarity with the Hiss home, household, and habits. As the case proceeded, Chambers accused Hiss directly of espionage and then produced some relevant notes in Hiss's handwriting as well as some typed copies of classified material allegedly copied by Mrs. Hiss. These copies matched some other letters typed by Mrs. Hiss.

Finally, Chambers produced a set of microfilms which he had temporarily hidden in a hollowed-out pumpkin on his farm in Maryland. The camera scratch marks on the film matched those of the camera used by the spy ring's photographer.

Hiss continued to claim that the typed documents were forgeries, but he was indicted and convicted of perjury in 1950. He was never charged with treason and he only served four years in prison on the lesser perjury charge. Over the next half century Hiss made numerous but unsuccessful attempts to have his conviction overturned, while denying the overwhelming evidence of his espionage. Meanwhile, he continued to enjoy surprising sympathy from much of the media and even now many people are absolutely determined to deny his guilt. As late as the 1990s, following the break-up of the Soviet Union, a Russian official was in the news claiming in an ambiguous statement that no evidence of treason by Hiss was to be found in KGB files. The Hiss case was, without question, one of the great "causes" of the postwar era in American history.

1949
Judith Coplon

As a young woman, Judith Coplon was already an open activist for Soviet causes, writing pro-Soviet editorials in her school newspaper and working actively in Russian war relief and similar causes.

Coplon was nevertheless able to pass a government security check for federal employment in a sensitive position. She was employed at the Department of Justice where she had access to FBI reports on foreign diplomats required to register in the United States. She frequently took some of the reports home, copied them, and supplied them to her Soviet contact. Eventually, she was exposed because information given to the Soviets was traced back to her and because of her requests for documents which were not germane to her job.

Although Judith Coplon was sentenced to twenty years in prison, her conviction was later reversed because of questions about the use of illegal wiretaps in investigating her.

1951
Morris Cohen

Morris Cohen was the son of Eastern European immigrants to the United States. He became a Communist sympathizer in his college years, fought on the Republican side in the Spanish Civil War, and later joined the U.S. Army. He and his wife, Lora, began performing espionage services for the Soviet Union before World War II. They served as a communications link with the Rosenbergs.

After the Rosenbergs were arrested, the Cohens fled the United States. In 1954 they turned up in Great Britain under the assumed names of Peter and Helen Kroger; there they continued to carry on their spying activities, serving as a communications link among several Communist networks. They were not arrested until 1961 when a tip from a defector led to the exposure of one of the rings with which they were connected and hence to the exposure of the Krogers themselves. They were convicted and sentenced to twenty years in prison. In 1969, however, they chose to go to the Soviet Union in an exchange of prisoners.

In 1994, at age 86, Cohen acknowledged his role in the theft of atomic secrets. The Russians substantiated this and that he had been the link to the unidentified Soviet mole, physicist "Perseus." The confirmation of the stolen data's authenticity had been that the notes of Klaus Fuchs and "Perseus" matched page-for-page.

1951 - 1983
Larry Wu-Tai Chin

Larry Wu-Tai Chin, a native Chinese, began serving as a translator for U.S. Army units in China in 1948. With the fall of Nationalist China to the Communists in 1949, Chin, who had joined the U.S. Consulate, moved to Hong Kong with that office.

Chin was first recruited by the Communist Chinese during the Korean War and provided them with information concerning the location and interrogation of Chinese prisoners of war. Later, Chin worked with the CIA's Foreign Broadcast Information Service (FBIS) on Okinawa. His job was to monitor Chinese broadcasts. Although Chin had never been granted a security clearance, he was nevertheless used to translate highly classified materials. In 1961, Chin was transferred to the FBIS facility in Santa Rosa, California, and, in 1970, he was transferred to Washington, D.C. At that point, routine security checks turned up nothing derogatory about him, and Chin was given a high security clearance.

Translators were often borrowed by the CIA from the FBIS and in this way, Chin came to see all manner of even the most sensitive documents. Moreover, compartmentalization requirements were frequently ignored. Thus, for years and on a continuing basis, Chin was able to remove, photograph, and then return CIA documents. To meet his handlers he traveled to Toronto and even to Hong Kong. In 1982, a Communist Chinese defector identified Chin as a turncoat. Although he had been paid between $500,000 and $1,000,000 dollars by the Chinese Communists over the years, and had recommended at least one man's relatives for potential use as hostages by the Chinese, Chin was still able to rationalize to others, and to himself, that the real motive for his espionage was to increase "understanding" between the United States and China. During his trial, after more than thirty years of active espionage, Larry Wu-Tai Chin committed suicide in his prison cell.

1952 - 1964
Robert Lee Johnson and James Mintkenbaugh

Army Sergeant Robert Lee Johnson first contacted the Soviets in 1952, offering to spy for them and then perhaps later defect to the Soviet Union. For a period Johnson photographed various materials from the U.S. Army's Berlin headquarters. Johnson recruited an Army buddy, Sergeant James Mintkenbaugh, to assist him.

After finishing their respective three-year hitches in the Army, both Johnson and Mintkenbaugh returned to the United States and were discharged. The Russians, however, contacted Johnson and instructed him to re-enlist in order to enable him to continue espionage work for them. In 1956, they gave orders to Mintkenbaugh to become a courier between certain Russian agents in the United States and Johnson. In 1959, Mintkenbaugh went to Moscow to attend a special spy school. Later, he returned to the United States and took a position in real estate as a cover for his espionage.

Domestic problems, as well as alcoholism, resulted in Johnson's disappearance in 1964. It was while investigating his disappearance that the FBI first learned from Johnson's wife of his treason. He was eventually found, tried, and sentenced to twenty-five years in prison. He was murdered in prison by his own son during a visit in 1972. Mintkenbaugh turned himself in, was tried and convicted, and was also sentenced to prison.

1957
George H. French

Air Force Captain George H. French actually promoted his brand of traffic in U.S. secrets by throwing a letter onto the grounds of the Soviet Embassy in Washington soliciting offers for the information he was able to provide on nuclear bombs. However, he was observed, and then captured, tried, convicted, and sentenced to life in prison.

1957
Nelson C. Drummond

Navy Yeoman Nelson C. Drummond supplied the Russians with defense-related dossiers and operations manuals taken from the Navy base in Newport, Rhode Island. It has been estimated that the U.S. Navy had to spend up to twenty million dollars in order to try to recover from some of the effects of his activities. Drummond was sentenced to life imprisonment.

Following the exposure of Aldrich Ames as a traitor to the United States, it became known that Drummond's identification had been due to the efforts of one of Ames's victims, Soviet GRU Major General Dimitri Fedorovich Polyakov, who served the United States from 1961 until his retirement in the late 1960's. General Polyakov was executed in 1988.

1959 - 1963
Jack Dunlap

Jack Dunlap was a U.S. Army enlisted man who served in Korea and was then assigned to the highly secret National Security Agency (NSA) as a chauffeur. Later he was promoted to a messenger position with the NSA. In 1959, he began to deliver secret information to the Soviets which he had acquired by concealing documents under his shirt.

At a certain point, the Dunlaps began to exhibit a much more lavish lifestyle, but NSA officials did not even notice the evidence of increased wealth and extravagance. However, some of his neighbors did. Dunlap put them off by claiming to have inherited a plantation.

In 1963, in order to avoid being transferred, Dunlap resigned from the military, but promptly went right back to work for the NSA as a civilian. Since the NSA, unlike the military and most government agencies, required civilians to take lie-detector tests, according to the official story of the time, Dunlap ended up incriminating himself. However, it was later reported that Dunlap had been uncovered by Soviet double agent Polyakov. Once a formal investigation of him began, he twice attempted to commit suicide. He succeeded on the third attempt. But even to the end his case was not considered to be a particularly serious one until his widow discovered a huge stock of classified materials in their home—documents which his supervisors and agency security officials had either lost track of or did not bother to control through proper security measures.

1960
William Martin and Bernon Mitchell

William Martin and Bernon Mitchell were cryptologists in the highly secret National Security Agency (NSA), where an apparent homosexual relationship developed between them. They had secretly joined the Communist Party in 1958, and, in 1959, they traveled without authorization to Cuba, which had recently fallen under the control of Fidel Castro. They openly criticized American intelligence activities. None of these actions aroused any suspicions. But in 1960, they both suddenly defected to the Soviet Union. The case was quite sensational at the time, and many questions were asked. There is no evidence, however, that any suspicions about them were ever aroused at the NSA prior to their defection, nor were the effects of their betrayal ever revealed if, in fact, these effects were ever properly assessed.

1961
Bay of Pigs and Publicity Leaks

Under the Eisenhower Administration, the CIA had developed a plan for the invasion of Castro's Cuba by Cuban exiles but with American air cover and logistical support. After his election in 1960, President John F. Kennedy decided to go ahead with the plan, which also included secret training of Cuban exiles by the CIA. In the weeks and days before the planned invasion was scheduled to occur, a number of newspapers in the United States predicted the coming invasion, providing extensive details about the planned military operation.

By the time the invasion took place, President Kennedy had himself been influenced by all the publicity about the operation, and he decided to cancel the originally promised American air support. It was therefore not surprising that the invasion was a disaster, resulting in the loss of many lives. In any case, Fidel Castro had clearly been alerted in advance—by the American media, which were more efficient in this regard than any spy network could have been. Someone "in the know" had to have given to the press and media those details which were then publicized by the press and media. Although this is perhaps not *espionage* in the classic sense, it is *treason* in the classic sense—the divulging of military secrets which resulted not only in the loss of lives but in the defeat of a U.S.-backed military operation decided upon after due reflection by the Commander-in-Chief responsible for the security of the United States.

1962
Joseph P. Kauffman

Joseph P. Kauffman was an Air Force captain who supplied military secrets to the East Germans. He was caught and tried and received a twenty-year sentence.

1962 - 1981
Joseph G. Helmich, Jr.

U.S. Army Warrant Officer Joseph G. Helmich, Jr., a cryptographic specialist, went into the Soviet Embassy in Paris and offered to sell secrets to the Soviets. Apparently, his immediate motivation was the threat by his commanding officer that, unless his overdue military club debts were substantially paid off, he would be court-martialed. Over the next three years, he carried out espionage against his own country for which he received more than $100,000 for American and NATO technical communications information, manuals, rotors, and keylists.

Despite being questioned about his lifestyle in 1964, serious suspicion was not aroused until sixteen years later. He was questioned in 1980 and brought in again the next year for questioning when he was seen with known Soviet agents. At this point, he began to cooperate with investigators, and eventually he was convicted and sentenced to life imprisonment.

1963
John Butenko

John Butenko was a civilian electronics engineer who conspired to provide data concerning the Strategic Air Command's communication system to the Soviets. He was sentenced to thirty years' imprisonment.

1964
William H. Whalen

Lieutenant Colonel William H. Whalen, a U.S. Army intelligence specialist assigned to the Office of the Joint Chiefs of Staff, provided "information pertaining to atomic weapons, missiles, military plans for the defense of Europe, information concerning the retaliation plans of the United States Strategic Air Command, and information pertaining to troop movements, documents, and writing relating to the national defense of the United States." Whalen was identified through the efforts of Soviet Major General Polyakov, the American agent in the GRU betrayed by Aldrich Ames. He was arrested in 1966 and sentenced to fifteen years' imprisonment.

1965
Herbert Boeckenhaupt

Air Force Sergeant Herbert Boeckenhaupt, while on duty at the Pentagon, provided the Soviet Union with U.S. military secrets the details of which were never released. Boeckenhaupt also was identified by Major General Polyakov. He was sentenced to thirty years' imprisonment.

1967 - 1985
John A. Walker, Jr., and Associates

We have already made mention in the Introduction of the sensational case of John A. Walker, Jr., and the various associates he recruited to assist him. The Walker case was, of course, one of the most sensational cases of the century. Walker came to trial in 1985, but his espionage activities had begun eighteen years earlier. The case of Walker and his accomplices may constitute the quintessential example of treason in the latter part of the twentieth century, in terms of the types of people involved, the venal and squalid motives revealed, the potential for grave damage to American interests, and, finally, the failure of the responsible officials and others to detect, report, or prevent a criminal activity that continued regularly for many years. The Walker case also vividly illustrates how apparently unrelated occurrences sometimes can be exploited to the full by a skilled foreign intelligence operation—always to the greater detriment of the United States.

In 1968, the United States spy ship *Pueblo* was hijacked by Communist North Korea. On board were several models of the KW-7, the workhorse cryptographic machine of the U.S. Navy and the other U.S. military services. Efforts to destroy these machines after it was apparent that the ship was at risk either came too late, or were incompetently carried out. At any rate they proved ineffective. From that time on, the United States was well aware that the Communists were in possession of these machines. It was believed, however, that, so long as the Communists were not also in possession of the daily translation keylists, they would never be able to decipher secure American communications. Even when thirty or so additional machines were lost during the Vietnam War, U.S. defense officials were unwilling to expend the resources or make the effort which would have been necessary in order to develop an entirely new cryptographic system. As long as we had the keylists, and the Communists did not, we were still all right; so the reasoning went.

What our defense officials did not know, but should have known, or at least suspected, was that the keylists themselves might have been compromised in some other way. In fact, in December 1967, Walker, a Navy cryptographer, had begun doing just that—*providing the daily cryptographic translation keylists to the Communists*. In other words, "secure" American communications were *not* secure during the eighteen years Walker was at work.

A fascinating question arises here: Did the Communists seize the *Pueblo* specifically to acquire the machines for which they already had access to the keylists? Certainly the rewards obtained justified the seizure of the ship. Walker labels this theory as "absurd," stating that it would have been easier for the Soviets to build copies of the cryptographic machines rather than steal them. In Walker's words:

All Registered Publication System (RPS) Custodians, which

was my position then, held both the crypto key lists and the equipment maintenance manuals. These manuals contain both the complete schematic (wiring diagrams) and a detailed theory of operation for each component. Construction of a duplicate could be accomplished in a matter of days by any industrialized country.

During my debriefings by FBI and NSA, I admitted providing copies of all manuals requested by the Soviets. It would make no sense to give them keylists for equipment they did not possess.

Thus, to attack a spy ship to obtain actual equipment, when the maintenance manuals were already in hand would be completely stupid and counterproductive. Firstly, the equipment would be destroyed or at least damaged in the capture. Secondly, any captured equipment would surely be modified after capture, as it was. Of course, I later provided the modification details.

In fact, my activity should have saved the *Pueblo*. Had the Soviets actually been in control of North Korea, they would have forbidden any action that would, and did, cause an equipment redesign and interrupt their flow of classified material.

The *Pueblo* story was surfaced by the FBI shortly after my arrest. Like you, they seemed to be searching for an uncomplicated story for public consumption that could show some combat loss as a result of my activity. Originally, they focused on the USS *Scorpion*, sunk by an internal accident in the Atlantic following an intelligence mission. Since I had no access to intelligence crypto systems, I could not have compromised the *Scorpion* mission. The government would also reveal later that the sinking was an accident.

They eventually settled on the *Pueblo*. By simply avoiding the facts behind the maintenance manuals, it seemed plausible to the uninitiated public even though informed professionals found the story preposterous . . ."

Of course, the fact remains that whether they built cryptographic machines, stole them or used those captured from the *Pueblo* and South Vietnam, the Soviets, with Walker's assistance, were able to decode our secure communications.

When it came time for his obligatory five-year "security re-investigation," Walker, no doubt fearing both the anticipated lie detector test as well as a possible review of his increased income and expenditures, simply went to the personnel file kept on him by the Navy and *forged* a re-investigation code, making it appear that he already had been re-investigated and thereby escaped scrutiny. It was that simple.

As he neared retirement from the Navy, Walker recruited a friend, radioman Jerry Whitworth, to carry on his profitable business by delivering secret information to him to be turned over to the Soviets. Later, Walker recruited his brother, Arthur J. Walker, and even his own son, Michael L. Walker, to help him in his operations. Walker did fail, however, to persuade his daughter to spy for him, though this was not for lack of trying. Nevertheless, neither she nor anyone in whom Walker confided was ever motivated by patriotism or ethics to report his treasonous activities to the authorities.

Thus, for eighteen years the Russians were able to monitor some of our supposedly most secure communications and obtain priceless defense and military secrets and information. The effect of such a capability on the part of the Communists on the conduct of the Vietnam War—to take one dramatic instance—could well have meant the difference between a possible victory and the defeat we in fact suffered in that war. Even the attempted helicopter rescue of the American hostages in Iran in 1980, which had to be aborted, may have failed because of the advantage John Walker provided the enemies of the United States.

In *Merchants of Treason*, Thomas B. Allen and Norman Polmar have this to say on the issue:

> . . . the planning for a hostage rescue received such high national security priority that the fear of cryptographic penetration, so long ignored and so deeply held inside the U.S. intelligence community, was again aired.
>
> As planning went forward for a rescue attempt, concern increased that military aspects of the operation would be discovered by the Soviets through the decrypting of U.S. military communications and then passed on to the Iranians. A virtual radio blackout was ordered. So secret was the concern, however, that all that could be handed down to lower military planning levels was the warning: Be extremely careful about communications before and during the rescue.
>
> The result, said a semiofficial review of the rescue, was that "the imposed silence on radio transmission was an underlying cause of the mission's collapse." Delta Force had "achieved communications security, but at too high a price." The extraordinary radio-silence orders had puzzled and exasperated planners because they had not been given the tightly held knowledge that the U.S. cryptographic system was suspected of being compromised.
>
> And that is at least why one intelligence official who heard

the *Nimitz* "launch" signal could only hope that the mission would succeed. He suspected, by April 1980, that many, if not all, of the top-secret messages that had been flowing for days into the communications center on board the *Nimitz* could be read in Moscow. He and the others who shared the awful suspicion could cling to only one long-shot possibility: that the Soviets were not being supplied keying materials promptly—in "real time"—but long after the keylists had been used.

If that was what was happening, then Soviet AGI, satellites, and other electronic monitoring systems would be recording all of the U.S. rescue-mission traffic (along with countless hours of useless administrative traffic) in anticipation of *later* possession of the keys for those days. They would then decode what they had recorded. If that was the way U.S. cryptography was being penetrated, then the Soviets would not have the ability to *act on* the rescue information. But Soviet analysts would be able to understand and interpret U.S. naval operations in a crisis and could advise Kremlin strategists about the best ways to counter future U.S. naval action. Political-military analysts would be able to infer information about how U.S. decision-making machinery works. "It's like playing poker and knowing what was in the guy's last hand," a U.S. communications officer later said.

As the *Nimitz* launched the rescue helicopters, she was receiving and sending messages with some of the same types of cryptographic machines that had been on board the *Pueblo* when she had been captured twelve years earlier. Incredibly, the machine-keylist cryptographic system of 1968 was still in use in 1980. Keylists still were the key to the code machines on board the *Nimitz* and the code machines on every U.S. warship, on every U.S. military base, and in every U.S. intelligence communications center in the world.

The precautions against cryptographic penetration had been considerable: virtual radio silence in the *Nimitz* much of the time, meager communication between units of the ill-fated rescue operation. But communications continued to be received by the carrier, the hub of information affecting the mission. Radio messages to the *Nimitz* included highly sensitive information that had been obtained by intelligence agents, at great risk, from friendly and unfriendly foreign embassies in Teheran. Such knowledge would provide extremely valuable secrets to Soviet military and diplomatic analysts. Yet, the messages had to be sent because, ultimately, the needs of the mission transcended the fears of betrayal.

Thus, the April 1980 rescue mission failed, in part—if not primarily—because of severe restrictions on communications due to the fears of Soviet intercepts. Under President Carter's direction, planning then escalated to a more ambitious, massive military assault on Iran for possible execution in October—on the eve of the presidential election. Preparations for this operation ended abruptly when U.S. intelligence indicated possible Soviet knowledge of the plans.

In several meetings, John Walker disclaimed any responsibility for the failure of the Iran hostage rescue attempt, pointing out that his delivery of encryption lists was always months after the dates on which they were used by the United States. Moreover, he believes that the mission was undermanned, suffered all of the coordination problems of the "typical joint military operation involving more than one service" and would have been under "radio silence" anyway. He stated further that the military could have used various other communications alternatives, including:

- Issue an exclusive and special cryptographic system for that particular raid. Since it had never been issued to anyone by NSA, its security would be guaranteed. This is not an uncommon practice.
- Utilize intelligence crypto systems which are much more narrowly distributed and therefore more secure. Also, a common practice.
- Super-encrypt all raid messages. This process involves encrypting the message by one system, then encrypting the result yet again using an entirely different system. Also, a common practice.
- Modify the equipment used in the raid.

Regardless of the extent of Walker's guilt, at least equally culpable were the military command personnel who, knowing that the Soviets had penetrated our communications shield, did nothing to replace that shield for more than a decade.

Throughout the entire period of his operations, when Navy people saw Walker improperly using copying machines, they assumed he was breaking security rules *merely* in order to print Little League notices or something of the sort. They did not interfere, nor were their suspicions aroused, even though Walker had regular access to the most sensitive kind of classified material. It apparently never crossed anyone's mind that suspicious and improper actions on his part ever meant anything serious. Awareness—so crucial to good security—was totally lacking.

When Walker's son, on sea duty, wished to prove that he, too, was able to acquire classified material, he merely went to his commanding officer and said that he had a security clearance, which he did not. He was taken at his word with no questions asked and *was actually made responsible for the collection and destruction of old classified communications!* Rather than destroy them, he merely hid them and delivered them to his father at the end of the voyage. The physical volume of the documents involved in these operations was staggering. And no one in the "security system" ever suspected.

In typical fashion, when Walker finally was caught, it was not because of any U.S. security officer, supervisor or security program in place. None of the procedures ostensibly established, and at great cost, to protect all the highly classified material to which this man had access, availed in the slightest. Navy security was basically inoperative. Walker carried out his sustained and lengthy treasonable activities with total impunity. He was only exposed because of discord within the Walker family itself. Walker was finally turned in by his wife, who had known about his traitorous activity for years. Had there been no family discord she might never have reported him to disbelieving and incredulous federal authorities.

During plea-bargaining with the Government, Walker's primary motivation appears to have been minimizing the sentence his son Michael would receive, and the Government offered some reduction in Michael's sentence in return for cooperation from Walker. In the end, Walker received a sentence of two life terms, plus 100 years—which means he has a possibility, albeit remote—very remote—of eligibility for parole after approximately ten years of time, which means 1995. More likely, however, is parole in 2015, after serving 20 years, since the regulations recommend serving two-thirds of the sentence before parole under the language of "life or 30 years or more." In Walker's case, a parole hearing is likely on or about May 20, 2015. For his part, Jerry Whitworth received a sentence of 365 years and was fined $410,000. Arthur Walker was sentenced to life in prison and given a $250,000 fine. The sentencing judge declared that Arthur Walker's greatest culpability had been his "silence." Michael Walker received two 25-year terms and three 10-year terms, all concurrent, making him eligible for possible parole in about eight years time.

The Walker case, one of the most serious and sensational espionage cases ever, was also one of the most disturbing in that so many persons approached by Walker were willing to betray their country for money, and not very large amounts of money at that. Of even greater concern was the utter and total failure of the government "security system" in the Walker case. Its purpose—the reason for having such a system—was to protect against successful espionage. Obviously, it failed completely.

1971
Walter Perkins

Air Force Master Sergeant Walter Perkins, an intelligence specialist assigned to the Air Defense Weapons System Center at Tyndall Air Force Base in Florida, attempted to supply U.S. air defense plans to the Soviets. Arrested on his way to deliver these plans to the KGB in Mexico, Perkins tried to claim that he intended to trade the information for the freedom of American POWs in North Vietnam. Perkins was tried, convicted, and sentenced to three years' imprisonment.

1973
Sadag K. Dedeyan and Sarkis O. Paskalian

Sadag Dedeyan was a naturalized U.S. citizen born in Lebanon. He was employed as a senior mathematician and was granted a security clearance for his work at the Johns Hopkins University Applied Physics Laboratory. In March 1973, in violation of security policy, Dedeyan brought home a copy of a document on which he had been working. It was entitled "Vulnerability Analysis: U.S. Re-enforcement of NATO." He showed this document to a relative, Sarkis Paskalian. Paskalian, who had been recruited and trained by the Soviet KGB eleven years earlier, photographed the document, presumably without Dedeyan's knowledge, and sold the photographs to the Soviets.

When apprehended, Paskalian pleaded guilty to espionage and was sentenced to twenty-two years in prison. Dedeyan was also convicted for his failure to report the illegal episode after he had become aware of it and was sentenced to three years' imprisonment.

1973
James D. Wood

Air Force Sergeant James D. Wood was a special agent in the Air Force Office of Special Investigations. He was arrested when he brought classified documents to a meeting with Viktor A. Chernyshev, who was a first secretary at the Soviet Embassy. More classified documents were found in Wood's car. Wood was apprehended through the FBI's long-favorite technique—monitoring known Soviet agents and embassy personnel as well as anyone ever seen in their company.

James Wood decided to cooperate during the subsequent investigation. He was dishonorably discharged and imprisoned for two years.

1973 - 1974
Harold Farrar

Highly secret and critical industrial technology can also be compromised when effective security programs are not in place. Harold Farrar was a manager for the Celanese Corporation at one of the company's plants in South Carolina. Farrar resented the position he held and felt he had been ignored and passed over for promotion. In addition, he was having financial problems. These, by the way, are among the classic characteristics found in a potential traitor.

At the time, the Japanese Mitsubishi Corporation had been trying unsuccessfully to match the capability of the Celanese Corporation to produce top-of-the-line industrial film. Mitsubishi went looking for a potential turncoat ready to betray company secrets and found him in Harold Farrar. Farrar provided Mitsubishi with no less than fifty thousand rolls of the microfilm, with technical advice and assistance, and also with access to the Celanese plant. Mitsubishi paid Farrar $150,000 for these "services."

When the Celanese Corporation finally discovered what was going on, Mitsubishi and Farrar were charged with racketeering and conspiracy to transfer stolen property. Mitusbishi ended up being fined $300,000 and Farrar was sentenced to four years' imprisonment. Meanwhile, however, some multi-millions of dollars worth of critical technology had been stolen and transferred to Japan.

1975
Philip Agee

Philip Agee, a former CIA case officer, published a book entitled *Inside the Company: CIA Diary* in which he identified several hundred CIA employees, local agents, and organizations. He then began a campaign of public identification of CIA agents, causing their names to be published in the magazine *Counterspy*. Agee was also once quoted in the magazine as saying, "the most effective and important systematic efforts to combat the CIA that can be undertaken right now are, I think, the identification, exposure, and neutralization of its people working abroad . . . Having this information, the peoples victimized by the CIA and the economic exploitation that the CIA enforces can bring pressure on their so-often compromised governments to expel the CIA people. And, in the absence of such expulsion, which will not be uncommon, the people themselves will have to decide what they must do to rid themselves of the CIA."

A number of CIA agents whose names had been publicized by Agee had to be withdrawn as a result of these revelations. At least one, Richard Welch, CIA Chief of Station in Athens, Greece, was murdered on December 23, 1975, evidently as a result of Agee's treachery.

In 1976, Agee was deported from Great Britain, where he had been living since 1969. In January 1981, the Supreme Court ruled that he could be stripped of his United States passport, although this was small punishment for the magnitude of Agee's offense.

1975 - 1976
Christopher J. Boyce and Dalton Lee

Christopher J. Boyce, a low-ranking clerk in the employ of TRW Systems Group, a space and defense communications enterprise, had access to the TRW code room. He was responsible for changing the cipher key settings each day. The code room contained telephone scrambling equipment, cryptographic machines, and numerous secret communications on various technical subjects.

In 1975, Boyce conspired with Dalton Lee, a marijuana dealer and drug addict, to deliver to the Soviet Union pictures of cipher key cards and messages concerning two advanced and important satellite projects, "Rhyolite" and "Argus." The photographs were delivered by Lee to the Soviet Embassy. Subsequently, the Soviets provided Lee with a two-month photography course in Vienna.

These activities continued for more than a year. At that point the Soviets offered to finance Boyce's continuing education, in order to make him a more valuable spy. Boyce accepted the offer, but first he was to photograph a report on the development of a new satellite network then under development, bearing the code name "Pyramider."

Lee attempted to deliver the negatives of this report to the Soviets in Mexico, but arrived too late and missed his contact. Needing money for drugs, he became desperate and threw a book cover with the initials "KGB" through the fence of the Soviet Embassy. This attracted the attention of the Mexican police and he was arrested as a possible terrorist. Discovering the negatives, they turned Lee over to the FBI, and thus he was finally brought to justice, convicted, and sentenced. Lee was sentenced to life and Boyce for forty years. Boyce escaped from jail a few years later. He was recaptured in Washington state after committing a number of bank robberies. He was convicted and was given additional sentences for these crimes.

When cases such as this one are brought to light, it is impossible not to wonder, considering the sieve-like nature of our government security system, how many other traitors have betrayed American security with impunity.

1975 - 1985
Clyde Lee Conrad and Roderick James Ramsey

Army Sergeant First Class Clyde Lee Conrad was assigned to the U.S. Army 8th Infantry Division in Bad Kreuznach, fifty miles west of Frankfurt, Germany. He was introduced to agents of the Hungarian and Czechoslovakian secret services in 1975 by his supervisor, Sergeant Zoltan Szabo. Over the next ten years, Conrad delivered massive amounts of classified information to the Eastern European intelligence services.

Sergeant Roderick James Ramsey also served in the 8th Infantry Division between 1983 and 1985. Ramsey had a top-secret military security clearance and was assigned to work under Conrad as Assistant Classified Documents Custodian. The documents in their custody principally related to plans for the military defense of the central part of West Germany.

Conrad quickly recruited Ramsey into his espionage ring, which also included two Swedish doctors of Hungarian origin and at least five other persons. Ramsey provided a great amount of classified material, including "General Defense Plans" for the defense of Central Europe, documents dealing with the use of tactical nuclear weapons by the United States and its NATO allies, documents related to the coordination of various NATO forces, technical manuals, and documents concerning military communications technology. Conrad received between $2.2 and $5 million for his work. Ramsey received about $20,000.

In August 1988, Conrad and seven others were arrested in Germany. A German court found Conrad guilty, the judge stating that Conrad had "endangered the entire defense capability of the West" and that, had war broken out, what he had supplied "could have led to a breakdown in the defenses of the Western alliance," to capitulation, or to the use of nuclear weapons on German territory. Conrad was sentenced to life in prison for spying for the Hungarians, and to four years in prison for spying for the Czechoslovakians.

Shortly after Conrad's arrest, the FBI had begun questioning Ramsey, and he was arrested in June 1990. Agent Joe Navarro, the lead investigator in the case, stated that during the investigation, Ramsey had actually tried to recruit him into the service of the Eastern Bloc. It seems that Ramsey had also robbed a bank in 1981 and had attempted to crack a hospital safe while working as a security officer, but ultimately no charges of any kind were ever brought against him.

1976
Edwin Moore, Jr.

Edwin Gibbon Moore, Jr., was employed by the CIA from 1952 to 1973, except for a six-year period between 1961 and 1967 during which he was charged, tried, and acquitted of arson.

Shortly after his re-instatement, he was sent into a war zone, although this duty was abruptly cut short for psychiatric reasons. Apparently these were not considered to be disqualifying, since he continued to be employed by the CIA. In December 1976, Moore threw a package over a fence surrounding a Soviet residence in Washington. A Soviet guard, fearing a bomb, called American officials.

The package contained secret CIA telephone directories and other classified CIA documents, along with a written offer of more information for the sum of $200,000. The FBI arranged for a dummy drop, and then arrested Moore when he attempted to pick it up.

The FBI searched Moore's home and discovered hundreds of CIA documents, including items whose dates were later than 1973, the year that Moore had retired and left the CIA. Moore was brought to trial, convicted, and sentenced to fifteen years' imprisonment. He was paroled after only two years.

1976 - 1980
David H. Barnett

In 1976, David Barnett, a former CIA officer who had served between the years 1958 and 1970, including time as a member of the Directorate of Operations, was facing the failure of his exporting business. So he sold to the Soviets the names of some thirty CIA intelligence officers as well as the names of some CIA informants. Later, he provided the Soviets with secret information concerning the American ability to jam the Soviet SA-2 surface-to-air missiles; the Americans had been able to hinder the operation of these missiles during the Vietnam War. Then Barnett provided the names and psychological profiles of CIA employees who might be "turned" by Soviet diplomats and also of Soviet employees or representatives whom the CIA wished to "turn."

Barnett received a total of $92,000 for his work, and, at the direction of his handlers, attempted to secure a staff position on either the Senate or the House Intelligence Committee.

In April 1980, American agents spotted Barnett meeting with KGB agents in Vienna. When brought to trial, he pleaded guilty to the charge of selling U.S. secrets and was sentenced to eighteen years in prison.

1977
Ronald L. Humphrey and David Troung

Ronald L. Humphrey was an official of the United States Information Agency (USIA) and David Troung, a Vietnamese national, was the son of a South Vietnamese peace candidate. Troung founded the Vietnamese-American Reconciliation Center in 1975 and used it to gather and pass intelligence to the Vietnamese Communist government in Paris. His courier was a double agent working for the CIA, and when this courier was provided with classified U.S. documents, a wiretap was placed on Troung's telephone. The monitoring of Troung's calls through this means led to Humphrey at USIA.

When confronted, Humphrey said that he had been supplying Troung with classified material in order to convince the Vietnamese to release his Vietnamese common-law wife who was being held hostage in Vietnam. Troung, for his part, claimed that his actions had been motivated by a desire for improvement in relations between the United States and Communist Vietnam. Both men were convicted and sentenced to fifteen years in prison.

1977
William P. Kampiles

William Kampiles was a watch officer with the CIA who quit the agency when he received a negative performance report. He took with him a Keyhole (KH-II) reconnaissance satellite System Technical Manual, the CIA "Big Bird" Satellite Manual. He then sold this manual to the Soviets for $3000.

Kampiles then sent a letter to the CIA detailing his actions, which, according to then Attorney General Griffin Bell, "remained unopened at the CIA for two months."

When brought to bay, Kampiles was convicted of espionage and sentenced to forty years in prison. Sadly, among other deficiencies, this case demonstrated the extent of laxity and vulnerability even in the supposedly security-conscious CIA. The agency's Director, Admiral Stansfield Turner, admitted in this case: "When we learned that one [KH-II] manual was missing, we found that we could not account for thirteen others."

1977 - 1986
Unknown

For some nine years beginning around 1977, an employee of Fairchild Semiconductors stole secrets concerning corporate strategy and computer capabilities and delivered this sensitive data to certain Japanese corporations, including Fujitsu. An incredible volume of approximately 160,000 pages of data reportedly were stolen in this manner and passed into Japanese hands. The culprit has never been identified and apprehended.

1977 - 1981
William Holden Bell

William H. Bell was an engineer at Hughes Aircraft Company who had a secret-level defense-industrial security clearance. In 1977, Bell became friendly with Marian Zacharsky, a Polish national. This was a very difficult period in Bell's life. His nineteen-year-old son had recently died and he and his wife had divorced after twenty-nine years of marriage. In addition, he had recently filed for bankruptcy.

Marian Zacharsky offered help to Bell in the form of both friendship and some payment for modest favors. The favors increased and soon Bell began to provide documents classified Confidential and Secret for Zacharsky to review. The payments increased. In time, Bell was bringing home classified documents, photographing them before returning them to their places, and then delivering the photographs to European contacts. The photographs were passed to the Polish Intelligence Service, and from there to the Soviet KGB.

Bell was finally fingered in 1981 by a Polish defector and agreed to cooperate with the United States in order to convict Zacharsky. Zacharsky was sentenced to life in prison and Bell to eight years. (Two years later Zacharsky was freed in a spy exchange.)

1979 - 1983
James D. Harper

In 1979, James D. Harper was newly divorced, unemployed, and badly in need of money. He was dating a woman named Ruby Louise Schuler, an executive secretary to the president of Systems Control, Inc. (SCI), a small defense contractor. SCI was developing methods to protect U.S. missiles from Soviet attack.

Harper prevailed upon Schuler, who had a Secret-level clearance, to provide him with classified documents from the company president's safe, to which she had the combination. She would open the safe after hours and smuggle classified documents out to Harper. Since the company president traveled frequently, Schuler was also in a position to request specific documents on her own from the Huntsville ballistic missile center. For two years these activities continued. During this time no supervisor or fellow employee apparently ever noticed the continuing treachery; nor did Schuler's increasing drinking problem and display of large amounts of cash attract any particular interest. Finally, in August 1983, Schuler, who had meanwhile married Harper, lost her security clearance, not because of her drinking or any other abuse of the clearance, but simply because SCI had been acquired by another firm.

At this point, Harper began trying to extricate himself from his espionage career. He called an attorney and instructed him to attempt to make a deal with the government which would preclude a jail term for him. He provided this attorney with a number of oral tapes in which he described certain aspects of his espionage career. At about the same time, a source in Polish Intelligence was reporting that an American was providing large amounts of data concerning American missile systems.

The FBI then conducted a painstaking investigation in which information on the oral tapes was analyzed and compared with information emanating from the Polish source. Eventually the FBI investigation led them to Harper and conclusive proof of his guilt.

On June 22, 1983, Ruby Harper died from complications resulting from cirrhosis of the liver. In 1984, James D. Harper was sentenced to life imprisonment.

1979 - 1985
Ronald W. Pelton

Ronald W. Pelton was an electronic signals (communications) intelligence analyst for the National Security Agency. Pelton was cleared for specialized compartmentalized information. However, like so many such experts, he made it a point to learn whatever could be learned in the position he held, whether or not the subject crossed boundaries into areas which did not pertain to his own work. He had a photographic memory and was frequently asked to share his knowledge with other compartments.

Pelton was also a user of illegal drugs. In 1979, financially over-extended, Pelton declared bankruptcy. Looking for a quick way to re-cover financially, and concerned that he might lose his security clear-ance because of his heavy debt, Pelton resigned his position in the NSA, and shortly thereafter telephoned and then visited the Soviet Embassy.

Pelton called upon his memory to describe for the Soviets a highly effective, secret capability whereby American submarines could listen in on Soviet military communications being transmitted through an under-water cable extending between installations on the Kamchatka Peninsula and the Siberian East Coast. Pelton was paid $15,000.

When Soviet KGB officer Vitaly Yurchenko defected to the United States in 1985—only to return to the USSR three months later!—he told his interrogators about Pelton. Only then was this particular case of treason discovered.

Ronald Pelton began to be wiretapped and interrogated by the FBI, and eventually was tried and convicted for espionage in a trial in which great care had to be exercised to avoid any further revelations of vital technical information. In fact, segments of the press covering this case were very nearly charged with violation of the statutes protecting U.S. intelligence communications. Pelton was sentenced to two concurrent life terms.

1980
Christopher M. Cooke

Air Force Second Lieutenant Christopher M. Cooke was Deputy Commander of a Titan Missile crew. On his own, Cooke approached the Soviet Union through its embassy and provided the Soviets with classi-fied information which seriously compromised the security of U.S. missiles.

Cooke made a telephone call from the Russian Embassy during which he identified himself. Of course, since such calls are routinely wiretapped, the FBI became aware that something serious was amiss. Assuming that Cooke was actually part of an espionage ring, the Air Force Office of Special Investigations granted him immunity from pros-ecutions in exchange for a confession and full cooperation. Cooke ac-cepted the offer, and, as a result of this "deal," the government in the end was unable to bring any charges against Cooke.

1981
Stephen Baba

Stephen Baba, a U.S. Navy ensign, wanted money so that his fiancée in the Philippines could attend college in the United States. Baba mailed classified electronic warfare documents to the South African Embassy. The South Africans, however, returned the documents to U.S. officials. Baba was arrested, court-martialed, and sentenced to eight years at hard labor.

1981 - 1986
Glenn Souther

Glenn Michael Souther served as a Navy enlisted man from 1975 to 1982, and then went on to study Russian at Old Dominion University in Virginia. In 1982, as a naval reservist, he worked at the Naval Intelligence Center in Norfolk, Virginia, where he had a Top-Secret security clearance and had access to highly classified intelligence data.

For several years Souther provided intelligence data to the Soviet Union.

It was Souther's wife who eventually tipped off naval investigators about his activities. Nevertheless, after interviewing Souther's brother-in-law, a shipmate, who quickly discounted the spy charges, the naval investigators dropped the probe. Only after the Walker case had broken, and at the instigation of the brother-in-law himself, was a joint investigation by the Naval Investigative Service and the FBI resumed. But the investigators were too late: Souther himself suddenly disappeared in May 1986.

On June 27, 1989, the KGB in Russia announced the death by suicide of KGB agent Mikhail Yevgenievich Orlov, alias Glenn Michael Souther.

1983 - 1985
Sharon M. Scranage

CIA employee Sharon M. Scranage volunteered for assignment in Ghana in part to forget an unhappy love affair. She served as a CIA operations-support assistant, and had a Top-Secret clearance for this job.

Shortly after arriving in Ghana, Scranage decided that she had made a mistake. She did not speak the local language or relate to the local culture, yet her living quarters were located among the local populace at some distance from the embassy. Also, she did not feel that there were others with interests and background similar to hers among the employees at the embassy. In short, she was lonely and apprehensive.

On her second day at work, Scranage met Michael Agbotui Soussoudis, and they soon became lovers. Soussoudis, a first cousin to Flight Lieutenant Jerry Rawlings, Ghana's dictator, asked for and received classified information from Scranage. The documents in question at first included transcripts of CIA cables, then the names of CIA employees, and finally the names of Ghanaians who were agents or informants of the CIA in that country.

At a certain point Sharon Scranage was told by the CIA station chief to break off the relationship gradually, but she did not. By the time she returned to the United States, the CIA had put the whole thing together. Scranage and Soussoudis were arrested at a motel rendezvous in Virginia.

Scranage was sentenced to five years' imprisonment (later reduced to two), while Soussoudis received a twenty-year sentence. Soussoudis was then exchanged for the Ghanaians arrested for working with the CIA.

1984
Jonathan J. Pollard

Jonathan J. Pollard was an intelligence research specialist with the Navy Field Operational Intelligence Office. He held a Top-Secret clearance, and had access to sensitive—but supposedly compartmented—information. Nevertheless, Pollard made a habit of browsing through classified files—files containing sensitive information which he had no valid job reason to "need to know." He was considered to be so conscientious, however, that virtually free access was accorded him to look at whatever he wanted to see.

Pollard had made a practice of lying about his background and career. He told friends in college that he had escaped from Czechoslovakia in 1968 because his father had been exposed as a CIA operative. He also claimed that he was connected with Israeli Intelligence. He told Navy officials that he had lived in South Africa where his father had been CIA Station Chief. None of these things was true. He also included false job and education credentials on his federal application forms. None of these falsehoods was identified during his security investigation, or, if recognized, no action was taken.

Jonathan Pollard did have a contact with a military attaché in the South African Embassy which he had not reported. When this was discovered, Pollard's immediate superior withdrew his Top-Secret and special compartmented clearances. As soon as that particular officer was assigned elsewhere, however, Pollard appealed the ruling. In a bureaucratic "turf battle," the commanding officer of the Naval Intelligence Support Center (NISC), Captain Chauncey Hoffman, insisted on restoring Pollard's clearances in spite of strong opposition on the part of the Director of Naval Intelligence, Rear Admiral Sumner Shapiro, and several key NISC department heads.

As his career advanced, Pollard continued to use his compartmentalized clearance to view far more classified material than was appropriate for his responsibilities. He even bragged to friends about the access he had and began giving out secret information on his own authority. An Australian Navy officer was given much more information than he was authorized to receive, as was a member of the Afghan *mujahideen.* At least two friends of Pollard's received classified information intended to assist them in business (facts largely ignored in the later, highly publicized attempts to secure Pollard's release from prison).

In 1984, Pollard began *selling* classified information to the Israelis, including information about locations in Iraq and Syria where chemical weapons were being made, as well as data on U.S. weapons systems. Pollard used systems which ran computerized searches of various data bases, again regardless of the limitations of his specific clearances. Between June 1984, and November 1985, Pollard maintained a routine involving the removal of up to a briefcase of documents three times a week and delivery of these documents to the Israelis approximately twice a month. In all, Pollard received approximately $50,000 in payments. He also made several trips to Israel and across Europe, which he explained to friends as having been gifts from a rich uncle.

It appears that when Israel bombed the headquarters of the Palestine Liberation Organization's Yasser Arafat in 1984, the Israelis used technical materials supplied by Pollard.

In the meantime, Pollard's wife, Anne, a public relations specialist, went into business for herself, making use of classified documents about China which Pollard had stolen for her.

Surprisingly, Pollard was actually identified through the attention and interest of his co-workers and his superior officer. In September 1985, it was reported to Pollard's commanding officer that he was conducting computer searches on the Middle East, which was far from his assigned responsibility. Then, on October 25, a fellow employee reported seeing him carrying classified documents out of the NISC complex.

Pollard was put under surveillance at that point and was eventually detained while carrying out a briefcase full of classified material. However, he was able to telephone Anne, who quickly bundled additional material in a suitcase and left it with a neighbor, foolishly admitting that it contained classified material on China. It turned out, though, that this neighbor was the daughter of a career Navy officer; she delivered the suitcase to the Naval Investigative Service. Later searches turned up classified material in Pollard's apartment and even in his trash.

Jonathan Pollard pleaded guilty to espionage and was sentenced to life in prison. Anne Henderson Pollard was sentenced to five years in prison.

Despite the damage done by this espionage, and despite the resistance of intelligence and security officials, enormous pressures have been exerted both by the Israeli government and by some American Jewish leaders to secure Pollard's release from prison.

1984 - 1986
Edward L. Howard

Officially, the CIA holds that its potential agents should be intelligent, articulate, honest, honorable, and trustworthy. However, there is a second school of thought which holds that for some positions, such as those which involve direct espionage or management of foreign national agents, candidates should be amoral, unscrupulous, and basically without standards of personal moral conduct.

Edward Howard was intelligent and educated, fluent in German and Spanish, a cum laude graduate and a Peace Corps volunteer. However, he had also abused drugs and alcohol, and was a liar and a petty thief. He was hired by the CIA and assigned to the Directorate of Operations, the unit which directs clandestine activities.

Howard's early training provided him with substantial information concerning CIA operations in Moscow, including the names of at least one Soviet national spying for the CIA. This training also included techniques to evade surveillance. Mrs. Mary Howard was also trained in techniques which would enable her to support her husband.

Some of Howard's deceptive tendencies eventually came out and he was discharged, first from the Directorate of Operations and finally from the CIA itself. Even though the agency assisted Howard in finding another job, he nevertheless harbored deep resentment against the CIA.

In September 1984, Howard received money from KGB officials in Austria. He told two CIA employees at that time that he was considering espionage. The CIA's response to this revelation was to pay for Howard to see a psychiatrist.

In February 1985, apparently using information provided by Howard, the Soviets arrested CIA agent Paul M. Stombaugh and a Soviet missile expert, A. G. Tolkachev. It is believed that Tolkachev was executed.

When Vitaly Yurchenko made his short, aborted defection to the West, one of the things that he told U.S. agents was that there was a former CIA agent providing the Soviets with information about CIA agents in the Soviet Union. Since Yurchenko did not know the name of this turncoat, the FBI and CIA began more assiduously investigating possible American traitors. But as suspicion fell towards Howard, he successfully executed a carefully developed plan for defecting.

Even after Howard's successful defection, several more American agents in the Soviet Union were arrested, and even more long-term harm may have been done by his activities. CIA Director Admiral Stansfield Turner told the Foreign Intelligence Advisory Board that "Howard [had] devastated the CIA's human intelligence operations in the Soviet Union." However, in 1994, it turned out that there was a more highly placed mole in the CIA, Aldrich H. Ames, who was responsible for some of the damage attributed at the time to Howard.

1986
Moscow Embassy Marine Guards

Marine Sergeant Clayton J. Lonetree was a bored and lonely Marine security guard whose first assignment abroad was the American Embassy in Moscow. In spite of the fact that he had signed a non-fraternization agreement and was under strict orders to report any contact with Russians, Lonetree became involved with a female Russian translator, Violetta Alexandrovna Sauna. Lonetree later admitted that he realized that it was not safe to be seen with her and hence he actually resorted to utilizing counter-surveillance techniques (varying routes, back-tracking, changing coats, etc.) in order to avoid being followed by the KGB, or, for that matter, by the CIA.

Before long Violetta introduced Lonetree to her "Uncle Sasha," whose name was really Aleksiy Yefimov, a KGB agent. Yefimov asked Lonetree if he would like to be a "friend" of the Soviet Union. When Lonetree said yes, Uncle Sasha began asking him questions concerning embassy personnel and the layout of the building. Lonetree answered all the questions. Lonetree was even prevailed upon to sign a paper proclaiming his friendship for the Soviet Union.

Later, when Lonetree was transferred to the American Embassy in Vienna, his Russian friends "followed" him there. They asked for, and got, such things as photographs of American employees, the embassy floor plan, names of Austrian cleaning personnel, the embassy telephone directory, the names of other Marine guards with personal weaknesses, and even some classified documents. Lonetree received several thousand dollars for his cooperation.

As Lonetree found himself drawn deeper and deeper into the abyss, he eventually decided to report his activities to the CIA Station Chief. There ensued an "interagency dispute"; the CIA wished to turn Lonetree into a double agent, while the Department of Defense insisted upon prosecution.

On the basis of Lonetree's confession, five other Marines were detained on suspicion of fraternization and of espionage. There were even accusations that Lonetree and another Marine, Corporal Arnold Bracy, had permitted KGB agents entry into the embassy at night, giving them free rein. After a panicky investigation, it was decided that, while the Marine guards perhaps had allowed enemy agents entry into the embassy, there was no way to establish final proof of it.

Lonetree was court-martialed, convicted of revealing the names of CIA agents to the Russians, and sentenced to thirty years in prison. Only one other Marine was punished in this widely publicized case. He received a demotion for drinking off limits.

1989
Charles Edward Schoof and John Joseph Haeger

Petty Officers Third Class Charles Edward Schoof and John Joseph Haeger were radar and communications specialists aboard the U.S.S. *Fairfax County* docked in Norfolk, Virginia. They surreptitiously opened a safe containing classified documents, and removed and smuggled out classified information which had been maintained on microfilm.

Schoof telephoned the Soviet Embassy and invited the Soviets to come and get the material. Since Norfolk was beyond the area in which Soviet personnel assigned to the U.S. were permitted to travel without special permission, Schoof visited a number of Norfolk bars, openly trying to find someone to drive him to the Soviet Embassy. A former shipmate reported this activity.

Taken into custody, Schoof and Haeger were tried by courts martial; they were convicted and sentenced to twenty-five and nineteen years imprisonment, respectively.

1989
Frank Arnold Nesbitt

Frank Arnold Nesbitt left a high-paying computer job in the summer of 1989 and traveled to Central and South America seeking inexpensive land. According to Nesbitt, he accidentally met a Soviet agent in Bolivia, who first entertained him and then began badgering him for technical information.

Nesbitt had been in the U.S. Air Force in the 1960s and in the U.S. Marine Corps in the 1970s. He had taken and retained in his possession top secret communications intelligence. He eventually offered to provide this information to the Soviets. It was still classified information when he delivered it to the Soviets. He was paid $2000.

After his apprehension, Nesbitt pleaded guilty to a charge of passing top secret defense information to the Soviets. He claimed that he had been motivated by concern for the safety of his family in Tennessee and also that of a new friend he had met in Guatemala. He further claimed that he thought he could help the American intelligence community by gaining the confidence of the KGB. Finally, he said that he had hoped and assumed that the information he passed on was in any case outdated.

1989
John Vladimir Hirsch

John Vladimir Hirsch was of Czechoslovak origin and became a captain in the U.S. Air Force. He was assigned to the Electronic Security Command, a unit which monitored Warsaw Pact radar and communications. During a routine security update, polygraph operators became convinced that Hirsch was not telling the truth. His apartment was then searched, yielding bank account records showing a balance of $120,000, photographs of NATO military installations, and other classified documents (according to a Pentagon source).

Nevertheless (again according to the Pentagon), the investigation did not "substantiate espionage, and the case was closed." Hirsch then asked for and received a voluntary early honorable discharge.

1990 - 1992
Joseph Garfield Brown and Virginia Jean Baynes

Joseph Garfield Brown was an American living in the Philippines where he was engaged in teaching martial arts. Virginia Jean Baynes was a secretary employed by the Criminal Investigations Division,

Department of the Army, in Manila. Baynes took lessons from Brown and soon became quite friendly with him.

Instigated by the Philippine government, Brown asked for and obtained through Baynes sensitive information gathered through covert U.S. sources concerning Philippine officials targeted for assassination by leftists as well as information concerning the use of briefcase bombs by Iraqi terrorists.

According to a federal affidavit, release of this material "threatened grave consequences to United States national defense interests, including exposing critical covert sources and endangering the lives of sources and of United States government officials."

Baynes was the first one caught. In May 1992, she pleaded guilty to one count of passing national secrets and was subsequently sentenced to forty-one months in prison. In order to apprehend Brown while avoiding complications with the Government of the Philippines, however, the FBI had to create an elaborate cover in which several undercover agents traveled throughout Southeast Asia pretending to be conducting a search for a martial arts instructor to teach CIA employees. Eventually they "selected" Brown for the non-existent position and gave him instructions to fly to Washington. Dreaming of a remunerative new career ahead of him, Brown readily boarded the airplane. He was arrested upon his arrival at Dulles International Airport in December 1992. Brown pleaded guilty in February 1993.

1990
Albert Sombolay

U.S. Army Specialist Albert Sombolay, stationed in Kaiserslautern, Germany, passed deployment data concerning U.S.-led allied forces during the Gulf War. He had himself initiated the first contact with the Jordanian and Iraqi embassies in Belgium and Germany, seeking an "outlet" for his wares. He also provided samples of chemical-weapons protection equipment and identification documents. All this material was directly handed over to a Jordanian intelligence officer.

After indiscreetly speaking of his activities to an undercover officer, Sombolay was apprehended, tried, and convicted in July 1991.

1990
Charles Francis Anzalone

Charles F. Anzalone was a 23-year-old Marine Corporal in Yuma, Arizona, serving as a telephone lineman. In November 1990, he called the Soviet Embassy to offer his services as a spy (under the pretext of inquiring about a college scholarship. Anzalone was later contacted by an FBI agent who posed as a KBG agent. Anzalone gave the agent two technical cryptographic manuals, a security badge and guard schedules. Anzalone, who is part Mohawk, told the FBI agent that he hated capitalism and the American government, apparently in part because of the treatment of the American Indian.

At his trial, Anzalone testified that it was all a scam to get money from the Soviets. He was convicted of attempted espionage, as well as of possession of marijuana and adultery with the wife of another Marine.

1991 - 1993
Frederick Christopher Hamilton

Frederick Christopher Hamilton, an employee of the Defense Intelligence Agency, was stationed at the U.S. Embassy in Peru in 1991 when he met secretly with members of the government of Ecuador and gave them U.S. intelligence reports evaluating the military readiness of the Peruvian security forces. His motive, as stated by his attorney when he was later brought to trial, was his belief that the information he leaked would defuse what he saw as a possible conflict between Ecuador and Peru. These two countries had a long-standing border dispute which had already led to violent confrontations. Tensions were particularly high in 1991. "What he thought he was trying to do was prevent a war," his attorney later said, attempting to justify the illegal passing on of security information by someone who had no right to divulge it and a responsibility to protect it.

When discovered, Hamilton agreed to cooperate with the FBI agents investigating the case. Brought to trial, he pleaded guilty in February 1993 to two counts of communicating classified information to a foreign country by a government employee.

1993
Steven J. Lalas

Steven J. Lalas was a ten-year State Department employee with a Top-Secret security clearance serving at the American Embassy in Athens, his fourth overseas diplomatic post. His duties included processing incoming and outgoing embassy communications and preparing and receiving diplomatic pouches. He had access to a large volume of cable traffic about Bosnia, Turkey, Greece, and the United States in a volatile part of the world where such sensitive diplomatic information was of vital importance. Athens had recently been the scene of tense negotiations over a proposed peace pact among the warring factions in Bosnia.

According to the evidence against him, Lalas was paid to pass information to a Greek official during most of the two years he was stationed in Athens. It was reported that he had received $20,000 in exchange for handing on some 240 classified documents. This security breach apparently came to light in conversations between U.S. and Greek officials, after which State Department Security and FBI investigations were instituted and Lalas was identified. Lalas was brought back to the United States in May 1993, questioned intensively, and then arrested and charged with passing sensitive military information to Greek officials.

1993
Geneva Jones and Dominic Ntube

Geneva Jones was a State Department clerk whose job was to sort and distribute classified cables received from around the world, including documents related to U.S. military operations. According to the FBI, Jones smuggled out copies of many documents in her purse, in a bag, or in a rolled-up newspaper and gave them to Dominic Ntube, a West African journalist who had become a permanent resident of the United States. Ntube transmitted some of the documents obtained through Jones to the Liberian insurgent army leader Charles Taylor. The fact that there was a security leak in this case became known when some of the stolen State Department cables ended up being printed verbatim in West African magazines.

When FBI agents went to West Africa to investigate, they found fourteen State Department cables classified "Secret" or "Confidential" in a command post in Liberia which had been evacuated by the insurgent Charles Taylor forces. They had been faxed to Liberia by Dominic Ntube. When the FBI searched Ntube's apartment in Washington they found, according to press reports, not only the same fax machine which had transmitted the documents to Liberia, but "several thousand classified State Department documents and approximately thirty-nine Central Intelligence Agency documents classified as 'Secret.'"

According to the FBI, Geneva Jones had also delivered some of the stolen classified documents to a native of Kenya, Fabian Makani, at the offices of a publication called *The African Mirror* published in Silver Spring, Maryland.

In August 1993, the State Department cable clerk was arrested, held without bond, and accused in federal court of stealing thousands of classified documents from State Department and CIA files.

1985 - 1994
Aldrich H. Ames

It is almost poetic that the Parade of Traitors would conclude (for now) with Aldrich Hazen Ames. This case graphically demonstrates just what the United States has accomplished in more than fifty years of "improvement" in its Security capabilities.

In 1985, just as the Walker ring was being exposed, a new story of treachery was just beginning. In terms of suffering and deaths of persons loyal to the United States, the Ames case dwarfs those of all other known traitors.

Aldrich Ames would seem to be the perfect CIA recruit. Born in River Falls, Wisconsin, in 1941, he was the son of a college teacher and grandson of a college president. In 1951, the Ames' moved to Washington, D.C., where Ames' father became an analyst in the Counterintelligence division of the CIA. Ames joined the CIA in 1962, without a college degree. He continued his education, receiving a Bachelor's Degree in History in 1967. Like his father, Ames worked in Counterintelligence, attempting to identify and capture or "turn" spies of other countries. He was considered to be a mediocre agent. Ames was assigned to Ankara, Turkey; then to headquarters outside Washington, D.C.; to New York City near the United Nations; and then in 1981 to Mexico City. By this time his marriage, to another CIA employee, was in trouble, and he went to Mexico alone.

In 1982, Ames met Rosario Casas Dupuy, a cultural attaché at the Columbian Embassy. Rosario is a member of a prominent Columbian family and a brilliant student and teacher of Classical Greek language and literature. Ames had an obvious drinking problem and, in violation of CIA policy concerning foreign nationals, he began sleeping with Rosario in a CIA safe house. In short, Ames fit the classic profile of a problem agent. In 1983, with Ames' assistance she became a CIA informant. In late 1983, Ames was transferred back to headquarters in Langley, Virginia, not to be disciplined or for treatment of his alcohol addiction, but to be promoted to a very sensitive position running counterintelligence operations against the Soviets. Even after he was transferred out of counterintelligence, Ames continued to hang around the offices of other counterintelligence officers, discussing their activities and related issues with them. (After Ames's arrest, some CIA employees mentioned that, as a member of the Intelligence Community, Ames was privy to many types of classified information, beyond that for which he had a "need to know.")

In 1985 and 1986, a series of disasters befell the CIA. Several Americans had been identified as traitors. The circumstances of Edward Lee Howard's escape suggested that he had been tipped off concerning his impeding arrest. The first two double agents ever recruited from the Soviet Embassy were ordered back to Moscow and executed. Eventually, at least seven American agents were tortured and killed. The Soviet Union began to identify and shut down CIA covert operations. In all, about thirty operations within the Soviet Union were compromised. In spite of all this, the CIA and FBI did not aggressively search for a mole, or even cooperate with each other, until 1991. Some sources claim that investigative efforts were stymied by the CIA's insistence that all of its recent failure must have been due to the moles who had already been identified. The real impetus for cooperation may have been the arrest and execution of an important double-agent in Russian counter-intelligence known as "Prologue."

In 1986, Ames was given a routine polygraph exam. Although the polygraph operator believed that Ames had exhibited weaknesses, Ames's superior decided that there was no reason for concern, and refused to permit further investigation. Although his name was on the CIA/FBI list of possible double agents, it was near the bottom and he did not become a serious candidate until another CIA insider being questioned by the FBI suggested that they examine Ames's spending habits. In fact, Ames had received nearly two million dollars from the Soviets and later the Russians, and had lived lavishly, paying cash for a Jaguar automobile and a $540,000 home. Once the investigators began their examination in earnest, Ames's financial and other records were damning. Tapped telephone conversations provided additional proof.

From March 1984 until July 1986, Ames had been authorized to conduct phone conversations with Soviet officials, as long as the conversations were approved in advance or reported afterwards. What should have been discovered at the time was that Ames was having both telephone conversations and meetings which he was not reporting. These factors were not noticed, or acted on, until the investigation began in the early 1990's. When his office was finally searched, investigators found stacks of top-secret documents which Ames was not authorized to see or possess. Once again, the arrogant and elitist attitude that, if you are a member of "the club" you can do no wrong and therefore should not be subject to the rules for protection of classified material, had excused the improper release of critical documents to a traitor. In fact, the release of such documents and oral information may have caused the death of "Prologue."

The Ames case was so shocking and severe in its repercussions that intense pressure was exerted upon CIA chief James Woolsey to finally take the action that, in spite of its obvious necessity, has been avoided in such cases for so long: disciplinary action against those who should have noted and acted upon the various signals and clues which Ames and other traitors have left. Woolsey sent letters of reprimand to eleven CIA supervisory employees (seven of whom are retired), and ordered that they receive no commendations until further notice. But even this modest action was too much for the CIA elite, and two other employees ignored the order. Woolsey demoted these two employees, who promptly resigned.

Even the Senate Intelligence Committee recognized that more severe action was necessary, and in its report of investigation of the Ames case, it criticized Woolsey for his mild disciplinary actions, specifically because none of the 23 current and former CIA officials identified as accountable by the CIA Inspector General were fired, demoted, suspended or even reassigned. Twelve did not even receive a reprimand and the letters of several who did also contained laudatory remarks on other subjects. The Committee report stated, "The committee found a bureaucracy excessively tolerant of serious personal and professional misconduct among its employees, where security was lax and ineffective, and we found a system and a culture unwilling and unable to face, assess and investigate the catastrophic blow Ames had dealt to the core of its operations."

Woolsey was quoted in *The Washington Post* as saying "We should put cases and decisions behind us and move on to the challenge of managing counterintelligence." One of the primary problems, of course, is that the CIA has too often put its security failures "behind" it, instead of critically examining the failures and changing the behavior and the personnel which permitted the failures to occur. Woolsey's reputation was damaged by his taped response to the scandal and he resigned.

In his interview with Committee Chairman Senator Dennis DeConcini on August 5, 1994, describing the ease with which he removed classified material, Ames stated that classified material "came into my inbox" and he would "just scoop" it out and provide it to the Soviets. Ames went on, "It was very easy [to walk out of CIA Headquarters with the documents]. There's no search . . . [The Soviets] couldn't understand how I could [remove classified material] without damaging

my security . . . But eventually they came to believe me when I said,
'Well, this stuff is just floating around.'"

Once again we see officials expressing shock that this could occur
and promising improvements to come. We also see the arrogance of "the
club" in that, while regulations mandate strict controls and government
officials pretend that these regulations are observed and enforced, classified material is handled in the most cavalier fashion, with virtually no
control exerted by those responsible for its protection.

According to former CIA Director Richard Helms, recovering from
the damage done by Ames will be like "cleaning out the Augean stables".
Any activity in which Ames may have had any part or of which he may
have had knowledge must be considered suspect. Every agent the United
States has in Russia may well be compromised. Recruiting new agents
in the Soviet Union, considering the fates of previous agents, may be
virtually impossible for some years to come. Finally, the question remains:
"Is there another mole, or moles, in the CIA?"

The above represents only some of the more notable cases of betrayal by Americans in sensitive positions that have come to light over
the past half century. Numerous additional cases have been identified
and, considering the strictly fortuitous manner in which many of the
particular crimes enumerated here were discovered, we must assume
that many more similar crimes have not been discovered. Moreover,
since many of these same crimes were only discovered years after they
occurred, we must also assume that most of the security scandals and
tragedies of the 1990s have not yet even come to light. As with crime
in America, where we know that only a small percentage of the crimes
committed are ever detected, and only a small percentage of the criminals are ever arrested and convicted, so is it also with regard to espionage and treason: There is no reason whatsoever to believe that all the
traitors in our "Parade" are the only ones who have ever engaged in
espionage and treason. Probably the number caught is but a small fraction of the total. Our security system is a failed system.

What is indisputable is that security breaches clearly represent an
ongoing problem for the U.S. government. They are quite unlikely to go
away in the future, at least under our existing "security system." The
cases we have cited establish beyond any doubt that breaches of security
can neither be ignored nor considered to be of little importance. No
American can be indifferent to the cumulative effects on our national

interest and on our national security that have resulted from these and similar cases of treason.

The average American may believe that all these cases we have been reciting were merely unfortunate "accidents" which somehow escaped the normal and usual high vigilance of the U.S. government security apparatus. Surely the government has an effective security system in place. Surely all that can be done to protect our legitimate security interests has been done and is being done. The citizen must believe that the stakes are just too high for negligence and apathy to exist. Moreover, our elected leaders are not traitors, after all, and they would surely not be standing still if American security was really in any serious danger. As a matter of fact, our high government officials, after nearly every disastrous security breach comes to light, regularly promise that the system will be fixed and that such a breach will never happen again— a promise they know will not be—has not been—kept.

Americans have repeatedly been assured that all is well with regard to security. Responsible government officials have periodically testified to this truth. Yes, the U.S. government does have a security system in place. It has had the *same* system in place throughout most of the period we have covered with our "Parade of Traitors." But the very fact that all the cases we have reviewed, and more, occurred, in spite of the security system that was in place, demonstrates that the security system the U.S. government has had in place all this time has simply not been adequate to the task.

This chapter concludes with a break in the chronology for a discussion of one final marcher in our "Parade of Traitors," a U.S. Government official with whom I was personally involved in trying to expose and have removed from the government for disloyalty. In addition to the intrinsic interest of the case, it is also illustrative, I believe, of a number of the more important issues we will be dealing with in following chapters.

1942 - 1947
George Shaw Wheeler

In the early 1940s George Shaw Wheeler was appointed to a highly responsible position on the Board of Economic Warfare (BEW). His government appointment, like so many of the appointments made in those days, was made "subject to investigation." The idea was that the services of some individuals were so vital to the war effort that the prewar standard practice of hiring an individual only after a clearance had been granted was suspended; it was assumed that the clearance would be granted in due course to the employee already on the rolls once the requisite suitability and loyalty investigation had been completed.

In those days, suitability investigations were conducted by the old Civil Service Commission (now the Office of Personnel Management), the agency charged by law with investigating, rating, adjudicating, and thus approving or denying applicants the right to work in the federal service. As an investigator for the Commission, I conducted many such investigations. It was not an easy job. Obtaining hard evidence of disloyalty can border on the impossible. No one intent upon undermining the government employing him is generally accustomed to leaving an oral or written trail which proves him to be a traitor.

One engaged in betraying his country for the interests of another country—who also possesses the training and skills to be employed in the upper echelons of his own government—is careful to avoid revealing actions. The task of building a case which can stand up within the framework of our constitutional protections of due process is normally a monumental task.

Nevertheless, in the Wheeler case, I succeeded in establishing, after an extensive investigation over a long period of time, that George Shaw Wheeler was a key member of the "Ware Group," a group named after one Harold Ware, who organized it as an underground operation; it consisted of a coterie of ultra-leftist ideologues and active apologists and advocates for the interests of the Soviet Union. Wheeler was a prominent member of the group. Another member was Max Loewenthal, who was also a highly placed BEW official who wielded enormous influence in our wartime planning. Both Wheeler and Loewenthal were already looking ahead to the post-war period and the shape Europe would then take under the influence of the Soviet Union.

The results of the investigation of Wheeler, however, convinced the Civil Service Commissioners that, on grounds of disloyalty, he was unfit to continue working for the U.S. Government. A notice of termination went out from the Commission to the BEW. However, Wheeler's appointment was not terminated. What ensued in this case illustrates the extent to which the federal employment and security system in those days of our wartime alliance with the USSR proved to be subject to manipulation by pro-Communist and pro-Soviet government officials. There followed a long and elaborate cat-and-mouse game between the Civil Service Commission seeking to terminate Wheeler's employment, and those who conducted a tenacious defense of Wheeler's continued employment in the agencies where he worked (for he continued to be employed by the government in a succession of increasingly responsible positions in different agencies, including the War Department, in spite of the established derogatory information on record against him).

The Wheeler case was typical of something which occurred only too frequently during those wartime years. A person would initially be recruited and provisionally hired by officials in a department or agency who already shared the same "political" philosophy, that is, a commitment to pro-Soviet Communist objectives. When a security investigation later turned up hard evidence of the disloyalty of this employee already on the rolls "subject to investigation," the superiors and sponsors of the employee within the department or agency where he was working would then proceed to exert maximum bureaucratic pressure to insure that the employee was not terminated. Like the protracted appeals process in our criminal courts today, pretexts and excuses for delay in staving off a final termination decision could be devised almost endlessly; interminable correspondence was exchanged. Time was normally on the side of those simply attempting to delay an action ("termination") from taking place.

In Wheeler's case, he enjoyed important protection from officials in powerful positions such as Max Loewenthal of BEW and David A. Morse, at that time an army major, but later a General Counsel of the National Labor Relations Board, an Assistant Secretary of Labor, and finally highly lauded for his leadership as director general of the International Labor Organization (ILO) after the war. The pressure they exerted was intense. If someone like Wheeler could be successfully terminated on security grounds, others could be placed in jeopardy on the same grounds.

The decision to terminate Wheeler had been made by the Civil Service Commission as a result of my investigation, and hence it was up to the three-member Board of Commissioners to enforce the ruling. They included Harry B. Mitchell, the chairman, a Mid-Westerner of advanced years; Lucille Foster McMillan, the widow of a Tennessee senator who had been appointed to the position as a sinecure; and the Republican member, Arthur S. Flemming. This third commissioner was able, intelligent, energetic—and liberal for a Republican in the 1940s, which may have been the reason President Roosevelt appointed him to be the required Republican minority member of the Commission. He enjoyed a long Federal career and later became much better known, serving as President Eisenhower's Secretary of Health, Education, and Welfare.

In the case of George Shaw Wheeler, the commissioners proved unequal to the task of standing up to those in the government who did not wish to see Wheeler's employment terminated. Thus his employment continued, even though the evidence of his disloyalty was conclusive. It is worth quoting the text of the decision made in Wheeler's case (from a Civil Service Commission Memorandum dated January 2, 1945):

> The Commission's investigation disclosed evidence from reliable and reputable sources which indicates that Mr. Wheeler has followed the Communist Party line in its changes from before 1939 to date. Evidence relating directly to this matter is supported by other evidence that shows Mr. Wheeler's active participation and sympathetic interest in policies and programs directly and indirectly further the objectives of Communism. The position to which Mr. Wheeler was appointed, subject to investigation, is of such importance to the Government of the United States in the establishment and maintenance of proper official relations with other countries that singular care must be exercised to assure that the incumbent will be entirely in harmony with the democratic principles of this Republic. When the testimony of responsible witnesses is weighed, a reasonable doubt persists as to Mr. Wheeler's absolute loyalty to these principles when confronted with situations involving pro-Communist elements. This doubt must, of course, be resolved in favor of the government.
>
> Mr. Wheeler has been rated ineligible, his pending applications and existing eligibilities have been canceled, and your agency is instructed to terminate his services, advising the Commission when such action has been taken . . .

In spite of this judgment, Wheeler was not only not dismissed; he went on to other important government positions. He was employed successively by the Labor Department, the War Production Board, the State Department, and the United States military government in Germany. It was only in 1947, and after pressure from Senator Styles Bridges of New Hampshire and Congressman George Dondero of Michigan, that he was finally dismissed from the job he then held in the U.S. military government in Germany, and the War Department was ordered to return him to the United States to be terminated.

What Wheeler did then stunned even his severest critics, he traveled to Prague, behind the Iron Curtain—which was still being constructed at precisely that time—and sought and received asylum in Communist

Czechoslovakia. He remained there until his death, teaching in that country's educational system.

Thus, the original Civil Service Commission decision was finally vindicated in the Wheeler case—but only after Wheeler had been able to go on for years exercising important functions in the U.S. Government, and this *after* evidence of his disloyalty had been established by a security investigation. As Congressman George Dondero declared on the floor of the House of Representatives in 1950: "Wheeler was found ineligible for a job with the occupation forces in Germany, but the Civil Service Commission then reversed itself as a result of left-wing pressure."

TWO

History of America's
Security Programs

I t is important to present a brief history of the successive security
programs of the U.S. government in order to make possible an understanding of the changes—sometimes the erratic lurches—in emphasis and direction which have occurred in response to particular events.
There have been periods of apathy and lackadaisical performance alter-
nating with periods of high tension and frenetic activity, the latter usually precipitated by revelations of security lapses, with abuses of due
process and violations of employee rights also usually accompanying
these latter periods. Moreover, these periods of intense concern for proper
security have not generally been matched by the effectiveness of the
security measures put in place. One main constant in the history of the
various U.S. government security programs, in fact, is the losses and
lapses resulting from security breaches.

As a generalization—which happens, however, to be true—our security concerns have not been driven so much by a genuine concern for
effectiveness as they have by suddenly enhanced levels of patriotism
and hatred for America's enemies that have usually been stirred up by
external factors, including revelations of espionage.

Meanwhile, it may be indicative of America's general lack of understanding of the very concept of "security" that most of us are probably
unable even to define the term; nor are the distinctions among such related
concepts as "espionage," "intelligence," or "counterintelligence" always
completely clear. It may therefore be helpful at the outset to supply several important definitions in reasonably clear layman's terms; understanding what these key words mean will be helpful as we proceed:

Intelligence—As applied to nations and other organizations, the body of information concerning other nations, groups, and subentities, gathered or being gathered as an organized effort. This information may concern enemies, allies, or neutrals; it may be political, economic, military, or technical; and it may be gathered through overt or covert methods. Depending on the type or content of the intelligence, subject countries or other organizations may or may not object to its acquisition.

Counter-intelligence—The entities and processes through which one nation or organization seeks to prevent, minimize, or otherwise thwart the gathering of that information which it considers critical or sensitive by the intelligence agencies or other representatives of other nations or organizations.

Espionage—That portion of intelligence gathering which is performed secretly, in violation of another country's laws and, usually, at least partially, within that country's borders, by intelligence agencies, private businesses, or other organizations.

Counter-espionage—The effort, programs, and organizations through which a country attempts to thwart any espionage efforts directed against it.

Security—The effort(s) or program(s) through which a country attempts to identify that information which it considers important to safeguard from release to the public, the press, and, especially, to other nations and actual or potential enemies; and which it endeavors to protect through a variety of formal and informal systems and techniques. Security programs, systems, or entities may be distinguished from counter-espionage programs, systems, or entities by the fact that the security effort seeks primarily to protect its assigned material against compromise, deliberate or accidental, while the counter-espionage effort operates actively to identify, thwart, mislead, and destroy an opposing espionage capability.

Classified Material—That information which a country deems vital enough to its interests and security to wish to safeguard from release to the public, the press, or other nations and which is so designated by a classification assigned by a government agency or other entity with the legal authority to do so.

Contact—Any person representing an espionage entity to whom a spy or traitor is to deliver materials or from whom he or she picks up materials and instructions.

Handler—Person directing the efforts of a spy or traitor actively engaged in espionage.

Spymaster—Individual responsible for setting up and running an espionage effort, ring, network, or agency.

Agent or Secret Agent—Person performing the actual function of espionage data-gatherer, usually in the territory of the country or entity being spied upon; or, in counter-espionage, attempting to counter such data-gathering efforts.

Double Agent—Person who is believed by a nation or entity to be a loyal agent of theirs but who in fact is working for the opposing side.

Treason—The offense of attempting by overt acts to overthrow the government of the state to which the offender owes allegiance; or of betraying the state into the hands of a foreign power (from Black's Law Dictionary). Treason consists of two elements: Adherence to the enemy and rendering him "aid and comfort."

Aid and Comfort—As an element in the crime of treason, the giving of "aid and comfort" to the enemy may consist in a mere attempt. It is not essential to constitute the giving of aid and comfort that the enterprise commenced should be successful and actually render assistance. An act which intentionally strengthens or tends to strengthen enemies of the U.S., or which weakens or tends to weaken power of the U.S. to resist and attack such enemies. Any intentional act furthering hostile designs of enemies of the U.S. (Black's Law Dictionary).[2]

---

[2]Several times in our discussions, John Walker has strenuously objected to identifying his activities on behalf of the Soviets as "treason." He advances the following argument:

> Treason is a crime defined by the U.S. Constitution. It states in part, "treason against the U.S. shall constitute only in levying war against them, or in adhering to their enemies, giving them 'aid and comfort.'" The courts have supported that language in numerous actions, and nowhere is espionage defined as treason.

Without getting into lengthy legalistic arguments, there is no question but that delivering classified military information to a country committed to destroy the U.S. not constitute giving "aid and comfort" to the enemy. Walker is not the only traitor who prefers to have his activities defined as "espionage." We are convinced that stealing America's vital secrets by U.S. citizens to whom they have been entrusted and turning them over to the enemy does constitute a betrayal and "adherence to the enemy," the second element of "treason."

Traitor—Person who betrays his own country, community, or group by turning over its vital security information to agents of another country or entity; or else by defecting to that country or entity taking along with him security information and knowledge to divulge.

Mole—Person, either agent or traitor, who has succeeded in positioning himself within an important agency of the target nation. This is sometimes accomplished by avoiding communication with contact, handler or spymaster for prolonged periods, until the mole has reached a position of responsibility and trust. At this point the mole can provide substantial classified information to his employing country with relatively little risk.

Espionage and covert action have been with us since pre-history. From Jericho's Rahab, the harlot who aided the spies sent out by Joshua, from the nameless traitor whose disclosure to the Persians of a hidden mountain pass brought about the annihilation of Leonidas and his Spartans at Thermopylae, up through Benedict Arnold to Rosenberg, Walker and Ames in our own day, those who have been willing to betray their trust and their countries have had an enormous impact on the affairs and security of nations. Many of history's most famous spies—and most traitors—were not career "intelligence officers," unlike most of their contacts and handlers. Spymasters have operated highly developed espionage and counter-espionage networks as far back as the time of Sun Tzu in China in 500 B.C. In the sixteenth century, Sir Francis Walsingham developed England's first secret service, and Cardinal Richelieu had even earlier performed the same service for France. Alan Pinkerton developed the first true American intelligence network during the Civil War.

Until the early twentieth century, the effort of protecting secrets from espionage was much less complicated than it is today. State secrets primarily related to diplomatic overtures and military plans which need only be known by a few persons. Compared with today's world, involving millions of pieces of secret and sensitive technical and diplomatic information, and thousands of weapons systems and contingency plans, scores of thousands of persons handling this information, and ubiquitous electronics copying and communications capabilities, protection of secret information before World War II was quite simple. If one of a special few persons turned traitor or was duped, let a secret slip or lost control over sensitive material, great harm could result. Otherwise, the secrets were safe.

THE ADVENT OF ESPIONAGE IN AMERICA

Before World War II, there was little in the way of formal United States government security. Perhaps even more significant was the fact that there was very little intelligence and counter-espionage capability possessed even by the combined military services, and virtually none in the civilian government agencies.

When we consider that European countries have carried out organized, continuing intelligence, counter-intelligence, and espionage activities for hundreds of years—and on a fairly sophisticated basis too—we must marvel at the backwardness of our own executive and legislative leaders during the earlier years of the American Republic. Even when some intelligence capabilities came to be developed during wartime, the onset of peace usually saw them quickly reduced or eliminated, as was the case with the impressive network developed by Alan Pinkerton during the Civil War.

In the 1920s, the State Department's "Black Chamber," originally begun as an Army counter-intelligence unit in World War I, enabled the U.S. delegates to decode the secret instructions from Tokyo to the Japanese delegates at the Washington Disarmament Conference in 1922, thus successfully undermining Japan's negotiation strategy. However, in 1929, President Hoover's Secretary of State, Henry L. Stimson, cut off the funds for the Black Chamber with the comment: "Gentlemen don't read other's mail" As Roosevelt's Secretary of War during World War II, Stimson would be one of the first to suffer from the neglect of the U.S. intelligence capability which he himself had earlier helped to foster.

Nevertheless, during all the years between the two world wars, the legendary and brilliant William J. ("Wild Bill") Donovan, our most decorated soldier in World War I and later a successful lawyer, carried out several secret missions while in and out of government, for every sitting president, Democrat or Republican, under the guise of business, humanitarian, or other missions. In the course of these presidential assignments, Donovan developed a network of his own in countries throughout Europe. As a result of Donovan's activities, Roosevelt asked him to create the office of the Coordinator of Information (COI) to provide analysis and reporting to the policy makers in the Government. The COI came into being on July 11, 1941 as a presidential office, but was renamed the Office of Strategic Services (OSS) on July 13, 1942, given an operational responsibility, and placed under the Joint Chiefs of Staff. Donovan, now a Brigadier General, pushed ahead over the objections of the military services and the FBI. With a bureaucratic commitment to self-preservation and the status quo, these agencies opposed what they saw as a threat to their satrapies, regardless of the threat to the nation. Their attitudes fostered a continuation of the fragmented, inadequate, and feuding bureaucracies working at cross purposes with one another concerning intelligence and security.

With the establishment of the COI, long years of preparation and anticipation on the part of Donovan paid off and the embryo of our present intelligence services came into being. Generally backed by FDR in bitter and uneven battles with the services as well as with the entrenched bureaucracies of the State and Treasury Departments and the FBI, Donovan played his British card for synergistic effect and drew upon his extensive associations on Wall Street, in the Ivy League, in the Social Register and elsewhere to flesh out the skeleton structure he had designed to provide America with an intelligence capability. Not only did his concept envision intelligence gathering, it also envisaged operations in areas of military, economic, geo-political, cultural, ethnic, demographic, industrial, and agricultural interests—all on a world scale. In the short span of just a few years, the initial trickle of intelligence had swollen into a veritable deluge, all masterminded by the genius of "Wild Bill."

AMERICA'S SECURITY—THE EARLY YEARS

Until as late as FDR's "Preparedness Program," the prelude to the "Defense Program," on the eve of the Japanese attack on Pearl Harbor on December 7, 1941, government "security," as we know it today, was virtually non-existent in this country. In 1869, the Army issued orders that certain information should be restricted on military bases. In 1911, Congress passed the Defense Secrets Act, which forbade the dissemination of "National Defense Secrets," without defining the secrets. In 1912, the Department of War developed procedures for marking and protecting certain "confidential" documents. The Espionage Act of 1917 replaced the Defense Secrets Act and prohibited certain types of information-gathering. The War Department established "Secret," "Confidential" and "For Official Use Only" terminology in 1917, later replacing "For Official Use Only" with "Restricted." The Air Corps Act of 1926 dealt with the confidentiality of military aircraft contracts and provided that: "No alien employed by a contractor . . . shall be permitted access to plans or specifications."

Outside of the War Department, no formal program existed for the identification of sensitive information and material or its systematic protection. However, a few pioneers, literally on their own, went ahead and operated in a "secure" manner anyway. They protected the operations of the organizations in which they worked with controls and verifications; they made systematic inquiries regarding people and problems; and they shared information among themselves as needed, while attempting to limit the dissemination of sensitive information generally. Sometimes it was on a decentralized and informal basis that some data was simply determined to be "restricted information."

In 1938 Congress forbade drawings, photographs, etc. of military bases or equipment defined by the President, without prior approval. Even at this point there were no such programmatic features as a centralized security authority, a consistent classification system, and a structured method of sharing sensitive data with other government agencies or other governments.

The important concept of "need to know" was also not yet a part of any government security system, or even our lexicon. This concept was finally developed not only to restrict access to classified information to persons whose suitability, character, loyalty, and security worthiness had been established up to appropriate levels, but also to deny specific classified information even to adequately cleared persons unless their immediate assignment required it. During the days before World War II, the community of persons with access to security information functioned like a private club in which sensitive information was shared among those belonging to the group because each member of the "club" was deemed to be a person of integrity and could, in general, perform his or her requisite duties more effectively when in possession of the entire confidential or sensitive body of knowledge. Of course, the "club" in question was much smaller and more manageable. The pre-World War II Army, for example, numbered no more than 125,000 men, and the entire Departments of State, War, and Navy were comfortably located in the modest-sized building known today as the Old Executive Office Building.

In Great Britain, this "club" attitude held sway up to and even after the betrayals by such insiders as the "Cambridge Five," Kim Philby, Guy Burgess, John Cairncross, Sir Anthony Blunt and Donald McLean—impeccably British "establishment" figures from the best schools.

In the United States, the "club" system officially went out of existence because of the massive growth of government agencies and functions once the war had begun although the 'club' attitude continues to be an unfortunately popular conceit. The number of persons employed by the government requiring some type of access to classified information skyrocketed and the need for a systematic security system therefore became overwhelming.

The concept of granting formal "clearances" to individuals did not yet exist. When it did come into being, it did not include the current, rather strange distinctions involving security clearance at various "levels." This assumes, in essence, that an individual may be reliable up to the level of the security classification, "Confidential," but not "Secret"—or loyal up to the level of "Secret," but not up to "Top Secret"; and so on.

THE U.S. CIVIL SERVICE COMMISSION AND THE BEGINNING OF A SECURITY DATA BASE

What did exist and function quite well in those early decades was a small but perceptive and efficient agency of government: the U.S. Civil Service Commission, now long since a casualty of power politics and bureaucratic empire building.

Established by the Civil Service Act of 1883, the Commission came into existence as a direct result of President James A. Garfield's assassination by a disappointed office seeker. The Commission administered examinations and verified qualifications for employment of potential civil servants, thereby correcting some of the more egregious failings of the political spoils system.

Over a period of years, as the Commission discharged its responsibility for examinations and certification of eligibility for federal employment of those who had passed the requisite examinations, it determined that merely rating the professional, administrative, or clerical proficiency of job applicants was not enough. Rather, an individual must also meet established standards of "suitability" for federal employment.

In our supposedly more enlightened and progressive era, it may seem quaint that our government would have concerned itself with the character, honesty, temperament, sobriety, marital status, morality, reliability, and other such personal attributes of prospective government employees. But it did. Perhaps we still need to recall that, in those years, government employment was a privilege and an honor, eagerly sought. Personal conduct and moral behavior could be, and were, qualifying or disqualifying. The Civil Service Commission therefore played a major role in establishing the facts upon which an applicant for federal employment would be judged qualified or unqualified.

Throughout the 1930s, the Commission's Investigations Division directed a staff of investigators who traveled throughout the United States verifying the educational claims, the employment history, the reputation, and the personal habits of applicants for federal employment. These investigators tapped a variety of sources: schools, former employers, neighbors, police departments, and the like. Where their investigations turned up allegations of misconduct, questionable character, lack of integrity, or other such defects, the investigators pursued the leads until the allegations were either proved or disproved.

Questionable or derogatory information resulted in a "Special Hearing," at which the applicant was placed under oath and confronted with the information in question, and given the opportunity to explain, resolve, or acknowledge it. Finally, the Report of Investigation, as it was called, together with the written Report of Special Hearing, was forwarded to a Ratings Section where a judgment was made concerning the suitability of the person. In the case of applicants or nominees to high positions, specially qualified investigators were charged with verifying the presence of affirmative qualifications and characteristics as well as investigating negative allegations. No matter how long it took, the individual did not enter on duty until the process was completed. The author, a product of that era, passed the examinations in mid-1939, but was not appointed until July 1940, well over a year later, and became a Federal investigator in this system in 1941. It was a remarkably fair and efficient system, and it remained generally in place until the politicization of the federal security system which came about in the Eisenhower-Nixon years under the impetus of the sensational revelations of espionage and treason which surfaced and the public reactions they engendered.

With the beginning of World War II, investigators at the Civil Service Commission became more attentive to the possibility that certain subjects under investigation might be committed to countries or ideologies inimical to the United States. Certainly an individual's support for the German or Japanese bid for world domination was understood to disqualify that person for U.S. government employment. Nevertheless, there were remarkably few Americans with these particular alien loyalties, despite large numbers of Americans of German origin and a more moderate number of Japanese Americans.

More prevalent were those people who turned out to be loyal to the relatively new idea of international Communism—and hence to the revolutionary state that was supposed to be the embodiment and guardian of that idea, the Union of Soviet Socialist Republics. The Soviets effectively portrayed Communism and, by extension, the Soviet Union itself, as a benign force trying to lead the world into a new and better social order. The appeal of this fantasy, coming as it did after the worldwide devastation of the Great Depression, was so compelling as to enthrall the more credulous. As with the treatment of the Jews in Europe by the Nazis, accurate reports concerning the Soviet Union's atrocities against its own peoples were disbelieved by the faithful disciples.

Many factors conspired to create a climate in which Communism could be sympathetically portrayed. There was widespread anger because of the public perception that American business had brought on the Depression and had resisted many of the initiatives of President Roosevelt to put America back to work. There was also media-inspired sympathy for the Republican side in the Spanish Civil War, which was dominated by Soviet communism.

Meanwhile, the film industry and other media extolled all types of collectivism, "The Grapes of Wrath" being only one example. Also, the immediate threat of Nazi Germany clouded the more long-term threat of the Soviet Union, and the Soviets themselves were skilled propagandists, able to elicit sympathy and support for Communism while concealing its true totalitarian nature and goals. American idealists did not always look behind the facade of the ideal being "packaged and sold," as happened in the case of Communism. This was not true of its close kin, Fascism. Although it often rivaled and surpassed Fascism in its cruelty, oppression, and suppression of freedom, Communism nevertheless succeeded in acquiring its desired utopian allure in the minds of many.

The commitment to world Communism was so great on the part of some sympathizers that, when the Nazi-Soviet non-aggression pact was signed in 1939, they either excused, or refused to believe, the obvious fact that the "peace-loving" Soviet Union was joining with Hitler in the conquest of Poland and the division of Europe. American Communists vigorously demonstrated during this period for the party line that America should not get involved in the war in Europe. When Hitler, in violation of the pact, launched Operation Barbarossa and attacked the Soviet Union two years later, these same Communist sympathizers were transfigured. Suddenly, every effort had to be made to save "our brave ally," the Soviet Union, including involvement in the war.

One of the crucial indicators that alerted security investigators that a subject might be a Communist or a Communist sympathizer was a marked reluctance to condemn the Nazi-Soviet pact and resulting aggression, followed by extreme agitation and condemnation of Hitler after he attacked the Soviet Union. A history of "Following the party line" in its tortured twistings and turnings as it reflected the politically expedient objectives of the Soviet Union became a recognizable litmus test for investigators seeking to identify Communists and Communist sympathizers.

In the early 1940s, the investigators of the Civil Service Commission began to construct indices linking Communists, pro-Communists, fellow travelers, dupes, and other sympathizers, as this information became available to them through their investigations. These files served the Civil Service Commission well in the ensuing years. Empathetic contacts and linkage with other government investigative organizations—notably not the FBI, by the way; in the author's personal experience, the FBI was still neglectful of the communist threat at this early period—created an unofficial but effective government network of investigators who were aware of the threat posed by Communists in the American government; an awareness, incidentally, not shared by the political leadership in the agencies and departments where the investigators worked. The informality of the linkages made possible the sharing of information among the various security and counter-intelligence organizations, including Army Military Intelligence (G-2), the Office of Naval Intelligence (ONI), the Washington Metropolitan Police Department, and the Martin Dies Committee in the House of Representatives (later the House Un-American Activities Committee). Investigators from the various agencies actually searched one another's files informally—something that would be impossible today.

THE EFFECT OF THE NEW DEAL

With the advent of the New Deal, not only were the Federal rolls inflated by over a million new appointments but, given the nature of the New Deal philosophy, with its strong socialistic overtones, and the attraction of the New Deal to the liberal academicians and social-engineers, a dramatic swing to the left was inevitable in the make-up of the new personnel swelling Agency and Department rolls. The levers of power underwent radical political and social charge.

Out of the Works Progress Administration (WPA) ranks they came. Out of the college teaching ranks, the law schools, the social workers rolls. And many came with an orientation toward the great new revolutionary experiment in the Soviet Union.

These were, for the most part, liberals and radical liberals, many from academia, who wittingly or unwittingly, accepted the twists and turns in the Communist "Party Line" without questioning. They remained "faithful" even when Stalin entered into alliance with a kindred ruthless dictator, Adolph Hitler, in their June 1939 pact.

For the trained loyalty investigator, the extent to which the individual under investigation "followed the party line" was significant in determining whether the subject's loyalty to the United States was in question and required further probing.

Some in the U.S. did become disenchanted at particularly egregious turns in the "Party Line," but most retained their ability to "see no evil" and to rationalize the actions of a regime which denied every basic human right and freedom to its own people. This was the era of the bright new world—Utopia—where economic and political freedom would be brought to all humanity by International Communism. Its American adherents therefore lived and breathed and fought for the extension of international Communism. Their primary loyalties were to the Soviet Union and not to the United States. Even so there were others who recognized the danger. Many knowledgeable Sovietologists issued repeated somber warnings concerning the ultimate price that would have to be paid for these eager self-delusions; nevertheless, the same delusions continued, sometimes in the highest reaches of the U.S. government.

Despite the influence exerted elsewhere by certain radical New Deal appointees, the Civil Service Commission remained unreconstructed, particularly at the working levels of its investigative and rating examiner echelons. Commission investigations and the Commission's investigative process were therefore able to evolve into examinations of the loyalty, as well as the suitability, of applicants and employees. This was exactly what happened. Beginning in 1942, however, the flood of appointments to the federal service became so great that it was no longer possible to recruit, examine, investigate, evaluate, rate, and clear all personnel prior to appointment, as had been the normal practice prior to the outbreak of World War II.

Unfortunately, while the Civil Service Commission methodically carried out its legal mandate from Congress, it was increasingly pressured and thwarted in its efforts by officials in the defense-related Departments of War, Navy, State, and Treasury, as well as in wartime agencies such as the Board of Economic Warfare, the Office of Price Administration, and the Office of War Mobilization—these latter agencies were particular targets of the Soviet espionage apparatus because they were developing economic and supply policies crucial to the Soviet Union, and along with dedicated, loyal employees, they attracted social reformers and academics committed to application of "progressive" ideas and practices. In many cases, New Deal officials seized upon the inevitable investigative and clearance delays as an excuse to demand that appointments be made "subject to investigation." This turned out to be a way of getting people on the federal rolls who, because of their political leanings, would not otherwise have been appointed.

Once these employees, still subject to investigation, were on the rolls, they could then be kept on through a series of appeals, arguments, transfers, delays, and further demands arising out of the claimed status for certain employees as "essential" to the war effort. A new set of bureaucratic maneuvers evolved in this situation, in contrast to the prior government practice of withholding appointments until the applicant had been cleared. The applicant was already on the job and had suddenly became so valuable to the government as to be "irreplaceable." If the Civil Service Commission had come up with any disqualifying information on the subject, the Commission would now be instructed by higher-ups to reinvestigate further specific aspects of the case, or else further questions would be presented requiring further investigation. The Commission might also be requested to postpone the hearing, or the subject himself would be transferred to another agency, or overseas, or otherwise made unavailable for proper adjudication of the case according to the established rules. Too often, the importance of a given individual to the war effort was deliberately exaggerated in order to justify retention of the employee.

One example was the case of George Shaw Wheeler, discussed in the last chapter. Even in such an open-and-shut case as this one proved to be, well-intentioned government officials could justify their delaying tactics because most of them simply found it inconceivable that others espousing the same philosophy they themselves believed could ever really be disloyal to the United States and to its government. Open and aggressive support of Soviet interests was accepted in some circles. No conflict was perceived in practice between the social goals of the New Deal and Moscow's "alternate route" to what were naively believed to be the same social goals. Thus agencies were able to dismiss evidence of Communist sympathies as unimportant and irrelevant.

The predictable result was that a small number of the employees that were kept on the government rolls and even advanced while still "subject to investigation" turned out to be not merely Communist sympathizers, but in some cases, actual Soviet agents. Unfortunately, as is often the case in a large bureaucracy, the pattern was not clearly perceived and understood until it was too late—until after the war in fact, when the true face of international Communism was revealed in Eastern Europe. Moreover, it is not easy, even today, to accept the idea that your colleague and friend might actually be a spy and a traitor; it was even less so in the atmosphere of the early and mid-1940s.

From a government administrative and management point of view, however, the major cause of the failure of the Commission's suitability review process to prevent the placement and retention of persons disloyal to the United States was a deliberate weakening of the clearance authority of the Commission itself which came about during that same period, and the placement of authority and responsibility for clearance adjudication and final decision on hiring in the hands of each individual department and agency—in the very organization where the employee worked and was known. This proved to be a disastrous development in practice, even though it was supposedly justified by emergency wartime conditions. It placed too many suitability and loyalty decisions in the hands of people in departments and agencies who were not competent to make those decisions, or who saw no need for the process.

Administrative personnel of each individual department and agency, in the main, had little or no understanding or appreciation for either the sensitive security issues involved or the relevance of membership in innocuous-sounding Communist-front or related organizations or of association with others known to be Communists or Communist sympathizers. Indeed, the administrative personnel of each individual department or agency had little appreciation of the significance of derogatory information in security investigations generally. Placing authority and responsibility for clearance adjudication and final decision on hiring in the hands of each department or agency thus meant, too often, that information concerning an individual that was in fact damning was often not even considered relevant.

For many government officials, suddenly called upon to adjudicate security cases for the first time, it was simply inconceivable that a valiant wartime ally such as the Soviet Union could or would organize and utilize a massive espionage system using U.S. citizens occupying positions of trust and power to spy upon their own government. Many simply would not accept this. (A reading of the "Report of the Royal Commission," issued in 1946 detailing the success of the Soviet Union's efforts in Canada, provides a stunning revelation of this phenomenon).

In any case, rather than using the criteria and standards already developed by the government to determine suitability for government employment, many officials preferred to base their judgments on social, political, ideological, and personality factors. Once individual departments and agencies were left to make their own security decisions, all that was necessary to ensure that some Communist-leaning people would be hired was an agency administrator (or top aide) who was himself left-leaning or socialistic in his views.

Moreover, once department or agency leadership began to accept people for employment on the basis of one's philosophical or ideological views, and not on the basis of the federal government's published standards, the end result proved to be a serious erosion of federal standards. It allowed, as history has recorded, the hiring of a significant number of persons who later turned out to be disloyal to the United States and in some cases outright foreign agents.

THE QUESTION OF LOYALTY

It may seem strange, looking back, but during the 1920s and the 1930s, virtually no one imagined that an American citizen would actually be disloyal to his country. From the moment an immigrant landed at Ellis Island, no matter what his origin, no matter what the hardship he or she might have experienced in adjusting to the new land, loyalty was assumed—and was almost a universal fact. Disloyalty was as foreign as the land and the allegiance the immigrant had voluntarily left behind.

That the Irish, for example, despite the bigotry and discrimination they encountered with the ubiquitous NINA ("No Irish Need Apply") policies and hostile signs, would ever be anything other than loyal to America was inconceivable. The loyalty of African-Americans, whose ancestors were brought here in chains as slaves, was similarly assumed and relied upon. So, too, with the Poles and the Italians and the Greeks and other nationalities. America was the real land of promise; it was not some "experiment" off in Eastern Europe.

During World War I, there was a period of hysteria in which German immigrants were subjected to suspicion and not a little harassment at times. There was even some suffering which resulted from apprehension in some small minds concerning the basic loyalty of German immigrants at a time when we were at war with Germany. In fact, it turned out that there was little cause for concern because German-Americans really had accepted their new home in place of their old allegiance to their original homeland.

Things changed, however, during the late 1930s and '40s. Automatic loyalty to the United States on the part of all could no longer be assumed. Three major elements contributed to making the question of loyalty a significant new issue in America. Ironically, in the first two of the three instances, those concerning the loyalty of persons of German and Japanese ancestry, initial suspicions of possible disloyalty were virtually unfounded. Both German-Americans and Japanese-Americans turned out to be overwhelmingly loyal during the course of the war.

The third element concerned ideological commitment to the Communist cause. This element was largely unsuspected and overlooked by naive leaders, and was exploited by conspirators to the great detriment of the United States and the entire world.

Let us look a bit more closely at each of these three groups.

German-Americans

During the 1930s, in cities like Milwaukee and St. Louis with large German-American populations, people tended to live in communities of homogeneous ethnic background. For the Germans, the tavern was not merely a place to buy a stein of beer; it was a place for socializing where beer, food, and *Gemutlichkeit* all flourished. It was inevitable that the existence of this kind of ethnic camaraderie would encourage the formation of societies and associations similar to those which had existed in the homeland; and thus many singing groups, sports groups, and other similar social groups sprang up composed exclusively of German-Americans.

It was probably also inevitable that, considering the zeal commonly exhibited by Germans for the German Fatherland, some enthusiasm, perhaps even excessive enthusiasm, should have surfaced for the reported early accomplishments of the Nazis. As Germany extended its dominance and influence, it was probably also to be expected that a certain amount of pride on the part of German-Americans should have become manifest. Following the brutal takeovers of Austria and Czechoslovakia and the *Blitzkrieg* invasions of Poland, Belgium, the Netherlands, and France, however, German-Americans en masse turned against Nazi Germany, and often began to exhibit a deeper revulsion for the works of Adolf Hitler than did other Americans. Except for a minuscule portion of them, German-Americans were as solidly dedicated to America's war effort as any other ethnic group.

Our investigative and security agencies were required to scrutinize

German-Americans, among others, concerning their suitability to serve their country, either in the military or in the federal civilian agencies, and hence timely investigations had to be conducted into the activities of the German-American Bund and similar associations thought to be pro-Nazi. What these investigations revealed was that the members of these organizations were remarkably free of disloyal elements. The Nazi government had little success during World War II either in creating an effective espionage apparatus in America, or in placing their agents in the upper levels of the American government or military in order to exert influence on policy. The German lack of success in this regard, except in a few isolated and inconsequential cases, was especially striking by comparison with the Soviet success in their subversive efforts. Unlike its early neglect of pro-Soviet activities, the FBI did place suspected German-Americans under heavy scrutiny and the record could not be more clear. The FBI's performance in this area was highly creditable, in fact; and so was the performance of the German-American community.

Japanese-Americans

Readily identifiable as Asiatics, and as Japanese, both the Issei and the Nissei (immigrant and first generation Japanese-Americans) were inevitable targets in the highly charged reaction to the attack on Pearl Harbor and the inhuman treatment of the defenders of Corregidor. The climate was heated even more by the balloon bombs and float bombs sent on the winds and tides toward the West Coast of this country.

Certainly investigative groups had to be prudently aware of pro-Japan activities and potential subversive actions by persons of Japanese descent to the same extent as for German-Americans. And certainly it was logical to be more vigilant and suspicious of Japanese-Americans than of British-Americans, for example, or of French-Americans, because we were in a life and death struggle with Japan.

Given the shock and confusion resulting from the attack on Pearl Harbor and the fact that America had no margin for additional error in its now perilous exposure in the Far East and the overwhelming readiness of Japan to conduct its war against an ill-prepared United States, no rational assessment would fault super-caution by this country. The tragedies of Pearl Harbor, Corregidor, the "Bataan Death March" and the slaughter of civilians and military prisoners had left a weakened American government uncertain that its population could safely withstand further defeats. Moreover, the mood of isolation, coupled with more than a decade of Depression, had left a nation consumed with concern over economic survival, oblivious to the need for sophistication and expertise in conducting every facet of governmental action on a world scale, and without the talents and even the concepts of what was required to cope with subversion, espionage, and worldwide military and naval operations.

America lacked everything: knowledge of the areas of the world within which it must operate politically, militarily and, culturally; specialists with language and travel experience; a governmental structure to support the rapidly burgeoning bureaucracy made up of academics and amateurs flooding into the Federal service.

After nearly fifty years of contemplation, and considering the influence of an activist leadership, press and legal system, it is not surprising that legal and moral concepts have since been devised to support a finding that rights were denied by a government which, even in extremis, took pains to be judicious and fair.

What is lost in the wave of criticism of America's defense action in creating the War Relocation Authority and interning Japanese citizens and Japanese-Americans while they were "screened," was that this process did proceed with dispatch and with equitable processes, and that the internees were released quickly, Japanese-Americans were admitted into the military services and Japanese-Americans were recruited and hired into the Federal civil service. On the latter point, the author has some considerable personal knowledge since he was responsible for the investigative and clearance program of the U.S. Civil Service Commission under the War Relocation Act. It is not accurate to allege that the U.S. Government was insensitive to the rights and sensitivities of Japanese-Americans. Almost immediately, a program was initiated to aid in the release of Japanese-Americans and to assist in their obtaining employment in the Federal government. In this effort, the investigative and clearance process was carried out with efficiency and due respect for the persons under consideration for release and hiring and not a single case of alleged discrimination or harassment came to the author's attention, by direct, or indirect, complaint.

In the end, Japanese-Americans proved to be loyal to the American war effort. Cases of disloyalty, espionage, or subversion were virtually non-existent.

Communists in the Federal Government

The one area in which substantial disloyalty to the United States did become actively manifest, of course, was in the successful infiltration and corruption of the American system that was carried out by Communists and Communist sympathizers during and after the war years; in particular, infiltration into sensitive government positions. Many Communists and Communist sympathizers obtained sensitive government positions, in which they were clearly in a position to influence important and critical policy decisions. In 1944, the special Committee on Un-American Activities of the U.S. House of Representatives completed an investigation of the primarily communist-driven un-American propaganda activities in the United States and formally documented the many Communist "front" organizations operating within our nation and the subversive activities which proved their disloyalty.

The investigations of the companion "Subversive Activities Committee" in the U.S. Senate corroborated the House Committee findings. Attorney General—later Supreme Court Justice—Thomas C. Clark established the Attorney General's List of Subversive Organizations. Membership in any of the listed organizations was henceforth a basis to question the individual's loyalty to the U.S.

History will no doubt marvel at the success Communism had in recruiting and retaining sympathizers of the sort which Lenin himself termed "useful idiots." American public opinion has been shocked at having to keep on learning exactly the same lesson over and over again about Communist ruthlessness and brutality. This lesson became clear at the end of World War II in Poland, Czechoslovakia, Hungary, Romania, Yugoslavia, Bulgaria, and Albania; then again in 1953 in East Germany; in 1956 in Hungary; in 1968 in Czechoslovakia; throughout the 1960s in Cuba; in the 1970s in Cambodia, Laos, and Vietnam; in 1979 in Afghanistan; in the 1980s in Nicaragua; in 1989 in Tienanmen Square in Beijing; in 1991 in Lithuania and Cambodia; and in 1993 again in Cambodia and also again in North Korea.

During World War II, we "forgot" the Soviet Union's liquidation of millions of its own people from 1917 on. Then, at the end of World War II, we were suddenly shocked to see Eastern Europe taken over by force and subversion exercised by the agents and army of the Soviet Union. Our illusions were dashed (though only for a little while). At this time, some of the consequences of the obstruction of established security procedures which had taken place during the war began to be apparent. These were the years when Communist sympathizers and agents began to defect or otherwise be exposed or publicly identified, usually under heavy pressure from Republican members of Congress, victims of Communist oppression, investigative reporters, and veteran government security and intelligence agents. There even followed a series of sometimes sensational revelations concerning the infiltration and subversion which had been carried on by Communist agents. The extent of the Soviet espionage activity within our own government began to be realized by the American public at large and this put tremendous heat on President Truman.

Testifying before the House Un-American Activities Committee (HUAC), ex-Communist agent Elizabeth Bentley identified the Communists and the fellow travelers with whom she had worked while committing espionage. Most prominent among those she identified were Harry Dexter White, who had been until very recently an Assistant Secretary of the Treasury and who had presided at the Bretton Woods Conference, and Abraham George Silverman, Research Director for the Railroad Retirement Board. Others such as Benjamin Mandel, former member of the American Communist Party and former editor of *The Daily Worker*, the official organ of the party, brought mountains of evidence concerning American Communists to the Congressional committees. Mandel himself became a key staff member of the Senate International Security Subcommittee. The knowledge of such ex-Communists enabled Congressional investigators to know in advance something about the sympathies and activities of those being interrogated. This helped explain the constant flood of Fifth Amendment defenses taken by witnesses ("I decline to answer that question on the grounds that it might tend to incriminate me"). The issue of "Communists in government" eventually became the stick of dynamite which precipitated the Truman Loyalty Program (Executive Order 9835), and may have motivated Truman's decision not to seek another term of office.

The most sensational of all the revelations were those of ex-Communist agent Whittaker Chambers concerning Alger Hiss, a former assistant to the Secretary of State and aide to President Roosevelt at the Yalta Conference. Chambers first identified Hiss as a member of a "sleeper" Communist underground apparatus as early as 1939. As we noted, Chambers went to Adolf A. Berle, a senior State Department official with his revelations about Hiss. When no action was taken he went, two years later, to the FBI. Mr. Berle apparently saw no reason to consider any action even though what he had been told by Chambers was seriously incriminating. When called to testify at the HUAC hearings nine years later, Berle stated that he had not taken seriously any "idea that the Hiss boys and Nat Witt were going to take over the government" (referring also to the brother of Alger Hiss as well as to an NLRB official also named as part of the apparatus by Chambers)—as if "taking over the government" by a handful of foreign espionage agents had ever been the issue. The issue was that espionage in the interests of a foreign power was being carried out by high government officials. Chambers had provided evidence of criminal espionage in the higher reaches of sensitive agencies of our government. In addition, Chambers' testimony confirmed information already in government files concerning Alger Hiss, Donald Hiss, and Nathan Witt. *That* was what Berle, as a responsible official, had really not "taken seriously." No further action had been taken as a result of Chambers' revelations to the FBI, either.

Berle simply filed away the notes he took during his meeting with Chambers—until he passed them on to the FBI as a result of Chambers' visit there two years later. This list, to which both the State Department and the FBI thus had access, may not have been a complete list of all the Communists in the U.S. government at the time, but it was lengthy enough, and it should have served to provide some substantial leads to anyone serious about investigating the problem. Only in 1945, with the defection of a Soviet agent in Canada who revealed that a high State Department official was a spy, did the FBI call Hiss in for questioning. Even then the FBI took no action until the explosive HUAC hearings at which Chambers testified concerning the Communist-party affiliations of Hiss.

The lack of any proportionate official response to the grave charges lodged by Chambers and the antagonism displayed towards Chambers himself by some Democratic members of Congress once the HUAC hearings got underway, as well as by some officials in the executive branch of our government and segments of the press and media, surely provide an additional illustration of the pervasive influence in our society of many of the ideas and interests of leftists and Communists. Often people are influenced in a certain way without even being aware of the fact that they are being so influenced. Chambers himself examined this phenomenon in his dramatic book *Witness*. Because of his unique qualifications to provide a clear and in-depth insight into the nature of Communist influence on the U.S. government in the 1930s and the 1940s—and also because of the enormous impact this Communist influence had on our government security program—it is worth dwelling briefly on the experience of Whittaker Chambers. Chambers wrote, for example:

For me the Hiss Case did not begin in 1948. It began in 1939 when I talked to Adolf Berle. As a result of that incident and later observations, I concluded that there were powerful forces within the government to whom such information as I had given Berle was extremely unwelcome... From time to time, rumors and reports had reached me of what I could only regard as a fitful struggle going on out of sight, among those who sought to bring the facts behind the Hiss Case to light and those who strove to keep them hidden. Sometimes the struggle reached a peak, as when, shocked by what Isaac Don Levine had told him of my story, Walter Winchell again took it to President Roosevelt. Again nothing happened. It reached another peak when Ambassador William Bullitt took the same story to the President.

Chambers believed that the official antagonism he encountered constituted the reason why, with allegations in the possession of the FBI for years to the effect that Alger Hiss and the rest of the Ware Group were Communists, no action of any kind had been taken. He therefore came to believe that only an entity such as the House Committee on Un-American Activities, and not some agency of government more directly concerned or even implicated, had to force the issue. Convinced that Communist infiltration had penetrated to the heart of the nation's security, Chambers believed he was obliged to respond to HUAC's summons to testify when it came, and to appear before the Committee to testify about what he knew in a forum where it might have some chance of being heard. At that time, he was a Senior Editor of *TIME*. Chambers wrote further in *Witness*:

> Once I had begun that testimony, only the existence of that higher apathy seemed adequate to explain why the full weight of official disapproval was directed at first against me, and not into following on up my charges, and why the Hiss Case was a "red herring." It explained why the violent resentment of public and official persons was concentrated on me...

Thus Whittaker Chambers was beset by conflicts that arose as a result of his decision to say publicly all that he knew. The controversies which surrounded the Hiss case were believed by some merely to be manifestations of partisan politics. Chambers himself, however, thought that most of those who supposed this were merely being influenced by the traditional—and familiar—pattern of American politics; but his point was, precisely, that the traditional pattern of American politics no longer held good. Of course, American politics may have been one of the factors in play, but it was not, according to Chambers, decisive. The real explanation lay deeper. Chambers explained:

> The simple fact is that when I took up my little sling and aimed at Communism, I also hit something else. What I hit was the forces of that great Socialist revolution, which, in the name of liberalism, spasmodically, incompletely, somewhat formlessly, but always in the same direction, has been inching its ice cap over the nation... It was the forces of that revolution that I struck at the point of its struggle for power. And with that we come to the heart of the Hiss Case and all its strange manifestations...
>
> It was the forces of this revolution that had smothered the Hiss Case (and much else) for a decade, and fought to smother it in 1948. These were the forces that made the phenomenon of Alger Hiss possible; had made it possible for him to rise steadily in government and to reach the highest post after he was already under suspicion as a Communist in many quarters, including Congress, and under the scrutiny of the FBI. *Alger Hiss is only one name that stands for the whole Communist penetration of government.* He could not be exposed without raising the question of the real political temper and purposes of those who had protected and advanced him, and with whom he was so closely identified that they could not tell his breed from their own (emphasis added).

In the early days of the Hiss case, Hiss had successfully denied any association with Chambers and airily dismissed Chambers' charges as fictional products of a deranged mind. However, when Chambers and his wife were able to describe, separately, the Hiss household in great detail; produce classified papers copied before 1939 on a Hiss typewriter; and then produce old microfilms of the typed copies, the Hiss defense collapsed. The comment made by Hiss on being presented with this evidence was: "I am amazed, and until the day I die I shall wonder how Whittaker Chambers got into my house to use my typewriter."

As we have already seen, Alger Hiss was convicted for perjury, *but he was never indicted on the espionage charges.* He was not the only high-level official identified by Chambers as a Communist or fellow traveler in the U.S. government, however. Chambers named others as well, including:

- Lee Pressman, formerly General Counsel of the Works Progress Administration (WPA) and of the CIO.

- John Abt, formerly Assistant General Counsel of the WPA and Special Assistant to the Attorney General of the United States.
- Nathan Witt, formerly Secretary of the National Labor Relations Board (NLRB).
- Donald Hiss, brother of Alger Hiss.
- Vincent Reno, a mathematician assigned to the U.S. Army Ordnance Corps' Aberdeen Proving Grounds in Maryland.
- Philip Reno, formerly with the Social Security Administration and the Securities and Exchange Commission (SEC).

Ironically, while the FBI received credit for "breaking" these cases, the fact is, once again, that they were really only "broken" because a former Communist came forward and told all. One of the most surprising aspects of the whole affair was that the FBI often could not even confirm what these spies had revealed. Certainly, without Whittaker Chambers, Alger Hiss himself would have continued in his role as advisor to presidents and secretaries of state, perhaps with even more destructive effect. As in the Walker case thirty-five years later, Hiss and his associates were not exposed by the operations of America's security system but by a third party who knew about their activities—yet who had immense difficulty convincing those who were charged with the responsibility of protecting America to act properly in the performance of their duties. To this day this kind of blindness remains the most incredible single aspect of our whole security problem.

The Soviet Union, meanwhile, reaped enormous benefits from the disloyalty of these American traitors—and from the failure of America's security system in their regard. The costs of all this have been staggering, not only in monetary terms for us, but also in terms of human misery.

It was all part of the blindness of the times that the Soviet Union and its Communist allies were in so many related ways given a new lease on life. Stalin was given a remarkably free hand by the Yalta Conference, for example, at which Alger Hiss was present as a senior advisor to the dying President Roosevelt. As a result of the theft of America's atomic secrets, the Soviet Union was empowered to face off America for far more than a generation, meanwhile unleashing its revolutionary and de-stabilizing forces around the world.

The phenomenon of those who are in a position to know better continuing to disbelieve even the possibility that threats to our security might actually be real resurfaces whenever security requirements come into conflict with popular political currents or causes. In the Carter years, after the Vietnam War, for example, in the face of what proved to be major intelligence assaults by the USSR (combined with failures and betrayals within the American security system), the CIA substantially reduced its presence in the Soviet Union. The Church Committee in the United States Senate undermined the CIA and related agencies and almost destroyed our intelligence-gathering capability. Similarly, today, following the break-up of the Soviet Union and its satellite states, many people appear to have concluded without evidence that our espionage and security systems are a greater threat to our nation than are any of the antagonistic forces still arrayed against America.

EXECUTIVE ORDER 9835—
THE TRUMAN LOYALTY ORDER

The "heat in the kitchen" on President Harry S. Truman eventually became so intense—because of all of the sensational revelations of Communists and fellow travelers in the government—that he was forced to act. Successive security embarrassments were destroying the credibility of the Truman Administration and putting in jeopardy continued Democratic party control of the White House and Congress.

On March 21, 1947, in a move aimed at restoring some semblance of control and confidence, President Truman issued Executive Order 9835 (Appendix A), which became known as the "Loyalty Order." E.O. 9835 revoked E.O. 9300, which had been issued in 1943. From this point on, the loyalty of employees in the executive branch of the government was to be assured by the following provisions:

1. Investigation of Applicants

There was to be a loyalty investigation of every person entering civilian employment in any department or agency of the executive branch of the government. Investigations of persons entering the competitive service were to be conducted by the Civil Service Commission, except where this investigative function was delegated by special agreement to another department or agency. Other persons entering the executive branch, as well as current employees, where appropriate, would be investigated by their own departments and agencies, except that those departments and agencies without investigative units of their own would utilize the investigative facilities of the Civil Service Commission. Persons entering employment before completion of the investigation would be hired subject to a favorable loyalty determination.

The normal security investigation under the Truman Loyalty Order was to be limited to a National Agency Check, which simply involved checking the files of the FBI, the Civil Service Commission, the intelligence units of the armed forces and other government intelligence or investigative entities, as well as the files of the House Un-American Activities Committee. Whenever derogatory information was turned up, or on request of the department or agency head, a full field investigation was to be performed.

2. Investigation of Employees

The responsibility for an effective program to prevent the retention—as distinguished from the hiring—of disloyal civilian officers or employees was assigned to the head of the departments and agencies themselves. E.O. 9835 was to be considered by them as presenting *minimum* requirements regarding their investigative and security responsibilities, which also included prescribing and supervising loyalty determination procedures.

The department or agency head was to appoint one or more loyalty boards, each with at least three department or agency representatives. These loyalty boards were to hear loyalty cases and make recommendations concerning the possible removal of any officer or employee. The department or agency head was similarly to prescribe regulations concerning the conduct of security proceedings.

Any officer or employee charged with disloyalty was to be served with a written notice in sufficient time and with sufficient specificity to enable him to prepare his defense. Persons so accused had the right to reply in writing. They were also to be given an administrative hearing, before a loyalty board, at which they could personally appear, with counsel, witnesses, and evidence as necessary. Moreover, a loyalty board recommendation for removal could be appealed to the department or agency head or his designated representative. Rulings could be further appealed to the Civil Service Commission's Loyalty Review Board for an advisory recommendation. While employee rights were to be observed and maintained, employees could be suspended at any time pending a determination.

3. Responsibilities of the Civil Service Commission

A Loyalty Review Board consisting of at least three impartial Commission officers or employees was set up to review cases of persons recommended for dismissal from the federal service and to make recommendations to the head of the department or agency concerning the cases brought before them.

The Loyalty Review Board was empowered to develop implementation rules and regulations. It could also:

• Advise all departments and agencies on problems relating to employee loyalty.
• Disseminate pertinent information to employee loyalty programs.
• Coordinate employee loyalty policies and procedures of the various government departments and agencies.
• Make reports and submit recommendations for transmission to the president.

A central master index was to be established and maintained in the Civil Service Commission covering all persons whose loyalty had been investigated by any department or agency since September 1, 1939. The reports and investigative material, however, were to be maintained by the investigating department or agency.

The Department of Justice was to furnish the various loyalty review boards in the individual agencies with the names of foreign or domestic organizations determined by the Attorney General to be totalitarian, Fascist, Communist, subversive, advocating a use of force to deny others their constitutional rights or seeking, unconstitutionally, to alter the form of government of the United States of America.

4. Security Measures in Investigations

At the request of an agency or department head, an investigative agency was to provide him, or a mutually approved delegate, with all material concerning any current or prospective employee. Confidential informants could be protected when necessary, provided sufficient evaluation material concerning the source was provided.

Each agency or department was also charged with developing a capability not only to gather and analyze loyalty information, but also to protect this confidential information.

5. Standards

Activities or associations involving any of the following factors

qualified applicants or employees for rejection under the Truman
Administration's E.O. 9835:

a. Sabotage or espionage, or any attempts or preparations for
them, or knowingly associating with spies or saboteurs.

b. Treason or sedition or advocacy of them.

c. Advocacy of revolution or the use of force or violence to
alter the constitutional form of government in the United States.

d. Intentional, unauthorized disclosure to any person, under
circumstances which might indicate disloyalty to the United States,
of any documents or information of a confidential or non-public
character obtained by the person making the disclosure as a result
of his employment by the government of the United States.

e. Performing or attempting to perform his duties, or otherwise acting, so as to serve the interests of another government in
preference to the interests of the United States.

f. Membership in, affiliation with, or sympathetic association
with any foreign or domestic organization, association, movement, group, or combination of persons, designated by the Attorney General as totalitarian, Fascist, Communist, or subversive, or
as having adopted a policy of advocating or approving the commission of acts of force or violence to deny other persons their
rights by unconstitutional means.

6. Miscellaneous

Each department or agency under the Truman Loyalty Order
was to submit the names and other identifying data of all employees to the FBI, which was to check those names against its records
and provide the department or agency head with any pertinent
information. The agency head was then to be the one to order
investigations when he considered this to be advisable.

Finally, and almost as an afterthought, E.O. 9835 directed the
Security Advisory Board of the then State-War-Navy Coordination
Committee to draft rules applicable to the handling and transmission
of confidential documents. These rules were to become effective
for all departments and agencies upon approval by the president.
As a further consequence of the order, the files of all current employees were to be examined by the employing federal agencies,
and derogatory information, whether in the files or in the form of
allegations, was to be submitted to the appropriate loyalty boards
to make determinations against the new standards whether any em-

ployees should be terminated. Where an investigation was considered necessary, it was to be performed by the FBI.

E.O. 9835 relied on a mechanism which was already a demonstrated failure, namely, the creation of loyalty boards in each department and agency. This meant that the clearance decision-making power would remain in each individual department and agency, that is, under the control of the very people whose ideological bias or lack of interest in security and lack of knowledge about Communism, subversion, disloyalty, political bias and the like had already resulted in myriad faulty security judgments, some of which had been responsible for bringing on board or maintaining there the very disloyal people whose presence had largely caused the Loyalty Order to be issued in the first place. It was precisely the faulty evaluations about loyalty and suitability made by the individual agencies which had resulted in the clearance and hiring (or retention) of so many employees who were neither suitable nor loyal. The cases were merely sent back for review to the same people who had initially "processed" them, but with one positive additional ingredient: they were subject to review by the U.S. Civil Service Commission's Loyalty Review Board, and this Board did have seasoned, qualified and objective members.

Not only did the potential for poor judgments within the agencies persist, but the same people who had made them now had an additional need to justify their original decisions, or, at any rate, to obfuscate the whole issue. Moreover, the agency loyalty boards normally included no loyalty or security specialists; all the decisions were to be made by laymen, whose normal tendency in such matters—shown time and time again—was almost always to assume the innocence and good faith of all subjects of investigation, usually their co-workers. In any case, the performance of the loyalty boards was normally determined by the political make-up of the agency involved, especially that of its leadership. In the more liberal agencies, for example, such as the Federal Security Agency, later the Department of Health, Education, and Welfare, and at present the Department of Health and Human Services, no instances of disloyalty were ever likely to be found.

The Civil Service Commission still had jurisdiction in certain cases (persons still under hiring probation or for whom the suitability investigation had not yet been completed). In these cases, the Commission was able to pursue its investigations and adjudications to a just and reasonable conclusion.

In summary, then, the Truman Administration's E.O. 9835, although it recognized that there was a problem of security and loyalty, did not really result in an improved government security capability. It left gaps which could be abused by those determined to infiltrate government ranks and who knew how to work the system. More importantly, time was running out. The evidence of subversion and treason that kept coming out was beginning to effect Congress, the media, the public, and, especially, the voters. The country's mood was clear: action was demanded against those who had betrayed their trust.

HOUSE UN-AMERICAN ACTIVITIES COMMITTEE (HUAC)

From the late 1930s on, elements of government recognized both the seriousness of the security question and that the Communist threat was the major security problem facing America. On May 28, 1942, Attorney General Francis Biddle, in a deportation order for the radical leftist labor union leader of Australian origin, Harry Bridges, issued a "finding of fact" that the Communist Party of the United States advocated the overthrow of the U.S. government by force and violence. This finding of fact also included the observation that proven Communist "front" organizations represented to the public as seeking some legitimate democratic reform were actually engaged in Communist subversion while simply awaiting such time as the Communists might be able to seize power through revolution.

As a labor leader, Harry Bridges had achieved a position where, even in wartime, he was able to shut down vital docks by strikes. His activities were unquestionably harmful to the country, but he was also a thorn in the side of FDR. Deportation to his native Australia seemed the most practical and painless way to extract that particular thorn. The case showed that there were at least instances when the Roosevelt Administration would move against the left—when the threat might endanger the war effort. Moreover, Attorney General Biddle's finding of fact concerning the American Communist Party was an important precedent.

Nevertheless, the most significant entity in the U.S. government that was both aware of and attempting to meet the Communist threat in those years was the House Un-American Activities Committee. HUAC engendered the most bitter, unrelenting hatred by the liberal left, led by the media.

In 1944, hearings held by this special committee of the House of Representatives resulted in an impressive tabulation of Communist front organizations. In 1946, HUAC's Representative (later Senator) Everett Dirksen of Illinois directed the preparation of an equally impressive "Report on Communism in Operation in the Soviet Union."

On May 11, 1948, HUAC submitted another report, entitled "Report on the Communist Party of the United States as an Advocate of the Overthrow of the Government by Force and Violence." While most Americans by then had already been disabused of any naive pro-Communist sentiment by Stalin's post-war actions in Eastern Europe, this report laid bare the reality of Communism and its international attack on democracy. The report covered such topics as:

- The writings of Lenin, Stalin, and other Communist leaders openly advocating the use of force and violence for the overthrow of the governments of the United States and of other democratic countries.
- The activities of the American Communist Party and its relationships and subservience to International Communism, i.e., to the Soviet Union.
- The systematic infiltration of the governments and infrastructures of other nations by Communist agents; and the subsequent overthrow, or attempted overthrow, of the governments of Bulgaria, China, Czechoslovakia, Greece, Italy, Hungary, Poland, Romania, and Yugoslavia.
- Legal determinations concerning the Communist Party and its advocacy of the overthrow of governments by force and violence, including Supreme court and other federal court decisions, other legal findings of fact, some brief excerpts and some historical precedents.

The Introduction to this HUAC Report ably summarized the whole situation at the time:

The Communist Party of the United States of America advocates the overthrow of our government by force and violence. As documentary proof of this, the Committee on Un-American Activities submits the following Report:

The Committee hopes that this report will dispel any confusion on the question that may presently exist in the mind of the American public, demonstrate the urgent need for enforcing existing legislation dealing with the Communist Party, and illustrate the voluminous evidence available for such enforcement.

This Report will show that:

1. The teachings of Marx, Engels, Lenin, and Stalin consti-

tute the credo of the Communist Party, U.S.A.—in fact, of the Communist movement throughout the world. The doctrine of forceful and violent overthrow of anti-Communist governments is a basic premise of these teachings.

2. The model party of the American Communist Party is the Communist Party of the Soviet Union, whose history forms a basic guide or textbook for American Communists on the practice of force and violence.

3. The American Party is now and always has been under the direction of an international Communist organization dominated by the leaders of the Communist Party of the Soviet Union. This was true under the Communist International and now under the Communist Information Bureau. This world movement has consistently advocated forceful and violent measures against anti-Communist governments. It is no mere coincidence that in every one of the countries recently overthrown by such Communist violence, leaders of the Communist International have seized positions of power.

4. The Communist Party, U.S.A., and its leaders, both present and past, are on public record as advocates of the forceful and violent overthrow of the American government, despite their recent disavowals. Many of these leaders have received training in Moscow on the practical application of such methods.

5. The Communist Party, U.S.A., has encouraged, supported, and defended, without a single deviation, the ruthless measures of foreign Communist parties to overthrow their legally constituted governments by force and violence. In other words, what the Chinese or Greek Communists are doing today is what the American Communists plan to do tomorrow under similar circumstances.

6. While the United States Supreme Court has not yet made a judicial determination on the question, numerous lower federal courts have, with unusual consistency, handed down decisions which characterize the Communist Party, U.S.A., as an advocate of overthrowing our government by force and violence.

The threat offered to our national security by the continued, almost unrestricted operation of such a movement within our own borders should be obvious to everyone.

As earlier stated, HUAC was not universally honored at the time for calling attention so powerfully to the true nature of the threat posed by Communism. It was not always so honored either within the U.S. government, or among the American public at large. In retrospect, though, few can claim to have been either as accurate or as prescient as HUAC on the subject of Communism.

THE EISENHOWER ADMINISTRATION AND E.O. 10450

The Truman Administration's Executive Order 9835 and the loyalty boards it established were not enough to save the Truman Administration from the embarrassment that followed the continuing revelations of pro-Communists in government. Ex-Communists such as Whittaker Chambers, Benjamin Mandel, and Elizabeth Bentley not only identified specific Communist infiltrators, but also exposed the ease with which these same Communist infiltrators had been able to get themselves hired and promoted and also illustrated the obstinacy with which, in too many cases, New Dealers had continued to defend and protect them.

There were, of course, during these years, those in the government trying to combat or prevent the hiring, retention, and promotion of persons with Communist affiliations. One of them was Raymond E. Murphy, a long-time security expert working in the State Department as special assistant to the director of Western European Affairs. Murphy had devoted a lifetime career to the State Department and had become an expert on Communism. His specialty was Soviet intentions and activities in Western Europe.

Working in concert with the American labor movement, and, in particular, with the American Federation of Labor, Murphy helped mobilize resistance to the Communists in countries such as Italy, where he played a major role in helping thwart a Communist takeover of the government in the immediate post-war years. At a moving ceremony at the Italian Embassy in Washington, Murphy was decorated by the Italian Ambassador for his contribution to saving Italy from the Communists.

Nevertheless, anti-Communist government insiders such as Murphy were continually disappointed and frustrated in their efforts on behalf of world security. Murphy himself had been a strong supporter of Whittaker Chambers at a time when the latter was still vainly trying to get anybody in the State Department to believe his revelations concerning Communist infiltration in the government.

Former influential members of the American Communist Party

including Benjamin Mandel, the former editor of *The Daily Worker*, were weaned away from their Communist allegiance by Murphy and ultimately placed in positions where their experience and knowledge of Communism and Communists in the government could be used in the defense of this country. Mandel, for instance, served for many years on the staff of the Senate Internal Security Subcommittee and was instrumental in developing the critically important indices which linked Communists and Communist sympathizers into a single network consisting of all those actively aiding the Soviet Union.[3]

Raymond Murphy died in 1963, having accomplished much in his efforts to combat Communism but also fully aware of many failures. The Communist threat had not disappeared, after all.

Some progress, however, was made. Disillusionment on the part of many former Communists brought them out into the open to tell what they knew. The intensity and sometimes sensationalism of the media coverage about the Communist agents—infiltrators—had aroused the public. The hearings of the House Committee on Un-American Activities were being widely followed and believed. Even E.O. 9835 was beginning to work after a fashion; it certainly served to call attention to the fact that the Communist threat was real. Even so, the attention span of Americans concerning any movement, cause, or issue is notoriously short; the media and the opinion-formers contribute to this short attention span because, although they may cover an issue thoroughly while it is immediately before the public, they are easily distracted. In time this is what happened to the issue of "Communists in government"; the media and the public lost interest and went on to other things.

In the meantime, while public attention was still focused on the revelations concerning Communists in government, the Truman Loyalty Program came into effect and was working to some degree. Some momentum was being created by the glare of publicity which so often

---

[3]It was Mandel and Murphy who once helped this author in securing the services of a young Congressman from California, Richard M. Nixon, as a speaker in connection with his experiences as a HUAC member confronted with the famous "pumpkin papers" of Whittaker Chambers. The occasion was the annual banquet of the National Center, now part of the George Washington University Law School. The program for which I was then responsible meant securing a banquet speaker and Nixon filled the bill. While driving the Congressman to and from the dinner and sitting next to him at the head table, I learned a great deal about his determination to rid the government of Communists.

surrounded it. Some security risks were identified and removed; others just "faded away"—resigned. Still others lost influence in the new climate.

The government was finally beginning to make up for the years of neglect of the security function. Yet it was just at the moment that greater security consciousness was beginning to take hold, both in the government and among the public at large, that the whole issue of security and "Communists in government" was suddenly about to be politicized in a far more dramatic way than had been the case. The entire country was about to pay for its previous security laxity with a backlash of gigantic proportions.

Government security and "Communists in government" were about to become election issues. Before the smoke of the electoral battles cleared away, the Truman Administration would be discredited, largely on these very issues. A Republican administration would be in office, and a new era in American history would come to be named after a new word that was added to the language—"McCarthyism," referring to unproven and irresponsible accusations of security laxity and "Communists in government" which Joseph R. McCarthy, Republican Senator from Wisconsin, would soon turn into national media sensationalism.

Republican Congressman Richard M. Nixon of California was already in the field. Nixon had come into national prominence principally by championing Whittaker Chambers at the time of the latter's HUAC testimony against Alger Hiss. The visibility Nixon gained at that time would win him first a Senate seat and then a place on the Republican national ticket with General Dwight D. Eisenhower.

Back in 1948, at the beginning of his remarkable political career, Nixon had recognized both the drama and the political potential of the Hiss case (he also knew at that time how to benefit from the labors of William Stribling, the able chief investigator of the House Un-American Activities Committee). In his 1950 California Senate race, in which he defeated the liberal Helen Gahagan Douglas—thereby earning himself the undying enmity of the media—Nixon had already made himself master of the loyalty and anti-Communism issues, and he was especially persistent in his attacks on the Truman Loyalty Program.

Dwight D. Eisenhower, popular military victor in Europe, was certainly not unaware of the national concern over Communists in government, nor did he fail to recognize the tremendous boost a young "Communist fighter" would bring to the 1952 national Republican ticket. Thus, after Eisenhower was nominated for president, Nixon was selected for the vice-presidential slot and was quickly assigned (or volunteered for) the role of gut fighter against the Democrats on the loyalty and Communist issues. This was very much his "cup of tea"—as it was not Eisenhower's. The issues may have been legitimate, but what followed in the election campaign went far beyond the bounds of propriety and accuracy. In the vehement attacks he launched, Nixon made allegations that were not only unsustainable, but—like those of Senator McCarthy— actually did harm to the efforts of the professional security, intelligence, and investigative people in the government who had responsibly been trying to carry on the fight against the Communists.

Although many excesses ended up being committed in the 1950s, it is also wise to recall that the security failures of the 1930s and 1940s were all too real. Neither Nixon nor McCarthy could have successfully launched their campaigns against "security risks" if the atmosphere in the country had not been what it was. In his book *The Glory and the Dream: A Narrative History of America—1932 - 1972*, author William Manchester confirms much about the history and events of the period of the Loyalty Program cases and describes the temper of the times during the late 1940s and 1950s, documenting the grievous extent of the penetration of the American government by American Communists; particularly worth reading is Manchester's chapter entitled "The Age of Suspicion."

In the summer of 1950, for example, Julius and Ethel Rosenberg were arrested for their part in the acquisition of atomic bomb secrets from the Manhattan Project and the delivery of these secrets to the Soviet Union. With reference to the espionage achievements of the Rosenbergs, David Greenglass, Henry Gold, Klaus Fuchs, Allan Nunn May, *et al.*, Manchester writes:

> That was real treason, not the paranoid fantasies of superpatriots demanding loyalty oaths of kindergarten teachers and movie extras. Beyond doubt the Rosenberg-Greenglass-Gold-Fuchs-Nunn May ring was one of the most successful in the history of international espionage. In Moscow it disgorged charts, formulae, and hundreds of pages of closely written data describing in detail everything from Oak Ridge's gaseous diffusion process for separating U-235 and U-238 to blueprints of the missile itself. The Russians could scarcely have learned more about nuclear weapons had they been full partners in the undertaking. At the cost of two billion dollars, America had assembled the best scientific minds in Western Europe and the United States, mobilized American industry, and united the two in a three-and-a-half year search that culminated in success . . . By then the Soviet director of

intelligence had a full account of the making of the bomb... The information was beyond price. USSR physicists could not have duplicated it then. They grasped the theoretical physics involved, but in the 1940s Russia simply did not have adequate industrial resources for so huge a venture. Treachery permitted them to close the nuclear gap. The Anglo-American traitors had hastened the onset of the Cold War by at least eighteen months.

Manchester points out that the crimes of these spies were so enormous, and the British and American counter-espionage nets through which they slipped so ineffective, that public opinion in both Britain and America, if it had realized both the enormity of the crimes involved and the drastic nature of the consequences of them for the future of the world, might well have demanded immediate changes of government at both 10 Downing Street and 1600 Pennsylvania Avenue. Instead, little happened. Although security failures were naturally lamented, there was no real effort to inquire how it had been possible for such security failures to come about and who was responsible for them. The public at large lacked the scientific and industrial knowledge to realize exactly what had occurred or its impact. Again, William Manchester remarks, pertinently:

> If [the other] Communists-in-government had not betrayed atom bomb plans, it was only because they didn't know any. All were cut from the same cloth as the spies in the labs—intelligent, sensitive, and idealistic men who had been born shortly after the turn of the century and witnessed the collapse of the economy after the [1929] Crash, the unchecked aggression which had followed in Spain, Ethiopia, China, and central Europe, and the shame of Munich. Despairing of the western democracies, they had embraced Communism as the faith that would remake the world. Like religious fanatics they would do anything for the cause. Most of them were denied the golden opportunity of the physicists, but everyone could do something. Those in the Administration could filch state secrets. If in the sub-cabinet one might recommend Soviet solutions such as the plowing under of Germany's Ruhr. Even ordinary people could serve as couriers. Harry Gold was a courier. Whittaker Chambers was another.

As recounted in Chapter One, I had to deal with one of those "subcabinet"-type officials recommending "Soviet solutions" from where he sat in high positions within the U.S. Government: George Shaw

Wheeler. There were many others like him. But so deeply did the penetration of such people into the U.S. government challenge cherished beliefs and assumptions of the time that the evidence for it and even actual confessions of espionage activity were disbelieved. Dean Acheson, President Truman's Secretary of State, went to his grave believing that high Treasury official Harry Dexter White was innocent and the Hiss case a "mystery." Many members of the "establishment" displayed similar traits. Manchester writes:

> Early in the Age of Suspicion liberals and intellectuals tried to drown the Red Bogey in laughter... As the summer wore on, they became less amusing. In sworn testimony, Miss Bentley and Whittaker Chambers accused thirty-seven former government employees of participation in Soviet espionage. Of these, seventeen refused under oath to say whether they were Communists or spies... None of them had been known to the public before 1948, but all had been close to the seats of power and decision. Six were not called to testify. Of those remaining, Harold Ware had died in 1935; Lee Pressman and John Abt admitted they were Communists but denied espionage. Laurence Duggan, a fourteen-year veteran of the State Department, either jumped or fell to his death from a sixteenth-floor Manhattan window after two witnesses identified him as a Communist... Harry Dexter White, against whom the evidence was formidable, died of a heart attack; and the other twelve then swore that the charges against them were false. Two of these were then accused of perjury. The first, William Remington, was found guilty and later murdered in prison. The other was Alger Hiss.

This, then, was the atmosphere at the beginning of the Eisenhower Administration. This was the climate in which Richard Nixon saw his opportunity to exploit the tragically real failures of the government's security system in order to advance his own personal agenda. If Nixon had been able to resist the temptation to lash out at security failures during the many years of domination of the national government by the Democratic party, and had conducted his campaign on a more accurate and temperate basis, he could have achieved the desired effects without inflicting damage to the government's ongoing security program. Instead of referring to the known cases of treasonable activity in an objective, factual, and dispassionate manner, leaving it to the media to carry the stories of the Rosenbergs, the Alger Hisses, the Harry Dexter

Whites, and the George Shaw Wheelers, Nixon fired broadside after broadside, often consisting of wild, generalized accusations. According to the Nixon of that era, the U.S. government, and particularly the State Department, was filled not only with Communists, but also with sexual deviates, "blabbermouths," and other undesirables whom it was the intention of the Republicans, as soon as they had captured the presidency, to remove wholesale as "security risks."

It is true that Senator Joseph McCarthy had already launched his own free-wheeling exploitation of the loyalty and "Communists in government" issues by the time of the 1952 presidential campaign. It could be that those managing the national ticket felt they could not afford to be perceived to be "weak" on these issues with McCarthy also out on the stump. Accusations were flying thick and fast in those days. In any event, Eisenhower and Nixon were just storing up trouble for themselves for later when they would have to deal with a McCarthy by then gone completely out of control.

After twenty years in power, tarred with the brush of numerous scandals, faced with a war hero in General Eisenhower as the Republican candidate—and with Adlai Stevenson, a tepid former governor of Illinois as their own standard bearer—the Democratic party went down to defeat in 1952, and, for the first time since 1928, a Republican was elected president. It was hard to specify exactly how much the loyalty and "Communists in government" issues influenced the election, but it was clear that they had had considerable impact. As a result of positions taken by their vice-presidential candidate, the Republicans were now firmly committed to cleaning up "the mess in Washington" and rooting out security risks from the government.

It was probably never Eisenhower's intention—certainly it was not his style—to get into the nitty-gritty of government operations as president. He carried over his established military habits into the White House and delegated massive responsibilities to subordinates. In the area of security, this "hands off" attitude of Eisenhower's was to have serious consequences, not only in the form taken by the security program put in place by the Eisenhower Administration and the way in which it was administered, but also in the way the loyalty and "Communists in government" issues continued to be handled generally, given the fact that there was a Republican senator vying for the headlines by exploiting these same issues.

Major responsibility for the government security program to be developed and put in place by the new administration naturally resided in the Department of Justice. As a result of the campaign, and also of conscious choice, another Administration figure would also be playing a major role in the Eisenhower security program: Vice President Nixon.

As both Congressman and Senator, Nixon had developed a close working relationship with the legendary director of the Federal Bureau of Investigation, J. Edgar Hoover. Hoover was famous for his ability to use the Bureau he headed to achieve his own national and personal ends. It was therefore no surprise that some of the tactics that would be employed in the Administration's new security crusade would be among the same ones that had normally characterized Hoover's style. It was also no surprise that Hoover would see and would seize the opportunity to accomplish some of his own long-standing power-seeking objectives within the executive branch. What greater expansion of FBI power could there be than the creation of a vast new security network composed of former FBI agents placed as security officers in many government departments and agencies, individuals who would be in possession of background information on every single person working in the executive branch? This situation was exactly the result the Eisenhower Administration brought about with its new security program.

It is important to realize that the FBI under J. Edgar Hoover was not just another agency which conducted investigations whose professionals, when they had completed their careers, would fade quietly back into private life. No. The networking system established within the FBI linked agents directly with the FBI director by a lasting personal commitment which was expected to supersede all other loyalties. Woe to the FBI agent who ever ran afoul of the harsh, petty and unforgiving spirit of J. Edgar Hoover.

Reacting to the real weaknesses and duplicity, and—as history records, sadly, even the treason—which had characterized some of the left-leaning, social-engineering of New Deal activists, the Eisenhower Administration knew what it wanted as its favorite target: Communists or pro-Communists in government. After twenty years in power, the Democrats had placed many sympathizers with their own agenda in the ranks of the career federal bureaucracy into policy and decision-making positions. The effects of such an entrenchment would even continue for many years after the Democrats had left office, aided by the fact that the Republicans did not always understand that another and different kind of bureaucratic war was being fought and that the realization of their stated aims was being thwarted by Eisenhower's policy of extensive delegation of authority. Senator McCarthy, for example, could chew up members of the Eisenhower Administration such as Secretary of the Army Robert T. Stevens, a well-intentioned political appointee totally unused to Washington's usual jungle warfare simply because Eisenhower's practice was to remain aloof and unconcerned. After all, as a soldier, he was used to battle casualties.

From the Administration's point of view, the main issue was to appear to move decisively against the "security risks" in government against whom the 1952 Republican campaign had so vehemently inveighed. Moreover, the campaign pledge had been "to remove all security risks" once elected. Almost as soon as the Republicans took office on January 21, 1953, a strategy was devised: there would be a new security Executive Order issued by President Eisenhower under which the government security system would be drastically changed and control would be placed in the hands of the Eisenhower Administration faithful. In reality, it was a Nixon program.

As evidence of the new administration's expanded commitment to security, there would be a vast expansion of security investigations. Millions of such investigations would be performed, in fact, one for each and every U.S. government employee! That was the concept. In truth the vast majority of these expanded security investigations would be simple name checks. Nevertheless, after all the ballyhoo of the election campaign, the Republicans had to make good in some fashion on their promises to "root out security risks" from the government rolls. It was for this reason that a plan was devised based upon conducting vast numbers of "security investigations" so as to find and remove all the alleged security risks.

On April 23, 1953, President Eisenhower issued Executive Order 10450 (Appendix B). This new executive order revoked the Truman Administration's E.O. 9835 Loyalty Program and ostensibly strengthened substantially the official standards which a current or prospective government employee must meet in order to be hired for or retained in the government. While E.O. 9835 had required that reasonable grounds should exist for belief that a person was disloyal to the government of the United States in order to trigger termination or refusal to hire, under E.O. 10450 the individual's employment, or retention in employment, had to be "clearly consistent with the interests of national security."

No longer would "security" merely be an overall idea that classified data must be protected. Rather, the aim was to establish an attitude of positive loyalty throughout the government. A security investigation of every employee was to be performed, from the most senior intelli-

gence and military personnel down to, say, animal caretakers in the
National Zoo. Every position would affect the "National Security."
Moreover, every government department or agency, no matter how remote from the defense or national security interests of the country would
now have to have its own director of security. The opportunity to extend
his influence into every department and agency of the government was
attractive to FBI Director J. Edgar Hoover. Vice President Nixon could
never have put into the hands of his friend a bigger plum than this and
Hoover was quick to take advantage of the opportunity afforded him.
What ensued after the Justice Department planning sessions early in the
Eisenhower Administration was that FBI agents and retired FBI agents
were appointed to director and senior security officer positions throughout the government. In sum, FBI people ended up filling these new
positions in great numbers.

The fact is that what made an FBI agent a good agent, i.e., the
ability for fact gathering without any exercise of judgment concerning
the meaning of the facts discovered and assembled, was virtually the
antithesis of what was really required in a good government security
officer, namely, the ability to assess, appraise, and judge the significance
of the facts collected. The Eisenhower Administration's security program thus got off on the wrong foot from the outset. The debacle that
followed was inevitable.

The scope of each employment investigation for the federal service
was to be determined according to the degree of adverse effect which an
occupant could bring about given the nature of the job occupied. Department or agency heads or their representatives were to designate as "sensitive" every position whose occupant could bring about a "materially"
adverse effect on the national security. A full field investigation, including on-site verifications of upbringing, education, and previous employment as well as personal interviews with co-workers, friends, and neighbors, was required to be carried out before the person could be assigned
to a "sensitive" position.

For all employees on whom a full field investigation had previously been performed, the file material was to be supplemented, if appropriate, and the case re-adjudicated according to the new standards.
Each department and agency was directed to establish and maintain an
effective program to perform and support this security function. Adjudication meant and required the application of analysis and judgment on
all of the facts generated by the investigation; this adjudication was to
be based on specific standards. The newly appointed former FBI agents

were seldom trained or prepared to carry out the security function properly as agency security officers. They merely assumed office from day one as Directors of Security and Security Officers.

For every employee whose position was not designated as requiring a full field investigation, a national agency check, as it was called, was to be conducted. This involved a search based on name and social security number checked against the existing records of the FBI and other federal investigative and intelligence agencies; if any derogatory information was turned up by means of such a check, it would have to be investigated further, evaluated, and then adjudicated.

Adverse information under E.O. 10450 which would disqualify an individual from government service went far beyond the obviously disloyal and even treasonable actions which had been identified under the earlier Truman Administration E.O. 9835. For the Eisenhower Administration, disqualifying adverse information included, "depending on the relation of the government employment to the national security," the following:

(i) Any behavior, activities, or associations which tend to show that the individual is not reliable or trustworthy.

(ii) Any deliberate misrepresentations, falsifications, or omissions of material facts.

(iii) Any criminal, infamous, dishonest, immoral, or notoriously disgraceful conduct, habitual use of intoxicants to excess, drug addiction, sexual perversion, or financial irresponsibility.

(iv) An adjudication of insanity, or treatment for serious mental or neurological disorder without satisfactory evidence of cure.

(v) Any facts which furnish reason to believe that the individual may be subjected to coercion, influence, or pressure which may cause him to act contrary to the best interests of the national security.

Actions or behavior which constituted evidence of disloyalty to the United States, according to E.O. 10450, were any of the following:

• Commission of any act of sabotage, espionage, treason, or sedition, or attempts thereat or preparation therefor, conspiring with, or aiding or abetting, another to commit or attempt to commit any act of sabotage, espionage, treason, or sedition, or attempts thereat or preparation therefor, or conspiring with, or aiding or abetting, another to commit or attempt to commit any act of sabotage, espionage, treason, or sedition.

- Establishing or continuing a sympathetic association with a sabo-teur, spy, traitor, seditionist, anarchist, or revolutionist, or with an espionage or other secret agent or representative of a foreign na-tion, or any representative of a foreign nation whose interests may be inimical to the interests of the United States, or with any person who advocates the use of force or violence to overthrow the gov-ernment of the United States or the alteration of the form of gov-ernment of the United States by unconstitutional means.
- Advocacy of the use of force or violence to overthrow the govern-ment of the United States, or of the alteration of the form of gov-ernment of the United States by unconstitutional means.
- Membership in, or affiliation or sympathetic association with, any foreign or domestic organization, association, movement, group, or combination of persons which is totalitarian, Fascist, Communist, or subversive, or which has adopted, or shows, a policy of advocat-ing or approving the commission of acts of force or violence to deny other persons their rights under the Constitution of the United States, or which seeks to alter the form of government of the United States by unconstitutional means.
- Intentional, unauthorized disclosure to any person of security infor-mation, or of other information disclosure of which is prohibited by law, or willful violation or disregard of security regulations.
- Performing or attempting to perform duties, or otherwise acting, so as to serve the interests of another government in preference to the interests of the United States.

Not much appears to have been left out here: in its intent as well as in the extent of its coverage, E.O. 10450 apparently aimed to com-pletely "solve" the government security problem. However, appearances can sometimes be deceptive. For one thing, the new standards were much less specific than the old. For another thing, they required the employee to prove loyalty rather than for the government to prove dis-loyalty. One thing we can confidently say about them is that they defi-nitely did not solve the government security problem.

EFFECT OF EXECUTIVE ORDER 10450

One of the things that the Eisenhower Administration's E.O. 10450 did accomplish was the rather remarkable feat of raising the profile, image, authority, and responsibilities of the government security func-tion while, at the same time, trivializing and stultifying it. Moreover, in what was the distressing "McCarthy period," it also elevated the role of the agency director of security and placed the position near the seat of power in the agency or department, thus increasing its influence.

Prior to E.O. 10450, if derogatory information or allegations pertaining to loyalty were turned up before, during, or after an individual's suitability investigation, this information or these allegations were adjudicated by a loyalty board and a judgment was then made concerning employability.

Under E.O. 10450, *every position in the federal government* had to be determined to be either sensitive (3b) or non-sensitive (3a) and then so designated. Even potential employees for non-sensitive positions required at least a national agency check. Potential employees for sensitive positions had to undergo a full field investigation as well as have a national agency check done on them. No position, no matter how far removed from the opportunity to do any damage to the interests of the United States, would be spared the national agency check.

Moreover, the distinction between sensitive and non-sensitive positions could be changed with each incoming administration, or, indeed, with each new department or agency head. In practice, this meant that even people in menial jobs with no access whatsoever to classified material—housekeepers, clerks, cooks, drivers, and a hundred other classifications—had to undergo the same "investigation," i.e., a name check, as those requiring access to "confidential" or "secret" documents in their jobs. In reality, then, there was no "custom tailoring" of security investigation procedures to fit the job requirements, as proponents of the new system often claimed. Among the effects of instituting this new security system, therefore, was an enormous increase in paper shuffling combined with a lowering of prestige, morale and respect for the security function. There was also a loss of morale on the part of the old security professionals who saw the security function being perverted for political purposes.

The requirement that every single agency and department have its own security office and director of security was usually implemented by hiring a current or former FBI investigator, as we have already noted. Yet almost without exception these Bureau agents were incompetent to manage, nor were they trained to perform analysis or evaluate the significance of the material collected. The skills they possessed from their generally excellent FBI training were oriented towards fact gathering, not assessment of the facts gathered; indeed the very idea that the information gathered was supposed to be interpreted or evaluated had generally been hammered out of them in the course of their FBI training and experience. Thus the new departmental security offices were generally weak, or incompetent, in evaluating the material they collected.

These new decentralized security offices were also weak in understanding or applying judicial processes or procedures. This would soon lead to charges of discrimination, unfairness, and denial of rights and of due process in the implementation of E.O. 10450. When these deficiencies were added to the general confusion which reigned concerning the relevance, as well as the application, of the new security standards to, for example, medical or nursing personnel, the government security function began to acquire—and, unfortunately, to deserve—a lowered reputation which impeded its effectiveness.

Nor did E.O. 10450 even address the management and operational failures of the system which still permitted traitors to have both access and opportunity to come into the government and proceed with their crimes. This executive order may have been intended to solve the problem of infiltration and preserve the federal government from the influence of people prepared to betray the interests of the United States, but it exacerbated the situation. It did not curtail the frequency of abuses but became the "system" under which such abuses were actually fostered.

THE NUMBERS GAME

It is ironic that the man who served so prominently on the House Un-American Activities Committee, playing such a key role in the hearings which led to the trial and conviction of Alger Hiss, should also have been instrumental in helping undermine the very government security program which the administration he represented had put in place. I refer, of course, to then Vice President Richard Nixon. With the promulgation and the beginning of the implementation of Executive Order 10450 came a series of actions as irresponsible as anything recorded in the history of personnel administration in our government.

The Eisenhower Administration created, designed, implemented, and administered a security program in large part to justify and prove, after the fact, some of the wild and unfounded charges that were made in the course of the presidential campaign the previous autumn. From the cabinet level on down, the new administration very early decided to put its prestige behind a mammoth falsehood that it attempted to sell to the entire nation and which caught up in its web a large number of innocent persons.

In our national memory it has seemed, as it did even to some at the time, that the typical crude and mendacious exploitation of the issue of "Communists in government" and the cynical politicization of the issues of loyalty and security in government were principally to be associated with the actions and accusations of Senator Joseph McCarthy. What has often been forgotten is the role the Eisenhower Administration played from its earliest days, in turning the issues of loyalty and security and Communists in government into so many political footballs, weakening and even discrediting the very government security system the administration was claiming to strengthen.

The implementation of E.O. 10450, as spearheaded by the Justice Department and the Civil Service Commission, and designed by the White House, presented a number of the very evils associated with what was already being called "McCarthyism." First of all, the new security system was ushered in to the accompaniment of a loud and systematic belittling of the earlier Truman Loyalty Program, followed by the public disclosure of figures intended to demonstrate how efficiently the new administration was removing "security risks." As a matter of fact, however, the figures and statistics in one of the Eisenhower Administration's first important instances were actually contrived and mostly false. They were issued solely for public consumption in order to justify earlier campaign promises.

The "numbers game," as this self-serving claim of the Eisenhower Administration was eventually and contemptuously tagged by the media, became a dramatic source of confrontation and embarrassment. It began with the White House announcing that 1,456 security risks had been removed from government employment. At the time this remarkable announcement was made, however, none of the required procedures for investigation, evaluation, adjudication, hearing, and final decision had even been promulgated in most agencies, much less implemented and executed. Nevertheless, it was reported to the public that all these security risks had been removed from some of these very same agencies.

The Director of Security for the Department of Health, Education and Welfare (HEW) was Frederick Schmidt. Mr. Schmidt was one of many former FBI agents who had left the Bureau for any one of many reasons, favorable and unfavorable, and who had been recruited en masse to be placed in control of Government security offices following the sudden birth of E.O. 10450.

Mr. Schmidt entered on duty as Director of Security for HEW on May 6, 1953. At the time, I was director of Security for the U.S. Public

Health Service. In August 1953, over the strenuous objections of the U.S. Surgeon General and his staff, all security in the Department was centralized under Mr. Schmidt and I and my entire office transferred to the Office of the Secretary of HEW. Concurrently, numerous former FBI personnel, including Clifford Letcher, the newly appointed Deputy Director, were appointed.

In order to appease Congressman Busby, HEW Under Secretary Nelson Rockefeller agreed to my appointment to a newly created position of Chief of the Personnel Security Division in order to bring some professional capability into the clearly disorganized security program.[4]

All personnel security cases—the core of the programs—were placed under my responsibility. As we shall see, that did not protect the security function from the corruption of the "numbers game." Nor did Mr. Rockefeller convince me, during our meeting at which he offered me the position, that he had any commitment to effective security. In fact, I was convinced that he just had no interest in the subject.

When the White House announced the "removal of 1,456 security risks from the government," the media immediately wanted a breakdown of the removals by government agency and department. After some resistance and delay, a breakdown was released and included 110 "removals" from HEW. Not only were these figures false, but not a single case had been adjudicated. In fact, the HEW's Office of General Counsel had not yet even completed and released its regulations for handling the process of removals.

The "removals" that had been announced were simply the result of the government-wide decision to cull files and tabulate the names and numbers of persons who had recently resigned, retired, been transferred, or died, and in whose files there had been some allegation or other derogatory information in order to support the claims of "security risks removed." In most of the cases concerned, the employees in question had been cleared in spite of the information in the files, since all the files

---

[4] By early 1954, the Department's Security Program had come under the scrutiny of Congress, specifically, the Chairman of the Department's Appropriations Committee, Honorable Fred Busby of Illinois. An intensive and extensive investigation was conducted by George Norris, of the House Appropriations Committee. The report was not only devastating in its criticisms of the quality of the new security program, but recommended the termination of the Director, the Deputy Director, and the three next highest level persons appointed by the Director.

were those of employees, not of new applicants for a government position; for all anybody knew, all of the persons in question could also have been cleared again under the new standards of E.O. 10450.

The list of HEW "removals," in particular, included at least one person who had resigned and had then returned and been put back on the payroll and was therefore still there at the time of the announcement of his removal as a security risk. Personnel files in which any derogatory information at all was contained, no matter how innocuous, and regardless of whether the information would really have resulted in any adverse action in any serious security adjudication, were counted in the tabulation as security risks removed. This was simply fraud.

I confronted Schmidt, the morning after the government announced the removal of the 1,456 security risks. Schmidt knew as well as I did that not one person had been removed from HEW, that not one single security case was even being processed, and that the proper procedures for such removals were not yet in place. (See Exhibit C.)

What had happened, in the case of the particular 110 HEW employees is that the files had been culled at night by the Director of Security himself, with the assistance of some of the former FBI personnel he had hired for the HEW security office. Clearly, I was not trusted to participate even though Personnel Security was my responsibility.

Schmidt himself had, typically, not come out of a professional security background and was bewildered by the complexities of his new job. The Congressional criticisms of the program made it impossible for him to accept any advice. The program was suffering badly. Nevertheless, he was one of the men supplying the data which the Eisenhower Administration was then representing to the public in order to demonstrate that the government was being purged of its disloyal elements.[5]

The fraud of the Eisenhower Administration "numbers game," while greeted with considerable skepticism and criticism in much of the press

---

[5]There ensued over a year of contentious and often bitter disagreement over the conduct of the HEW personnel security program with my original staff (which had been brought under the FBI-dominated Office of Security) struggling to preserve the professional direction of the program. It finally culminated in a lengthy memorandum prepared and directed to Mr. Schmidt after a particularly vigorous confrontation during which I detailed again the deficiencies, wrongdoings and actions required to correct the weaknesses. Mr. Schmidt finally requested that my accusations and recommendations be put in writing. See Appendix E, memorandum dated November 30, 1954.

and media, was never fully exposed and discredited, nor did any of those associations and individuals normally concerned with the protection of civil rights and the preservation of equal justice seriously challenge this particular miscarriage of justice. Powerful voices, including some which existed solely for the purpose of insuring justice, were silent. At the time, the American Bar Association, and the District of Columbia Bar Association right on the Washington scene, as well as other influential organizations, failed to speak out against the administration's exploitation of the loyalty, security and the Communist issues at the expense of the rights and reputations of individuals. They either feared being attacked themselves as pro-Communists, given the climate of the times, or perhaps felt that the laudable end of protecting the government against subversion justified the means of fraud employed. It was a time of fear.

The wild and unsubstantiated charges of Senator Joseph McCarthy being made around the same time have generally become known and documented and suitably deplored and inveighed against. What is less recognized and remembered is the way in which our government leadership engaged in similar fraudulent tactics.

One of the most distressing lapses of all was the silence of government security officers who often were in a position to know that a fraud was being perpetrated on the public for imagined political gain. The security profession had the most to lose. Already in questionable repute, many of its practitioners helped provide additional ammunition to those opposed to having any effective government security program at all by participating in, or remaining silent in the face of, a gigantic fraud engineered in the name of "security."

THE "NUMBERS GAME" UNDER ATTACK

Initially, the media reported the government's story of all the Communists, who had been discovered and terminated by the Eisenhower Administration, with all the drama and sensation it deserved. It does not require much imagination to realize the effect of more than 1,000 Communists, spies, or security risks burrowed deeply into the vitals of the government.

Conversely, if the U.S. had had over a thousand agents in the Kremlin acting on our behalf, the Soviet Union would probably have been in serious trouble long before it finally did fall apart. In short, the numbers used in the "numbers game" were implausible from the beginning.

When the announcement of these numbers was first made, however, it had the effect of verifying what people such as McCarthy and

Nixon had been contending all along, namely, that the Democratic Party had been a party of treason and that the Roosevelt and Truman Administrations had been criminally weak and lax, if not actively collaborationist, and that they had loaded the federal rolls with all these subversives. Moreover, these 1,456 security risks supposedly represented only the beginning. *The Eisenhower Administration security program had just begun!* If over 1,400 dangerous agents had been discovered in just the early months of the new Eisenhower Administration, how many additional thousands were still lurking in the bowels of the government just waiting to be rooted out by this new security program?

By the summer of 1954, the key jobs in the new department and agency security offices were now mostly in the "right" hands. A wide network had been established throughout the government which basically took its direction, as well as its "party line," from the Justice Department. This no doubt insured that all the fraud and pretense would be maintained, even in the face of critical scrutiny.

Once serious reflection began concerning the notion that the government had precipitously identified and axed no less than 1,456 security risks, however, skepticism began to grow and more and more reporters began to dig a little deeper into the facts and significance behind the government's startling claim. The Eisenhower Administration was not popular with segments of the press and media, and they would have been quite happy to be able to identify any discrepancy that constituted a story. Vice President Nixon, of course, had never been popular with the media, and many reporters would have been especially pleased to get something on him.

The following "numbers game" chronology demonstrates the manner in which the Eisenhower Administration claims were made, originally accepted, soon questioned, and finally subjected to all-out direct attack. *It illustrates the dangers of concentrating on the appearance of security rather than on its substance.*

On October 23, 1953, the White House announced that 1,456 government workers either had been dismissed or had resigned while facing action against them in the Federal Employee Security Program which had become effective on May 27 of the same year, the first year of the Eisenhower Administration. The White House announcement said that 863 employees had been dismissed and that 593 had resigned; the figures were complete up to September 30, 1953. "In all of the resignation cases," it was announced, "the agencies and departments had unfavorable reports on these employees."

The story on the White House announcement run by *The Washington Post*, on October 24, 1954, however, already included something of a skeptical, argumentative note: "The reason for believing that the 863 persons dismissed are not largely permanent or other employees who had Civil Service 'status' under the Truman Administration is that these employees would be entitled to hearings," the *Post* reported. "The hearing process requires considerable time, and as a matter of fact, very few federal agencies had even issued their new security regulations when the present program went into effect on May 27th". This news story also related that the number 1,456 included many employees hired on a temporary basis in the last months of the Truman Administration, hired, that is, "pending investigation."

On October 29, 1953, Postmaster General Arthur Summerfield announced that the jobs of 166 employees of the Post Office investigated under the new security program had been "terminated." In addition, he said, ten other employees had been suspended as "security risks." The announcement indicated that although the 166 had been credited to the 1,456 total, they were actually individuals who had been dismissed under normal Civil Service regulations, and that only ten dismissals were properly related to the new security program (*The Washington Post*, October 29, 1953).

On November 7, 1953, *The New York Times* carried the following headline at the top of its back page: U.S. AIDE REPORTS 1,456 REDS OUSTED. The story carried a Newark dateline, and contained this lead paragraph: "Bernard M. Shanley, special counsel to President Eisenhower, deviated from the text of a prepared address today to observe that '1,456 subversives had been kicked out of government jobs since the president assumed office'."

A month later, on December 2, 1953, President Dwight D. Eisenhower himself read the following prepared remarks at a press conference: "I repeat my previously expressed conviction that fear of Communists actively undermining our government will not be an issue in the 1954 elections. Long before then, this administration will have made such progress in rooting them out under the security program developed by Attorney General Brownell that this can no longer be considered a serious menace. As you already know, about 1,500 persons who were security risks have already been removed . . ." (*The Washington Star*, January 3, 1954).

Anyone with any knowledge of the facts could only have concluded here that Eisenhower had evidently been duped by his own people, and perhaps did not even suspect the truth.

Also on December 2, 1953, the same day as the Eisenhower press conference, a Veteran's Administration announcement claimed that 134 out of the 1,456 total had been terminated by the VA or had resigned from it (108 terminated and 26 resigned); this VA announcement admitted that its figures, as in the case of the Post Office, included those who would have been fired under normal Civil Service proceedings anyway (*The Washington Post*, January 1, 1954).

On December 8, 1953, *The Washington Post* quoted a Navy spokesman to the effect that an undisclosed number of the Navy's 192 separations under the new Federal Employee Security Program "left their jobs without knowing that there was derogatory information against them."

On December 13, 1953, the United Press quoted Attorney General Herbert Brownell, Jr., in a rather provocatively headlined article, as follows: "BROWNELL SEES REDS ALL OUT OF U.S. JOBS." Brownell predicted that the Federal Employee Security Program would be completed during the coming year. He said the objective was to rid the government of anyone suspected of Communistic tendencies. "We think they are all out of government now," Brownell said, "but the president has promised that within the coming year we will have completed our employee security program so the people can be sure none of them is left in government" (*The Washington Post*, December 14, 1953).

On December 21, 1953, the *Washington Daily News* began a series of eight articles disclosing individual cases of persons fired or charged under the new security program. The cases described included one of a woman discovered to have borne a child less than nine months after marriage to her present husband ten years earlier and one of a man who had not yet gotten his job back although he had been cleared in a hearing by a loyalty board and reinstated. The writer of the series concluded that the program was "not working perfectly," either for the individuals concerned or for the government.

On January 1, 1954, *The Washington Post* in a column by Murrey Marder declared that the administration, "in its zealousness to show that it has been cleaning security risks out of government" has produced "a series of statistics which has been transformed into a seriously distorted political issue."

On January 3, 1954, the *Washington Evening Star*, in a three-column review of its own efforts to analyze what its reporter, L. Edgar Prina, called "an almost meaningless figure," wrote that "it appeared that the figure 1,456 included some persons who never were fired or forced to resign, as the White House announcement implied, but who instead were separated through voluntary resignations, reductions in force, even by death, without ever knowing they had been accused of anything."

The *Star* story also reported that the Navy had originally prepared a release announcing eight persons fired and twelve suspended as security risks, but after learning that the Civil Service Commission had counted the Navy for 192 of the 1,456 security risks, the Navy dutifully prepared another press release announcing the separation of 192 persons "against whom a security question existed." Finally the *Star* story revealed that the Air Force had rebelled against conforming to the official administration figure and had canceled a press release on the subject entirely.

By January 5, 1954, the *Washington Evening Star* was declaring editorially that the Civil Service Commission "owes the public a full explanation of how this total was arrived at and what it covers." Questions, in short, were beginning to be raised; it should have been clear to a perceptive administration that its figures were not going to stand.

Instead of backing off, though, the administration plunged heedlessly forward. On January 7, 1954, President Eisenhower included the following statement in his State of the Union message: "Under the standards established by the new employee security program, 2,200 employees have been separated by the federal government." Now the fraudulent figure had been escalated.

Commenting on the president's claim, a *Washington Post* editorial on January 17, 1954, declared that "those 2,200 separations . . . do not afford any meaningful index to the administration's security vigilance. It looks," this editorial concluded, "as if the president has been handed a phony figure. We wish he would demand a breakdown of it and give the results of that breakdown to the public."

At this point the House Un-American Activities Committee decided to ask the Civil Service Commission to issue a breakdown on the figure. The House Committee on Post Office and Civil Service also agreed to ask the Civil Service Commission for such a breakdown.

Syndicated columnists Joseph and Stewart Alsop then reported in their column that the State Department's total of 306 out of the total supposed security firings had been swollen in two ways. Files of department employees who were resigning anyway were carefully scrutinized for derogatory information, they said, and "wherever the raw files provided the slightest excuse for so doing, the names of those who were resigning anyway were added—without their knowledge—to the total of security firings." The Alsops described a second technique which they averred was "just as dishonest." Many employees who were being transferred from the State Department to the Mutual Security Agency were "transferred with the warning flag up," the columnists said, and then listed as State Department "risks" taken off the payroll as such, although the majority of these same people were later cleared and never fired at all.

On January 23, 1954, *The Washington Post* again asked editorially for a breakdown of the administration's figure.

Then, two days later, on January 25, 1954, Senator Olin D. Johnston (D-SC), a member of the Senate Post Office and Civil Service Committee, introduced a resolution directing the Senate Civil Service Committee to require the chairman of the Civil Service Commission to supply a detailed statement of the reasons for separation in all of the 2,200 cases which the president had cited in his State of the Union message. At the same time Johnston accused the administration of "deceit and demagogism."

Senator Johnston cited the oath which every government employee must sign and have notarized before entering the federal service. He then cited the section of the Criminal Code providing penalties for making false, fictitious, or fraudulent statements. "If," Senator Johnston asked, "the new administration has found one single government employee who is disloyal or engaged in subversive activities, or is a member of the Communist party or a Communist-front organization, then why has it not used the violation of this oath as a basis for prosecuting to the full extent of the law? If the administration has found one violation, then the Attorney General of the United States has been derelict in his duty in not using the violation of the oath to obtain an indictment." Senator Johnston went on to suggest that, if there were no indictments to back up the 2,200 figure, the Attorney General should resign.

It can be revealed that I did assist Senator Olin Johnston, Chairman of the Senate Civil Service Committee, in that Committee's line of inquiry into the truth concerning the "numbers game."

I took this very difficult course of action because I knew the numbers were false and that great damage was being done not only in the persons accused, but to the reputation and performance of the government's internal security program.

As Chief of all Personnel Security for the Department of Health, Education and Welfare (HEW), no case could be processed without my knowledge and action. Not a single case had begun the adjudication process and yet the Administration had claimed that among 1,476 persons "removed," 110 were employees of the HEW. That was false. However, my efforts at confrontation of the issue within the Department to halt the false claims and restore the facts failed.

The Congress was the only avenue, albeit at some risk, that I saw open to me to correct the record. I took it to William (Bill) Brawley, later Deputy Postmaster in the Eisenhower Administration and then Clerk of the Committee, who deserves great credit for his efforts to bring out the facts of the "numbers game," through his role as long-time Administrative Assistant to Sen. Johnston.

On February 8, 1954, Representative George M. Rhodes (D-PA) introduced a resolution in the House of Representatives requesting the president to furnish the House with the exact number of removals under the Federal Employee Security Program in each department of each agency. Among the questions he had were these: how many, if any, were removed for espionage, treason, or sabotage, or for current membership in the Communist Party of the United States? How many were removed under other provisions of the new security executive order? How many were notified in writing? How many were discharged and how many resigned?

This resolution of Congressman Rhodes was referred to the House Committee on Post Office and Civil Service under a preferential status requiring House action within seven legislative days regardless of committee action. Committee Chairman Ross (R-KS) was quoted in *The Washington Star* of January 12, 1954, as remarking about the whole affair: "There should be no lumping together of those who are separated because of disloyalty and those who are separated because of doubt as to their stability or suitability as federal employees."

Joseph and Stewart Alsop returned to the subject in their column published in *The Washington Post* on February 10, 1954, and probably succeeded as well as anyone in summing the whole thing up: "The public has been grossly misled about the infiltration of subversives into the government," the Alsops wrote. "The best witness to this fact is none other than W. Scott McLeod, Senator Joseph R. McCarthy's personal ambassador to the State Department. According to testimony before a congressional committee, McLeod has failed to find Communists lurking anywhere in the State Department, despite twelve months of untiring effort."

There we pretty much have it: the fraud of an administration resorting to the crude manipulation of data in order to convince the American public of its anti-Communist zeal without any regard for fact, truth, or the reputations of those injured in the administration's scatter-gun blasts. Such was the "numbers game." The issue was never properly resolved but simply got lost and was then forgotten.

MCCARTHY AND THE HEARINGS

During the general period from 1950 to 1954, encompassing the activities of Richard M. Nixon on the issues of loyalty and security and Communists in government, the issuance and the beginning of the implementation of E.O. 10450, and the introduction and eventual debunking of the "numbers game," another series of events was taking place which would also do serious damage to the image of U.S. security. Joseph R. McCarthy, a Republican Senator from Wisconsin, made his name a household word which became the name of a whole era through his ability to exploit the media, in a perverse but instinctively clever way, creating the impression that there was a titanic struggle going on in which he was the sole protagonist fighting for America. As a result of this uncanny ability, McCarthy was able to initiate a "reign of terror" during which virtually anyone could be accused with impunity on the floor of the U.S. Senate of being a Communist or Communist sympathizer. Wide publicity was then given in the national media to the accusations thus voiced, usually without a shred of anything resembling evidence to substantiate the charges. In the end, McCarthy's impact on the nation's security interests and problems was actually quite minimal. While he was around, however, because of the tactics he successfully employed, the hysteria he exploited, and the fear he engendered, he succeeded in sensationalizing and emotionalizing practically everything related to the question of government security. He succeeded at nothing but giving security a bad name.

Worse, he did so at a time when there really were Communists and Soviet agents in positions of trust within the federal government. By his wild and irresponsible actions and attacks, McCarthy seriously impeded actual efforts to remove Communists from the government. Among other things he gave credibility to the frequent claim that "security" consisted of nothing but a gigantic witch hunt. McCarthy himself was poorly served by his own aides, his chief counsel Roy Cohn, and his chief investigator, G. David Schine. He was also undone both by his own ambition as well as his serious drinking problem. Senator McCarthy recognized a problem when he focused on Communists in government, but in seeking to exploit it for political gain, he ended up serving the Soviet cause instead.

A bit of prior history: in December 1949, a poll of Senate correspondents had branded Joseph McCarthy as the "worst" member of the United States Senate. McCarthy was therefore searching for a means to enhance his reputation and ensure his re-election. There are at least two stories explaining his choice of Communist infiltration into the government as his big issue. One of them appeared in a book written by John G. Adams, Counselor of the Army, who was eventually to be quite instrumental in McCarthy's downfall. Adams stated in his book, *Without Precedent*, that the idea of attacking communist infiltration was suggested to McCarthy by Father Edmund Walsh, S.J., Dean of the School of Foreign Service at Georgetown University and a world authority on geo-political issues. On the other hand, Mr. Robert Goldsborough, an intelligence expert and columnist, recalled a strategy meeting at the beginning of the 82nd Congress at which Senator Robert A. Taft of Ohio and some of his Senate colleagues requested a volunteer from among newly elected senators who would be willing to lead an attack on the Democrats on the issue of Communists in government. Goldsborough recalled that Senator McCarthy responded that he was quite willing to lead such an attack.

I am not personally knowledgeable concerning these incidents. However, I do have personal and intimate knowledge concerning the character and integrity of the late Father Edmund Walsh. Father Walsh and I served together as members of the OSS assigned to the International Military Tribunal, at the trial of the major Nazi war criminals in Nuremberg in 1945-46. We were thus closely associated for an extended period of time, working daily on the preparation of the brief on the "Persecution of the Christian Churches." Our daily association began early in the morning on the way to the Palace of Justice, continued throughout the day and on through our travels back to the Grand Hotel, where we were both billeted, and it sometimes extended into the dinner hour for our evening meal. Father Walsh was an exceptionally learned man who had served the Jesuit Order and the Catholic Church in many capacities, clandestine and otherwise, with skill, fidelity, and always with the utmost discretion. He was a man of the highest integrity and decency.

Certainly Father Walsh would have been knowledgeable concerning Communist infiltration into the American government, and it is probably reasonable to suggest that he may have recognized the problem as one deserving of special national attention. However, it would have been totally out of character for Father Walsh ever to have imagined, much less counseled, a course of action even remotely comparable to the one which Senator McCarthy actually embarked upon. In the entire period of my association with Father Walsh in Nuremberg, and in our continued association after we had both returned to Washington, I never detected the slightest suggestion of meanness or duplicity in either his speech or his actions. Of course these comments are offered on behalf of a friend, but they are also made in the confidence that all who knew him would readily recognize his exceptional qualities of character and decency.

In his book *Without Precedent*, Army Counselor John G. Adams described Senator Joseph McCarthy's plan of action, once he had decided upon "Communists in government" as his big issue. Adams wrote about McCarthy:

> First . . . he had to find some Communists. He called up the *Chicago Tribune* reporter—Willard Edwards—and asked if he knew of any. Edwards told him of an old congressional investigation that had looked at the files of 108 State Department employees suspected as bad security risks. As of 1948, 57 still worked for the department. McCarthy also checked in with Congressman Richard Nixon's office. He was referred to an issue of the *Congressional Record* where he learned that in 1946 the State Department had recommended against the permanent employment of 284 wartime employees. Of these, 79 had been discharged. McCarthy subtracted 79 from 284 and got the magic number of 205.

McCarthy was scheduled to speak at several Lincoln Day dinners, in Wheeling, West Virginia, Salt Lake City, and Reno, Nevada. The speech was the same before all three audiences, discussing the communist threat to America. In fact, it was not an original speech at all, but a modified version of a speech given by Richard Nixon several weeks earlier. It certainly contained no substantial material in addition to what Nixon had said..

In *The Glory and the Dream*, William Manchester compared McCarthy's speech at Wheeling, and one Nixon had delivered on the floor of Congress two weeks earlier. Here are the two speeches in question:

"NIXON IN CONGRESS" (1/26/50)

The great lesson which should be learned from the Hiss case is that we are not just dealing with espionage agents who get 30 pieces of silver to obtain the blueprint of a weapon . . . but this a far more sinister type of activity, because it permits the enemy to guide and shape our policy.

"McCARTHY IN WHEELING" (2/9/50)

One thing to remember in discussing the Communists is that we are not dealing with spies who get 30 pieces of silver to steal the blueprint of a new weapon. We are dealing with a far more sinister type of activity because it permits the enemy to guide and shape our policy.

In his book *Without Precedent*, the army's John G. Adams added this further comment:

> McCarthy did add at least one paragraph of his own. Waving a wad of papers above his head, he exclaimed: "I have in my hand a list of 205 card-carrying Communists who are now employed in the State Department and whose identities are well known to the State Department as being members of the Communist party."

The whole charge was nonsense, of course, but McCarthy's timing could not have been better. He fired his broadside just one month after the conviction of Alger Hiss for perjury. The Hiss case had certainly proved that there were high-level Communists in government. More-over, within the next few months, an even more chilling story of Communist spying was to unfold.

America was soon to receive the shocking news that the Soviet Union also possessed the secret of the atomic bomb, delivered courtesy of the Rosenberg spy ring. Americans had considered the atomic bomb to be its greatest protection against the Soviet Union's drive for world domination. Now, the Soviets possessed the bomb as well. America was enraged at these betrayals and ready to identify and punish any additional traitors.

McCarthy continued to exploit the public anxiety brought about by the instances of real espionage and treason that had been and were being uncovered, and before long all the ingredients of what came to be called "McCarthyism" had emerged: make accusations from the floor of the U.S. Senate where he was immune from possible libel suits for anything he said. The media would then dutifully report the accusations as if they were real and serious; as a result a very large public came to believe in the Senator from Wisconsin as a crusader trying to save America from the Red Menace.

Senator Joseph McCarthy was able to continue unchecked for three years. Government personages accused by McCarthy and his committee of being closet Communists ranged from anonymous government employees to former Secretary of State and wartime Army Chief of Staff General George C. Marshall as well as Secretary of State Dean Acheson. Eyewitness accounts describing McCarthy's interrogation of witnesses before his Investigations Subcommittee of the Senate Government Operations Committee relate scenes of bullying, cruelty, and misrepresentation of fact. Few Americans could stand up to McCarthy, however, and the Republican Administration was even reduced to clearing its executive branch appointments with him.

Beginning in mid-1953, McCarthy began to attack various representatives of the United States Army. The new Secretary of the Army, Robert T. Stevens, had offered to cooperate with McCarthy whenever McCarthy and his staff identified personnel whom they considered subversive. In the months to come, however, McCarthy would demonstrate that cooperation was not what he intended.

In September, 1953 McCarthy brought about the transfer of an Army general over the issue of an Army Intelligence library book on Siberian folkways. McCarthy considered the book subversive. Then McCarthy's staff received what was to become known as the "purloined letter" from a supporter in Army Intelligence. The document was represented as a letter from J. Edgar Hoover to General Alexander Bolling, Chief of Army Intelligence. It was in fact a two-and-a-half page condensation of a fifteen-page letter written in 1951. Whereas the original letter had listed some unsubstantiated and trivial allegations, but had contained no definite accusations, the condensation did appear to contain definite—and serious—accusations against thirty-five people working at Fort Monmouth, New Jersey. Their cases were illustrative both of how the Eisenhower Administration's E.O. 10450 was working and of McCarthy's by then famous "methods."

Over the preceding three years, all the employees mentioned in the "purloined letter" had been cleared by loyalty boards which had access to the unfavorable allegations against them, and had therefore had the chance to consider and reject these allegations. Because of McCarthy's sudden interest, however, 26 of the 35 were now again held to be security risks under the new Eisenhower Administration standards which, as we have seen, were actually less specific than the earlier ones but which required the employee to prove loyalty rather than requiring the government to prove disloyalty. Once again it was John G. Adams, Counselor of the Army, who best described the proceedings followed in the eight most serious of these cases in his book *Without Precedent*:

> Their Loyalty Board hearings made a mockery of due process. Each was advised that the charges against him came from confidential sources. (These "confidential sources" were such things as

the unevaluated Hoover-to-Bolling letter of 1951—a collection of hard-to-prove or disprove insinuations, including neighbors' gossip, and the hostility of jealous employees.) They were told they could not cross-examine their accusers or even know their identity. The could not see any records, certainly not the FBI report. In fact, as they were to learn, there were to be no witnesses against them, only papers they mustn't see. [One] was asked questions like these:

"Would you consider the religious beliefs and opinions of your parents to be too strong?"

"May I ask what are the religious beliefs of you and your wife at the present time or during your married life?"

"Do you and your wife attend services regularly?"

"Do you as an individual believe in God?"

Other Fort Monmouth employees among the unfortunate eight were asked these questions:

"What party did you vote for?"

"What is your philosophy of life?"

"Have you ever thought about the problem of whether or not public utilities, like big power and light companies, should be owned by the government?"

It was on the basis of their answers to such questions as these, as well as on the basis of allegations they had never seen, that all eight of these Fort Monmouth employees were fired. The fired employees all sought relief through the courts, and, over the next few years, all of them were re-instated through court orders—court judgments which merely underlined the original irresponsibility and injustice of their firing. What they were all "guilty" of, of course, was getting caught in the web of Senator McCarthy's ambition and lust for power, and being so unlucky as to share the same web with petty and irresponsible bureaucrats prepared to sacrifice the jobs and reputations of other employees to their own fear of McCarthy. For it needs to be stated that McCarthy was only able to reach as far as he did because the Eisenhower Administration was not yet prepared to stand up to him. Meanwhile fundamental constitutional rights of American citizens were most certainly being violated in these and similar cases.

At this juncture, McCarthy learned of an Army dentist, Irving Peress, who had written "federal constitutional privilege" on his loyalty questionnaire in answer to the question about possible membership in subversive organizations. This answer had somehow been missed in the course of his suitability/loyalty investigations, and, when a service-wide grade-adjustment bill was passed by Congress, Peress received an adjustment. McCarthy, though, insisted that his subcommittee must examine as a witness the person who was "responsible" for "promoting" somebody McCarthy characterized as a "Fifth Amendment Communist."

McCarthy vilified Brigadier General Ralph W. Zwicker, a bona fide war hero from the Battle of the Bulge; Zwicker had been the commanding officer of the unit to which Peress was assigned. McCarthy declared that Zwicker did not have "the brains of a five-year-old child" and was unfit to wear the military uniform. At length a private meeting was held between McCarthy, some of the other senators on his subcommittee and Secretary of the Army Robert T. Stevens. McCarthy maneuvered Stevens into signing a settlement agreement that was so one-sided that McCarthy later bragged to reporters: "Stevens could not have surrendered more abjectly if he had gotten down on his knees."

In going up against the U.S. Army, McCarthy was attacking one of the few institutions almost universally admired by Americans; the men and women of the U.S. Armed Forces were the ones principally responsible for having just fought and won the world's greatest war. The Army quickly counter-attacked, and released a written summary of all the investigative proceedings against the Army before McCarthy's subcommittee in the course of the previous year. This summary amply illustrated his improper methods and his loaded questions. Included in the material was documentation of continuing efforts by McCarthy and his staff assistant, Roy Cohn, to influence the Army's treatment of another McCarthy assistant then serving in the Army, G. David Schine.

The accusations between McCarthy and the Army finally led to another series of Senate hearings, this time on live nationwide television. Although these hearings were conducted by McCarthy's own Investigations Subcommittee of the Senate Government Operations Committee, it was agreed that McCarthy himself, as one of the principals in the dispute with the Army, should not preside. This task was given to the number-two man on the subcommittee, Senator Karl Mundt of South Dakota. Other subcommittee members who had generally avoided attending McCarthy's hearings were in attendance for these Army-McCarthy hearings. They constituted one of the great "media events" of those years.

The old cases in the running dispute with the Army were first reviewed, but the hearings themselves soon degenerated into wrangles over who had tried to provide favors for Army Private Schine. Indeed the Mundt Report on the hearings was anti-climactic: McCarthy was blamed for having allowed Roy Cohn to get out of hand in seeking Army favors for David Schine; Secretary Stevens and Counselor Adams of the Army were faulted for their vacillation and appeasement; Adams was criticized for having released the summary of all McCarthy's abuses in investigating the Army; and McCarthy, again, was criticized for having encouraged government employees to appropriate classified material to be passed on to him and his subcommittee.

But the real meaning and outcome of the Army-McCarthy hearings did not reside in the formal report of the hearings. Rather, two months of such hearings on national television had served to exhibit to the nation at large the characteristic features of McCarthyism. Practically everyone in the country got a good look at both McCarthy and Roy Cohn, and a pronounced negative reaction against them was widespread. It had even become evident to the Eisenhower Administration—not to speak of the U.S. Senate itself—that McCarthy had to be stopped. He was out of control.

Senator Ralph Flanders of Vermont, one of the few members of the Senate who had ever dared to criticize McCarthy up to then, introduced a motion of censure in the Senate: "Resolved, that the conduct of the Senator from Wisconsin, Mr. McCarthy, is contrary to senatorial traditions and tends to bring the Senate in disrepute and such conduct is hereby condemned."

This was the beginning of the end for McCarthy. He faced thirty-three separate charges which a Senate Select Committee was named to adjudicate. His attorney, the criminal lawyer Edward Bennett Williams, who consistently throughout his career had been able to win many "hopeless" cases, orchestrated a defense in this one in which he successfully compared each of the charges to something some other senator or congressman had been able to do with impunity. One by one the charges had to be dropped until only one remained—a charge relating to McCarthy's actions in contempt of the Senate's Gillette Subcommittee on Privileges and Elections chaired by Iowa's Senator Guy Gillette.

At a key moment, Vice President Nixon, presiding over the Senate, changed the wording of the resolution, replacing the word "censure" with the phrase "relating to." The resolution then passed the Senate 67 to 22. The date was December 2, 1954.

In spite of the mildness of the rebuke, it was clear that Senator

Joseph R. McCarthy had been disgraced before the whole country. His mystique was gone. His influence was destroyed. He had lost all of his allies in the Senate. He no longer inspired fear either in the Congress or within the Eisenhower Administration, nor did the media any longer consider everything he said an automatic "story." He lived out his remaining life in the Senate as a pariah, dying within a few years of cirrhosis of the liver.

In the years since McCarthy's death, there has developed a myth that in fact, there was no real threat of Communists within the American government, the film industry or anywhere else. As we have seen, the infiltration into the government was real and massive in scope. And there were men of character and noble purpose, including Senators, Robert A. Taft of Ohio, Everett Dickson of Illinois, Karl Mundt of South Dakota and Styles Bridges of Vermont, who led the legitimate battle against the menace. Respected syndicated columnists like David A. Lawrence and Constantine Brown wrote extensively and with great feeling concerning the extent of Communist penetration citing specifics by names, agencies and actions. Certain members of the House of Representatives such as Congressman Ashford of Ohio and Fred Busby of Illinois made equally important contributions concerning the menace.

Because of his position as Committee Chairman, it was McCarthy who led the fight in the Senate and by his irresponsible behavior diverted attention from the basic issue.

Professionals in the field of security lamented, even at the time, the damage McCarthy was doing. But it needs to be understood that the Junior Senator from Wisconsin struck terror in the hearts of bureaucrats, even department heads. And security, so necessary when fighting a formidable enemy such as the Soviet Union of the 1950's, suffered.

Nevertheless, McCarthyism has left its flawed legacy. It is not too dissimilar from the one left by the Eisenhower Administration's exploitation of real security issues and concerns for short-term political gain. Exploiting public anxieties about loyalty, security, and "Communists in government" in such a fashion can only result ultimately in irreparable damage to the security program. This is what happened in fact, and, as a result, America's security system was compromised and in some quarters even discredited.

ABUSES IN THE SYSTEM (1954 - 1968)

The time is 1954 - 1955 . . .

You are called "in" and confronted by a security investigator (or a hearing officer) in connection with the conduct of his investigation to determine whether you can be cleared for access to classified information, or to occupy either a sensitive (3A) or non-sensitive position (3B).

"We have information that you have engaged in immoral activities. What comment do you wish to make?"

Whether it involved a matter of morals, false statement, drinking to excess, arrest, membership in organizations on the Attorney General's List, or any form of conduct, association, or allegation reflecting on reputation or character, the "hearing" was conducted in the same manner.

The "subject" was brought into the hearing room with the interrogator and his witness present. The information was presented in the form of an allegation, without attribution, with a request for the response of the applicant or employee.

Almost without exception, the questioners were male. The setting was an almost bare room, with a clear desk and the questioner, backed by the full power of the Federal Government, paging through a dossier representing your life's record as viewed through the lens of Government security.

You have no counsel, or even a colleague or witness. You do not know the evidence, if any, against you. You have not been provided with any statement of facts, charges, or a list of questions or topics. There is no established, agreed upon, framework or set of conditions within which the proceedings will be conducted, except that this is the way the government has determined it shall be done.

You must decide on the spot, without preparation, without options, without knowing where the questions will lead you, whether to lay bare your inner life and secrets—even to giving evidence against yourself.

"We have information that you signed a petition . . ."

"We have information to the effect that you had a sexual relationship with a woman to whom you are not married."

"We have information that you had difficulties with your last employer," or that you are emotionally disturbed, or you were unable to get along with your supervisor at your former job. etc., etc.

Your natural impulse is to ask "Who told you this?" or "What is the evidence, or the basis for the allegation?"

If asked, the answer, under the security system put in place by Executive Order 10450, would have to be: "I'm sorry, but we cannot divulge the sources of our information. However, we will be glad to consider and put in the record and evaluate anything you may wish to tell us."

Your fate lies in the hands of those you have never seen before, whose qualifications, training, compassion, or sense of justice are apparently not established in accordance with any fixed standard. The setting is certainly not a courtroom subject to established procedures, rules of evidence, and due process. Nevertheless, in a few split seconds, you must decide whether or not to open parts of your life "for the record"— for the file on you which will be added to and "pulled" over and over again down through the years, usually for the purpose of decisions vital to your career and well being. In that file there may well be, and very probably are, statements about you sometimes made by persons unknown to you regarding your personality, character, morality, honesty, or loyalty to your government. These statements may not be measurable against any fixed norm, or standard, or rule of evidence, and yet the very same statements can serve as the basis of a judgment about your loyalty to your own government or your suitability for government employment. Indeed it is all too likely that such statements *will* serve as the basis of the government's judgment about you. Yet the furnishers of such statements remain immune from any question or challenge. There are no penalties for false statements, mistakes, innuendoes, or colored or otherwise misleading testimony, nor are there even any disincentives included in the process that might possibly discourage anyone from making false statements or innuendoes.

During the 1950s and 1960s, once the system established by E.O. 10450 was solidly in place, employees of the federal government were routinely spied upon, tested, questioned, and questioned again; their friends and associates were questioned too; sometimes their telephones were tapped, their offices bugged or their mail opened and read. Allegations of fellow employees they may have opposed in some "turf battle" or of subordinates they had failed to promote could find their way into the same growing "file." In some jobs, the more conscientious the performance, the greater the likelihood of making enemies, and hence the greater the vulnerability.

In such a system, such things as due process and equal protection of the laws, and the enjoyment of rights supposedly guaranteed by the Constitution, hardly enter in. The fact is that criminals charged with serious crimes have greater protection in the American court system than government employees routinely had under the American security system of the 1950s.

The initial abuses under E.O. 10450 faded from the public consciousness. The "numbers game" ended "not with a bang but a whimper," in
the phrase of T.S. Eliot. Despite Congressional demands and even threats,
no breakdown of figures was ever provided by the Eisenhower Administration. Nor was any falsification ever admitted. Nor did Vice President Nixon suffer any lasting damage for the part he played in the
cynical and opportunistic manipulation of numbers. McCarthyism soon
passed into history. On the other side of the Capitol, the House Un-
American Activities Committee also wound down its activities—less
and less considered a "story"—and eventually it too passed from the
scene. The media and the politicians went on to other things, without
ever having resolved the questions earlier considered so urgent.

A major casualty of the security battles we have been covering in
these pages was *security itself*. Security had always had to struggle for
respectability within the government. Always suspect, it was first considered merely a "gumshoe" function, and, later, as a result of the
McCarthy-Nixon approach, as some kind of heavy-handed Gestapo type
of operation. Always disliked before, during the reign of E.O. 10450 it
came to be feared for both its power and its lack of accountability, and
it often came to be regarded with disdain and contempt by the managers
of the very government agencies it was supposed to be serving.

Security was unique among government managerial specialties in
that its operations were based upon specific statutes and executive orders, rather than on general management principles, and its functions
were almost always carried out in an atmosphere highly charged with
emotion and fear. "Big Brother" had joined the federal service! Given
the history of the security function within the government, it was perhaps impossible for it to have avoided acquiring at least something of
the reputation that it did, but the situation was considerably worsened as
a result of all the abuses.

Meanwhile another problem arose from the huge expansion of
government security that took place within a relatively short time frame.
Due to misunderstandings concerning the skills and qualifications necessary for a security officer, security practitioners were usually drawn
from pools of persons with limited academic backgrounds and professional training. Typically, police forces and the military were sources for
the recruitment of security personnel. What the positions really required,
however, were persons with capabilities in the areas of analyzing and
evaluating data and materials and making judicious, reasoned judgments
about them. These latter skills needed to be developed through training

in such subjects as philosophy, the social sciences, history, and, at least in the upper echelons of security administration, in the law and judicial practice.

Lacking an established discipline, or even a defined structure or prescribed course of study, security became a catch-all function. Just about anyone could become a security officer. E.O. 10450 had prescribed that every government job required a security clearance, and hence security officers had to be hired in droves to do all the clearances. They were thereby placed in positions of authority over the reputations and careers of virtually everybody in government—"little men rattling about in big jobs," to borrow the late Governor Thomas E. Dewey's indictment of government bureaucrats in general. With the advent of E.O. 10450, the government had never seen so many little men rattling around in such big jobs and with so much power to do harm to reputations and careers.

Even after the fall of Senator McCarthy, little effort was made to control the abuses that had now become almost endemic to the system. The mere hint of an allegation of being "soft on Communism" was still enough to send some administrators, however able, into hiding. Even when obvious injustices arose in the administration of the program, most agency senior bureaucrats were too cowed or too frightened to take a stand against any decision ever made on "security" grounds. It was in this way that security officers and directors of security acquired power which some were not loath to wield—sometimes with startling ineptitude.

The new department or agency security officers themselves now made all the security decisions on a de-centralized basis, and the problem was now not so much failure to act in security cases as it was injecting "security" into virtually everything through the power the security officers had within their agencies. Sometimes they exercised their power with little discernment.

It was in this fashion that many basic rights of American citizens were ignored. E.O. 10450 placed the burden upon the employee or job applicant to prove that he or she was *not* a security risk—a rather difficult task when hearsay evidence and casual associations dating perhaps back to college days were given the same weight in some security decisions that hard evidence is given in a court of law.

Under the advent of E.O. 10450, the practice became common that an accused was virtually never given the opportunity to confront the accuser. It was the rule not to divulge the source of any derogatory information. In such a situation, it is obviously the suppliers of derogatory information who quickly come to exercise a disproportionate influence. After a while, it was no longer clear how all the "security risks" really were to be handled. It quickly became common government practice in cases where derogatory or questionable information was turned up simply to tell the applicant that the job opening had been closed for budgetary or program reasons, whereupon the applicant would go away never realizing that he had been disqualified on the basis of security, and, indeed, that the government now possessed a negative dossier on him that quite possibly could follow him around for the rest of his life. While loss of a job—or failure to get one—is not comparable to loss of life, or grave injury, a regular government practice such as this cannot be characterized as anything but an abuse and an injustice, yet one that our government came to engage in rather routinely and without considering whether it constituted an injustice.

In the period from the mid-1940s to the mid-1950s, the government security function went, in too many cases, from protecting and covering up for the guilty to punishing the possibly innocent accused without even requiring that there be any substantial evidence for the accusation or affording any right of appeal or redress. Such has been our government security system. It would be ironic if it were not so tragic. To leap ahead for a moment: today virtually no one is ever denied employment on security grounds—or denied a security clearance regardless of evidence of character defect, or other cause, but more on that later.

During the period when these abuses were becoming established features of our security system, efforts were made to resist the trend. Reporters and columnists increasingly wrote of specific instances of abuse. Government security determinations were often successfully challenged in the courts. Some attorneys were willing to take on clients at minimal compensation for the principle involved, including Byron Scott, a former Democratic Congressman from California, Donald Dalton, and Sam Sherwood.

I was responsible for bringing to the attention of the American Bar Association, as well as of the District of Columbia Bar Association, the depth and magnitude of the denial of legal rights taking place in the implementation of the new government security procedures and practices. I interested Byron Scott in the "cause" and, through our efforts, committees of both bar associations, called "Civil Service Law Committees", were organized to examine cases and hear complaints of these abuses. I served as a member and later as Chairman of both of these Bar

Association Committees, and I am proud to say that the legal profession came down four square against the abuses in question and was instrumental in obtaining recognition of the problem as well as a measure of agreement from the government that corrective action needed to be taken.

For example, Byron Scott, a long-time friend and law school classmate of mine, responded instantly when the abuses of the security program were described to him. He lent his very considerable weight to a corrective campaign by serving as the first chairman of the D.C. Bar Association's Civil Service Law Committee. A long list of other lawyers in Washington, including Neil Kabatchnik, Oliver Gasch, and Joseph D. Hannon (the latter two both subsequently appointed to the bench) all served the D.C. Bar Committee with distinction, as did the members of the ABA Civil Service Law Committee. It was a fine instance of the legal profession responding in an orderly, disciplined manner to governmental abuses of power directed against its employees, and, indeed, against American citizens in general. Of inestimable help in the whole process was the able and experienced Civil Service Director of Investigations, Kimball Johnson, an implacable foe of the direction our government took with the issuance of E.O. 10450.

By 1968, recognition of the need for reform was so well documented, and the role of the bar associations so widely accepted, that the Civil Service Committees of the two associations had begun to work with some government agencies, notably the Civil Service Commission itself, to bring about reform, or at least amelioration. Legal reversals of some agency security actions, as well as continuing pressure from the bar associations and Congress, resulted in substantial reforms of certain security policies and practices, although it did not, unfortunately, result in any rethinking of the current basic security concepts or in any in-depth re-assessment of the whole system. These issues were not addressed. Incidentally, I was still in the Federal Service and my efforts at reform, I am pleased to say, were never curtailed.

The media weighed in with stories documenting egregious abuses and denials of due process. A leading champion of employee rights was a long-time friend and colleague from the mid-1940s until his recent death, John Cramer, for many years the writer of a government column in the *Washington Daily News*.

When great national issues are at stake and disaster strikes, the very people who have most contributed to the disaster are too often the very ones who rush forward to offer themselves as the experts we must continue to rely on in coping with the disaster they have helped design.

We have all noted this phenomenon in the field of education, for example, where the same educational experts who produced a generation of illiterate children are always right up front explaining the reforms required and the direction to be taken—and especially the new public money to be expended—in order to be able to deal with the situation which they themselves have so largely brought about. We see exactly the same thing in the programs brought forward to combat drug abuse: no matter how great the number of failures recorded in one drug prevention and treatment program, the same experts who designed and implemented it can be counted on to present themselves the next time around as the most competent people to develop and implement the next favored solution to the drug addiction problem in society.

So it was with prospective reform of abuses in our government security system. It has not been recorded that any security officer ever lost his job or was censured or disciplined for the egregious abuse of employee rights that had manifestly become a feature of the government security program. Even more disturbing, however, was the fact that no centralized authority within the executive branch ever took a serious look at what was happening or recognized that what was needed was an intensive scrutiny of the whole security system, and development of a truly rational approach to the function. Careful thought needed to be given to the basic question of just what a security system was and what it was supposed to do; what standards were required for a truly rational security program; what qualifications were required in those security people who would be passing judgment on the employability, suitability and loyalty of others; what jobs really required specialized security clearance because of their actual or potential impact on the nation's safety and welfare and, perhaps, what jobs did *not* require such specialized security clearance; and, finally, careful thought needed to be given to the question of how a person should be determined to be "secure," and, equally important, to remain "secure."

Not only were no answers to these absolutely fundamental questions ever developed, but the questions themselves were never even raised. It is true that E.O. 10450 did set forth standards for clearance and for determining sensitive positions, but they were vague, inadequate, and totally lacking in any of the judicial elements or safeguards which determinations of the importance of personnel security adjudications required.

What happened in practice in our government security program was this: when the instances of abuses reached a level which pretty nearly everyone admitted, at least tacitly, was intolerable, there was nevertheless no change in the concept, the standards, or the basic framework of the program. *Instead there was merely a change in the practice or application of the standards.* Bowing to the fierce winds which had begun to blow concerning abuses in the security system, security practitioners simply eased up in the way they applied the standards. Those who had been security "extremists" suddenly became security "moderates." An employee would henceforth not necessarily be "bounced" because of all the hearsay in the file (although all the same hearsay was still in the file). What changed was just the practice. The official standards and procedures remained—and remain—intact.

CONTINUING FUTILITY (1969 - 1995)

Since 1953, Executive Order 10450 has remained the primary directive on which the executive branch's personnel security program has been based. Over the years, as a result of all the media attention as well as of the various congressional hearings inquiring into the extent to which constitutional guarantees were being observed in the administration of our government security programs, some amelioration has resulted. The government's overall security clearance program has gradually been modified to give greater recognition to basic constitutional rights and due process, and to reduce the number and seriousness of the abuses of the system.

In addition, as our society has become more morally permissive, and more tolerant of what were formerly considered types of immorality which disqualified people from government employment (adultery, fornication, cohabitation outside of marriage, illegitimate births, active homosexuality, and the like), these situations have ceased to be disqualifying for government employment. Although the written standards have not changed, in general, the standards have not only come to be applied much more leniently, but to be largely ignored.

At the same time, however, the official and written security standards, procedures, and modes of evaluation of investigative data and other security information have remained essentially unchanged from the Eisenhower-Nixon era. Both the security process, and its results, still remain shrouded in a vague aura of secrecy, despite congressional demands for correction. Of equal concern when looking at the U.S. government security program as a whole, there has been a consistent—and, really, incredible—lack of any serious executive branch oversight. Especially to be noted is the absence of any cost-benefit performance results.

The sad fact of the matter is that our U.S. government security program is operationally ineffective and managerially obsolete.

In addition to the relaxation of security *standards* over the past several decades, there have also been some other changes in *security* generally. Continuing refinement of the Security Classification System, as well as greater specification of the classification/declassification authority, and also improvement of declassification procedures, have all occurred, as a number of executive orders over the years have modified and extended President Eisenhower's E.O. 10450:

- President Eisenhower's 1960 E.O. 10865 directed the creation of a security program to cover DoD and other government contractors and related industry.
- President Kennedy's 1961 E.O. 10964 amended President Eisenhower's original executive order by improving declassification procedures. Four information categories were created, each of which was distinguished by whether automatic downgrading and declassification was permitted and specifying the time intervals at which this would occur.
- President Nixon's 1972 E.O. 11652 made a number of major changes in the security program, restricting the authority to classify information to those offices in the executive branch which were concerned with matters of national security. For example, the number of offices with authority to classify information as "Top Secret" was decreased from 31 to 12. This order also forbade classification for purposes of "concealing inefficiency or administrative error, to prevent embarrassment to a person or department, to restrain competition or independent initiative" or for any reason other than national security. It also included a requirement to classify individual portions of documents where appropriate and applicable; and it further included an automatic downgrade/declassification schedule providing for automatic review of exempted material. Finally, foreign affairs was added to national defense as subject matter for classification.
- President Carter's 1978 E.O. 12065 further reduced the agencies given the authority to classify information and identified seven topics, at least one of which had to be involved if material was to be classified. This executive order encouraged increased declassification and required that material classified for longer than six years must contain the name of the official who authorized the longer time period, and the reason for the extended classification. Derivative classification, for extracts, summaries, or copies, was recognized and the approval process for classification guides was described.

The National Security Council was given responsibility for overall policy direction for the program and the Information Security Oversight Office (ISOO) was created to replace the former Interagency Classification Review Committee. The ISOO forms an administrative part of the General Services Administration, but is directed in matters of policy by the National Security Council.

• President Reagan's 1982 E.O. 12356 restated, expanded, and increased the specificity of virtually every aspect of the previous executive orders; it will be discussed in more detail in the next chapter.

There were a few other occurrences and trends which impacted the U.S. government security function during these same years. The Senate committee hearings conducted by Senator Frank Church of Idaho in the 1970s reduced the freedom and independence with which the intelligence agencies had been able to operate. These hearings produced some negative emotional fallout which brought about a further reduction in the respect and regard in which the security function in general was held. The Vietnam War and its aftermath had a similar effect.

The one realistic attempt to strengthen America's ability to protect its secrets during these years came as a direct result of the public revelations of espionage and treason that continued to come to light in the 1970s and the 1980s: President Reagan appointed the Stillwell Commission to examine the state of the nation's security program. The report of this Commission, *Protecting America's Secrets*, contained a variety of technical and procedural recommendations intended to tighten up day-to-day security operations, and some of the recommendations which did not require the expenditure of money were actually implemented (those considered too expensive were never acted upon). Unfortunately, this Commission report brought about no substantive improvement in the basic concept and structure of U.S. government security.

Thus, while considerable effort was expended over more than three decades in trying to improve certain specific security procedures and techniques, little or no original thinking was ever applied to its basic philosophy and components to determine what would comprise a truly effective program. Similarly, little was accomplished which would improve managerial performance in successfully identifying and preventing actual instances of leaks, theft of information, and espionage. The popular phrase, "re-arranging the deck chairs on the Titanic," inevitably comes to mind.

Moreover, it appears that the Clinton Administration is looking at the U.S. Government's security program mostly in terms of achieving a reduction in costs. This is surely short-sighted, considering the continuing threats to American security described elsewhere in these pages. The only way in which costs can be reduced without placing our security interests in jeopardy would be through a complete re-design of a fundamentally defective security system, including major changes in principles and techniques, not in the tinkering with an unfixable system.

In a number of important ways, the security threats and problems faced by the United States are *worse* today than in the 1940s and 1950s when there was so much public concern and anxiety about America's security that the Eisenhower Administration felt obliged to put in place with great fanfare the failed system we have had ever since.

Yet there is little public concern about security today even as the system itself continues to fail. Neither the security investigation process, nor the security clearance standards, nor the managerial and operational systems for the protection of our national secrets can be said to be working effectively. It *has*, unfortunately, been "fifty years of failure."

THREE

Security Today

In the more than fifty years since the government security function first became recognized as requiring some kind of continuous, formal, and structured approach for its accomplishment, a litany of procedures as well as several armies of investigators, adjudicators, and regulators have all been created in order to verify the loyalty and character of applicants and employees and to insure that appropriate security policies and procedures are developed, implemented, and observed. The authority, responsibilities, and practices of these various agencies which aim at protecting America's secrets normally involve three major groups of people:

- Employees of the federal government and of Congress.
- United States military personnel.
- Federal government contractors.

FEDERAL AND CONGRESSIONAL EMPLOYEES

The Office of Personnel Management (OPM), the successor federal agency to the old Civil Service Commission, is currently responsible for the creation of employment and security clearance standards and the performance of suitability investigations (under Title 5 of the U.S. Code), as well as for security investigations (under Executive Order 10450), for all persons hired, or seeking to be hired, through competitive Civil Service examination procedures. The director of OPM sets the standards based upon E.O. 10450 for security and upon the Civil Service Rules (5 CFR Part 731) for suitability. OPM may delegate the responsibility for the performance of security clearance investigations and, following the lead of its predecessor agency, it has frequently done so. For excepted Civil Service positions, it is the head of the agency to which the person is applying or works who has the authority and responsibility to set standards and assure compliance, although such an agency may ask OPM for guidance. The Federal Bureau of Investigation (FBI) and the Central Intelligence Agency (CIA) are both excepted agencies and therefore they administer their own security programs without OPM participation.

The security investigations for agencies and departments of government other than the FBI and the CIA are carried out as follows:

- Department of State—OPM.
- Department of the Treasury—OPM, except for the following Treasury bureaus, which perform their own investigations:
  Secret Service.
  Internal Revenue Service.
  Bureau of the Customs.
  Bureau of Alcohol, Tobacco, and Firearms.
  Bureau of Engraving and Printing.
- Department of Defense (civilians)—OPM for "Sensitive" and "Non-Critical Sensitive"; and the Defense Investigation Service (DISCO) for "Sensitive-Critical" positions.
- Department of Justice—Apportioned between OPM and the FBI. (During the long tenure of former FBI Director J. Edgar Hoover, the FBI attempted to carry out all Justice Department security investigations; in 1973, one year after Hoover's death, the Justice Department returned the responsibility for most of these investigations to OPM.)
- Nuclear Regulatory Commission, NSA, USIA, etc.—OPM.

While the Defense Investigation Service investigates Congressional staff members desiring security clearances, members of Congress themselves require only a "need to know" clearance.

It is now also permissible to "contract out" the security investigation function to private organizations. In such cases, if the investigations are for competitive civil service positions, OPM must approve the investigation, even in the cases with delegated investigative authority.

The responsibility for the decision *to grant or decline* a security clearance, based upon the results of the investigation conducted, rests entirely with the specific agency involved, whether or not OPM has delegated the responsibility for the investigation to the agency. This has been a consistent principle of government security administration since the Eisenhower Administration's E.O. 10450 was promulgated in 1953. The only instance in which OPM has any input into the actual clearance decision is when a potential new government employee is involved.

Although the Appraisal and Assistance Branch of OPM provides training to the adjudicators assigned by the other agencies and conducts audits of the performance of adjudicators of the other agencies, the training is voluntary and addresses the suitability issue almost exclusively, essentially ignoring security clearance adjudications. OPM representatives have stated that the quality of the adjudications and the application of the government-wide standards vary tremendously among various agencies and adjudicators.

The statute on which the government security clearance requirement is based is 5 USC 7532, which has been extended to cover all federal agencies. Under this statute, a person failing a security clearance may be turned down or removed from a position only if it is a designated *security* position. As determined in the court case *Cole vs. Young* in 1957, applicants or incumbents for non-security positions can only be refused or removed from employment for causes not related to security. Furthermore, in the case of *Navy vs. Egan* in 1988, the Supreme Court ruled that the security clearance decision is entirely dependent upon executive discretion.

OPM representatives have stated privately that there *has not been in recent years a single case of proven betrayal of this country's secrets coming out of any of the government's civilian agencies*, and, therefore the system as a whole is obviously effective. Unfortunately, this is not the case. At the very least the system has never prevented leaks of what is clearly security information to the press by Congress, the White House, or executive departments. One notorious—and harmful—example of this was the apparent betrayal of security information concerning the imminent invasion of Panama in 1989 by sources in the State Department.

Furthermore, this is the same government security system which has failed to prevent the outright sale of secrets by people working within the military or the military-industrial complex. It should also be obvious that, given the existing major differences among departments and agencies in the application of government security standards, and their varying capabilities for the evaluation and adjudication of security cases—not all agencies can really be fulfilling their obligations with respect to the proper implementation of the existing standards.

Finally, since every U.S. government department and agency sets its own priorities for carrying out its security responsibilities, as directed by each agency or department head, it is simply impossible that all of these varied units are carrying out their security responsibilities with equal and appropriate vigor. In practice, agencies will only do what the

agency heads demand, and most agency heads today are generally unconcerned with the subject of security, which continues to be considered
as a low priority and sometimes even slightly disreputable.

Another factor to be considered is that, under the constant pressure
that comes from Congress and elsewhere, OPM has been steadily modifying its application forms, including both its standard application for
employment forms and its security clearance request forms, in order to
make them more acceptable to those who believe that the information
currently required on these forms is too "invasive." During 1990 and
1991, for example, Standard Form 85 (Questionnaire for Non-Sensitive
Positions), Standard Form 85P (Questionnaire for Public Trust Positions), and Standard Form 86 (Questionnaire for Sensitive Positions)
were all modified to be more in keeping with what was described to us
as "today's environment."

Since Standard Form 86 is the form used for security clearance
requests, it is worth identifying the changes which have been made:

1. Organizational memberships, including foreign organizations, are
   no longer required to be listed.
2. Continuing contact with foreign nationals is only required to be
   listed if this information has been specified by the employing
   agency. (It was previously required for any contacts in all Communist countries.)
3. Concerning police records, the form has been changed from
   requiring information concerning any arrest, charge, or conviction to information concerning a charge or conviction only.
4. Concerning drugs and alcohol, the item noting the use of alco-
   holic beverages has been changed from "habitually to excess" to
   instances "causing formal problems."
5. With respect to foreign travel, reportable travel has been changed
   from any and every foreign trip to that taken only in the previous five years.
6. Concerning financial records, reportable problems (bankruptcy,
   liens, or judgments) now only include those instances occurring
   in the previous five years, rather than all such problems that ever
   occurred, as before. Reportable late payment conditions are defined as more than 180 days, rather than as 90 days late, as before.
7. Membership in organizations committed to the overthrow of the
   United States government by force and violence are required to
   be reported only if the subject has the intent to further these
   same objectives.

All these items may appear to be petty and innocuous. In reality, they are very significant, especially taken cumulatively. These particular changes represent precisely the kinds of things which make it more difficult for investigators to arrive at true and accurate judgments about people and their backgrounds. The purpose of a security investigation is not to try to "dig up dirt" that will reflect badly on the people being investigated and perhaps do harm to their reputations. The main purpose is to identify information that might help in resolving any possible questions about a person's character and background, might have a bearing on that person's suitability for government employment, or would disqualify him for a security clearance. A properly trained security investigator would know how to use the information that was once requested on these forms without doing improper harm. What is troubling about some of these recent changes in OPM's forms is the virtual invitation under these now watered-down questions to withhold information concerning such things as membership in groups or organizations antagonistic to the United States. To specify, as the form does, that unless the subject withheld the information "knowing that the organization engages in such activities with the specific intent to further such activities," is not only to guarantee a dishonest answer for all practical purposes from anyone who belongs to such an organization, but to void this part of the questionnaire—and hence this part of the investigation as well—of any real meaning. Inclusion of this kind of question means that we are only pretending to be asking a serious question or conducting a serious security investigation.

Cumulatively, all the changes made on the new OPM form thus significantly inhibit any security investigator from conducting a serious probe into the backgrounds of applicants or employees.

Considering all the expressions of concern and intention to take corrective action after each revelation of yet another damaging espionage case, the limitations of investigative scope which the government has in fact been voluntarily placing on its own ability to conduct serious investigations speaks volumes about the real commitment to effective security, both in Congress and among the higher-ups in the executive branch of all recent administrations.

DEPARTMENT OF DEFENSE AND FEDERAL DEFENSE CONTRACTORS

The Department of Defense is responsible for the security investigations of all military personnel, and of most of its own civilian employees, as well as of all defense contractor employees (and the employees of most other federal contractors). Since 1972, when the investigative arms of all the military services were combined into one, all DoD investigations have been performed by DoD's Defense Investigative Service (DIS).

Requests for clearances are sent to the Personnel Investigation Center (PIC), which separates this investigative material geographically and dispatches appropriate portions of it to the various regional offices. The separated portions are returned to the PIC upon completion, where they are re-assembled into a single investigative report. Each military service branch then performs its own evaluation and adjudication. If a decision is made to deny the request for clearance, a letter is sent to the individual stating this intention to deny the clearance and giving the reason for it. The individual is permitted to write back to the adjudicator to rebut or explain the findings. Each service has some level of review above that of the adjudicator.

For employees of federal contractors, the initial adjudication is performed by DoD's Defense Industrial Security Clearance Office (DISCO). The adjudicators at DISCO are permitted to grant clearances, but not to deny requests for clearance. Initially, eighty to eighty-five percent of all requests for clearance are granted by DISCO. Next, those cases which the DISCO adjudicators believe should indicate "termination" or should be looked at more carefully are sent to the Office of Industrial Security Clearance (ISC), where additional expert adjudicators can review them. Final adjudication is performed there. ISC will either direct DISCO to grant the clearance or will write to the individual concerned, sending a Statement of Reasons. If the individual wishes, he may either respond in writing or request a hearing, attending it with counsel. There is one level of appeal beyond this, but it is only a review of the record by the appellate board. No personal appearances are permitted at this higher appeal level.

Like all other federal adjudicators, the Department of Defense uses the language of Executive Order 10450. The standards applied are laid out in DoD 5200.2-s, and are no more specific than those of the civilian sector. The standards are as follows:

2-101 Clearance and Sensitive Position Standard

The personnel security standard that must be applied to determine whether a person is eligible for access to classified information or assignment to sensitive duties is whether, based on all available information, the person's loyalty, reliability, and trustworthiness are such that entrusting the person with classified information or assigning the person to sensitive duties is clearly consistent with the interests of national security.

2-102 Military Service Standard

The personnel security standard that must be applied in determining whether a person is suitable under national security criteria for appointment, enlistment, induction, or retention in the Armed Forces is that, based on all available information, there is no reasonable basis for doubting the person's loyalty to the government of the United States.

2-200 Criteria for Application of Security Standards

The ultimate decision in applying either of the security standards set forth in paragraph 2-101 and 2-102 above must be an overall common-sense determination based upon all available facts. The criteria for determining eligibility for a clearance under the security standard shall include, but not be limited to the following ...

At this point there appears a list of reprehensible actions and personal frailties which is nearly identical to the one that appears in E.O. 10450 (Appendix B). After more than forty years of experience, we are still giving our security adjudicators no more guidance than simply that they are to make a "common-sense determination" with reference to a list of improper activities and weaknesses. It would seem that, with all the experience accumulated, the government should be able to give much more specific guidance concerning the things security investigators need to be looking for in particular, the weight to be given to various factors, the application of due process, etc., if the objective of the whole exercise is really to try to identify those who might possibly be the ones to betray their trust and America's secrets. The security establishment itself does not seem to have faith in this process and therefore does not bother to provide specific guidance.

EXECUTIVE ORDER 12356:
THE INFORMATION SECURITY OVERSIGHT OFFICE

President Ronald Reagan issued Executive Order 12356 on April 2, 1982 (Appendix D), which brought clearer definitions and specificity to the process of classification and declassification, codified the responsibility of agencies and others to control access to classified information, and provided continuing authority to the Information Security Oversight

Office (ISOO) which had been established by President Carter's E.O. 12065, issued on June 28, 1978. This Reagan Executive Order 12356 concerning the ISOO included provisions concerning the following areas:

1. Restatement of the classification levels with an update of the classification categories, the duration of classifications, and the design and content of the classification identification markings that are to be placed upon documents; and also the limitations on the use of classification itself.

2. Official introduction into the whole security system of the concept of "derivative classified information" (secondary, tertiary, etc., that is, documents containing or paraphrasing classified material).

3. A requirement that departments and agencies with original classification authority must prepare classification guides to facilitate the proper and uniform derivative classification of information.

4. Requirements and procedures for the declassification and downgrading of classified material, including mandatory and systematic reviews of such material.

5. Provisions for the treatment and control of transferred classified information.

6. Principles concerning the safeguarding of classified material, including a restatement of who is authorized to receive access to classified information and a reiteration of the requirement that controls must be established by each department and agency to ensure that classified information is used, processed, stored, reproduced, transmitted, and destroyed only under conditions that will provide adequate protection and to prevent access to it by unauthorized persons; prohibitions on dissemination of classified information are also included, as are authorities and primary conditions for "Special Access Programs" and "Access by Historical Researchers and Former Presidential Appointees."

7. Assignment of responsibility for policy direction (to the National Security Council) and program implementation and monitoring (to the Administrator of the General Services Administration).

8. Authorization of the Information Security Oversight Office (ISOO), and allowance for the delegation of the implementation and monitoring function to the ISOO Director.

    Among the responsibilities of this ISOO Director are the following:

- To develop, in consultation with departments and agencies, and to promulgate, subject to the approval of the National Security Council, directives for the implementation of E.O. 12356 which will be binding upon departments and agencies.

- To oversee agency actions to insure compliance with E.O. 12356 and any implementing directives issued pursuant to it.
- To review all agency implementing regulations and agency guidelines for systematic declassification review with directions for modification if necessary, subject to appeal to the National Security Council.
- To conduct on-site reviews of the information security program of each agency or department that generates or handles classified information and to require of each agency such reports, information, and other forms of cooperation as may be necessary for the ISOO Director to fulfill his responsibilities.
- To review requests for original classification authority from agencies or officials not granted such original classification authority; and, if deemed appropriate and supportable, to recommend presidential approval of these requests.
- To consider and take action on any suggestions and complaints received.
- To prescribe standard forms, after consultation with the affected departments and agencies.
- To report at least annually to the President through the National Security Council on the implementation of E.O. 12356.
- To convene and to chair interagency meetings to discuss matters pertaining to the information security programs of agencies.

9. Identification of general responsibilities for agencies handling classified information (these are essentially the same as in previous Executive Orders and other pertinent directives).
10. Provisions for response to instances of non-compliance.

The Information Security Oversight Office has also concerned itself with creating materials such as videos and booklets explaining the purpose and the various elements of the security classification system, the federal Nondisclosure Agreement (SF 32), and other related forms and documents. It has encouraged departments and agencies to decrease the number of their classified documents and to increase their declassification programs on the documents they have. The Office compiles and submits to the President an annual report which includes data concerning review of classified documents for adherence to the standard classification standards and procedures, the numbers of documents classified and declassified, and the number of infractions found in the course of the self-inspections conducted by the departments and agencies. Although the Office has the authority to perform direct security inspections, it has currently taken the position that it does not have the manpower to perform this inspection function properly.

On February 16, 1993, the ISOO issued its Report for 1992. Some of the data reported included the following: the Office examined 10,933 classified documents, of which 53% were electronic cables or messages, 25% memoranda or letters, and 22% other documents; 2,878 discrepancies were identified, which is considered to be an error rate of 24%, even though there may have been more than one discrepancy in some of the documents. This rate is lower than the 42% rate recorded for the period 1986 through 1989 and the 33% rate recorded for non-Gulf-War documents in 1991. These Gulf War documents experienced an error rate of only 8%. Authorities reported original classification decreased significantly, to 5,793. Reported derivative classification decisions decreased 11% to 5,868,689.

According to the Report, under the systematic review program, departments and agencies reviewed 10,715,290 pages of historically valuable records; this was 32% fewer than in FY 1991. Meanwhile, departments and agencies declassified 9,426,011 pages, 33% fewer than in FY 1991. 4,431 new mandatory review requests were received; under mandatory review, agencies declassified in full 101,814 pages and in part 118,655 pages, and retained classification in full on 13,224 pages. As for mandatory review appeals, agencies received 207 new ones, and on appeal, agencies declassified in whole or in part 15,248 additional pages.

Finally, according to the Report, agencies conducted 21,233 self-inspections during 1992, and reported 21,071 infractions, 1% fewer than in the previous year, FY 1991.

One area of concern identified in the report is that 94% of the classified documents reviewed had no release date but instead contained the code "OADR" ("Originating Agencies Determination Required"); this represents an over-use of the indefinite release date. More serious still is the fact that the self-inspections by agencies of their Safeguarding Systems decreased by 1% in 1992, and this followed a decrease of 11% in 1991. It should be noted that all of these inspections were *self-examinations*, a system with few incentives built in to motivate the agencies to take security very seriously. *There appears to have been no inspections by outside experts.* This latter type of inspection would necessarily have been more stringent and much less self-serving.

For its part, the ISOO appears to have been quite pleased by the declassification figures reported and, particularly, by a program carried out by the Air Force to declassify Vietnam-era documents.

EXECUTIVE ORDER 12829

As part of the continuing effort to streamline the federal government security program, President George Bush issued Executive Order 12829 (Appendix E) at the very end of his Administration on January 6, 1993. This Executive Order established a National Industrial Security Program intended to better safeguard federal government classified information released to contractors, licensees and grantees of the United States Government, by simplifying and standardizing requirements and procedures. For example, while contracts with different agencies now may require multiple investigations for a single individual and differing physical security specifications for identical functions, standardization would eliminate these duplications. A single, integrated program is to be developed to replace the former Defense Industrial Security Program. It is designed to function identically for all defense related agencies and contractors. A 260-member task force has been established to implement the program over the next five years. It remains to be seen what level of improvement will be reached.

SECURITY CLASSIFICATION

Security classification systems, and their management and operation, have become quite difficult and complex. One instructive current document addressing the classification process is the four-volume series entitled *Security Classification of Information*. (Volumes Three and Four are still under development). The series is authored by Arvin S. Quist for the Oak Ridge K-25 Site of the Oak Ridge National Laboratory, managed by Martin Marietta Energy Systems, Inc., for the U.S. Department of Energy.

Volume One of this series provides a history of security classification, and includes the results of the various executive orders and also discussions of issues such as the constitutionality of security classification and its impact on scientific and technical progress. It also includes a discussion of the impact of the Freedom of Information Act. Some modest (and obsolete) classification cost data are also included.

Volume Two describes the types of classification systems and classification levels, and examines the "balance" of disclosure risks versus benefits. It also provides both guidelines and instructions for classification and declassification of material.

Volume Three of the series will address classification management, including the preparation of guides and manuals, training and education, and penalties for unauthorized disclosure of classified information. It will also address the question of over-classifying or under-classifying security information.

Volume Four will cover control of certain unclassified information, including nuclear, scientific, and technical information as well as information controlled by private organizations.

In the prefaces to both Volume One and Volume Two of this series, the author, Mr. Quist, makes polite and matter-of-fact, but telling, comments concerning the skills and experience needed in order to make effective classifications. He points out that the federal government neither provides training nor produces effective written materials to guide and assist classifiers in their efforts. He writes:

The classification of information, documents, or materials is a complex activity. It is not an exact science but requires subjective determinations (judgments) by classifiers. To reach sound classification decisions, the classifier (1) must be knowledgeable in the field in which the classification decision is made, (2) must be provided with adequate classification guidance, and (3) must understand and apply the principles of classification. A classifier generally acquires knowledge of the field in which he or she provides classification guidance (e.g., uranium enrichment technologies) by education, training, and experience. Written classification guidance is provided to a classifier in the form of classification guides. However, a classifier's knowledge of the principles of classification, and how they should be applied to reach classification decisions, is usually acquired only by self-study and on-the-job experience. There is no formal educational program for training classifiers.

A document that broadly covers the classification of information would be very helpful to classifiers in their "self-education and training" and in their preparation of classification guides. Such a document would also assist classification managers in establishing sound classification programs. To the author's knowledge, no single document, or small number of documents, provides background information on classification of information in the United States, describes classification principles, provides guidance in the selection and training of classifiers, presents information to aid in preparing classification guides, discusses employee classification education, and considers other important aspects of classification and of a sound classification program for an organization. This series of documents is being prepared to remedy that situation and thereby to assist classifiers in becoming better at their jobs and to help classification managers in improving their organization's classification program.

In the Abstract of Volume Two of this series on security classification, Mr. Quist states further:

This document is expected to be particularly useful to Department of Energy (DOE) and DOE-contractor personnel concerned with the security classification of information. Classification of scientific and technical information is extensively discussed because this is of major importance within DOE. However, this volume contains a significant amount of information that will be useful to classification personnel in all federal agencies because the basic classification principles are the same for any activity.

This document was given to my associate by the director of the Federal Information Security Oversight Office as being among the most effective documents available for training classifiers or describing the security system. Yet, printed on the inside cover of each volume is a disclaimer by which the federal government disavows any responsibility for, or concurrence with, the document's contents or conclusions:

This report was prepared as an account of work sponsored by an agency of the United States Government. Neither the United States Government nor any agency thereof, nor any of their employees, makes any warranty, express or implied, or assumes any legal liability or responsibility for the accuracy, completeness, or usefulness of any information, apparatus, product, or process disclosed, or represents that its use would not infringe privately owned rights . . .

The example of this disclaimer is all too typical of the federal government's approach to security generally: no specific training or guidance is provided by the government to those persons with security responsibility, and yet, even when a valuable training document happens to be produced, the government explicitly declines to support or endorse its contents.

SECURITY MANAGEMENT

The current state of security management in the government is exemplified in the various security manuals of the Department of Defense. These include: DoD 5200.1R, Information Security Program Regulations; DoD 5200.28, Information Security Directive; DoD 5200.28M, Security Manual for Safeguarding Classified ADP Information; DoD 5220.22M, Industrial Security Manual for Safeguarding Classified Information; and a multitude of other manuals more specific to particular tasks.

These manuals do not lend themselves to summarization, since they primarily consist of policies, directives, and specific instructions for the proper storage and transport of classified material and information, and specify the kinds of actions to be taken when dealing with classified or security information or materials in the course of one's work.

What they do not include—and what it also must be said is lacking from the normal security training given either to security personnel or to regular employees—is any philosophical or historical grounding in the need for and the basic structure of the government's security programs. There is no training program anywhere intended to provide the specific management and operational security knowledge which would provide the employee with the ability to make the right decisions when confronted with a set of circumstances not predetermined in the manual. Nor is there any prepared training material which would develop skills both in training personnel in their obligations to protect classified material and in managing other employees handling classified material so as to be able to detect and identify incidents of misfeasance or malfeasance. There is nothing concerning the discipline or punishment of supervisors who fail to prevent or detect security violations on the part of subordinates. Security is scarcely even considered as an area where judgments ever have to be made! The judicial aspect critical to sound judgments is lacking.

In addition to the lack of any indepth training with respect to managerial and technical capabilities for improved physical and procedural protection of secrets, there is also a lack of continued research and development concerning physical and technical capabilities. There is a refusal to acknowledge and respond to even the possibility of abuse, threat, or espionage. When the 3M company approached the Department of Defense several years ago with an idea for the prevention of unauthorized copying of classified documents, the company was rebuffed; the Department of Defense was not interested. The system would have provided for a permanent label to go on documents in such a way that any attempt to remove the label would noticeably and permanently damage the document and any attempt to copy the document would cause the copying machine to "lock up" the document and sound an alarm.

Apparently the Pentagon believed that since a technical approach such as this could not provide a guarantee against *all* methods of espionage, there was no reason to be interested in implementing this one particular technique. It was decided that current classification techniques, clearances of personnel, and access control and other physical security procedures would remain the relied-upon methods. In reality, however, effective protection of secrets involves a discipline which should include the development of many different techniques and the utilization of any or all of them as appropriate in any given area. Moreover, technological measures are constantly developing in every area and security must be open to their use and application. This is true in the case of security management as it is in any other management discipline.

The other area in which management training is deficient is in the *awareness* on the part of all employees and contractors involved in using classified material. There already exists, of course, some manuals, videos, and orientation programs which outline the need for certain security methods and procedures and encourage vigilance. In real life, however, the attitude which is too frequently encountered is one where the entire security classification system is considered to be merely a waste of time. Many employees only observe security requirements by going through the motions, while ignoring the real goals of the security program, and, at the same time, few managers are inclined to attempt any serious correction of this common state of affairs. Federal employees have recounted stories of security classification markings being simply "whited out" before being copied and given out to persons from whom, in some instances, employees hoped to gain advancement or favors. This is more likely with political and diplomatic secrets than with scientific or technical secrets, but it occurs far more frequently than merely in the cases where espionage comes to light or charges are brought and prosecution instituted. Every available technique, not just a few orientation sessions, must be used to raise the awareness and understanding of both managers and employees of how serious their security responsibilities really are.

In practice, a lack of managerial involvement in the security system instituted for the protection of classified material can be verified in many areas. The following are some examples:

1. In most instances, the access control procedures and systems in place do not begin to approach the level of sophistication of the data being protected. For example, during the heyday of the Strategic Defense Initiative ("Star Wars") program, critical data was stolen from the internal disk of a standard personal computer in a contractor's office that was protected only by a standard coded-card and card-reader access system. Although many contractors will permit visitors only when accompanied by an assigned employee, many of these same contractors invite the technical community to programs and seminars, frequently sales oriented, which bring outsiders into or immediately adjacent to supposedly restricted areas. Moreover, the electronic access control and alarm systems which protect these restricted areas are frequently easily disabled, even if a person has access to the restricted area for just a few minutes. These systems can be disabled by shorting the leads to the magnetic door switches, for example, or by adding an additional magnet to the detection circuit. Meanwhile, more sophisticated detection devices which might defeat these simple techniques are not normally required to be installed. Managers just don't believe traitors exist in their departments and that constant vigilance is critical.

2. In the course of examining many individual cases, the author knows of no instances in which managers have been demoted, dismissed or otherwise disciplined when employees under their supervision disclosed or otherwise betrayed secrets.

3. Undercover or "sting" operations are virtually never utilized to identify those who might be willing to commit espionage, increase the awareness of others of the problem, instill in employees a healthy fear of the consequences of betraying secrets entrusted to them, or otherwise identify security weaknesses. Such operations have proved to be effective in law enforcement generally, however, as they have proved to be effective in keeping politicians and other public servants "honest." Similarly, "tiger teams," popular for a number of years in testing the integrity of computer systems as well as the security of facilities considered to be potential targets for physical attacks, have not been used to test the security provided to classified materials and data.

4. Discussions with government employees and even with government security officers have indicated that both groups continue to believe that the only real threat to classified material in their

departments or agencies is through accidental release of such classified material by well-meaning people. The possibility of deliberate and systematic espionage tends to be discounted. The very human tendency to assume that someone well known, such as a co-worker, could actually be a traitor or a criminal continues to be strong. So does an irrational and arrogant but widespread belief that if someone really were stealing or releasing material this would quickly be evident to the rare insight or the sharp eyes of the manager. Using a "gut feeling" about a person's integrity is simply an abysmal management technique.

5. All areas of government have been slow to implement Total Quality Management programs. These programs would be particularly beneficial for the government security function, since they require employee involvement, including "quality circles" and similar techniques for their successful execution.

6. Observance and *enforcement* of the principle and the application of the "Need to Know" concept is lax to nonexistent in many organizations. This is true at nearly every level of management. More often than not, classified information is freely discussed and shared within and among groups which are "trusted" or "cleared."

As long as many of these current attitudes persist and these current techniques are relied upon, government management will continue to fail in fulfilling its responsibility to protect America's secrets.

JOINT SECURITY COMMISSION

On June 11, 1993, a new Joint Security Commission was convened at the request of the Director of Central Intelligence and the Deputy Secretary of Defense to develop a new approach to Security which would "assure the adequacy of protection within the contours of a security system that is simplified, more uniform, and more cost effective." The primary emphasis of the Committee's directive is on efficiency and cost reduction. In fact, the Infrastructure Report of the Community Management Review, an earlier study ordered by then Director of Central Intelligence Robert Gates, identified current security policies and practices as the "greatest deterrents to major savings in infrastructure."

The Committee's inception occurred during a time of reduced tensions with Russia and of relatively few espionage scandals, at least considering the recent tempestuous past, and the study was to take these improved conditions into account. Ironically, however, by the time the Committee's report was presented, on February 28, 1994, the United States, and the CIA itself, had once again been rocked by a massive spy scandal, one which was more ruinous to America's intelligence capability and more damaging to its foreign policy than any before it. It is likely that, if the Ames case had come to light six months earlier, the tone of this report would be rather different. Nevertheless, the report contains a number of valuable insights and recommendations.

The report, titled "Redefining Security," addresses security practices in the Department of Defense, the Intelligence Agencies and defense contractors. The Study's areas of concentration and primary conclusions follow. The Joint Security Commission considers its recommendations to be cost-saving or cost-neutral except in the areas of Personnel Security and Information Systems security, in which it believes the most improvements are necessary.

Classification

The Committee has recommended a very simple classification system—one level with two degrees of protection. Currently there is Confidential, Secret and Top Secret based on potential for damage; but determining potential level of damage is very subjective. In addition, this leads to less vigilance in protecting material of lower classification. In addition, there is no relevance between an item's level of importance and the number of years for which it should be protected. In short, if it's classified, you cannot have it without authorization.

The two levels of the new system would be Secret and Secret-Controlled Access. Secret would be discretionary in terms of "need to know" and providing access to cleared persons. Secret-Controlled Access would be specific in terms of who could receive it. Currently, even Top Secret documents are not protected in terms of "Need to Know". If you have Top Secret Clearance, you can see them. The only Control Markings necessary are "Release To" markings.

Related recommendations include:
- All special access, SCI, covert action control systems, war plans and bigot lists should be integrated into the new classificationsystem.
- A single control channel for SECRET COMPARTMENTED ACCESS information, with a codeword for each "need to know" list, should replace all existing special control channels.

The report recognizes one of the key problems—that of poor oversight and management—in the following comments and recommendations:

"Nevertheless, no system can be expected to work very well if there is no one in charge. Today there are few government-wide standards and, even when standards are supposed to have general applicability they often are translated and interpreted in ways that do violence to the concept of standardization. Often there is no penalty for noncompliance. Moreover, we conclude that the Information Security Oversight Office simply is not positioned to ensure compliance. Without an effective policy and oversight structure, no coherent security policy is likely to evolve. Instead, inconsistent rules will continue to be formulated and disputes will continue to impede the development of a uniform policy."

The Commission recommends:

a) Strong centralized oversight by the security executive committee as well as more effective oversight at the agency level.
b) A strengthened Information Security Oversight Office as a part of the security executive committee staff.
c) A requirement that each agency appoint a classification ombudsman, establish a hot line for employee classification questions and complaints, and institute a spot check system.

Personnel Security

The commission found that the clearance process "is needlessly complex, cumbersome, and costly. Security clearances are sought for too many persons who have no real need for a clearance, There are too many different forms in use. There is insufficient automation and little interconnectivity between agencies. Investigation and adjudication are practiced inconsistently among agencies, resulting in reciprocity problems, delays, and increased cost to both government and industry. All too frequently clearances granted by one agency are not accepted by another, or even by another program manager within the same agency.

Virtually all of the commission's recommendations addressing Personnel Security would simplify, standardize and economize the clearance and adjudication process and increase its perceived "fairness". Several additional issues are discussed below.

The simplification of the Classification System would permit some simplification and standardization of the types of personnel clearances. There would be only two types of clearance, Secret and Secret Compartmented Access. However, the commission believes that, if its recommendation to downgrade a significant amount of information from higher to lower levels of protection is accepted, the investigative standard for a Secret clearance should be increased from a National Agency Check, with written inquiries to law enforcement agencies, former employers and supervisors, listed references and schools attended within the last five years (NACI) to an NACI plus credit check, with expansion as appropriate to follow up only on issues likely to result in adverse adjudication. Re-investigations should include the NAC, local agency check and credit check, performed at least once every 10 years on a periodic basis.

The Investigative Standard for a Secret Compartmented Access clearance would be a Single Scope Background Investigation (SSBI) with a scope of seven years. However, investigators would not be required to conduct education and birth record checks in person or neighborhood checks other than the most recent residence of six months or more. Re-investigations should include the SSBI, performed at least once every seven years on an aperiodic basis.

The commission supports the use of the polygraph, with "appropriate standardization, increased oversight, and training to prevent abuses . . . We believe that the intrusiveness of the procedure should be minimized and mechanisms should be put in place to resolve ambiguous results quickly and efficiently." The report contains recommended procedural safeguards and oversight "to ensure that the technology is used in a reliable, consistent, and ethical manner."

Physical Security

The commission recommends reductions and standardization in the concentric layers of physical security currently imposed over areas containing classified data. The report contains the following example, and implies that the security described is excessive:

"The physical security countermeasures at one industrial facility include a fence, roving guards, and automated building access controls. Inside the facility, there is also a specially constructed room to which access is controlled by cipher and combination door locks. Moreover, the program manager of a special access program required that the five-drawer safe used to store program material have each drawer alarmed even though the safe was inside an area already alarmed."

It is true that the great majority of thefts of classified information involve persons who already have been granted access to the physical area and even to the protected material, and we concur that substantial cost-saving can frequently be realized in this area *provided that complete physical and procedural analysis supports such reduction on a case-by-case basis.*

However, even the classified material in the example referenced by the Commission is not necessarily overprotected, The exterior and building perimeter measures may be necessary to protect from entry by outsiders, either to prevent crime in general, or because these or other building contents are considered to be at risk. *The room protection measures are primarily to protect the material from persons properly in the building who have no right of access to the room or its contents.* Similarly, the safe may need protection from persons properly in the room who have no right of access to the safe, and different drawers within the safe may be used by different people. Finally, there must be at least a certain level of concentric and/or redundant protection to ensure against complicity by persons controlling part of all of the physical or electronic security capabilities and against equipment malfunction.

This is not to say that many facilities cannot be more economically protected, simply that the needs and characteristics of each must be carefully addressed.

The commission also recommends Standardization of Physical Security Techniques, Facility Certification, Reciprocity of Accredited Space, continued use of containers and locks currently approved for use in the United States and replacement of routine industrial re-inspections with periodic, random inspections. These recommendations appear reasonable provided they are not used as an excuse to virtually eliminate re-inspections. Traditionally, the level of readiness of security systems rapidly declines without outside review.

Technical Security

The commission's recommendations concerning technical security are limited to two areas. First, that domestic TEMPEST countermeasures not be employed except in response to specific threat data and then only in cases authorized by the most senior department or agency head. Second, that routine Technical Surveillance Countermeasure Inspections (TSCM), searches for technical surveillance devices or "bugs", be eliminated in favor of overseas inspections, except where specifically threat driven, and that a coordinated TSCM R&D and training program be funded to support overseas inspections and as a defense against future technological advances in technical surveillance equipment.

Procedural Security

The commission recommends creation of a Central Clearance Verification Data Base, abolishing separate certification of need to know for every contractor visit and development of a uniform community-wide badge system, each of which will increase efficiency.

Another recommendation addresses Operations Security (OPSEC). OPSEC is a formal Security program utilizing the risk management technique. It was institutionalized by National Security Decision Directive (NSDD) 298 mandating the implementation of a formal OPSEC program by each executive department and agency with national security responsibilities. A "robust" OPSEC community now coexists with, but separate from, the standard security structure. It is an excellent example of how the Federal Government creates an entirely new bureaucracy to acquire what should be instilled into its Security Program.

The Commission recommends that the normal security staff structure and risk management processes be incorporated into security and security awareness training programs at all levels and that the mandatory requirements for formal OPSEC programs be deleted from all contracts except in response to specific threats and then only when specifically authorized by the most senior department or agency head.

However, it must be recognized that the OPSEC Program became necessary because the security staffs were not interested in, or not capable of, performing these critical reviews themselves. This recommendation is reasonable and practical *only* if a continuing, viable program is implemented and managed by and through the security staff, with more skilled professionals brought in as appropriate.

The Commission also recommends the elimination of Document Tracking and Control, and Document Destruction Accounting and Verification Requirements, because of the ease with which documents can be copied, telefaxed and transmitted, thereby creating new documents and even delivering them without defacing or removing the originals. This recommendation is a poor response to a difficult situation and is a typical example of the manner in which both employees and contractors try to avoid the effort and responsibility for any control effort at all by complaining that since a control can be defeated, nothing at all should be done. In fact, this is a critical control problem and requires a solution even if the solution requires even more effort, at least for the most critical documents. This very important issue is addressed further at the conclusion of this section.

Protecting Advanced Technology

The Report recognizes the need for the United States to protect its advanced technology, and that the United States is losing more than it is gaining through participation in many foreign exchange agreements. The Commission offers the following recommendations:

- Foreign Ownership, Control and Influence (FOCI) Policy refers to the issue of foreign interest gaining control over American companies possessing classified technologies. There does not currently exist a coherent national policy on FOCI. This situation prevents America's Security forces from imposing consistent restrictions on foreign owned and influenced companies and contributes to a lack of reciprocity among government agencies. An FOCI Policy should be developed.

- The Secretary of Defense should review existing data exchange programs, using updated threat information, and determine whether the programs should be continued, canceled, or renegotiated to ensure they are in concert with current U.S. national security and economic goals.
- The Secretary of Defense should direct that comprehensive, coordinated threat analysis, intelligence, and counterintelligence support be provided to facilitate risk management to DoD critical technologies, systems, information, and facilities.
- Access to the Foreign Disclosure and Technical Information System (FORDTIS) data base should be expanded to command and other DoD consumers to support defense planning, programming, resourcing, analysis and information-sharing activities.
- Counterintelligence elements should cross-check critical systems or technologies against the FORDTIS data base to determine:
  a. The extent to which baseline technologies on each system have been released to foreign nations, and;
  b. The vulnerabilities posed to current or future weapons or weapons support systems if exchanges continue under the applicable Defense Development Exchange Program agreements.

Joint Investigative Service

The Commission recognized the costs in terms of dollars, efficiency, consistency and redundancy of the current situation involving separate investigative organizations for DoD, CIA, NRO, NSA and certain Navy and Air Force programs. In addition, there is a certain level of dissatisfaction with the performance of the Defense Investigative Service. In order to address both of these problems, the Commission recommended:

- That a Joint Investigative Service be established that performs all personnel security background investigations on a fee-for-service basis for the DoD, the NSA, the NRO, the CIA and other organizations that report to the Secretary of Defense or the Director of Central Intelligence.
- That a Joint Investigative Service perform industrial security services of common concern for the defense and Intelligence Communities, as determined by the Security Executive Committee and in accordance with a programmatic, customer service approach.

- That the Joint Investigative Service be established by the Secretary of Defense and the Director of Central Intelligence, that its resources be drawn from existing security organizations, and that it report jointly to the Secretary of Defense and the Director of Central Intelligence.

Information Systems Security

The Commission "found a number of problems hindering the effectiveness of information systems security. Problems include ineffectual and conflicting policies, failed strategies for obtaining the necessary computer security technology, poor mechanisms for obtaining timely threat information, inherent systems vulnerabilities, lack of effective audit data reduction techniques, and accreditation processes that are far too slow. The Commission also believes that there is a need to improve the quality and number of information systems security professionals and to increase training and awareness programs for management and non-security personnel.

"The policies and standards upon which the Defense and Intelligence communities base information systems security services were developed when computers were physically and electronically isolated." The report goes on to say that the policies and standards are therefore:
- Not suitable for networks.
- Developed for complete risk avoidance and therefore not suitable for use in a balanced mix of security countermeasures.
- Lack flexibility needed to address systems of today and the future.
- Do not differentiate between countermeasures needed in highly secure and less protected networks and environments.
- Are only beginning to combine computer science and encryption.
- Cannot respond in a timely manner to dynamically evolving information technology.

The Commission's recommendations all address managerial and program changes and development, rather than technical or operational improvements. Basically, they amount to a call for an entirely new Computer and Information Security Capability. The recommendations include that:
- Policy formulation for information systems security be consolidated under a joint DoD/DCI Security Executive Committee, and that the committee oversee development of a coherent network-oriented information systems security policy for the Department of Defense and the Intelligence Community that also could serve the entire government.
- The Secretary of Defense and the Director of Central Intelligence

develop an information systems security investment strategy including an emphasis on commercial production of computer security components at affordable costs. The goal should be to use 5 to 10 percent of the costs of infrastructure development and operations to ensure availability and the confidentiality and integrity of our information assets.

The report goes on to recommend that research and development programs be given high priority to create the secure products needed for protection of classified and unclassified data, that NSA be the executive agent for this effort, and that the Defense Information Systems Agency (DISA) be the executive agency for development of operational security management tools for infrastructure operations (including more powerful audit reduction tools and automated tools for use in assessing network and connected systems security) and improving security management support technology. The Commission also recommends the development of a systems security threat and vulnerability data base, that DISA's ASSIST program be the executive agent for DoD and the Intelligence Community emergency response functions and that a systems security professional development program be established.

What is not identified or explained in the report is why and how the management and supervisory structure of the DoD and the Intelligence Community would ignore the need for Information Security for so long and to such a degree that a sweeping call for an entirely new organization and new capability would be necessary. Systems and network security could and should have been a management focal point for the past ten years as personal computers and networks were developed, and as more and more information was loaded onto these systems. Even if these programs are initiated immediately, it will be five years or more before they will provide any realistic protection. *In the interim, short term technical improvement demanded by management and designed and developed by a team of computer auditors and other professionals should be implemented.*

Organizational Structure

The Commission accurately describes the near-chaos which has resulted from the manner in which the responsibility for Security has been fragmented among different government agencies, and the inconsistency which has resulted from placing the responsibility for development and implementation of programs and procedures with the individual agency and department heads. The Commission recommends:

The establishment of a national level security policy committee to

provide structure and coherence to U.S. Government security practices and procedures. The Committee would:
- Develop government security policy and standards,
- Ensure long term and continuing implementation oversight,
- Serve as an ombudsman to resolve disputes, and
- Monitor security resources expended and provide security program guidance.

As a first step, the Commission recommends that the Secretary of Defense and the Director of Central Intelligence immediately establish a committee to fulfill these functions for the Defense and Intelligence Communities.

This recommendation represents one halting step in the right direction. However, it is much too timid and limited to accomplish much more than a high-level advisory committee which would still leave the development of detail and implementation of programs to the same bureaucrats who have failed to recognize and act on the threats to this nation's security over the past fifty years. Of great concern is the fact that the corrections will take years during which time our vulnerabilities will continue.

Conclusions and Observations

The Joint Security Commission has provided a reasonably good, if incomplete, tool for the improvement of the some of the security deficiencies of the Department of Defense and the Intelligence Communities. It has recognized the duplication, inefficiency and inconsistency in the current investigative programs, and the lack of unified, consistent direction coming from the various agencies and departments. The consolidation of military and intelligence investigative arms would be an improvement, but the recommended Security Executive Committee will not have the necessary power and authority to ensure and enforce an effective program.

The Committee has made the mistake of looking primarily to the clearance process as the primary ensurer of continuing good conduct. The recommendation for reassessment on an aperiodic basis will provide some assistance *if it, in fact, is not cut or eviscerated for lack of operating funds.* However, the committee report has totally ignored the role of management and supervision, and the need for continuing development of tools and techniques, not by periodic committees, but by management itself as it fulfills its responsibility to protect the secrets under its care.

The neglect of procedural security within this report also demonstrates the lack of understanding that it is the day-to-day operating procedures and on-site supervision which provides the greatest potential for prevention, or identification of traitorous behavior.

The role of technical security has also been ignored in this report. Even though electronic mail is readily available, the office copier is still a major threat to the security of classified materials. In the early 1970's the government ignored the opportunity to create copiers which would be incapable of copying classified documents and continues to do so today. Similarly, little has been done to prevent dissemination of classified and sensitive information over communications networks other than the apparently failed attempt to require "clipper chips" in all computers.

It is still fair to say that there has been no real attempt at any re-examination of the system itself and its basic assumptions and techniques. This re-examination is vital to the creation of an effective security program.

PROBLEMS BLOCK PROGRESS

At the present time the federal government, taking its lead from the White House, seems to be overwhelmingly concerned with the cost and efficiency of U.S. Government security programs. Reasonable concern is legitimate here. Indeed, it is about time that the massive cost of our current security program became an issue.

However, it is questionable whether significant cost improvements will be made merely by carefully examining all the various facets of current programs and then eliminating the wasteful or duplicative aspects that are identified, seeking to improve current operations, and putting into operation various innovative approaches—or even merely by cutting back, which would result in a program that was essentially the same as the present one, only smaller.

Let us take some cases. In October 1991, President Bush issued a National Security Directive which was intended to define the primary characteristics of a "Single Scope Background Investigation" to be utilized for any and all full field security investigations performed by or for any agency or department of the government. However, this directive met with acceptance only in part because of differing and even contradictory views among the various agencies concerning the extent and depth to which security investigations should be conducted. The intelligence and investigative agencies, such as the Central Intelligence Agency, the National Security Agency, and the Federal Bureau of Investigation, all endorsed the idea of security investigations which would be both intensive and extensive, going into the past fifteen years or more of a subject's life. The Departments of State and of Defense and other non-intelligence agencies, however, preferred a less intensive—and less expensive—background investigation covering five to seven years of the person's life. The upshot of this difference in investigative philosophy was that neither group was willing to embrace the Single Scope investigation defined in President Bush's National Security Directive.

However, since under current executive orders the responsibility for the personnel security program of each department or agency continues to rest with the head of that department or agency, each head has substantial discretion concerning the manner and degree to which security investigations are to be performed and security standards applied, rendering consistency and uniformity impossible. While the Information Security Oversight Office (ISOO) oversees government-wide security classification and reports to the president annually on its status, there is no entity charged with independently enforcing compliance with what the president may direct in an executive order or even monitoring what the departments and agencies actually do. This omission provides tremendous leeway to individual departments and agencies; it also facilitates cover-ups of abuses and mistakes, unless and until the inevitable debacles are revealed by the media.

Another controversial issue which is currently helping to block standardization of security procedures is the question of "due process" for persons denied security clearances. There is considerable pressure today to provide government employees with the same degree of due process currently provided to government contractors, including hearings before an administrative law judge. The Department of Defense is very concerned about the cost of such standardization, while some of the other departments and agencies are more concerned about the publicity which could result in such cases. These complications proved to be formidable enough, some believe, to persuade President Bush to neither release the results of a study of Personnel and Information Security commissioned during his administration, nor send them to Congress for implementation.

The Clinton White House, it seems, has put a premium upon "openness of the investigation and adjudication process, standardization, and cost efficiency." Emphasis is to be placed on "risk management" rather than on "risk avoidance"—meaning that "reasonable" controls, but not "absolute" ones, are to be developed and enforced with respect to sensitive information. In other words, the "cost" of the damage that would result from the compromise or betrayal of secure information is to be compared to the cost of the various levels of protection to be afforded to such information, and an appropriate balance is then to be struck. In concept this idea is valid: it would hardly be logical to spend a fortune to defend innocuous secrets at all costs.

However, major considerations need to be addressed in connection with such a concept. How does one measure "cost" when vital information, sources, lives and operations are compromised or lost? How does one insure that appropriate judgments are being made? And how is one to distinguish among types of costs, political, economic, values, etc. Inherent in this second question is the issue of whether the "cost" of betrayal or compromise of security information is the actual basis on which the information is classified, or whether more complicated and subtle factors are involved. Also to be considered is whether it is possible to protect one set of information with less vigor than another set of information. Is it simply established that there is to be a certain cost for classified versus secret versus top secret information? Finally, it must be remembered that classified information is frequently stored and maintained in close proximity, and using the same physical, procedural, systematic and electronic features and systems used to protect all information. Given these kinds of questions, which inevitably arise, it would seem once again that to attempt to achieve mere cost savings without a complete re-evaluation of the nature, scope, and methodology of an effective security program could result in severe damage to U.S. security—at a "cost" far greater than any imagined savings.

There remains the question of the fundamental attitudes of those in the government departments and agencies which create, utilize, and maintain classified information. Security officials have privately reported a marked return to the old attitudes which tended to belittle the security function and its basic mission. The view is becoming more prevalent in this post-Cold War era that security is now simply unnecessary. In the past, the existence of such attitudes merely served to encourage, aid, and abet espionage and treason. These represent a cost we can surely not afford. Moreover, a confused, disjointed, ineffective security system is destructive of morale, commitment and professional growth and development.

FOUR

The Practice of Failure

A half century since the suitability investigations and evaluations ably carried out by the old Civil Service Commission; over 45 years since the loyalty investigations of the Truman years; over 40 years since Executive Order 10450 and the inception of the present security system; after all the revelations of security abuses and injustices and the protests lodged against them; after all the spectacular revelations of the failures of our government security system—after more than a half century of such experience, it would seem that our security system should have proved itself by now to be valid and effective, capable of accomplishing the purposes for which it was created.

However, while some technical improvements have been made and more are being considered, our security system today is probably on the balance more deficient, its results less assured, its mistakes more costly, and the danger to the Republic greater than during the worst days of the 1940s and the 1950s when the national anxiety about security was at its height and the hue and cry against subversives and traitors in government were the loudest.

We still have not learned from the cases of espionage and treason that have been revealed.

We have seen how John Walker, his friends and family members were able to steal and sell over a period of nearly two decades massive quantities of vitally important information which Defense Secretary Caspar Weinberger admitted constituted "a serious loss to this country." Every time a spectacular failure of government security comes to light, our leaders—government spokesmen, cabinet secretaries, members of congressional intelligence committees, and security specialists themselves—announce that the system is going to be reformed and tightened up and that nothing similar is ever going to happen again—until

155

the next espionage case comes to light when the entire identical process is repeated.

The scenario rarely varies. The media latch onto the latest juicy spy case, such as Aldrich Ames, as they might latch on to the latest murder case. Experts vie with one another to try to explain how the nation's vital secrets could possibly be stolen like goods from a warehouse or money from an open bank vault. Commentators marvel that anyone could be so base and venal as to be willing to sell out his or her own country. It is as if nothing like it had ever happened. Then, suddenly, the media and the experts and the commentators all simply drop the whole subject and go on to something else. Scandals about spies and worries about security evaporate into thin air as if they never existed.

CONVENTIONAL WISDOM—MISSING THE POINT

One explanation for why the government's security system never seems to improve has been provided by Guenter Lewy, a political science professor at the University of Massachusetts. In a book published by the American Enterprise Institute entitled *The Federal Loyalty-Security Program: the Need for Reform*, Lewy wrote that "well-meaning, but politically unsophisticated investigators [must work] without any central guidance or political training, and without any workable criteria of loyalty and subversion."

"The problem is basically economic," said Thomas J. O'Brien, director of the Defense Department's Defense Investigative Services, when testifying before Congress in 1985. "We just don't have the resources."

When Walker's treason was revealed in 1985, Senator Sam Nunn, Democrat of Georgia, and Senator William V. Roth, Jr., Republican of Delaware, who had just completed hearings in their Senate committee in April on security clearance problems, said in a joint statement that the current investigation being conducted for a Secret clearance was "woefully inadequate." It was revealed that individuals granted access to Top Secret material were "supposed to be" re-investigated every five years but that, in fact, the government was many years behind in these re-investigations.

Given the enormous backlog, Senator Nunn reached the conclusion that security officers and investigators could not, as he expressed it, "take their jobs seriously now." "It's a complete absurdity," he went on. "Nobody could possibly handle that number of files. If you were a good, con-scientious security checker, you'd probably be already berserk."

This kind of reaction, especially when exhibited by members of Congress, including such normally reasonable senators as Roth and Nunn, points to the real problem, namely, that our leaders do not really understand what a real security system is, how it should work, and what it should achieve.

The Walker case, in fact, brought out a number of such reactions by national leaders demonstrating their ignorance of what is involved in security and what the Walker case, in particular, should have demon-strated about our current security system. In June 1985, for example, Albert Gore, then a Senator from Tennessee and now Vice President, reacting to the disclosures of the Walker case, declared: "It is simply too easy to get a security clearance. It is fast-food security"—as if that had been the problem in the Walker case. Walker *did* find it easy to pass his security re-investigation, of course; he simply forged the results of one and put them in the file. His son found it easy too: he simply declared he had clearance and was taken at his own word.

So the failure in the Walker case had little or nothing to do with the prior clearance process; it had a great deal to do with the way security was managed on a day-to-day basis in the Navy unit in which Walker served.

Not too much more pertinent to the question were the remarks of Lawrence J. Howe, a vice president for security at Science Applications International, a California-based company, who told a Senate commit-tee: "The result [of the investigations workload] is that the employee finally throws up his hands and says, 'The heck with this security stuff.'"

David Martin, a retired Senate "intelligence expert" declared, in a book of his own on personnel security published by the Heritage Foun-dation, that because of what he called "the near total destruction of the intelligence data base"—along with a few other factors—the U.S. gov-ernment had become "virtually incapable" of weeding out subversives from sensitive jobs.

Security investigations of applicants and employees serve a pur-pose, but they are not the entirety of effective security. The record shows that today's traitor has often been yesterday's loyal and dependable citi-zen and employee. The history of espionage and treason of the last half century in America is replete with cases of highly trusted and "cleared" persons who nevertheless betrayed their trust. Either they were traitor-ous from the inception of their employment and concealed their true loyalties, or they became corrupted. In either situation, most cases simply could not have been uncovered in advance by even the best of security investigations. It can only be dealt with by designing and implementing a managerial security system which *prevents* criminal and negligent actions such as the removal or compromise of classified material and, through vigilance and awareness detects the tell-tale signs that lead to identification of the traitor.

Ames is the classic case. Signs of his sudden wealth, alcoholism and erratic behavior should have been obvious. His polygraph exams provided additional warnings. Such criminal activities really cannot be dealt with merely by investigating and clearing individuals and then allowing them virtually free rein.

Government security can, in fact, quite effectively ensure a low success rate for whatever traitorous actions corrupted (or "idealistic") individuals believe they can undertake with impunity. This preventive function should be the primary aim of government security. What has to be in place is a security system which is designed to prevent betrayal or at least to catch, at an early point, the individual who violates the established rules rather than a system which, like our current one, relies too heavily on trying to identify possibly disloyal employees far in advance by means of a pre-employment security investigation. No matter the quality of the initial investigation, this determination should not then serve as a guarantee of permanent loyalty.

Extending this analysis, we need only consider other major causes of financial losses or losses of sensitive documents. These kinds of losses, often as not, verifiably arise from poor and sloppy management practices, apathetic employee performance, employee disaffection, absence of adequate management controls to protect materials on hand, and lack of follow-up auditing. These failures cannot be corrected through better pre-employment investigations, but they can be prevented through more effective management, more effective monitoring of ongoing employee performance, and better operational and control systems.

This is not a book on weapons loss, yet we know that over the years since World War II, the loss of weapons, ranging from rounds of ammunition to anti-tank weapons, stocks of uranium, and vehicles of all sorts, has been both massive and continuous, all accompanied by little, or apathetic, response by persons charged with managing the programs. Poor record keeping, laxness, employee neglect, improper supervision, as well as cupidity have resulted in enormous losses. Such factors have often made it impossible even to recognize the nature and scope of any losses. Invariably such losses are the fault of those immediately managing the programs. Managerial neglect is almost always a major factor in any cases of mistakes, carelessness, loss, theft, and, ultimately, treason. As a matter of policy, such managerial neglect should therefore be dealt with harshly.

The response of Senator Sam Nunn to revelations of the criminal theft and sale of our state secrets to foreign countries, namely, to lament that we have not committed greater and greater financial resources to conducting even more background security investigations, is unfortunately typical of governmental responses generally. Scarcely a word is said concerning the abysmal lack of management controls imposed by those who oversee and manage the day-to-day activities of our government. Proper management control, if it had existed, could have prevented nearly every known theft or loss of classified documents, weapons, or sensitive information.

Conversely, in virtually every case of criminal espionage that has been revealed, the person who turned out to be the traitor not only had been investigated, but had a security clearance as well. And, as a result of having such a clearance, he or she had too often been granted virtual *carte blanche* to handle, copy, and even remove classified information from the premises.

An even greater responsibility for the security lapses and violations belongs to those who are in charge of the actual protection of existing classified data—physical security specialists and operational managers. These specialists are normally highly paid and fully endowed with appropriate authority. They exist in ample numbers in every department, agency, or branch of the federal service. Yet this is the area where our government security system has most often broken down, whether this breakdown is due to the incompetence, laxness, duplicity, inattention, casual attitude and/or simple unawareness, on the part of those immediately responsible for protecting the material under their care, or of those who supervise them. Whatever the specific cause, this is *where* the system fails. It may even be that too little attention is paid to elementary security precautions in the workplace *because* too great a reliance is placed on the fact that the individuals in the sensitive workplace are "cleared." The prevailing attitude is: what is there to worry about since everybody who is cleared is by definition automatically trustworthy?

Even more blameworthy than the security people who function in the workplace are the upper management supervisors who have a responsibility to manage and supervise all of the personnel and operations under them. These upper management supervisors are also responsible for insuring that all of the classified and sensitive information and material used in their areas of general responsibility are protected. This means that appropriate safeguards must be put into effect and enforced in order to be certain that they are functioning as intended and that they are properly administered by those directly responsible for administering them.

These senior managers and security specialists are not the same people Senator Nunn and Mr. Howe had in mind when they spoke of security people going "berserk" or "throwing up their hands" or saying "the heck with this security stuff." Nevertheless, it is these top people who are the most at fault. Among the worst deficiencies of our government security system is the commonly perceived notion that "security" is principally a matter for the security officer to worry about, and is not worth the attention of senior managers. The effect of this attitude is that once the manager has seen to the appointment of a security officer for his organization, he gives no more thought to the matter. As a matter of fact, after the statements quoted above were made, Howe and any other people who offered and accepted these excuses should have been immediately fired for their failure to understand even the basics of their responsibilities.

We saw how political officials at the highest level, for example, were even willing to fight the security system in order to keep George Shaw Wheeler on the rolls in spite of the conclusive evidence against his loyalty. The Whittaker Chambers case is notorious for the same kind of almost reflexive hostility which Chambers encountered at the highest levels of officialdom when he came forward and tried to tell his story of espionage. The present-day managers who overlooked or forgave the warning signs of Pollard and Ames demonstrate the continuation of these attitudes.

The damage that results from such management decisions to protect people in place regardless of their actions or the evidence against them is far greater than the common bureaucratic practice of leaving "deadwood" in place while the organization "protects its own." In security cases, the high officials who practice and condone protecting potential traitors are, in a very important sense, themselves equally, or more, responsible for the resulting damage to U.S. interests. Yet nothing offends equity and justice more egregiously than the fact that, while actual spies, when caught, go to prison, their negligent and malfeasant supervisors who are charged with overall responsibility for the operation and management of the offices and agencies are rarely disciplined. They are handsomely compensated for assuming the grave responsibilities which they fail to carry out. The ultimate obligation and responsibility rests with the agency head, and it is where both reward and punishment should begin.

There was not any public criticism, much less any official disciplinary action, for example, in the case of the American ambassador in Moscow, his administrative officer, or his security officer, all of whom allowed the whole squalid Marine guard episode to occur under their very noses. Their explanations for the security failure were puerile and foolish, yet went unchallenged. Through all the years of spying activity within the government by recognized traitors, and many others, we know of not one senior official or agency head in the agencies where these people were employed who was ever called to account or disciplined, openly and officially. Yet it was their official neglect or malfeasance which permitted conditions within their organizations where espionage flourished. It is not excessive to assert that it never even occurs to the Washington hierarchy that senior managers or agency heads should be held accountable for the breakdown of security.

Perhaps the following dramatic example can illustrate how this neglect of security can have globally damaging effects on the U.S. Government. The example also illustrates that when the head of an agency signals by his conduct unconcern about security, all the employees in the organization are similarly affected. It concerns the late President Franklin D. Roosevelt, at the height of World War II. In retrospect, FDR's naivete in dealing with Joseph Stalin has been confirmed by more than one observer or historian. He apparently considered "Uncle Joe" to be someone whom FDR could "charm" as effectively as he had charmed so many American "pols."

During the war, correspondent Helen Lombard wrote a book entitled *While They Fought*, now undeservedly forgotten. She included a chapter entitled "Termites," which described a number of incidents of how the Communists, successfully boring from within, penetrated the most sensitive levels of the U.S. Government *in wartime*. The Soviets were aided in doing this by decisions taken at the highest level, namely, by the President himself, which were evidently made without concern for the country's security:

> At Teheran, Roosevelt promised the Russians that a radio-teletype circuit would be set up in the War Department for their use. General George C. Marshall, Army Chief of Staff, called the President's attention to the fact that under Section 319A of the

Federal Communications Act proof of citizenship is required from anyone desiring to open and operate a radio in the United States.

Nevertheless, the general received a "chit" on White House stationery, signed "F.D.R." telling him, in effect, to: "Find some way to do it anyhow."

As a result, a teletype was set up within the War Department itself linked by direct wire to the Soviet Embassy in Washington and Consulate General in New York. A special room was set aside in the Pentagon to house the equipment. This equipment was manned by *Soviet Government* personnel; thousands of words were transmitted over this secure circuit every day. The messages were coded and enjoyed diplomatic status. American personnel not only had no access to or control over what went over this circuit, they also did not even have access to the room itself in the Pentagon when it was in use by Soviet personnel (the Russians were apparently deeply concerned about *their* security!).

Helen Lombard reported further on this singular Soviet communications link, illegally set up on the direct orders of a president apparently unconcerned about the security aspects of it all:

> Assistant Secretary of War [John J.] McCloy admitted in a letter to Representative George Dondero of Michigan that the teletype existed and claimed that it had been set up strictly as a war emergency. It was still in operation, however, in the spring of 1946.

After the Teheran conference between Roosevelt, Churchill, and Stalin, the War Department was actually ordered to cease to defend itself or the armed forces from Communist infiltration. This order came in the form of a directive issued on May 7, 1944, to destroy all copies of subversive records within the War Department. The pretext for this action was that some generals in the field were misusing these reports as instant "security checks." But the effect of the particular order that was issued was, in effect, to abolish any counter-subversive system within the Army. As Lombard records:

> The Counter-Intelligence Service, whose duty it was to protect the armed forces from subversive influences, was instructed to destroy its records on subversives. These records contained detailed descriptions and information about subversives of all types, Nazis, Fascists, and Communists.
>
> Members of the Communist Party learn, early in their training, that "a file is a weapon." The Communists were so anxious

to get rid of the possible weapons against them, in the files of Military Intelligence, that they were willing to have the records on Nazis and Fascists burned also.

Such questionable activities within the War Department itself only came to light because of Congressional queries and actions, particularly, on the part of the late Senator Styles Bridges of New Hampshire. For our purposes, however, the point is that enormous damage has been done, and can be done again in the future, when high government officials are uninformed and unconcerned about security and consider it unimportant, bearing no necessary relationship to the other responsibilities they have. Then, when the virtually inevitable exploitation of the exposures which they have created comes to pass, these officials are shocked and appalled that our security system could permit it.

In considering how most security lapses and losses really do occur, however, we need to return for instruction, once again, to the Walker case: for nearly two decades Walker had virtually unlimited access to the documents he coveted, and nobody ever questioned him. He was "cleared," after all. Returning to the understanding of security exhibited by Senators Nunn, Roth, et al., what does an "investigative overload" of security personnel have to do with the lapses and failures that made the Walker and Ames cases possible? *If they had been re-investigated, there is little doubt that they would have been cleared again. And again.*

The Walker spy case prompted a critical re-examination on Capitol Hill and among military and intelligence specialists not only of the Privacy Act of 1974, but also of an entire generation of laws, regulations, and court decisions restricting the government's ability to investigate individuals. There were other statements attributed to some conservatives and military officials to the effect that all these same laws and regulations had weakened America's personnel security program. Senator Roth of Delaware stated after the Walker case broke, for example, that there had "been concern even among the moderates and liberals that we've gone too far" in restricting the government from delving into personnel security matters, as if that had anything to do with the Walker case.

Statements of this kind, unfortunately, show that even many of those truly concerned about security do not understand the real issues. They focus on the wrong problem. If our legislators at the national level do not understand even the basics involved in an effective security system, how can its weaknesses and abuses be corrected? The answer is, unhappily, that they probably cannot in the present climate, circumstances and understanding. There will be no solid reform or correction until there is a better realization of what security really is and what it entails.

Too many members of Congress, like too many senior executives in the various agencies and departments of the government, still view security in terms of the supposed magic of more and more security investigations, conducted under even more stringent authority, perhaps, than even E.O. 10450 contains. As David Martin expressed it, the basic idea of security continues to be "to weed out subversives from sensitive jobs." This is exactly the same cry that went up in the late 1940s and during the 1952 election campaign. We have already examined at some length the results of conceiving of security primarily in these terms.

Let there be no mistake. Nobody can object to weeding out subversives from sensitive jobs. But first they have to be identified; it is not only far from clear, it is surely demonstrably incorrect, that a significant number of the subversives who have been identified have been identified as a result of a prior security investigation.

It is not the clearance procedure that is at the heart of our security failures (although even the current clearance procedure is misdirected, ineffective, and far too costly). At the heart of our security debacle is the failure of federal managers to manage where security is concerned—and the failure of our security personnel to provide the basic and often elementary safety measures needed to prevent wholesale looting of our nation's secrets.

INVESTIGATION AND EVALUATION

As currently designed and functioning, neither our investigation and clearance system, nor our security management process can successfully achieve the objectives intended. These objectives may be briefly stated as follows:

- First, to insure employment by the government only of persons of sufficiently high integrity to be able to resist the temptation of appropriating and selling America's secrets.
- Second, to protect those secrets from compromise, theft, and unauthorized disclosure to anyone, whether traitor, spy, or opportunist.

Investigation and Adjudication

The one technique which the American security profession utilizes above all others is the investigation and clearance process. Locked in by inertia, lack of imagination, and bureaucratic resistance to change, and assured of a comfortable salary as long as he does not rock the boat, the federal security officer is not about to challenge the basis of the whole security system by battling for more effective techniques, regardless of the magnitude of the problem or the genius of the solution. Besides, as with so many bureaucracies, the system seems to be working fine for those running it.

Our government has been carrying out for the past two generations a massive charade of endless, detailed, and enormously costly individual security investigations of government employees and applicants for government employment. The basic idea is that by investigating the background and habits of actual or potential government employees, the government will acquire the kind of information which will enable it to predict whether a given individual will end up betraying the country if a suitable opportunity to do so is provided.

Under this system, the security investigation distinguishes the level of risk, and therefore the scope and magnitude of the investigation, according to the classification level of the material to which the subject is expected to have access. If the level is Top Secret, a full field investigation, as it is called, is required, but then is not always performed because of limitations of time or resources or for other reasons; for example, the Department of Defense routinely grants Top Secret clearances not on the basis of a full field investigation, but merely on the basis of a name check. If the level is below Top Secret, a check of the individual's name is made against the files of the various federal intelligence, security, and law enforcement agencies, as well as, where applicable, local law enforcement agencies. The individual's name, social security number, and other identifying data are used; and then, if any derogatory information is revealed by the name check, and is of a sufficiently serious nature, a full field investigation may be conducted.

Conducting full field investigations on thousands of applicants or employees is a massive business; it involves many hundreds of investigators criss-crossing the country looking into the backgrounds of the subjects, as the persons undergoing the security investigations are called. Security investigators frequently must drive or fly hundreds of miles, stay in hotels, dine out on government expense accounts, in addition to drawing their salaries and benefits as well as reimbursement for most of the other costs they incur. And since a number of federal agencies refuse to accept the results of each other's investigations or evaluations, transfer of an individual from one agency to another may well require a completely new investigation!

There is no question that this veritable army of government security agents fanned out in all directions busily conducting security investigations succeeds in compiling an enormous amount of information and data—mountains of it. Security investigators regularly insure verifications of birth, education, employment, neighborhood residence (and reputation); they have conversations with friends, employers, co-workers, neighbors, and colleagues; they examine court records, newspaper files, whatever. Where allegations have been made, they pursue the evidence and attempt to arrive at the truth or untruth of the allegations. They are persistent. And they require massive supplies of paper, forms, files, and other office supplies and telephone and secretarial services. The whole operation requires an immense government outlay in terms of time, money, office space, and staff. The system is a bureaucratic make-work dream.

Where does it all lead? Almost without exception, it leads to the same conclusion for each subject. *It leads to a security clearance for that individual. Almost everybody investigated by our government security system today is cleared.*

All of the data, fact and fiction, is gathered and an evaluator, of limited training and qualifications and lacking any judicial qualifications, then applies the magic of the bureaucratic "common-sense determination" provided for by E.O. 10450 to decide whether or not the individual is suitable for hiring or retention as a government employee.

Few subjects fail to be cleared, except where grossly derogatory information is turned up and verified, and, even then, the subjects under investigation are often cleared anyway. This has become more and more common as our society has come to tolerate kinds of behavior once understood to violate existing standards of morality, honesty, integrity, and suitability for U.S. government employment.

On those rare occasions when the facts require a higher level of bureaucratic common sense applied to the material than the journeyman evaluator is able to supply, the case is moved up the ladder where the common sense in question is applied by a higher-ranking evaluator. However, the end result is almost invariably the same: the security clearance is granted.

On even rarer occasions, perhaps when derogatory information is revealed that not even common sense can ignore, the evaluator is faced with a dilemma. The granting of security clearances now has become so much a part of the modern government "culture" that it becomes difficult to deny any clearance which requires justification for the denial. In such situations, it has become a common security practice simply to drop the investigation quietly and perhaps even "deep six," i.e., "lose," the case containing the derogatory information, citing budgetary or program reasons why the employee can no longer be hired or retained. When a system spawns such dishonest and reprehensible conduct, it has become flawed to a fatal degree, and it corrupts those charged with judging the integrity of others.

Equally dishonest is the practice of suddenly "discovering," when questionable or derogatory information is uncovered that a security clearance is not really needed for the position after all. Such techniques are employed to avoid denying a security clearance. In part this is because agencies do not want to be taken to court by someone whose clearance has been denied. Applicants and employees who have hired lawyers to contest an actual or threatened denial of clearance, in fact, have generally been quite successful in the courts.

The above, in brief, describes how our security investigation and clearance system works. Is the system a failure? Yes. How do we know?

In the first place, as we have described, the system has been corrupted to a point that it no longer functions either as originally designed or as it is currently documented. In addition, after more than a half century to develop whatever expertise or techniques were required to make the system work properly and achieve its objectives, a parade of traitors continues. The official security clearance system in place bears little or no relationship to the cases of espionage that come to light. And, just as in the world of crime, those we see behind bars represent only a small percentage of the criminals who are out there and active. Knowledgeable security practitioners know that for every Walker, Pollard, or Ames who is exposed, there are others who have taken their thirty pieces of silver in payment for betraying America without ever being discovered. In virtually every case they have been investigated and cleared.

It follows that the investigative and clearance system is not achieving its stated objective of identifying potential subversives *in advance* and preventing them from being hired or retained by the government.

The cost for the operation of the system, involving scores of agencies and departments, often overlapping and duplicating one another, is not only incalculable, but is often hidden in other budget numbers. In spite of the massive cost, however, treason has not been deterred, secrets continue to be betrayed, and so we lose not only the secrets themselves, and whatever dollar value their betrayal represents. *We are burdened by costs of operating and maintaining a cumbersome and futile system which has almost no actual impact on our security at all.* Clearly, either the system should be made to work, or it should be abolished and the taxpayers spared its costs.

The very idea that potential traitors can be identified by a prior security investigation is a highly questionable idea in the first place. People change every day. Daily, people face new temptations. New opportunities arise where they suddenly might find themselves in a position to exploit their circumstances. Pressures from unpaid bills or sudden financial obligations or losses also arise to change the situation of a government employee who might, as a result, come to be willing to consider selling what he or she knows. Also, there is the matter of greed. Or alluring companions might appear on the scene. Resentment against supervisors, or the government itself, has often spawned acts of treason. Or pride, the desire to be important and not just a cog in a machine, might assert itself. People with access to classified information must actively affirm—on a continuing basis—that they are going to remain loyal and honest and continue to respect and safeguard what has been put into their hands. It cannot be assumed that loyalty will necessarily persist merely because somebody was once investigated and cleared.

There also remains the problem of the committed, trained, and highly skilled traitor—the Alger Hisses, the David Greenglasses, the Nathan Witts, and on and on. Does anyone really think that, under the present system of clearances granted on the basis of security investigations, whether full field investigations or name checks, that anything significant would have been uncovered concerning the motives or activities of such dedicated spies? The instances of uncovering such spies by prior security investigations are almost non-existent. These spies were caught only when somebody who knew of their activities exposed them, usually after they had years of successful espionage behind them. It was not the operation of the current security system which revealed their betrayals. Many of the other notorious spies caught were similarly not discovered through any investigative or re-investigative process. Rather, nearly every known traitor has been discovered or tripped up not by the security people or the investigative process, but by a bitter or estranged spouse, by envious friends and neighbors, by defectors from the other side, or, at least in the old days, by the guilty traitor when he or she has changed through remorse. Whittaker Chambers, for example, was unable to convince the State Department and the FBI that he himself had been a spy, and that he knew other spies whom he could identify. Nor could John Walker's wife at first make the FBI believe that her husband was stealing cryptographic lists and selling his ill-gotten acquisitions to America's principal enemy. Nor were Aldrich Ames's drinking problems, polygraph slips or sudden wealth enough to alert the CIA.

Louis Budenz, Benjamin Mandel, and Elizabeth Bentley were all ex-Communists who repented, confessed their guilt, and named other co-conspirators. But they were not always honored for it; as often as not they were pilloried. Yet, if they had not come forward, nothing would have been known of the dangerous activities of some of those they named, nor would the public have become aware to the extent that it did that subversion was even a problem.

There was a case in my own experience in which a high government official who was a member of the Communist party decided to return to his American allegiance. He came to see me since I was at the time the director of security for the agency which employed him. He revealed his party affiliation and named the cell and his fellow Communists who belonged to that cell. His security investigation had revealed none of this; a subsequent investigation could not even reveal what material had been compromised. His Communist party membership only came to light because he decided to come forward and reveal it. This man, now long dead, proved his ultimate loyalty after having committed a grave error—unlike most Americans whose loyalty is never tested. Much is owed to such Americans who paid for their mistakes and served the nation loyally thereafter.

Irrelevance of the Full Field Investigation

One significant reason for the investigation system's failure is simply this: at the beginning of their long careers, the people who have been investigated in order to be able to enter upon government employment have usually not yet had a chance to be tested by temptation. They have neither been sufficiently tempted to betray their trust, nor have they become sufficiently corrupt so that it even occurs to them. Even more, they have not normally been in a position or had the opportunity to commit the kind of crime or act for which clearance might have been denied if uncovered in a security investigation. Even the people who are prone to commit criminal or traitorous acts have not yet had sufficient experience in government at the beginning of their careers to know their opportunities. Most instances of traitorous activity begin as crimes of opportunity committed by persons who have not previously committed serious crimes. Their previous behavior, as least as it regards lack of criminal activity, is usually irrelevant.

It is, of course, true that common sense should preclude the granting of security clearances to convicted criminals, but such criminals can almost always be identified through a simple name check with the appropriate federal agencies and through a police record check; a full field investigation is hardly called for in the absence of derogatory information.

The people who must be stopped, if our government security system is to succeed, are generally those with no criminal background, who would nevertheless be prepared to commit espionage if given the chance. How could such people possibly be identified in advance? One way might be through the identification of personality or character traits which, while not illegal, might tend to precondition the subject to commit treason. But other traitors, such as some of those identified in Chapter One, apparently never exhibited prior character defects or performed actions which might have made possible predictions of their subsequent behavior.

No such predictions were made in any of those cases, nor, upon reflection, does it seem likely that they ever could be made. Alger Hiss had Supreme Court Justices and others of similarly high repute testifying as character witnesses for him at his perjury trial. This fact, coupled with the extremely low refusal rate of all applicants for government employment, argues strongly that, while agency name checks certainly deserve an important place in any security system, the routine and costly full field investigation, as it has been carried out for so long, should be reserved for the cases where fruitful results are predictable. Result of psychological testing, polygraph tests and name checks, including criminal records and past employment voucher results, as well as a detailed personal history statement examination, may all be predictors of the fruitfulness of further investigation, but at enormously less cost, time, and waste.

Failure to Deny Clearance—Lack of Standards

It is duplicitous and self-serving to keep talking about how the prevention of treasonable activity in government is a consequence of the security office's inability to conduct more and better investigations of applicants and employees. *More investigations would just result in more clearances, not fewer.* The government hardly ever denies security clearances any longer, except in the case of actual felonious conduct, and this trend is likely to be even more pronounced as time goes by, since there is scarcely any conduct any longer which is considered disqualifying for government employment.

Historically, under the old Civil Service Commission's suitability investigations, evidence turned up in the investigations which demonstrated a lack of morality, an absence of integrity, falsification of information concerning one's education or experience, an incidence of lying, or other character defects or lapses in personal conduct resulted not only in a denial of a security clearance but also in the rejection of the individual from any consideration for a government job. A decision was made concerning the person's unsuitability for employment and the name was "flagged" to preclude future employment. In those days such an individual was considered unfit for government employment. Later, under the Truman Loyalty Program, as well as early on under the Eisenhower Federal Employee Security Program, such persons continued to be rated ineligible, and they were either denied employment or terminated if already employed. This was the practice based on the government's published employment standards.

Today, in practice, there are virtually no standards of personal morality or character according to which an individual might be rejected for government employment. According to the most recent security clearance statistics available from the Office of Personnel Management (1980-1984) and the DoD (1993), departments and agencies served by OPM granted clearances to greater than 99% of applicants, and DoD approved 96.6%. Appendix I contains additional data.

Less than one percent (or 3.5% for DoD) were denied clearance in a process costing many hundreds of millions of dollars, consuming scores of thousands of work hours, office space, equipment, etc., etc., and backlogging, or denying more important investigations. Cost benefit analysis? Never heard of it. Quality management? Not that either!

Those who are not granted clearances are probably ineligible on the face of it, with drug or criminal records, falsification of applications, and the like, *things which can almost always be caught in any case by a reasonably intelligent and competent pre-employment interview.*

So the question needs asking: what possible purpose can be served by such an elaborate system? Senator Roth of Delaware was once moved to exclaim: "I sometimes think it's more difficult to get an American Express card than a security clearance." He was absolutely right.

"Loyalty is an ethereal concept psychiatrically," according to Steve Pieczenik, a psychiatrist who was Deputy Assistant Secretary of State for Management under Presidents Ford and Carter and in that capacity oversaw the State Department's security clearance program. He continued: "Investigations don't really point up characterological defects of the individual" that suggest disloyalty. "What constitutes a security problem?" If the man who directed and justified to Congress the enormous budgets for the program does not believe in the worth or effectiveness of the program, why in the world is it being continued? Why isn't it overhauled?

Professor Guenter Lewy pointed out how in our security system well-meaning but politically unsophisticated investigators have to work without any central guidance or political training and *without any workable criteria of loyalty and subversion.* Professor Lewy went on to add: "One can only hope that some day we will not have to pay a high price for this accumulation of neglect." The fact is that we are paying, and have paid, a high price already: first, in the enormous cost of operating our present futile program; second, in the loss of blood and treasure (billions of dollars in research and development costs, for example) resulting from compromised national security secrets which have been stolen and delivered to our enemies; and third, in the frustration of our military and foreign policy objectives.

We need to remember that a security adjudicator is expected to examine all aspects of an applicant's personal and moral characteristics and then make a common-sense judgment concerning the fitness of a subject to receive a clearance. This approach would be comparable to having our criminal and civil adjudications made simply on the basis of each judge's common sense judgment alone rather than on the basis of the law and precedent by which our judges are in fact bound. Nowhere in our security system is there any definition or delineation of those characteristics which would be *specifically* disqualifying or to what degree a particular characteristic might have to be present in order to be considered disqualifying. At one point in our history, adultery, homosexuality, and co-habitation of unmarried persons were all grounds for disqualification. Today, only active homosexuality has even a remote chance of disqualifying an applicant and even that is currently becoming more and more debated and problematical, especially with the advent of the Clinton Administration.

Histories of mental disorders and other medical problems which would have caused disqualification in the past are now often accepted. Credit problems now are unlikely to be disqualifying. In Colorado, in 1990, a woman was denied a security clearance by the Air Force because she had had three abortions. In that particular case, the Air Force stated that she would not have been rejected if she had only two abortions; but three indicated "a lack of stability." In the same news report disclosing this, it was stated that neither the Army nor the Navy would have denied the clearance. There was also, in the same case, an immediate public outcry by some groups at the Air Force's denial of a woman's "right." The woman was also indignant because she had been questioned about her credit and what she styled "some other ridiculous things." Standards, the basis upon which clearances presumably are granted or denied, are lost in all of this—a casualty to "rights".

In the face of organized, shrill outcries against what were once taken-for-granted moral standards, today's political leaders have now effectively vitiated the policies and standards by which the military and intelligence agencies must abide in security decisions. In doing so they have evacuated of nearly all meaning the application of the standards by which personnel were once supposed to be judged. This weakening, if not the actual jettisoning, of all standards has been accomplished while leaving the written standards on the books. Among other things that could be remarked about this result is the fact that it is yet one more example of dishonesty in a system which judges the honesty of others.

In Chapter Five of this book, we will examine the question of character and morality in more detail as it impacts, and should impact, upon the issue of access to classified information. With respect to our current topic, the reasons for the failure of the government's investigation and clearance system, the obvious question to be asked at this point is: if verified deficiencies in moral character are not to be an integral part of the evaluation criteria employed in security investigations, what is the reason for conducting these investigation at all, beyond carrying out the obvious agency and police name checks for any actual criminal convictions or similar information? Is it to turn up more information about an individual which is in any case not going to be used? Conversely, if moral or characterological criteria are to be used in any way, then fairness itself, not to speak of honesty and genuine professionalism, would seem to dictate that consistent, realistic, and defensible standards on the subject should be developed and promulgated and then consistently implemented.

The Collapse of Moral Authority

As we have seen earlier, the U.S. government has, historically, based its decisions concerning the granting or denial of security clearances on behavior, especially moral behavior. The behavior of employees or applicants for employment was heretofore required to be moral, decent, truthful, and honest. In practice, the moral standards required were those enjoined by what in our day has come to be called the Judeo-Christian ethic because they were the moral standards of the Ten Commandments, as they have been understood and practiced in Western history. This traditional moral and social code continues to be embodied in the government's published standards for security clearances.

However, since these published standards were put in place, a moral and social revolution has taken place in our society. There is now serious question whether these published standards have been or can be maintained; indeed there is little doubt that, in practice, and for the moment, they are not being maintained.

A belief in God and in a future reward or punishment for one's acts long provided a stable basis for moral behavior in the past. Many of our governmental systems, including our security system, assumed this basic morality and depended upon it. Not only has there been a collapse of moral order, but many other conventions and rules of behavior have gone by the board as well: civility, decency, respect for authority, even common courtesy. It has become almost *de rigueur* in some quarters to flout and violate almost all forms of traditional and conventional conduct.

A wide range of new statutes and regulations have been promulgated by our law-making and regulatory bodies which are seemingly designed expressly to undermine, or overthrow, practically everything that had previously been accepted. Authority, discipline, morality, obligation, religion, responsibility, tradition—all such words and concepts suddenly have no meaning or relevance. Old responsibilities and codes of conduct can no longer be relied upon. The only survivor from what had been a comprehensive and consistent moral and legal code is the concept of "individual rights," which has been vastly expanded. Persons now have an enhanced right to privacy, even in regard to security investigations, and the right to engage in intemperate and unseemly behavior which would formerly have resulted in refusals of clearance.

It has proved possible, in fact, to find new rights to satisfy heretofore unimaginable new demands. Along the way, our society has steadily become more fragmented, divided and morally irresponsible.

From childhood on, now, our children, from the earliest school grades, are exposed to permissive—yes, radical—attitudes on abortion, pre- and extra-marital sexual intercourse, and homosexuality which attitudes and teaching are in direct conflict with the moral tradition of America.

Chastity and virginity are denigrated even at the height of epidemics of AIDS and other sexually transmitted diseases, ignoring the fact that abstinence from sex is the most effective preventive against the disease.

The rejection of responsibility for social behavior and moral behavior has its counterpart in the ever-increasing desire for not just pleasure, but the expensive playthings that are considered essential to providing that pleasure. The bank clerk who embezzles, the store clerk who steals from the till, the lawyer who violates his trust, the government official who defrauds his agency, the cop who accepts the drug dealer's bribe, the Wall Street dealer who rigs stock transactions and the government traitor who sells his country's secrets all are indulging their appetites for self-gratification.

These dramatic changes in moral behavior, and how we now perceive the freedom of restraints on behavior, have far reaching implications for the government's security system and the administration of its investigative, adjudicative and clearance processes and standards.

Too late, our religious leaders have recognized that the loosening of moral bonds unleashes forces that lead to disintegration of the moral and social fibers that hold the country together and produce a system which makes it possible to prescribe standards of conduct upon which judgments can be made that an individual is predictably a "good security risk" or a bad risk.

Can a society which imposes no moral restraints reasonably expect its youth to grow up capable of resisting the appeal of vast sums of money available in taking bribes, thefts, or pay-offs?

At the end of the 19th Century, a European observer, James Bryce wrote: "Religion and conscience have been a constantly active force in the American Commonwealth . . . at the worst times inspiring a minority with a courage and ardor by which moral and political levels have been held at bay and, in the long run, overcome."

The Catholic Bishops of the United States echoed that theme in their statement:

"The history of our country has been generally infused with an ideal based on moral principles. The time has come to confess, however, that our national ideal no longer rests upon a foundation of broad and solid popular morality. Ignorance of moral principles and the rejection of the very notion of morality are on the rise today and threaten to undermine our nation and its most sacred tradition. The evidences of our moral decline are everywhere to be seen."

That statement was issued in 1961, well over a generation ago.

The Bishops continued:

"The conditions we face are unique. For many, the past gives neither precedent nor guide. Many men are questioning and often denying the objective distinction between good and evil and the ability of human reason to know with certainty what is right and wrong. They are cutting themselves off completely from moral tradition. For the first time in history they find themselves without a moral law to break." "Many modern men find themselves without God and religion, on a lonely eminence of their own making, left to create their own moral values, forced to determine for themselves what is good and evil, right and wrong."

Nearly every sector of our society, especially the professions, has seen, over and over, some public, highly embarrassing disclosure of massive dishonesty or misbehavior on the part of some of its members: bankers, lawyers, businessmen, doctors, scientists, the military, and even evangelists and our clergy who should be obligated by their callings to teach clearly the traditional moral tenets of their professed faiths.

In the midst of all this pronounced moral disintegration, the U.S. government's security program continues to maintain, at least in writing, the same old standards, based on "moral conduct, character, and integrity," just as has always been the case. Ironically, this remains true even to the point of continuing to require security evaluators and adjudicators to make judgments about the suitability, security, and loyalty of employees and applicants on the basis of the "common-sense determination" required by Executive Order 10450—issued in the climate of 1953.

Presently, it is far from clear what "common sense" really means and what it is supposed to decide. Society is now more or less saying that almost any kind of moral conduct is currently acceptable; that, for example, adultery, promiscuity, homosexuality, and at least certain types of dishonesty may all be practiced without putting the individual outside the pale of acceptable moral behavior. Other improper behavior is considered to be within the individual's "private life" and no longer germane to a security adjudication, and still other behavior is expected to be overlooked because it is simply part of the past. Thus the "common-sense" security yardstick, to be consistent, must now permit far more derogatory information or deviant behavior than would previously have been permitted. With current mores as a standard, subjects who formerly would have been rejected as "security risks" must now be granted security clearances.

The consequences of this we have already seen, namely, that nearly all those who are investigated are now granted security clearances. This means, in turn, that they are not only to be considered suitable for government employment; they are to be granted access to sensitive and classified information which could do harm to the United States if divulged or released to unauthorized persons.

There is clearly a basic contradiction at the heart of our whole security system as a result of how moral and social standards have evolved in our society. On the one hand, the system is supposed to depend for its effectiveness on the fact that sensitive and security information will only be available to persons proved by a security investigation to be of good conduct and character and attested to by the possession of a security clearance. On the other hand, modern society currently rejects the idea that any moral standards in particular can disqualify people from being given the required security clearance. Thus, virtually anybody today can be given access to sensitive and classified information.

To summarize: if honesty is one of the required standards for clearance but members of our society no longer consider it necessary to adhere to strict honesty, then the honesty standard is worthless. If morality is one of the required standards for clearance, but morality has been rejected by the near unanimous judgment of modern society, then the morality standard is also worthless. If homosexual relations are supposed to be a bar to clearance, yet society has now come to view them as not only licit but as even deserving of some special status (so-called "gay rights"), then this standard must now clearly be considered inoperative as well. It is contradictory to teach schoolchildren that homosexual activity is normal, and natural, and is to be protected and even advocated, and, at the same time, deny security clearance to homosexuals on the grounds of unsuitability.

Similarly, if thievery, dishonesty, falsification of educational attainments or employment records, or other personal aberrations cannot be bars to clearance (since all such things can easily be "excused"), then the published standards are, for all practical purposes, useless.

Our present security system relies heavily and uncritically on the security investigation and clearance as its fundamental underpinning. Yet, if little, or none, of the derogatory evidence turned up in the course of a security investigation can be used to deny a clearance, what further point is there in conducting background investigations to gather such evidence? Why pretend that anything is being accomplished? The traditional standards upon which common sense is supposed to guide clearance judgments bear little relationship to the judgments actually being made. The entire system is distorted, and must be redesigned.

The bottom line is that, if nearly all persons applying are cleared, the program is not worth the cost.

Reinvestigation

One practice through which the present elaborate investigative process might actually identify some instances of wrong-doing would utilize random financial and lifestyle investigations on persons holding current security clearances, particularly when evidence exists which might raise questions or cause suspicion. Persons living above their means, or with assets beyond what would be expected at their salary level, could be required to explain the source of their additional wealth. The activities of such persons in their workplace could be scrutinized more vigilantly to insure that the source of this wealth was not the sale of classified material to which they had access in their jobs. We have noted how the temptation to sell such classified material is a more and more frequent occurrence. The current security system does include a provision for reinvestigations, of course, but it is a purely mechanical one where the employee is in any case alerted to when it is scheduled; as we have noted, these required reinvestigations are currently many years behind schedule.

With regard to this backlog, even the least imaginative and competent manager must ask himself: "What good is a program which addresses a need years late?"

If reinvestigations are to be made, they obviously need to be kept current. Moreover, they should be conducted randomly, not on a schedule which will enable a guilty employee to resign, thus suspending the reinvestigation or otherwise take steps to cover his tracks. We saw earlier with what ludicrous ease John Walker evaded the reinvestigation requirement. Random investigations, however, have proved their worth in the case of IRS tax audits, for example.

In today's budgetary situation, it is in any event unlikely that reinvestigations can ever be brought up to date and maintained anyway. That fact alone constitutes a reason why the present investigative and clearance should be drastically reexamined and expeditiously changed.

SECURITY MANAGEMENT

Control of Behavior

For many, what used to be called moral behavior is an unattainable ideal. People are now seen as creatures of their various drives and desires, which must imperatively be satisfied. It is no longer clear how theft, espionage, liaisons with enemy agents, and other forms of dishonest and even criminal behavior can be prevented as far as security is concerned. Many of the readers of this book will not engage in the kinds of actions formerly deemed "immoral" but statistically, at least, many other people no longer see anything wrong in such actions, and society, at least at this time, seems increasingly prepared to tolerate these attitudes.

The most pertinent consequence of all this for security and for the preservation of classified and sensitive government material is this: relying on the character and integrity of people as the basic principle of our security system is no more realistic than expecting people not to act immorally or dishonestly in other situations where they are exposed to strong temptations. To rely primarily upon the honor and loyalty of people to prevent the theft and sale of the nation's secrets at a time when such honor and loyalty can no longer be depended upon, is comparable to placing gluttons before a huge spread of attractive and tasty food and then expecting them to walk away without eating anything—or of placing alcoholics or drug addicts in a room supplied with ample stocks of alcohol and drugs and expecting them not to abuse them.

It currently appears impossible for large numbers of people to control their behavior now that traditional moral underpinnings have been swept away. Many people today appear to have grown up with no idea or appreciation at all for what constitutes acceptable and unacceptable conduct. The consequences of trying to maintain a workable security system in the midst of such moral chaos cannot be underestimated.

The old moral constraints were unable to protect our secrets adequately in the past; they are even less capable of protecting them at the present; and they will probably be even less capable in the near future. If we cannot rely upon clearances and moral constraints for the protection of our nation's secrets, then we must rely upon the management and operation of security systems and procedures. Let us examine the current quality of performance in that arena.

Management Operational Performance

At first glance, we might imagine that the failure of our security management system results from the brilliant high-tech maneuvers of master spies working against our own courageous though not "perfect" defenders. It is true that there are high-tech measures and counter-measures utilized in the security, espionage, and counter-espionage businesses today. However, most of the past successes of foreign powers in this area have not resulted from particularly sophisticated techniques. They have simply purchased, usually at criminally low prices, the intelligence they wished to acquire from America. They purchased it from Americans without conscience who were in a position to exploit the deplorable managerial and operational weaknesses of the U.S. government security system, steal the intelligence in question, and deliver it to the interested foreign buyer.

Why are our security management and operational systems so defective that they can be circumvented? Part of the problem is the personal loss of our capacity to demand and ensure excellence in our endeavors. This development has been particularly manifested in the American workplace. There has been a loss of pride and personal satisfaction and identification with the work product which has been reflected in a too high incidence of shoddy and deficient articles produced in the United States in recent years. Frequently, this loss of integrity manifests itself in cases of outright dishonesty, fraud, and theft.

Too many American workers seem no longer to possess the capacity to sustain a concentrated effort in their work. They often become bored, uninterested, and resentful of its demands. Too often they bring personal antagonisms towards companies, owners, superiors, and even colleagues into the workplace. The primary focus of such people is usually turned towards their own personal satisfactions or pleasures.

The failure of contemporary quality performance is even more evident in the security business than in other areas of our professional and industrial society. All types of security are ignored or taken for granted by mid and upper-level management to an extent that would not be tolerated for any other function. We need only look at the frequent neglect and apathy of security personnel at airport security check points, entrances to government buildings or industrial plants, and elsewhere. The general problem is usually compounded by the abysmal quality of the supervision that is normally exercised over these security personnel. Often security guards and similar personnel are simply left on their own to do their jobs, well or badly—until a security failure occurs. Then there is hustle and bustle and talk of "reform." Soon, however, things return to their "normal," dismal state. In fact, in many environments it is an unwritten policy to avoid training guards and other security personnel concerning actions to be taken in specific situations, so that, whatever actions are taken in an emergency cannot be ascribed to the guard's training in the event of a mishap or mistake.

All of these factors help to explain why it has become relatively easy today to bypass security controls, not merely for espionage, but simply for convenience. Sophisticated and expensive access control and alarm systems are disconnected, damaged, or, sometimes, simply ignored across a whole spectrum of modern industry and activity, including hospitals, universities, government agencies, industrial plants, laboratories, and so forth. In sum, security is too often not taken seriously either by employees or outsiders today because *management* itself does not regard it as important. Regardless of official policy, employees quickly pick up on and tune in to such attitudes of indifference.

In some exceptional cases where security is taken seriously and therefore is designed and administered in an intelligent and consistent way, with security requirements being built in to operational requirements and considerations, there are virtually never any security breaches or failures; e.g., in the Federal Reserve Banks.

The single most damaging management failure of the present U.S. government security system is the failure to assign responsibility for the protection of sensitive or classified material to the normal management structure and, in the event of a security violation or failure, to assess responsibility among and apply sanctions to the appropriate line management supervisory personnel in the area where the violation or breach has occurred. Under the present structure security responsibility is assigned *solely* to the security officer of the department or agency. Normally, the government security officer is at a low enough level so that it becomes virtually impossible for him ever to enforce the security regulations in place or insure compliance by department or agency personnel, especially if senior management is unconcerned.

Even if the security officer is so disposed and qualified, he does not have the resources to monitor and oversee all the employees in an agency to determine whether they are or are not following the rules or carrying out the established security procedures.

In addition, security breeches and violations typically occur in operational and/or management sectors outside the purview and control of the security office.

Even more importantly, if higher management does not stand behind the concept of security and require compliance by all the staff with its requirements, it is impossible for the security officer to do it on his own. Examples abound of departments in which lip service is paid to the security concept and system. In practice, scores of violations occur daily and are not penalized, nor, for the most part, even discovered. This kind of situation is frequently to be found, primarily, because management, both higher and mid-level, refuses to take any responsibility in the area of security, and, too often, is an active collaborator in subverting the security system.

Conditions are even worse in defense industries where all of the weaknesses of the federal bureaucracy are multiplied. The specific excuses usually offered by line management are only too similar to those heard whenever management decides to abrogate its responsibilities. Some of these excuses are:

- "I am not a policeman. That's the security officer's concern."
- "I know my people. None of my people are foreign agents. That's absurd."
- "We are too busy doing our jobs here to have time for all that security stuff."

Where such attitudes prevail—and they prevail widely—employees quickly come to learn that observing the security requirements is not an essential part of their jobs. This is especially true in jobs where the employee or office worker is not subject to any kind of check or verification by outside auditors. Of all the traitors surveyed in Chapter One, only two were ever identified by awareness or observation on the part of their supervisors.

Until all levels of management begin to accept their responsibility for security, including being prepared to impose penalties for employee failure to observe the rules and carry out the established procedures, effective security management will continue to be impossible.

In addition to the points we have mentioned, a variety of other typical lapses and failures in security management can be identified:

1. While the concept of security management requires that each cleared individual be provided access only to that information which is necessary for the performance of his or her responsibilities, the reality is that any person with a security clearance can usually gain access to a vast array of classified material, sometimes above the level of his clearance level. This kind of situation arises in most agencies because of an "us versus them" attitude that simply assumes that all colleagues in a given organization, once initially cleared, must henceforth be considered "safe" for all time, and therefore can safely be entrusted with all the organization's sensitive information and data.

2. Mis-assignment of responsibility frequently results in lower-level employees with minimal clearances having access to higher-level material anyway, often material substantially above their clearance level. Several of the examples in our "Parade of Traitors" involve

employees who had such access in practice, even though their jobs merely involved copying, filing and delivery duties.

3. Failure to control removal of classified printed material, to identify its loss once it has been removed, or to identify the person who removed it if and when its loss *is* discovered. In essence, this is a failure to maintain adequate records.

4. Access control systems which fail to function either technically or procedurally. For example, during the course of some SDI "Star Wars" research, some microcomputer discs containing important research data were stolen both from a contractor's office and from the Pentagon itself by overcoming simple card-reader access systems.

5. Failure to control the use of copying machines—a matter of applying an utterly simple procedure, yet it has been one of the most damaging of all factors in espionage cases; failure to institute clear and enforced rules for all uses of copying machines in an organization is an incredibly gross act of management negligence. Now, with telefacsimile ("fax") machines, this has become one of the most critical of all problems where classified material is concerned. In fact, the whole area of telecommunications and computer security is one that will be increasingly important.

6. Failure to examine material carried or mailed out by employees.

7. Tendency to rely on complex and expensive equipment and systems to automatically protect the environment, so that management can avoid more time consuming, perhaps tedious, detailed involvement in the function and the performance of potentially embarrassing security audit reviews.

8. Willingness to turn over entire building complexes, after hours, to lower-level, unsupervised personnel, as occurred in the much publicized case of the Marine guards stationed at the American Embassy in Moscow.

9. Automatic assumption of unwavering loyalty of all employees in all circumstances which accordingly grants *carte blanche* access to unsupervised and uncontrolled employees, especially after hours.

10. *Obtuse refusal to understand that human beings, all human beings, can be corrupted.*

The Aldrich Ames case illustrates how management failures permitted his treason to continue unabated for nine years.

1. Ames never had difficulty explaining his extra income of $2.5 million because he was never asked. As Ames explained, "I never had to provide officially or unofficially any justification or rationalization. It was assumed, and I allowed it to be assumed . . . that my wife's family had money. I never told anyone that Rosario had inherited money from her father. But this was a reasonable as-

sumption that people would make." Instead of checking it out, obviously.

2. Ames claimed that there was no problem in passing lie detector tests. He stated "Confidence is what does it. Confidence and a friendly relationship with the examiner . . . rapport, where you smile and you make him think that you like him." However, Ames was tripped up on one question involving finances and the detector operator was overruled when he recommended that Ames be investigated.

3. In spite of Ames's drinking and personal problems and violation of CIA regulations by his relationship with Rosario while she was a CIA contact, and even despite the supposed low regard in which he was held, the CIA appointed him Chief of Soviet Counter-Intelligence. It would be fascinating to learn the rationale for this promotion.

4. Because Ames was highly knowledgeable concerning the Soviet Intelligence Service, he apparently was given access beyond what would normally be provided in certain instances, even after he was no longer responsible for Soviet or Russian Counter-Intelligence. Once again, the select "club" attitude prevailed.

Ames was never concerned that he would be identified by the CIA or FBI. He obviously understood the level of effectiveness of America's Security program. In Ames's words:

"Initially, my only fear was that a KGB officer knowledgeable of my relationship with the KGB would defect or volunteer to us . . . *Virtually every American who has been jailed in connection with espionage has been fingered by a Soviet source.*" (Emphasis added)

SECURITY VIOLATIONS BY CONGRESS, THE EXECUTIVE BRANCH LEADERSHIP, AND THE MEDIA

Who are the most frequent and dangerous violators of the espionage laws of the United States? Possibly, the members of the Congress of the United States, although senior officials in the executive branch may well run a very close second to Congress in this regard.

Congress—Our Greatest Security Risk?

The Congress of the United States enacts all federal laws, including the laws directed against engaging in espionage, yet members of the

Congress regularly consider themselves exempt from the very laws they enact and violate the federal espionage laws with impunity and with great frequency. The principal question here is not: "Why do members of Congress violate the law?" The principal question is: "Why is the law not enforced in the case of a violator who happens to be a member of Congress?" Both logic and morality would seem to dictate that those who make the laws ought to be the ones most assiduous in upholding and complying with them.

An employee of the federal government or one working on a classified government contract in private industry who divulges or releases classified information acquired in the course of his work is subject to penalties. Such an employee may be disciplined, suffer possible job loss, or even be prosecuted and jailed. No member of Congress or Congressional staff person who does exactly the same thing is ever likely to be penalized in any way. Rather, since the motive is generally political, the Congressional violator may even benefit from an enhanced political position or at least an improved relationship with the reporter to whom the classified information has been "leaked." Yes: "leaks" of classified material are violations of the espionage laws every bit as much as if the information were sold to the Russians.

In spite of this illegality, however, the "culture" and tradition in Congress takes it for granted that representatives and senators, as well as their staff people, can, in effect, unilaterally declassify whatever information they choose and leak it to the media for publication or broadcast. The failure of the United States government even to attempt to prosecute an offender for leaks of sensitive information has surely ensured that it would become standard political practice.

Actually, the harm done to the United States by some instances of congressional leaks of sensitive information, especially some of the leaks that have emanated from the intelligence committees, can be more dangerous than the work of traitors. Such leaks take on added significance because of their source and because of the official positions and responsibilities of the persons creating the leaks.

In 1988, then Speaker of the House of Representatives, Rep. Jim Wright of Texas, released classified information to the effect that the CIA was providing funding to assist internal opposition to the ruling Communist Sandinista government in Nicaragua. Such a statement from the leadership of the House linking the Nicaraguan opposition to the CIA was quite damaging to the cause of freedom and quickly invited repression. Nicaraguan resistance leader Adolfo Calero stated at the

time: "Why, I ask, is it so difficult for Mr. Wright to believe that conditions in Nicaragua can be so miserable that a mass, grassroots campaign of dissent cannot arise without the help of the CIA?"

Calero said more:

> This death and destruction to the opposition within Nicaragua
> that we have already begun to see as a result of Jim Wright's
> linking Nicaraguan civilians to the CIA is inexcusable. The dam-
> age has already been done. The Sandinistas will now be able
> systematically to blame all opposition activity inside Nicaragua
> on the CIA, thus giving another convenient excuse to the tyran-
> nical Communists in Managua to continue their campaign of ter-
> ror against the population of Nicaragua.

Jim Wright certainly had the right to criticize the Nicaraguan opposition and even to support the Sandinistas. But to release classified
information to accomplish this was not only to place his interests and
opinions above our organized government system through which the
nation legally determines and implements its foreign policy; it was also
deliberately to break the law of the land—which a member of Congress
ought to be particularly dedicated to uphold.

Actually, in obtaining the sensitive information he released, Jim
Wright had to conspire to evade House rules in order to receive the
information directly from Intelligence Committee Chairman Louis Stokes
of Ohio. Given the occurrence of an incident of this type in the Congress
of the United States, is it any wonder that President Ronald Reagan
feared informing Congress in advance of the planned American invasion
of Grenada? The President was afraid that "there would be some who
would leak it to the press together with the prediction that Grenada was
going to become another Vietnam."

In essence, if a representative or senator who receives sensitive and
vital national defense secrets enabling him to carry out the official duties
of his office elects instead to disclose that information in order to advance
his own political agenda or, worse, for his own personal advantage, what
penalty is assessed?

In practice, the penalty is nothing, nothing at all. The senator or
representative will walk away from the incident unscathed regardless of
the harm he may have done to the interests of the United States or our
friends or allies. This is true despite the fact that nothing either in the
applicable laws, nor in the president's executive orders on the subject,
exempts a member of Congress from the penalties prescribed for viola-

tions. When a Pollard or a Chin is caught divulging classified material, he is taken into court and prosecuted to the fullest extent of the law; when a Jim Wright—or a Senator Durenberger—signals to the world that he has done exactly the same thing, he may even see his position and his prospects advanced.

Senators and representatives ought to be subject to the law. If they violate it, they should be prosecuted. Or if such prosecution in the courts is deemed impossible because of the constitutional "speech or debate" clause, then other procedural protections and penalties should be developed and applied, including censure by or even expulsion from Congress itself. Obviously, the same principles apply even more strictly to Congressional staff; there is no excuse or justification for allowing them to break the laws with impunity.

In October 1988, syndicated columnist Bruce Fein addressed this very question of leaks by Congress, and made some pertinent comments and recommendations. He wrote:

> . . . Congress possesses plenary constitutional authority to expel misbehaving members by a two-thirds vote. It should establish an Office of Independent Intelligence Counsel to examine non-frivolous allegations of classified information disclosures by a member presented by at least 40 representatives or 10 senators.
>
> The intelligence counsel would be appointed by the comptroller of the General Accounting Office, an arm of Congress, and would possess the investigating powers of a U.S. attorney. Counsel would recommend expulsion or not, based on findings submitted in a report to the House or Senate. The recommendation would trigger a recorded roll call vote on the expulsion question.

Any such reform requiring the participation and approval of Congress might be difficult to achieve. However, nobody can argue that such a reform is unnecessary. About a year after Speaker Jim Wright abused congressional access to classified intelligence material in the way already described, his successor as Speaker, Rep. Thomas Foley, Democrat from Washington, conspired with the Democratic majority members on the House Intelligence Committee in order to circumvent the rules limiting his access to classified material. Committee rules limit the speaker's access to that which the whole committee (not just its Democratic majority) specifically agrees may be given out. In this instance, though, a senior aide to Foley was simply added to the Intelligence Committee staff as a clerk and henceforth was in a position to funnel any desired classified information to Foley without the requisite Committee approval, and without challenge.

While it was acquiescing in this rupture in the security wall built around classified material, the same House Intelligence Committee was allowing to die through inaction a number of proposals by Rep. Henry Hyde, Republican of Illinois, which would have strengthened that particular wall. The Hyde proposals, which were ignored, included:

- Secrecy oaths to be required for all Intelligence Committee members and staff. Violators to be investigated and punished by the House Ethics Committee staff, with conviction requiring permanent expulsion from the Intelligence Committee or, in the case of staff, loss of employment.
- House security clearances required for all members and staff, similar to those required for the executive branch.
- Return of the nineteen-member Intelligence Committee to its original 1981 size of thirteen persons, thus reducing the potential for leaks.

Later actions by Speaker Foley further demonstrated his disdain for the government security function. In February 1991, for example, Foley appointed six ultra-liberal members of the House to be members of the House Intelligence Committee. Syndicated columnist Cal Thomas, writing in *The Washington Times* of February 14, 1991, outlined some of the reasons against at least one of these appointments, that of Rep. Ronald Dellums, a California Democrat:

> Mr. Dellums, who was first elected in 1970 as an anti-defense radical from Berkeley with the help of the violent Black Panther party, has never seen a Marxist revolution he couldn't support or a U.S. military action he couldn't oppose.
>
> The publication *Human Events* reported that during a speaking engagement at Berkeley shortly before the 1980 election, Mr. Dellums told a symposium on "McCarthyism": "We should totally dismantle every intelligence agency in this country piece by piece, nail by nail, brick by brick."

The third highest official in the U.S. Government, Speaker Foley, thus considered to be an appropriate member of the House Intelligence Committee a man who presumably favored dismantling the committee itself along with "every intelligence agency in this country."

Cal Thomas pointed out further how Congressman Dellums had called for the impeachment of President Ronald Reagan as a result of the Grenada affair. Nor were Grenada's Communists the only Communists he liked. For example, he had supported the FMLN Communist guerrillas then fighting the government of El Salvador. He had also arranged for the brother of the FMLN Party Chairman Farid Handal to speak to the Congressional Black Caucus. Earlier the same Mr. Handal had met with the Cuban mission at the United Nations in New York and had also met with a representative of the Communist Party, U.S.A.

In the book *Destructive Generation*, authors Peter Collier and David Horowitz have reported on Handal as saying: "The offices of Congressman Dellums were turned into our offices. Everything was done there."

There have been many examples of disclosure of classified information for personal or political advantage by Members of Congress. None is more egregious than that by Congressman Robert G. Torricelli of New Jersey in late March 1995.

Charging complicity by the CIA in two killings in Guatemala, one of an American, Michael DeVine in 1990 and the other of leftist Guatemalan rebel Efrain Bamaca Velasquez in 1992, Torricelli revealed closely held government classified information that came to him as a member of the House Intelligence Committee. Despite testimony of the Acting CIA Director, Admiral William Studeman, before the Senate Intelligence Committee that directly disputed his statements, Torricelli not only conceded that he did reveal classified information, but arrogated to himself the judgment as to what information—given to him by virtue of his solemn oath of secrecy and high trust—he can reveal: "My most important duty was to tell the truth. I did what I thought was right." In other words, he was the sole judge of what classified information to reveal.

Walker and Pollard rightly languish in prison for revealing secret information. How much greater punishment is due a member of Congress to whom is given the highest trust, who takes no risk, and arrogantly discloses classified information for personal advantage, or political purpose?

The fact that a member of Congress has been elected to office by a local constituency should not mean that he henceforth has a free hand to undermine America's security nor should anyone in the Democratic or Republican leadership be free to do so. There should be fixed rules by which members of Congress and their staffs also have to abide. Any plan for the improvement of our security system should therefore include provisions for insuring that members of Congress too must respect the security system in place or pay an appropriate penalty.

White House Hypocrisy

Consideration of congressional security leaks points to similar leaks from the executive branch of our government, including the White House itself and the Executive Office of the President. Congress, even while it attempts to divert attention from its own leaks, sees the White House as especially vulnerable on this score, and there is a great deal of truth in this position. Congress and the White House are surely close to being equally guilty in the matter. The leaks in question tend to come out in four different guises:

- Selective release of classified information and data by named sources in support of presidential policies.
- Similar releases made with the understanding that, although the information has White House approval, the supplier will not be named.
- Information leaked with secret White House approval in order to retain "deniability," if the reaction is not what is wanted or anticipated.
- Information detrimental to official White House policy, released as part of an internal bureaucratic guerrilla campaign by someone on the inside who disagrees with the official position.

Thus, while leaks motivated by opposition to official policy are infuriating to the presidential incumbent and staff, and there are dire threats to identify and punish those responsible, most administrations themselves regularly resort to selective leaks of classified material in order to serve their own purposes. The selective leak has become practically a standard White House public relations tool. The result is, once again, that there are no truly safe secrets as each administration, group, or faction places its own opinion or agenda above the interests of the country.

One further consequence is that the emitting, or condoning, of leaks by the executive branch means that Congress can never be prevented from following the same practice. The Justice Department is hardly going to move against a member of Congress for something if its own President, or White House staff member, may be equally guilty. Similarly, the media remains immune from prosecution as long as the same administration which would have to bring in the indictment is itself violating the same laws, often in collusion with media professionals. The whole system, as it is now set up and functioning, encourages the breaking of laws which, however, still remain very much on the books.

Among the most serious of all the leaks emanating out of the executive branch were the 1960 leaks involving the Kennedy Administration's support of an invasion of Cuba by anti-Castro Cuban exiles. For weeks preceding the event, newspapers and television newscasts were predicting its imminent occurrence and speculating upon the extent, if any, to which United States forces might be directly involved. By the time the invasion took place, any reasonably competent dictatorship should have been ready for it, and, as things turned out, Fidel Castro was ready. The affair was the most spectacular setback of the early Kennedy Administration.

More recently, American efforts to topple the Panamanian strongman Manuel Noriega were consistently dogged by leaks concerning both tactics and timing. During the period when an anti-Noriega coup in Panama was still a realistic possibility, newspaper articles came out with such leaked information as the story that President Bush had agreed to back a coup plan. The newspaper stories identified the name and cost of the plan contemplated, and the number of previous plans. Even when President Bush declined to comment on these newspaper stories, other senior administration officials substantially confirmed them. *The Washington Times*, on November 29, 1989, was moved to editorialize:

> Forget the secrets. The U.S. government is as skilled at keeping them as a five-year old at Christmastime. Thanks to a legion of "officials who asked not to be named" as they leak the details of clandestine operations, secrets and spying are nearly obsolete.
>
> Last week, for example, the space shuttle Discovery blasted off on a military mission to place a spy satellite in orbit. It's hard to hide a shuttle launch from the public. But hiding the mission's goal, which was supposed to be a secret, was just as difficult. Journalists queued up around the launch site days before the takeoff to report the "secret" that the shuttle would be spreading more spy cameras around the heavens.
>
> A week earlier, President Bush signed off on a covert action plan to overthrow Panamanian Gen. Manuel Antonio Noriega. Enough detail to make that plan completely worthless showed up in newspapers and on the nightly news before the presidential ink was dry ... General Noriega must have gotten a good belly laugh ...

The newspaper believed that if the United States were ever to protect its interests abroad effectively, it obviously needed to let fewer people in on its plans. It singled out Congress in particular in this regard and spoke favorably of a pending intelligence authorization bill which would only require the President to give Congress "timely notification within a few days" of any American covert actions. *The Washington Times* concluded by noting that the best notice to Congress would be none at all and encouraged the President to continue to reserve the right to withhold notification entirely. This would appear to be an eminently sensible position in view of the Commander in Chief's overriding obligation to protect American lives.

After the successful U.S. military operation against Noriega was concluded a month later, intelligence officials revealed that information concerning this operation had also been leaked to Noriega two days before the operation began. Administration sources were apparently divided on exactly how General Noriega had received the warning, but there was no doubt that the Panamanian strongman had indeed been tipped off in advance. It was a tribute to our military that the American operation was successful.

The Washington Times reported on December 29, 1989:

> Administration sources were divided on exactly how Gen. Noriega received the warning . . . Once source said there is "hard evidence" that the leak came from the State Department in the form of a telephone call to Panama about 48 hours before the operation kicked off at "H-Hour," 1 a.m., December 20.
>
> The phone call was intercepted by a National Security Agency listening post near Panama City, sources said . . .
>
> However, Pentagon spokesman Bob Taylor said, "We don't have any indication at this time that there was a major OPSEC [operational security] problem."

Although administration sources thus disagreed on whether this phone call actually went out from the State Department to Panama or not (a whimsical question: would even Alger Hiss have dared to betray an imminent American military operation by making a telephone call from his office at the State Department?), the evidence does seem to point to the conclusion that, however he may have learned about it, General Noriega did know about the impending military operation in advance. This conclusion may be based, in part, on at least four other incidents:

- Cuban MIG 21s scrambled on the night of December 19 and "shadowed" the C-141 Starlifters ferrying U.S. Army paratroopers from Pope Air Force Base, N.C., to Panama.
- General Noriega significantly stepped up his nocturnal movements two days before the U.S. assault.
- Panamanian Defense Forces seemed to be lying in wait for Navy SEAL (sea-air-land) commandos who parachuted near Paitilla Airport, a small airfield where General Noriega maintained his personal 727 jet plane.

- A major aspect of the operation called for "neutralizing" Battalion 2000, General Noriega's most elite jungle warfare unit. But when U.S. forces arrived at the battalion's facility, those Panamanian forces had vanished.

Thus, it is not only members of Congress and their staffs who are capable of abusing and exploiting the classified information that comes into their hands as a result of their official positions. It is also members of the executive branch of the government as well. Many higher ranking officials appear to believe it is permissible to leak sensitive information in order to obstruct a policy or operation which they oppose. Should we then be surprised when lower ranking personnel, observing such actions, decide to follow the same example when it appears to be in their own interests? The result can never be anything but governmental and policy chaos, virtually nullifying the security function.

A logical question surely arises in connection with the degree of the offense being committed. Who is the worst offender? The spy who betrays his country for lucre, or the political "operator" who does it for political gain?

If our government security function is ever going to begin to be taken seriously again, prosecution should be considered, and, where sufficient evidence exists, should be instituted against *every* person who improperly discloses classified information, whatever the motive or pretext. In view of today's attitudes and conditions, it would seem that only a deterrent of this severity might possibly have any effect. In this regard, Bruce Fein suggested:

> A criminal penalty for executive branch disclosures of classified information should be complemented by a statute mandating dismissal of any employee found guilty of the same by a preponderance of the evidence in an administrative proceeding. The requirement of discharge will prevent a president from exonerating persons who leak classified information favorable to his popularity while denouncing leaks with the opposite effect.

A measure such as this would seem to be as sensible as it is imperative. Would anything less have any impact on the temptations that apparently arise regularly within the executive branch, and even within the White House itself, to leak sensitive information for personal or political gain?

The Issue of the Media—Ironic and Complex

The whole issue of security is riddled with all kinds of ironies, of course, but no irony is greater than the one inherent in the role played by the media. It is highlighted by the apparently common current opinion that, while individuals are expected to protect the nation's secrets confided to them, perhaps even at great personal cost, it is the right of the media to ferret out those same secrets, even though they are supposedly protected by law, and display them for all the world to see, even if American lives, treasure, or national policy objectives should happen to be at stake. Such a thing would never have occurred during World War II. The media was more responsible—unlike in the cases of the American actions in Panama, Grenada, Libya, and the Gulf War.

The individual who supplies confidential information to the media could very well be prosecuted; but nobody in the media is ever prosecuted. For example, after Samuel L. Morison provided classified satellite reconnaissance photographs to *Jane's Defense Weekly*, he was convicted and sentenced to two years in prison, but no attempt whatsoever was made to prosecute *Jane's Defense Weekly* for printing the classified photographs acquired. Similarly, journalist Bob Woodward's book *Veil* is replete with classified information. Its publication most certainly violated the Espionage Act, yet this fact has failed to arouse any prosecutorial interest.

The Justice Department avoids media prosecutions even under the Espionage Act, because it believes that society has accepted the concept that the media has the right, even the obligation, to decide for itself what information is fit for publication—even classified information. However, decisions to prosecute or not prosecute should not be made subject to a bureaucrat's understanding of society's opinion. And if society actually does believe that the media has the right to publish classified material, then society is mistaken! The media has already caused a number of American fiascoes and embarrassments by releasing information.

On the other hand, if media entities ever were prosecuted, even occasionally, they would be far less likely to accept classified material for publication from individuals within the government. Acceptance of a media "right" to publish classified material undermines the very concept that the government can "classify" material for protection. If the media can have access to it despite the government's classification of it, the government's authority to classify is already undermined, and the only question that then remains is why the media alone should have this declassifying privilege. In actuality, there is no evidence that there really is any such thing as a "societal consensus" favoring the publication of classified material by the media. It is more likely that the general public opposes it as reprehensible.

What is fairly apparent, however, is that the press and other media generally believe themselves to be above the provisions of the Espionage Act. Those who claim to speak for the industry on this topic appear to believe that there is a nearly absolute and unconditional right under the First Amendment for the media to decide what they will or will not print or broadcast. This position is both asserted and fairly regularly acted upon, and, for the most part, with impunity.

In an article printed in *The Washington Post* on June 8, 1986, commenting on the paper's reporting of the Ronald Pelton spy case, the *Post's* Executive Editor, Benjamin Bradlee, explained his position:

> First, we do consult with the government regularly about sensitive stories and we do withhold stories for national security reasons, far more often than the public might think. The *Post* has withheld information from more than a dozen stories so far this year for these reasons.
>
> Second, we don't allow the government—or anyone else—to decide what we should print. That is our job, and doing it responsibly is what a free press is all about.

Bradlee went on to say that the newspaper discusses those stories in which there may be national defense concern with representatives of the administration and then decides for itself whether and what to publish. The Pelton spy case involved an American capability to intercept Soviet communications. Since, at the time, the United States was uncertain of how much the Soviets knew about the capability, it was necessary to restrict what could be published. From December 5 to May 2, 1986, a number of meetings were held. In Benjamin Bradlee's words:

> We were determined not to violate the legitimate security of the nation, but we were equally determined not to be browbeaten by the administration, which has from time to time appeared to relish press-bashing, into not publishing something that our enemies already knew.
>
> The weapons of any administration in this kind of battle are formidable: presidents, admirals, generals, CIA directors telling you that publication would endanger the nation and the lives of some of its fighters, and ultimately threatening to prosecute you for violating the law.

> There are red lights that a newspaper goes through only with
> a deliberate lack of speed.
>
> The weapons of the press in this kind of battle are generally
> the reporters themselves and their facts, the First Amendment,
> and common sense.
>
> These are the green lights that make democracy the greatest
> form of government yet devised.

Notwithstanding Bradlee's opinion that the *Post* went to great lengths
to arrive at an appropriate resolution of the problem of how to handle the
public side of a case as sensitive as the Pelton case, the fact remains that
the interpretation of the First Amendment which he and most of the rest
of the media today insist on is an interpretation which is surely incom-
patible with the nation's very survival in the long run. The Constitution
does give to the government the authority and responsibility to conduct
the nation's business and provide for its defense and security, including
putting in place security systems and enacting Espionage Acts. It follows
that the Constitution, including the First Amendment, must be interpreted
in a way that does not hinder or prevent the government from exercising
its proper authority and carrying out its proper responsibilities, as determined by law and regulations under the Constitution itself.

Nowhere does the Constitution provide that the media or anyone
else is exempt from the normal application of the laws duly enacted by
Congress and signed by the president. The First Amendment, in particular, does not accord to the media or anyone else an absolute and unconditional right to print whatever they choose, laws and government regulations notwithstanding. Classified information is protected by law. In
the specific case before us, the media doesn't have the right, asserted by
Benjamin Bradlee, to decide which material, classified by legitimate
government authority according to regulatory standards established under
law, may be declassified and given to the public. To allow the media to
make such decisions on its own would mean that ultimately authority
resided in the media and not in the government, and this the Constitution
most emphatically does *not* provide for. Media arrogance can be no sub-
stitute for legitimate legal authority.

On a more practical level, it is quite unlikely that the American
people would approve giving such unlimited power to the media. Given
the reputation for biased reporting, does anyone believe that the media
would make such judgmentsevenhandedly? They frequently set out with
the frank intention of discrediting the government policies with which

they broadly disagree—policies legitimately arrived at by officials elected by the American people—such as the policies of the Reagan and Bush Administration towards Central America, for example. Moreover, there are other segments of the media that cannot be expected to put the welfare of the nation above political or monetary gain.

To allow the media to print and broadcast exactly what they please in the area of national security simply results in putting the media above the law. It means the creation of an unelected, unappointed, uncontrolled, and uncontrollable new political and social authority which the Founding Fathers never contemplated. Orderly—and just—government would necessarily be impossible where such a system held sway (which, indeed, may be precisely one of our problems at present!). In the fairly recent past, similar license has resulted in such debacles, clearly harmful to the national interest, such as the defeat at the Bay of Pigs, the publication of the so-called "Pentagon papers," and other instances where vital secrets were made public at the whim of an editorial staff. We can only be grateful that we do continue to have responsible members of the media so that the problem is not even greater.

Let there be no mistake, however. Nobody is advocating the abrogation of the First Amendment. Let newspapers and magazines and radio and television stations and other media go right on making their editorial judgments and printing what they like. If, however, in the process of making these decisions, they should violate the Espionage Act or other laws, let them be taken into court and prosecuted. Nothing would be more salutary for the media themselves in fact, than the acceptance of some kind of a requirement that they should be as responsible as everyone else. The present system in which, in practice, the authorities are afraid to touch the media for fear of violating the First Amendment, simply allows them to go on being as irresponsible as the recent record shows.

It is interesting that Benjamin Bradlee omitted a significant fact in the account quoted above. The one thing that induced the *Washington Post* to publish its coverage of the Pelton case *without* any of the details of the communications systems involved was a threat by the government to prosecute the newspaper under the Espionage Act, 18 United States Code 789.

In summary, there can be no doubt that the nation's ability to put in place and properly administer an effective security system requires that the media, like the White House and the Congress, respect and abide by the system put in place by valid authority. The media cannot

be allowed to decide on its own which national secrets may be declassified and published. In other words, the media cannot be permitted to
break the law.

It is, of course, both true and unfortunate that government officials
may misuse and even abuse the government classification system to
hide embarrassing or politically damaging information which has no
bearing on national security. The potential for that kind of abuse is
undoubtedly a very real problem, but it is nevertheless not a sufficient
one to allow the whole security system to be undermined in order to
combat it. We need a mechanism that will both minimize the potential
for improper classification and avoid reliance upon independent media
to "expose" the problems when they arise.

Coverage of the Espionage Laws

In view of all that has been discussed up to this point, it seems
clear that there is a need to update and expand our federal laws dealing
with the general problem of espionage. Bruce Fein has reflected on
these problems with great acuity. He describes several directions which
a revision of our laws concerning espionage would have to take:

> The impending launching of private reconnaissance satellites
> for use by the media will compound the problem of secrecy in
> national security matters. A wholesale revamping of laws and
> regulations governing classified information is imperative to bol-
> ster national security sinews.
>
> The Land Remote-Sensing Commercialization Act of 1984
> authorizes private commercial operation of remote-sensing space
> systems, subject to conditions prescribed by the Secretary of
> Commerce to safeguard the national security. The secretary should
> require prior review of remote-sensing information or pictures
> before transmission or publication. If the material would be clas-
> sified if possessed by the government, then no further revelation
> should be permitted. The Supreme Court's ruling in *Snepp vs.
> United States* (1980) justifies that prior restraint . . .

Fein points out that, at present, no statute actually makes criminal
the knowing publication or transmittal of classified information. The
Espionage Act is generally confined to punishing willful disclosures of
communications of intelligence information with reason to believe its
potential to disadvantage the United States. This statute would seem to

be drawn much too narrowly. Fein's view would seem to be in accord with both common sense and the true interests of the country:

By definition, however, all classified information is potentially damaging to the national security or foreign policy interests of the country. Further, improper transmission of such information invariably undermines the nation's ability to elicit foreign cooperation or maintain secret agents abroad, because it fosters a belief that no pledge of confidentiality from the United States can be trusted.

Accordingly, the Espionage Act should be amended to make criminal any knowing unauthorized transmission, publication, or disclosure of classified information.

The constitutionality of that prohibition seems unchallengeable under the federal appeals court ruling in *United States vs. Morison* (1987). There the court rejected a First Amendment attack on an Espionage Act prosecution.

The final point is an extremely important one, not nearly as widely known as it should be, perhaps in part because the media has succeeded so thoroughly in misleading the public into believing that the current media interpretation of the First Amendment must always necessarily take precedence over the law of the land as embodied, for example, in the Espionage Act.

In Chapter Seven, we shall propose some other specific recommendations in this same vein in order to provide greater and more effective protection for the classified material which has too often up to now been compromised by Congress, the White House, the rest of the executive branch, and the media. The basic tenet must always be, of course, that violation of the rules concerning such material is a criminal act and should be prosecuted even if the violations come from Congress, the executive branch, or the media.

FIVE

Why People Commit Treason

One of the many failures of security management today is that there is no effective continuing program devoted to examining deterrents, personality characteristics, motivations and rationalizations. An effort is needed to develop educational and awareness programs that maximize the deterrents, identify problem characteristics, minimize or eliminate the motivations for treason, and debunk potential rationalizations. Current education techniques appear to assume that all problems are the result of forgetfulness or lack of understanding.

It is important to understand what can motivate people to betray their country and, conversely what might effectively deter those who might be so motivated.

The decision of whether or not to take a particular action is usually made by comparing the action's deterrents and the person's motivations, which basically consist of the benefits which the person believes will accrue to him as the result of taking the action. In those cases in which conscience or emotion is involved, the rational process through which the decision is made may be twisted by the individual in order to avoid facing uncomfortable moral or other consequences.

Of course, in the case of illegal and normally immoral activities, such as treason, the perpetrator will likely seek to escape the shame of his action, both in his own eyes and in the eyes of others, by developing rationalizations which he hopes may excuse or mitigate the act. And, of course, all of the above factors mentioned will be affected by the individual's personality traits and particular problems.

Let us look in turn at some of the major deterrents, motivations, and rationalizations involved in the crime of treason.

DETERRENTS

Notwithstanding the breakdown of morality which has plagued our nation and the corresponding lack of a strong moral code—considerations that must be taken into account in the development of any government security program today—there are several other important identifiable factors which can still act as strong deterrents to treasonable activity. Some of these are:

- Patriotism.
- The fear of punishment.
- Pride in self.
- Shame and the fear of exposure.
- The human conscience, that quiet and steady arbiter between right and wrong which can still reliably guide us, even in the midst of the moral confusion.

Anyone setting out to commit treason must overcome restraints on his action arising from one or more of these deterrent factors. Until the 1950s, virtually all American traitors acted out of loyalty to a cause which they considered higher and more important than patriotism. However mistaken their understanding of the Communist system may have been, persons such as the atom bomb spies, the Ware Group, including the Hiss Brothers, and (before they decided to renounce their Communist allegiance) even Whittaker Chambers, Elizabeth Bentley and Ben Mandel, were, in their own minds, patriots to the "higher cause" of Communism. This was typical for the times. In fact, the only American traitor during the first half of the twentieth century identified as acting primarily out of greed was John Farnsworth, the former Navy man who committed espionage for the Japanese during the 1930s.

The Communist traitors in the 1930s and 1940s were apparently not troubled by their consciences until at least some of them began to recognize the overwhelming evidence concerning the true nature of Stalinism and Soviet power. For the Communists who remained committed, there was little feeling of shame about their actions. They were proud of what they were doing. Moreover, the Communist system of cells enabled them to encourage and support one another. Fear of capture and punishment appears to have varied depending upon the gravity of the crimes and the likelihood of detection. So long as they operated in good faith, believing in the cause of International Communism and of the Soviet Union as its embodiment, their consciences generally remained "in sync" with their actions. Similarly, those who defected from Communism usually did so for reasons of conscience. Those who remained faithful to the Communist line, observing the actions of Stalin during and after the Second World War, developed extremely complex excuse rationales.

Since the mid-fifties American traitors' motivations have almost universally involved greed or greed combined with lust, vengeance, ego and other similar factors. In these kinds of cases, it would seem that the deterrents would be more effective than they were in the heyday of Communist zeal. These new types of cases do not involve the allegiance adopted to the higher cause which Communism was believed to offer, and do not include the support system that party membership provided; nor, except in sex cases, is there usually any human fellowship involved in these kinds of cases beyond the artificial camaraderie provided by the traitor's contact or handler.

In today's society, the deterrents of patriotism and conscience are clearly much less effective than in former days. Even fear of exposure or punishment, or plain old-fashioned shame, are lesser deterrents today, since most people today are quite aware that a permissive society is all too inclined to forgive and forget with few or no recriminations to be expected. With crime and self-indulgence rampant today, the seriousness of almost any crime committed, not only the crime of espionage, is seriously downgraded in the public eye. Nevertheless, to the extent possible, today's government security programs must maximize the impact of these deterrents in the eyes of potential traitors.

MOTIVATIONS

Allegiance to Another Cause or Country

Allegiance to a higher ideal is by far the most difficult motive to be deterred, since the traitor not only avoids the deterrent normally supplied by conscience, but nurses an active belief that he is acting for a higher good. Thus, the Rosenbergs were not only able to commit a heinous crime for the cause but even to go to their deaths with apparent equanimity. Similarly, to the British, Nathan Hale was a traitor, but in his own mind his was a noble act; and in the minds of Americans, he was one of the heroes of the American Revolution.

Since the Communist system has now been largely discredited, even in the eyes of most of its apologists, the potential for such cases has greatly decreased. Even during the resurgence of belief in a Communist Utopia during the period of the Vietnam War, most of those who opposed America and favored her enemies were acting for other reasons than love of the Soviet Union as the embodiment of the Communist Utopia. The last known major espionage case involving betrayal out of direct allegiance to the Soviet Union and its satellites appears to have been that of William Martin and Bernon Mitchell in 1958.

Nevertheless, we have recently witnessed other instances of betrayal of secrets to other countries not considered direct, immediate military threats to the United States, which were due, ostensibly, to allegiance to or even affection for the foreign country in question. For example, the actions by Larry Wu-Tai Chin and Jonathan J. Pollard in support of the Peoples Republic of China and the State of Israel, respectively, were presumably committed out of affection for these countries, although it is apparent that greed was also a factor.

The best protection against those treasonable acts which are committed in the name of a higher cause include 1) strong and effective security management; 2) emphasis on the fear of a harsh punishment; 3) pride in self and job; and 4) continuing education concerning the actions of our enemies, the need to retain our secrets even from our friends, and the requirement that officials of an elected government, not private individuals, must always make the basic decisions concerning information to be released or withheld.

Disapproval of American Policy

At such times as the United States is obliged to pursue controversial policies, as was the case during the Vietnam and Gulf Wars, there is always an increased potential for treasonable activity by individuals who oppose the official policies and believe they must be thwarted at any cost. Certainly, money is also likely to be involved, along with ego in these kinds of cases. One of the most serious examples inspired by a combination of these motives was the case of Philip Agee, who in 1975 published a book, *Inside the Company: CIA Diary*, which revealed the identities of hundreds of CIA agents and employees and almost certainly caused the death of at least one American as well as major disruptions of American operations and objectives. In 1977, Christopher Boyce and Dalton Lee were similarly motivated at least in part by disapproval of U.S. policies.

Protection against betrayal motivated by disapproval of American policies requires the same techniques as for betrayals due to another allegiance or cause. Particular emphasis must be placed upon educating all employees on the rationale and necessity for particularly controversial policies and, even more importantly, upon the concept that, in the service of a democracy, the personal opinions of the individual must be subordinated to the policy of the employing agency or the employee must resign.

However, persons must not be forced on a condition of career employment to engage in conduct which egregiously violates a reasonably formed conscience.

Greed

In today's society, the motivation which is perhaps the easiest to understand, yet the most disconcerting and difficult to forgive, is that of greed. In the second half of the twentieth century, greed has been by far the most common motive for treason. Going down the list of thirteen traitors identified in the course of the years 1984 and 1985, for example, it appears that greed was a major motivating factor in at least ten of these cases: Thomas P. Cavanaugh, Larry Wu-Tai Chin, Edward L. Howard, Randy Miles Jeffries, Ronald W. Pelton, Jonathan J. Pollard and his wife Anne (who claimed to be motivated by loyalty to Israel, but who nevertheless proposed to sell classified information to Communist China), John A. Walker, Jr., Arthur Walker, and Jerry Whitworth. Sharon M. Scranage and Richard W. Miller committed treason on account of love affairs, while Michael Walker may have been drawn into treason out of misguided filial loyalty to his father, John Walker, as well as by greed.

With the erosion of the national morality that we have noted, greed is likely to figure increasingly as a causative factor. It would seem logical, then, for American security and counter-espionage programs to devote a reasonable amount of resources to education programs which emphasize the dangers and penalties of committing treason as compared to its possible rewards, as well as identifying and paying closer attention to the activities of people whose lifestyles or expenditures point to personal wealth or resources considerably above that of their peers or who exhibit serious money or credit problems. John Walker and William H. Bell did not get drawn into espionage until they found themselves in difficult personal financial situations. In fact, in the case of Army Warrant Officer Joseph G. Helmich, it appears that the "last straw" influencing his decision to commit treason was the threat by his own commanding officer of a court martial if he did not pay certain military club debts. Certainly the pressure of impending or current financial failure can greatly weaken one's normal powers of resistance to illegal and improper opportunities.

The critical need, therefore, is for a *security management system* that is capable of identifying in a timely manner factors such as financial crises which may make a subject susceptible to the temptation of treason for pay. Effective agency programs to identify, monitor, and perhaps assist employees in financial straits will prevent some people from ever succumbing to treason. But this requires real management effort. Management assistance could involve counseling, financial education, and help in debt restructuring and budgeting, etc.

In addition, an agency capability of identifying new unexplained employee wealth *as soon as it becomes apparent*, that is, not merely in the course of a security reinvestigation, followed by a rapid check intended to turn up improper liaisons, unusual activities or sources of funds, would have cut short a number of the traitorous careers. For example, the new wealth of Aldrich Ames, industrial spy Harold Farrar and James D. Harper accomplice Ruby L. Schuler (as well as the latter's obvious drinking problem) should have immediately alerted supervisors and even co-workers to the existence of a possible problem.

Love, Lust, and Loneliness

Love and sex, in all their many forms and appearances, have been powerful weapons in espionage, particularly in Europe. The Profumo Affair in the 1960s, involving a British cabinet minister, John Profumo, who became linked to Soviet diplomats through a call girl, Christine Keeler, was only one of many scandals which have rocked our European allies and had severe consequences. Perhaps the greatest comparable scandal in the United States was one which was never fully revealed at the time, and not even during the lifetimes of the major participants. It was the scandal involving President John F. Kennedy in an affair with Judith Exner, who was already the mistress of gangster leader Sam Giancana. This liaison, like other Kennedy liaisons that have come to light since his death, reveal a recklessness and contempt for presidential responsibilities that could have had enormous consequences for America's security. The reporters and media people who are now known to have "covered up" for the popular young president exhibited a twisted and perverted sense of responsibility to both their profession and their country. Determined on the one hand to be guided solely by their own professional judgment when deciding to publish state secrets, they appear equally determined, on the other hand, to exercise the same personal judgment when deciding to cover up information such as Kennedy's affairs, regardless of the effects of these decisions on America's security.

Whether heterosexual or homosexual, adulterous or not, sexual liaisons can entrap people in situations into which they never would otherwise venture. If a person feels lonely and abandoned, and someone offers attention, affection, and emotional warmth and security, the person's emotional obligation to return the gifts can become overwhelming and, moreover, may be easily manipulated. The Sharon M. Scranage case is a classic example of this. She was a CIA employee working in a foreign country of exotic culture and she felt abandoned. She was susceptible, and nothing was easier, or perhaps more likely, than for her to get caught up in a "romance" through which she was corrupted and then manipulated. It needs asking: Why did the agency not anticipate her vulnerability? Such cases abound and represent classic opportunities for subversion.

Lonely individuals can also be exploited in their own countries, as was demonstrated in the case of James D. Harper, who co-opted a female employee of a defense contractor and prevailed upon her to deliver secrets to him. While the Scranage case involved an employee working in unfamiliar circumstances in Africa and the Harper case occurred on home ground, both cases involved the exploitation of a fundamental lack of personal morality as well as sound judgment, exacerbated by loneliness which made the individuals susceptible to a tawdry romantic affair.

All countries have used the allure of sex to advance their intelligence and espionage agendas. The aim is to corrupt by offering overt sexual temptations. Victor Ostrovsky's book *By Way of Deception* details the extensive and painstaking methods of the Israeli Mossad in the use of sex as an intelligence tool. And the Soviet KGB, of course, was always a master in arranging romantic relationships between its agents and Americans and others with access to classified material. When necessary, the KGB surreptitiously filmed or videotaped love trysts for later use in forcing their victims to commit acts of treason rather than be exposed. The East German *Stasi's* photographic collection of German notables and others taken in compromising situations, now in Western hands, has turned out to be quite extensive.

There is much evidence, however, indicating that blackmail or threats are frequently unnecessary in cases of sexual liaisons. Richard W. Miller, an FBI counter-intelligence agent, *willingly* provided classified information to his KGB mistress. In the case of the American Marine guards at the American embassy in Moscow, Sergeant Clayton Lonetree swallowed unbelievable stories concerning his paramour's travails as justifications for treason.

Nor was this use of attractive female agents by the former Soviet Union a recent or isolated case. For many, many years U.S. government

employees, particularly those of the State Department, were systematically targeted by the Soviets, who regularly aimed at tempting them.

During the immediate post-war period, I had a personal experience
in investigating such a case. At that time, I was serving as an agent with
the Counter-Intelligence Corps and I was assigned under a cover to
work in the Eurasian Branch of the Intelligence Division of the War
Department. The investigation concerned a coterie of employees who
had worked in the American Embassy in Moscow during the war. One
subject in particular was a meek and unprepossessing official who, it
turned out, had been attracted to and formed a liaison with a female
agent of the NKVD (predecessor agency of the KGB), of great beauty,
while in Moscow. She ended up marrying him and came with him to the
U.S. as he moved into the highly sensitive innards of the War Department. Along with another traitor, a woman who was an American citizen, he continued to have access to classified material for quite a long
time. Though finally removed, the two of them remained much too long
in highly sensitive positions for the good of the country. In the end, they
were not punished but quietly permitted to resign.

Homosexual relationships must be recognized as at least as likely
as those of heterosexuals to lead to espionage problems. Although the
United States may have experienced relatively little of this type of espionage activity, we have already cited above the joint defection to the
Soviet Union of the homosexuals Martin and Mitchell.

During the ten years immediately preceding World War I, Colonel
Alfred Redl, Director of the Intelligence Service of Austria-Hungary,
was regularly supplying the Czarist Russians with the major secrets of
the Habsburg Empire, including potential battle plans against Serbia—
all to protect his secret homosexuality. When Redl was finally exposed,
he committed suicide.

From the time of the stories of Adam, Eve, and the serpent, of
Samson and Delilah, and of Salome, Herod, and John the Baptist, down
to the actions of the Marine guards at the American Embassy in Moscow,
history has insistently taught us that nothing else has the capacity to
cause us to lose our ability to make reasonable judgments as love and
sexual attraction. Any viable security program must provide reasonable
and effective training concerning the probability that such blandishments
are only too likely to present themselves, the nature of the attractions
themselves, and also the appropriate responses and resistance required.

No security program can tolerate dalliance with foreign nationals,
especially when it is realized that foreign agents are specifically trained

to take advantage of precisely these situations of temptation. Current security programs, like too many officials up to and including ambassadors, appear not to want to give much systematic attention to the determined and methodical efforts by foreign governments to achieve their espionage objectives by corrupting American personnel, particularly younger employees, with sexual temptations.

The current practice of assigning young, single Americans to critical foreign posts without any consideration for their social needs, and then simply leaving them to their own devices, must be stopped. Obviously, any effective security program must include a capability to:

- Select persons for classified overseas positions who are best able to withstand the inevitable loneliness and the blandishments, including the sexual advances, of possible foreign agents.
- Educate new assignees about what they must expect and what can be done to resist temptations and relieve their loneliness and boredom.
- Develop programs which will minimize these negative conditions as well as be able to identify and respond to any problems which do develop.
- Require quality supervision and management to anticipate and prevent Marine-guard type disasters.

Currently, there is apparently little being accomplished. For example, even though it was noted by her supervisors that Sharon Scranage was consorting with a questionable foreign national and she was actually warned against it, no follow-up or preventive action was taken at the local CIA station. Similarly, the fact that the egregious actions of several of the Marine guards at the American Embassy in Moscow, including their relationships with Russian females and allowing access to the embassy to Russians after hours, were able to go on without discovery or without any action on the part of embassy officials, simply boggles the mind. It speaks volumes concerning the gross dereliction of duty on the part of the American Ambassador, his administrative officer, and his security officer. The conditions of life in an unfriendly country with few social or recreational outlets present dangers which are already too well known for senior officials to ignore them. As a matter of fact, it has been long accepted that any female companions available to U.S. Government personnel in Moscow, Leningrad, etc. are "enemy" agents.

Friendship

Offering opportunities for friendship can be and is utilized in the espionage business in the same way as offering temptations involving love and lust. In fact, use of an agent to become the "friend" of the employee being approached may be even more insidious and effective, since it is usually considered appropriate and beneficial for American personnel to develop ties with citizens of a host nation, and there are not the automatic warning flags that exist in a sexual encounter. The beginning of friendship almost always appears to be totally beneficent, with none of the risks of a sexual liaison. Moreover, even though the sexual drive may not be there to distort judgment, the subject at the same time may be much less likely to imagine or recognize that an ulterior motive may be present in an offer of friendship which seems wholly altruistic.

The combination of friendship and money may be one of the most powerful of all inducements in today's world. Often, as in the case of William H. Bell, financial hardship and personal trauma engulf the individual simultaneously with a time of vulnerability. In this case, his nineteen-year-old son had died, his wife and his other son were estranged from him, *and* he was in deep financial difficulty. When the Communist agent, Zacharksky, offered both sympathy and cash for simple favors, it was too much for Bell to resist.

The necessary protection of American personnel from the possible abuses of friendship, whether or not combined with money, is the same in concept as in the cases of love and sex relationships. In fact, a single training program can and should be devised to cover the risks of all the possible relationships into which American personnel might enter with foreign nationals, especially abroad.

Coercion

In some instances, individuals may be susceptible to coercion even when they might not otherwise betray their country's secrets for money, sexual favors, or friendship. The most salient of these cases of "coercion" would seem to be those in which a loved one is under the control of the nation or other entity seeking intelligence. For example, Ronald Humphrey claimed that he cooperated with Vietnamese intelligence only because his Vietnamese common-law wife was being held hostage. While doubtful in his case, this is a bona fide hazard.

Once again, effective protection from espionage in this type of case would include effective identification of employees with this type of problem who would have to be considered at risk as well as a realistic, publicized ability to help personnel who might come under pressure to commit espionage. The agency's willingness and capability to help such persons should be well known in advance so that whenever an individual finds himself in a situation of potential coercion he will not be afraid to come forward and seek assistance.

A second type of potential coercion, even more difficult to deal with, is vulnerability to blackmail. Blackmail has been used quite effectively in a number of European espionage cases, although relatively few such cases have been revealed involving United States personnel. But the vulnerabilities are obvious. If someone has something unsavory or illegal in his background or conduct, he may be extremely reluctant to see it revealed even if his employer has a program to assist employees with various kinds of personal problems. Nevertheless, many persons potentially vulnerable to the pressure of blackmail could be dissuaded from yielding to it if they know in advance that the organization will stand behind and aid them to the extent possible if they are forthcoming with the problem. It must be clear that every effort will be made to enable the individual to continue in his position, or, if that is not possible, to assist in obtaining alternate employment. Both in employee manuals and in training, it should also be constantly emphasized that the consequences and repercussions from being convicted of espionage are much greater than those of having one's unsavory secrets revealed.

RATIONALIZATIONS

While the motive for a person's action would be the true, primary reason for that action, the person may also develop one or more rationalizations for the action. Consciously or unconsciously, traitors employ rationalization to mitigate or excuse the negative consequences of the act, thereby reducing the deterrents of conscience and, if the action is detected, shame and punishment. Given the reach of the human imagination, there may be no end to the rationalizations that persons may create, but a few of the more common are described below.

Loyalty to a Separate Cause or Country

Jonathan J. Pollard claimed that Israel required U.S. secrets for its survival and that therefore the United States had no right to withhold them from Israel, and decided to remedy the deficiency himself. Larry Wu-Tai Chin claimed that his actions were intended to create better understanding between China and the United States. It can be difficult to determine whether a person is providing the true motivation or is employing a rationalization. Several factors normally need to be considered in making a judgment about this. For example:

- If someone stands to make a profit on a deal, claims of idealistic motivation must be considered, at the very least, suspect.
- The United States government is in the best position to know what information in its possession needs to be kept confidential in its own self-interest. Moreover, the U.S. government has the legal authority and the moral responsibility to make just such judgments and not each and every employee. Any claim that surreptitious release of controlled information is really in the government's or the country's best interests must be considered highly specious at best and without justification.
- If someone is so interested in promoting another country or cause that he will damage American interests and betray an American trust in order to serve that cause, he is in fact an enemy of the United States and deserves to be treated as such.

The Information Delivered Is Valueless

Frequently, people permit themselves to be drawn into a web of treason by accepting the claim that the information which they are handing over is so innocuous as to be without value, and therefore no harm is being done. In some cases, the perpetrator may even start out by gathering and selling information which is not classified thinking that he has "fooled" the foreign intelligence service. In reality, however, he has been drawn into the espionage network of a foreign country or enterprise—financially, organizationally, emotionally, and morally—and thus he has already been compromised. If he continues to have access to secrets, he will in all likelihood be inextricably drawn in. Finally, the rationalization that the material being delivered is valueless can be, and has been, applied even to highly classified information. In this instance, the traitor is actually attempting to minimize security levels assigned by qualified, responsible classifiers, thereby putting the traitor's judgment and opinions above that of the entire security system. It is a usurpation of the authority of the responsible officials, in many ways equivalent to many other instances in which individuals consider themselves above the law. This potential rationalization must be attacked head-on in orientation and other training with the truism that, just as in the case of any other law or regulation, it is not and cannot be the right of any individual to place his own judgment above that of the persons with the responsibility and duty to assign these classifications. Foreign agents who recruit potential traitors are patient and persistent. Their first goal is to establish a relationship—any relationship—with the potential traitor. The second goal is to develop some claim on the subject, so that the subject will be beholden to the agent. Any favor will do at this point. It doesn't have to be illegal. A large sum of money, payment for an innocuous favor, readily available information, friendship, sex, etc., can be used to develop this first, critical involvement. John Harper first sold what was apparently a collection of unclassified documents to Polish Intelligence for $5,000 in 1975; four years later, in a difficult financial and emotional situation, he began his treasonable activities in earnest. In another espionage case, the suspect who was apprehended tried to claim, with apparent seriousness, that he was actually helping the United States by obliging the Russians to pay him in scarce hard currency for the worthless information which he was supplying to them!

Actually, foreign intelligence services typically know precisely what information they want to obtain, and that major objectives are sometimes achieved by piecing together seemingly unrelated and insignificant data. Therefore all data sought has value to the person seeking it.

The United States Government Doesn't Care

This claim usually relies upon the remarkable notion that, if the classified information were really worth protecting, the U.S. government would have an effective system in place that really did protect it; since the spy has in fact been able to steal the information, the self-serving argument goes that the government does not really care. John Walker used this rational to excuse his treason, but the review of his case demonstrates that great damage was, in fact, caused by his provision of cryptographic lists to the Soviet Union. This damage may well have included loss of secret information relevant to the then ongoing Vietnam war as well as requiring radio silence during the attempted hostage rescue in Iran. The unhappy truth of the matter is that while many protected secrets are indeed vital ones, and the government does care, the level of performance of U.S. security in protecting them is frequently so incompetent and lackadaisical as to lend some plausibility to this particular claim. Development of an effective security program would obviously greatly weaken this rationalization.

Unfortunately, one of the other things that can lend credence to the claim that the U.S. government really does not care is the cynical leaking by federal officials at the highest levels of government of information which a lower-level person would be prosecuted for divulging. Similarly, the use with impunity by the media of classified data further erodes the idea of the inviolability of classified material and re-enforces the notion that the government truly does not care about the secret information in its charge. Never has even one such case resulted in criminal prosecution or punishment and that is a blow to American security.

Perhaps the greatest hurdle to overcome in questioning whether our government cares is the failure to make serious and sound improvements to a failed security system despite years and years of acts of treason carried out with great harm to the nation.

Vengeance

The urge to "get even" is one of the most common of human motives and so it is perhaps not surprising that it has also been used as a rationalization for crimes committed. For example, in the security case of Sergeants Robert Lee and James Allen Mintkenbaugh, both men claimed revenge as a justifying motive—Johnson to get back at the Army for failing to promote him as he felt he deserved, and Mintkenbaugh to repay God and the world for the fact that he had been born a homosexual.

One of the most vicious instances of turning traitor for vengeance was that of Edward L. Howard. After being dismissed by the CIA— which did, however, assist him in acquiring another position—Howard went on to sell to the Soviets information which along with information supplied by Aldrich Ames, devastated the CIA's human network in the Soviet Union. Amazingly, early in his career of treason, Howard actually told two CIA employees that he was considering turning traitor; the CIA in response simply paid for him to see a psychiatrist, even though his knowledge of the agency's Moscow operations was well known. Moreover, no follow-up or surveillance of his activities was performed until he was fingered by a defecting Soviet agent.

Another traitor motivated by vengeance against the CIA was William P. Kampiles. After he had committed his crime, he actually *wrote to the CIA* documenting what he had done, and, as we have noted in Chapter One, his letter went unopened at the CIA for two months.

Probably everyone has at one time or other tried to blame others, or the world itself, for his problems. A viable security program accordingly needs to include the availability of counseling, without recrimination, for persons with real or imagined grievances and other problems, and programmatic reminders that actions taken against the nation, far from hurting the few people or the agency against which the subject has a grievance, might actually do harm to millions.

The security program must include training for middle managers to enable them to identify and respond to instances of anger and resentment as well as open threats as in the Howard case. Furthermore, if persons possessing sensitive or secret information leave a position in anger, steps should be taken immediately to change security and procedures; this is as obvious as changing the locks on one's house if one has reason to believe the keys have fallen into the hands of a potential burglar. Furthermore, such persons should be warned against disclosing confidential procedures, and their actions should be monitored. Apparently no such procedures were ever followed in the case of Edward Howard.

Espionage Has No Morality

Difficult as it may be for the aware citizen to believe, there are some who actually accept the nonsense presented by persons such as author John Le Carre who espouse the theory that the intelligence business is so intrinsically evil that it makes no difference which side you are on. In this perspective, it logically follows that no action taken within the scope of this vast amoral environment can be evil in itself, but merely amoral. Therefore everyone can act as he pleases.

Such a concept certainly provides a great psychological justification for the aspiring traitor. He is able to assure himself that, in the amoral world of espionage, whatever actions he may decide to take are immaterial and for him alone to decide.

Aldrich Ames appears to have employed a combination of the last two rationales to support his claim that all of espionage is simply a game and there are no negative consequences.

The response of an effective government security program to such a notion must be training and orientation which constantly points out the advantages of the American system, the tremendous differences in the political and security systems of the United States and its adversaries, the basic moral justifications behind the programs and policies of the United States and that it is a system that can be conscientiously endorsed and promoted. It must also be protected from harm. Similar public relations and communications campaigns should try to imbue all Americans with the same ideals and attitudes, and on a continuing basis. The constant criticism and belittling of America and American ideals that so often come from the media and certain elites can become a very serious matter when the question of possible disloyalty or espionage suddenly arises.

CHARACTERISTICS AND CIRCUMSTANCES

In their book *Merchants of Treason*, authors Thomas B. Allen and Norman Polmar describe the method through which one of the earliest American spies-for-money, Navy Yeoman First Class Nelson C. Drummond, was recruited by the Soviets:

> Drummond, a clerk at the U.S. Naval Headquarters in London, held Top Secret and Cosmic (NATO) security clearances. A Soviet-hired "spotter agent," who could have been a British barmaid or fellow serviceman, noted that Drummond, a chronic gambler, was constantly in financial straits and passed his name to Soviet intelligence. One night in 1957 he was invited into a pub by a stranger who, while picking up the tab, gave Drummond some money and asked for a favor: a Navy ID card so that his friends could use the Navy exchange. From there the demands escalated until Drummond was soon supplying actual classified documents.

On various occasions United States intelligence agencies have tried to develop a complete profile of the traitor or potential traitor, apparently with only partial success. However, a review of publicly available information on historical cases of espionage can provide some valuable insights. The characteristics identified in the list below have been noted as either being universally present in a large number of identified traitors, or have appeared as highly visible traits in a lesser number of them:

1. Selfish and arrogant.
2. Manipulative of others and of conditions around them.
3. Vain and susceptible to flattery.
4. Desirous of attention.
5. Aggressive, even imprudent with money.
6. Possessing characteristics which make the subject stand out and perhaps feel embarrassed or alone, such as race, job function, etc.
7. Sexually indiscreet and/or promiscuous.
8. Addicted to alcohol, drugs, gambling or other vice.
9. Huge ego.

Foreign agents habitually look for people to recruit who possess some or many of these characteristics, or who are in difficult personal or financial situations.

Merchants of Treason goes on to describe how, in addition to Americans involved with codes, the KGB attempts to recruit junior American embassy personnel and, especially, Marine guards, presumably because of their youth, isolation, naivete, and vulnerability, as well as their access to the embassy:

> According to the U.S. Government's classified manual, *Soviet Intelligence Operations Against Americans and U.S. Installations,* "It is this broad category of code clerks, secretaries, Marine guards, etc., which the Soviets regard as particularly vulnerable since (in the words of one KGB directive) 'they do not belong to the privileged class and are worse off financially.'"

The Soviets continually try to introduce "class wars" into their spy recruiting. This was evident in the KGB's attempt to recruit a black Marine and the Marine who was a full-blooded American Indian as major targets among the guards at the U.S. Embassy in Moscow in 1985 - 86. However, one Marine officer who served in the embassy during this period (without direct responsibility for the guards) was quick to point out that the Soviet effort to turn embassy staff as well as guards into spies is a blanket operation.

"These [American] people are in Moscow for a short time, two years," he told the authors. "The Soviets go after them all; certainly some appear more vulnerable to their attempts than others, but almost everyone at the embassy—especially the junior people and enlisted Marine guards—are the subject of KGB attention."

The classified manual on KGB interest in Marine guards is amazingly prophetic. it accurately notes the potential personality weakness of typical young Marines and, in describing what damage a recruited Marine can do, the report reads like a scenario for events that some investigators say actually happened:

"U.S. Marine enlisted men, assigned as guards at diplomatic installations abroad, are especially interesting targets to Soviet intelligence because of their frequent access to safe combinations, their presence (sometimes alone) in embassies while on night duty and their obvious capability—in the event of recruitment— to emplace microphone and transmitter listening devices.

Although hand-picked for their protective duty assignments abroad and given special training and security indoctrination, Marine guard personnel are, for the most part, young and unmar-

ried and often "on the town" in their off-duty hours. They are
inevitably exposed to temptations which the Soviets can put in
their paths. They are approachable by local nationals who are
recruited agents of Soviet Intelligence and often by Soviets themselves. There have been repeated approaches of both types in
every part of the world and also attempts at recruitment."

The manual describes an Austrian agent of the KGB who
"was told to cultivate persons of two categories within the embassy—local citizens working as switchboard operators and Marine guard personnel." Soviet intelligence officers had first conceived of this "cultivation" soon after Marine guards were assigned to embassy duty in 1949. The traditionalist KGB was still
issuing the same orders in Vienna in 1986, when the KGB approached Lonetree who had already been recruited in Moscow.

Another KGB gambit in Vienna involved a volleyball team of
Marine guards. A Soviet team challenged the Marines to a game.
That one was played at the Marine compound. The next one was
scheduled on Soviet territory. This, says the manual, was "an
unprecedented gesture which clearly was intended to give the
Vienna KGB American-operations specialists a chance to cultivate Marines socially and open the way for possible further contact, assessment and development.

"To make it a festive occasion, virtually the entire Soviet
colony turned out in force complete with wives and children, and
the game was preceded by a film showing and followed by drinks
and other refreshment." KGB officers circulated among the Marines, "sizing up potential prospects." Later the officers appeared
at a bowling alley frequented by the Marines and said they would
like to learn how to bowl.

The manual gives other accounts of similar KGB moves aimed at
Marines. U.S. counter-espionage officials charged with training and
monitoring the 1,300 Marine guards must either have negligently avoided
what should have been required reading for them, or else failed to learn
from it. Once again, we are left facing high levels of incompetence and
indifference. It recalls the rationale presented to me during one of the
extensive interviews I had with John Walker at his prison. More than
once during the course of our discussion, Walker said: "The government
doesn't care if it protects its secrets, so why should I?"

The Rationalizations of Aldrich Ames

America's most recently discovered traitor, Aldrich H. Ames, has provided a fairly comprehensive set of rationalizations and excuses for his actions. They serve as an appropriate conclusion for this chapter.

In an interview with *The Washington Post* at the Alexandria, Virginia jail on April 27, 1994 and, in pleading guilty to espionage on April 28th, Aldrich Ames provided significant insight into the thought processes which many traitors utilize in justifying their treason, both to themselves and, if they are caught, to the courts and the rest of the nation. Ames was motivated by money, pure and simple, but like most traitors he was able to use a variety of techniques to justify, or at least avoid concentrating on, the true motivations for his actions and their terrible consequences.

As for the fact that he was responsible for the deaths of ten people, who had undertaken personal risks far greater than those Ames will ever face, Ames exhibited remarkably little remorse or other emotion. His primary excuse appears to involve dragging those persons down to his level. Using the "spy novel" logic that betraying the Soviet Union was the same as betraying the United States, Ames claimed that the fact that both he and the agents he fingered ran the same risks and were in the same "game," and that he might be captured eventually, made them even. In Ames's words, "I have a kind of empathy with them, I really felt that we had given each other, that what I had done to them was what was going to be done to me. That, in a sense, my balance with them was even. Because . . . it's pretty sure this was not going to go on forever." Of course, it was no sure thing that Ames would ever be identified and, even now, he will not pay the ultimate price paid by each of the persons he betrayed. The Soviets at one time used a film clip in their training exercises showing a captured Soviet turncoat being lowered and raised—alive—in and out of a furnace. Yet, Ames could tell himself that he and Soviet agents were in similar circumstances.

The story of one of the Russian agents betrayed by Ames is illustrative of the difference between Ames and those he betrayed. GRU Major General Dmitri Fedorovitch Polyakov spied for the United States throughout most of the 1960's. He helped the FBI identify at least four American traitors: Army Sgt. Jack E. Dunlap, Army Lt. Col. William H. Whalen, Navy Yeoman Nelson C. Drummond and Air Force Sgt. Herbert W. Boeckenhaupt, once again demonstrating that American traitors are fingered by family and foreign agents or defectors, not our own security programs and personnel. Ames prosecutor Assistant U.S. Attorney Mark

Hulkower said Polyakov provided valuable information "utilized by every branch of the U.S. government" and that the general spied not for money but "because it was the right thing to do." In 1977 Gen. Polyakov was warned by the CIA that he was in danger of being exposed by a book being published in the United States, but he turned down an offer of asylum. When Edward Lee Howard defected to the Soviet Union, he tried to expose Polyakov, but thought Polyakov was in the KGB. Ames correctly identified Polyakov, who was then arrested and executed.

Ames also excused his actions by claiming that his actions did no damage to the interests of the United States, claiming that he is so knowledgeable and skillful that he could provide the Soviets and Russians with useless information and still be paid millions of dollars. Of course, his elimination of perhaps our entire network of Soviet informers speaks for itself.

Ames denigrated the entire intelligence system as basically useless. In his eight-page written statement he states:

"But I am compelled by my desire to be honest with this court and with the public to assure you that, as an intelligence officer with more than 30 years' experience, I do not believe that our nation's interests have been noticeably damaged by my acts, or . . . those of the Soviet Union or Russia noticeably aided.

". . . Two factors operated . . . to shape my sudden decision (to provide the KGB with the names of all Soviet agents known to him) . . . First, I had come to dissent from the decades-long shift to the extreme right in our political spectrum and from our national security and foreign policies".

In other words, disagreement with American foreign policy justifies treason.

Ames goes on:

"Second, I had come to believe that the espionage business, as carried out by the CIA and a few other American agencies, was and is a self-serving sham, carried out by careerist bureaucrats who have managed to deceive several generations of American policymakers and the public about both the necessity and the value of their work.

"There is and has been no rational need for thousands of career officers and tens of thousands of agents working around the world, primarily in and against friendly countries.

"The information our vast espionage network acquires at considerable human and ethical costs is generally insignificant or irrelevant to our policymakers.

"Our espionage establishment differs hardly at all from many other federal bureaucracies, having transformed itself into a self-serving interest group, immeasurably aided by secrecy.

"Now that the Cold War is over and the Communist tyrannies largely done for, our country still awaits a real national debate on the means and ends—and costs—of our national security policies...we need to question, as only a few have done, our real needs for intelligence collection including the highly suspect tool of espionage.

"Our counter-intelligence efforts have had dramatic success since the mid-1950's. Despite decades of scare-mongering by the bureaucrats who know better, American counter-intelligence, the CIA, the FBI and the military services have effectively penetrated and manipulated the Soviet and Warsaw Pact intelligence services on a massive scale. Though it had been considered important to conceal the scale of our successes from the other side, our counter-intelligence chieftains have routinely gone overboard, violating the truth in preferring to whip up hysteria on this topic. Frankly, these spy wars are a sideshow which have had no real impact on our significant security interests over the years. The government's case against me as represented on the Statement of Facts reflects this basic distinction between intelligence and counter-intelligence. The government concentrates upon the counter-intelligence compromises, and ignores the huge quantity of information on United States foreign, defense and security policies which I provided the USSR and Russia.

"I earnestly hope that an enlightened view of our nation's true and enduring security interests can emerge from a real debate on the issues. Intelligence collection, including espionage, is too important and costly an undertaking to be left to its traditional, self-serving managers."

The foregoing is an imaginative mix of truth and fantasy which cannot be considered to be either a reason or an excuse for betraying either programs or persons. Although United States espionage activities did not cause the fall of the Soviet Union, it is indisputable that intelligence and covert operations were critical in many American foreign policy successes (and failures) over the past fifty years, and it should be obvious by now that an effective intelligence capability is essential.

The claim that American counter-intelligence efforts have been more successful than the agencies have admitted is hardly an excuse for treason, any more than the statement that intelligence itself is unnecessary.

In summary, Aldrich Ames committed his treason for money and, both at the time of his crimes and later, tried to excuse his actions by telling himself, and us, that:

- It was permissible to cause the deaths of nine or ten people because he was at risk also.
- America's intelligence efforts are unnecessary and, perhaps intrinsically wrong. Since the Cold War is over, there is no more threat or need for security or intelligence.
- Counter-intelligence is insignificant.
- Ames is so knowledgeable that he could sell information which the Soviets and Russians wanted but would not really damage the United States.
- Ames had "transferred his loyalties," not to the Soviets, but to "the kinds of things that were happening." In other words, to the lifestyle that his blood money enabled him to lead. This he considered to be above the interests of the United States.

When asked how he could live with the knowledge that he had betrayed his country and his oath, Ames said "I tend to put some of these things in separate boxes, and compartment feelings and thoughts". Actually, although Ames may have a greater ability than most traitors to develop complicated rationales to excuse his actions, it all comes down to the same thing: an overwhelming ego and selfishness, and lack of standards, discipline and morality, which permitted him to sell out his nation and set himself above other human beings.

Finally, in his concern that the government is emphasizing his counter-intelligence betrayals too much, Ames admits the damage done by his release of massive amounts of foreign, defense and security policies to the Soviets and, later, the Russians. Ames himself thereby emphasizes the critical need for security—the protection of America's secrets.

SIX

Continuing Threats

The sentiment is often expressed: "The Cold War is over and we have won!" Those who represent themselves in this fashion usually mean a great deal more by it than what the words actually say. Often believed but not explicitly stated, for example, is the view that defense and national security are of vastly lesser importance now that the Cold War is over—as if the Soviet Union and its satellites were the only potential enemies the United States ever had or will have, and Russia herself is now a peaceful, stable democratic country instead of a highly unstable one with strong nationalist, absolutist, and aggressive tendencies.

The question of security may loom even larger in the future when it is no longer quite so clear exactly who America's actual or potential enemies are, or, indeed, whether America even has enemies. We began hearing about the "peace dividend" as soon as the Soviet empire began to come apart. Instead, what we very quickly got was the unexpected Gulf War (concerning which we have already cited an instance of successful espionage.)

No, America's need for improved security did not end with the Cold War. There is perhaps now even a greater need. To prove that this is indeed the case, we need only look at the situation in the wake of the break-up, first, of the Communist satellite empire in Eastern Europe, and then of the Soviet Union itself and its constituent republics, including Russia. We also need to consider the threat other countries may pose, as well as the prospects for technical and economic espionage, concluding this chapter by looking at what our response should be.

THE GLASNOST EFFECT

In 1985, Mikhail Gorbachev, the new leader of the Soviet Union, initiated two new and widely publicized programs: *perestroika*, or "restructuring," allowing increased political freedom, more entrepreneurial opportunities, and greater governmental honesty within the Soviet Union and *glasnost*, or "openness," involving a more open attitude and a new era of understanding and cooperation with the Western democracies. Over the ensuing five years, the Soviet Union pulled its troops out of Afghanistan. The Eastern European countries were allowed to go their own way, freeing themselves from direct Soviet domination. The Berlin Wall came tumbling down, and Germany was reunified after more than forty years of division.

The Union of Soviet Socialist Republics itself became substantially more cooperative, and, after much agony over opposing an ally, ended up supporting the coalition led by the United States in opposition to Iraq's occupation of Kuwait, at least to the point of agreeing that Iraq must evacuate Kuwait. Interestingly, the Russians did not entirely cease their intelligence or their military assistance, either to Iraq or to their Communist surrogates in Afghanistan. For the latter they continued to dedicate massive amounts of weaponry and munitions, even after the Soviet Union itself was dissolved in December 1991.

During the Gulf War, the old Soviet propaganda machine proved that it had lost none of its former virulence, issuing claims, for example, that the United States intended to destroy Iraq and install itself as a permanent imperial fixture in the area, a fabrication entirely worthy of those for which, in its heyday, it was famous.

In the era of *perestroika* and *glasnost*, the Russians were quite successful in portraying themselves as cooperative and even approached a New York public relations firm in order to discuss possible ways of improving their image. Mercifully, the firm was not engaged, although similar PR efforts continue today, and American security and intelligence types are now teaming up with "former" KGB people in various entrepreneurial ventures.

However, certain continuing realities regarding Russia suggest that perhaps the country's situation and long-range objectives do not always entirely coincide with the warm and benevolent image that has been projected. The West would love to love a new democratic Russia, of course, but it is far from clear that the next step for the West is simply to lay down its arms and embrace the new Russia. The Russian bear has not lost all its teeth.

As late as 1991, for example, Gorbachev was continuing to make clear not only that he remained a confirmed Communist but that Communism remained the only ideology permitted within the Soviet Union. Even though this stand ultimately failed, it was in response to external realities rather than to any change of heart. Gorbachev had permitted the Red Army to occupy the Lithuanian Ministry of Justice, murdering unarmed civilians in the process, at the very time Moscow was trumpeting its benevolent new intentions. Of course, the Red Army claimed that it had moved into Lithuania, and then into Latvia and Estonia as well, because ethnic Russians in these areas had asked for protection, and that the army had only fired when fired upon. Such pretexts were exactly the same ones employed by Hitler when aggressing against Czechoslovakia and Poland in 1938 and 1939. Could such things happen again? What would be the pretext? Ethnic Russians asking for help? We should not forget that ethnic Russians remain in all of the successor republics of the now dismantled Soviet Union. The Soviets had once again reverted to the hobnail foot, and the Big Lie was used as justification, just as in the day of Stalin.

Then, in the late summer of 1991, there came one of the most astounding of all the remarkable events in the East in those tumultuous years: a bevy of the old hard-line Communists in Gorbachev's government attempted a coup presumably intended to return the country to the old tired ways. For a few dramatic days the entire Soviet Union hovered on the brink, wavering between relative democracy and the type of dictatorship which had driven it for 74 years.

In the end, the courageous and steadfast actions of Boris Yeltsin and his supporters turned the tide. Yeltsin himself came into a new prominence as a result of the role he played against the attempted coup of the hardliners and shortly was to become unique as the first democratically elected leader of Russia. Meanwhile, on Christmas Day, 1991, the Soviet Union itself officially went out of existence, succeeded by fourteen Republics in a looser (and more unstable) Commonwealth of Independent States. A new day appeared to have dawned across the whole vast expanse of the Eurasian land mass that had been the Czarist empire and then the Soviet Union.

Boris Yeltsin's attempts to grapple with an intractable parliament and an intractable economy should not have given rise to the sometimes uncritical optimism that has been expressed about him. Hailed as "democratic," he has nevertheless been forced to rule largely by decree from the beginning of his presidency. His celebrated conflicts with the parliament elected under the old, Communist-era constitution were frequently the subject of front-page stories, leading finally, in October 1993, to an armed uprising against *him*. Again it was close. The issue was truly in doubt; the victory of the Yeltsin forces was not inevitable. And this time the coup was not bloodless; Russian troops and even tanks were called in to attack the armed insurgents, including elected delegates, who occupied the Russian White House, or Parliament, which was badly damaged in the shelling. A more extended civil war was narrowly averted, and the fact that Russian troops shed Russian blood will not soon be forgotten.

It is both significant and ominous that Yeltsin's regime managed to survive this second national coup attempt in the short space of two years only with the support of the Russian military. It provided an enormously enhanced role to the military in Yeltsin's "democratic" regime, resulting, for example, in a new Russian hardline against possible NATO membership for such former Communist satellite countries as Poland, the Czech Republic, Slovakia, and Hungary.

Even more ominously, the whole period of Yeltsin's term of office has witnessed more or less continuous armed conflict in such former Soviet Republics as Armenia, Azerbaijan, and central Asia—and even Siberia and the Russian Far East—in which the Russian military has perforce been involved. In the fall of 1993, the role played by Russia, apparently instigated by the Russian military, in helping to fight against the democratically elected government of Georgia, hardly represented a plus for democracy. At the beginning of 1994, Russian troops were operating in Moldova, Georgia, Azerbaijan, Estonia, Latvia, and Tajikistan, and their participation in these local civil wars was not calculated to enhance the independence of these former Soviet Republics. Most distressing of all was Russia's brutal assault on Chechnya.

The elections held in December, 1993, through which Boris Yeltsin had hoped to break the political gridlock between the president and parliament, were a mixed blessing at best. Although Yeltsin did succeed in securing voter approval for a new post-Communist constitution—a constitution providing sufficient presidential power for the incumbent to rule by decree in many important respects—the elections themselves illustrated the Nation's confusion and instability. Over 100 political parties competed within 13 broader coalitions. The ultra-rightists, some of them openly calling for the restoration of the Russian empire and Soviet-style power, together with the ex-Communists, actually garnered more votes than the two major democratic reform movements taken together. Further political stalemate and instability are the most likely results.

One troubling result of these elections was the success of the absurdly misnamed Liberal Democrats, a fascist-type party which won 23 per cent of the popular vote and control of nearly 15 per cent of the seats in the lower house in the new parliament. The leader of this party, Vladimir Zhirinovsky, called for Poland to again be divided up between Russia and Germany, for Latvia, Lithuania and Estonia to again be annexed by Russia, and even for Alaska to be returned to Russia—by force if necessary. Such results certainly demonstrate the degree of confusion and frustration which continue to exist in Russia. A return to dictatorship is not out of the question in such a country and such a climate. Zhirinovsky's power has since waned, but the attitudes which propelled him to parliament remain unabated throughout the country.

Still other external conflicts, some of potential military significance, also remain. There has still been no final settlement, for example, between Russia and Ukraine on either the division of nuclear weapons or the division of the Black Sea fleet. Such conflicts can be escalated at any time, and can even lead to possible armed conflict. Similarly, it should not be forgotten that, as civil war continues to rage in former Communist Yugoslavia, and as peaceful solutions have continued to elude the international community, Russia was once the historic ally of Serbia; their strong historic and racial ties have severely hampered the United Nations' peacekeeping efforts.

How things will ultimately turn out—how the vast Eurasian land mass will end up being organized politically—cannot be foreseen. Several things are clear, however: whether ruled over by one single state or divided into several states, this huge area, commanding enormous resources, will remain a significant factor on the world scene. Russia by itself is still the world's second power and is heavily armed with nuclear weapons. One or more of the former Soviet republics, including Ukraine, may also continue to be nuclear powers. Furthermore, the very process by which these political and military questions have to sort themselves out is not likely to be a stable one. The entire area has no tradition of democracy or peaceful settlement of differences. Historically, the area has been unified and stabilized by Russian military power.

Has the Russian Bear become a consistent and reliable advocate of democracy and peace throughout the world? In the Bush Administration, Secretary of State James A. Baker stated that he was confident that the Russian nuclear force was in reliable hands although vigilance was still necessary. His successor, Warren Christopher, has kept the Clinton Administration on the same pro-Yeltsin-regime tack, but this confidence has not always been supported by events.

In any case, how have we reached the point where we can take comfort in the fact that there are still 30,000 missiles or so in the hands of the Russians? There is no way to avoid the conclusion that it constitutes at least a potential threat to American security.

Evidence of that instability and the danger to not only Western Europe, but the world, was provided when, on August 10, 1994, two Spaniards and a Colombian man were arrested at Munich's airport when they arrived from Moscow aboard a Lufthansa plane with "up to 17.5 ounces of weapons-grade plutonium" in their luggage.

Security sources confirmed the seizure and the "alarmed German government on August 13, 1994 immediately sought talks with Moscow on the *growing problem* of nuclear smuggling from Russia." (Emphasis added.)

According to experts, 35 ounces of the extremely pure plutonium-239 is all that is needed "in the hands of an expert with sophisticated equipment" to "fashion a nuclear bomb."

The German Chancellor, Helmut Kohl, called the nuclear smuggling a "grave danger" and vowed that he would talk with Boris Yeltsin, the Kremlin leader, almost immediately.

The obvious fear, underscored by German authorities, is that the nuclear materials ultimately may reach terrorist groups in countries like Iraq and Libya. The equally great fear stems from such possibilities of de-stabilization as a result of "underpaid Russian atomic scientists" selling the capabilities for the manufacture of nuclear bombs, according to the Bavarian Interior Minister, Guenter Beckstein, in statements to the German magazine, *Der Spiegel*, on August 9, 1994.

The implications not only for the security of the Western world, but for the performance and readiness of our intelligence and security systems are enormous. Human intelligence is of greater importance in a period of instability, when it is almost impossible to know the minds of terrorists and terrorist nations, than in the time of the Cold War.

We are living in a time of great peril and the maintenance of the highest quality and excellence of our security system is of the greatest urgency.

At the height of the power of the Soviet Union, there were Americans who denied that there was any threat to America from the Soviet Union or from Communism generally. It is perhaps not surprising that there are those who believe that there is no threat today. Such people are not necessarily dupes or unduly influenced by leftism. Many observers always did believe the threat was exaggerated and therefore often deplored the tremendous military investment the United States felt obliged to make in its own defense. Many of these same people, and others, would now like to see this tremendous investment almost totally transferred to domestic needs. Still others have *always* emphasized these domestic priorities, while others yet have perhaps always lived on the elixir of "wishful thinking."

To keep things in perspective, we should not forget that there were some who were silent even when overt, armed Soviet aggression was at its peak, as when demonstrators were shot down by tanks in the streets of Budapest, when Prague was occupied, when Afghanistan invaded, or when Lithuanians were shot down in cold blood. Even in those days there were those who counseled the United States against opposing the Soviet Union. So it is perhaps not surprising that at the first hint of a smile from a Russian leader, they are ready to begin celebrating perpetual peace.

Certainly in the aftermath of the demise of Soviet tyranny—of a totalitarian dictatorship that oppressed over 200 million people for close to four generations—we may be permitted some genuine celebrating. However, there are a number of other important considerations we must never lose sight of even as we rejoice over an obvious turn for the better.

First, people who have never understood, or had experience of, a democratic system cannot easily or quickly move out of the cocoon of total state control into a world of political and economic freedom. While we may hope that the freedom now won by the peoples of the former Soviet empire will be a permanent acquisition, we cannot be certain of this, nor can we rule out further coups or takeovers, either in Russia or in some of the other former Soviet republics and satellite countries. Takeovers by hard-liners, military adventurers, or others whose rise would be inimical to the security of the United States remain a distinct possibility in a highly volatile situation.

Second, a working market economy does not rise up automatically out of the ruins of a state-controlled economy. There is bound to be enormous stress as well as continued instability in this whole vast territory which still lacks many essential means or structures for producing, distributing, delivering, and marketing the goods and services people need for economic stability and prosperity.

Third, many false starts and mistakes will inevitably be made by the new leaders in the successor countries to the former Soviet Union and its former satellites. Many have already been made. This has resulted in enormous resentment and agitation against these same leaders, again making for great instability, with some countries continuing in an almost permanent state of turmoil and unrest. None of this can be very reassuring.

Fourth, conflict among the successor states with Russia or among themselves could easily lead—indeed already has led—to local conflicts and even to "little wars," as we have noted in the cases of Armenia, Azerbaijan, Georgia, etc. Such little wars can have a big impact on American security.

Fifth, all the Communists and apparatchiks who administered the previous system are still there. Generally, their personal positions have not always been enhanced (although some of them have been among the first to get rich), and so some of them at least are perhaps ready and even eager to support any leader promising to restore their former privileged positions in society and their guaranteed jobs in place of today's uncertain freedom. Recent elections in Poland and Hungary returned many former Communists to office. The "old days" are probably already looking considerably better for many Russians, particularly those who enjoyed privileged positions under the old Communist system.

Sixth, it will be extremely difficult for Russia to reverse thousands of years of expansionism and resist the temptation to reconstitute the Soviet Union, perhaps under some other name and political/economic system. A return by Russia to a policy of forced annexation of other countries would certainly bring it into some type of friction, if not conflict, with the United States. This continuing desire for expansion is already surfacing in pronouncements of Russian leaders and in such documents as the report released in September 1994 by the Russian External Intelligence Service entitled "Russia-C.I.S.: Does the Western Position Need Correction?" Of course, its conclusion is that the West does indeed need to modify its opinion that the Soviet Union will not be reconstituted.

The article, which obviously represents the position of some in power in Russia, includes the following points: The West is attempting to prevent Russia from strengthening itself as a world power; The process of reunification will be a long one which may result in some "alienation" with the West but will not result in a resumption of the Cold War; Either the reunification will occur, which will bring "stabilization, democratization and . . . reforms" or groups favoring separate development will gain power in the C.I.S. States "with assistance from abroad," resulting in "growing authoritarian, anti-democratic tendencies . . . society's criminalization, violation of the rights of ethnic minorities, and massive abuses of human rights"—all because they didn't become Russian protectorates.

All these considerations suggest that things are far from settled in the territories of the former Soviet Union and its Eastern European satellite empire. They suggest that the American stance should be one of watchful waiting for some time to come. Rarely has it been as important to continue to "be prepared" as it is now. These considerations further suggest, as a matter of common sense, that our own intelligence activities with respect to the area must actually be increased, if we expect to be successful in knowing what is going on there and dealing with events from the standpoint of our own best interests. And to the extent that the present level or perhaps even an increased level of intelligence is the issue, then the question of the security of our intelligence and communications again becomes a topic of the foremost importance.

Unfortunately, not everyone in the United States is thinking along these lines. For example, in February 1991, a conference was held by a coalition of activist groups under the auspices of the American Civil Liberties Union (ACLU). This conference aimed at developing strategies for phasing out all government activities which, presumably for "Cold War" reasons alone, involved secrecy or counter-intelligence. Now, with the end of the Cold War, many of these activities are thought to be wholly dispensable. Senator Bill Bradley, Democrat of New Jersey, for example, said at this particular conference: "'Economic espionage' by foreign powers in the U.S. must not become a pretext for a new counter-intelligence surveillance by the FBI on either foreigners or Americans."

It may not be too clear to the average American why America should not protect herself from what is conceded to be "economic espionage" directed against her. Things seemed to be crystal clear for this ACLU-sponsored conference, however. The conference's goals included:

- Reduction or elimination of government classification of documents and information in order to permit full public access.
- Unrestricted free exchange of ideas and information and unrestricted travel with all countries of the world.
- No future secret, warrantless searches of homes of suspected agents of foreign powers.
- A change of FBI Counter-intelligence Guidelines to prohibit surveillance of law-abiding Americans opposed to U.S. policies.
- Full disclosure of the U.S. intelligence budget.
- Prior public debate, or at least congressional approval, for all overt and covert U.S. operations.
- No future CIA censorship of writings of former intelligence officials, particularly when the items deleted are essential to any public discussion.
- Narrowing of government employee secrecy agreements.
- No questioning of employee political beliefs and affiliations.

• No continued exemptions for nuclear weapons procedures from environmental impact statements or laws.

One of the sponsors of this ACLU conference, Senator Daniel Patrick Moynihan (D-NY), introduced a Senate bill on January 22, 1991, which he subtitled "The End of the Cold War Act of 1991." This proposed bill called for the abolition of the CIA, and the transference of all its functions to the Department of State. The bill would also have eliminated the president's right to deny immigrant status to those vocally opposed to the American way of life and to those in favor of the violent overthrow of the U.S. government. The bill would further require publication of the total national intelligence budget. Senator Moynihan was quoted as saying when introducing this bill: "With the Cold War over, we must re-define ourselves and purge our bureaucracy of the vestiges of this struggle."

The assumption behind such proposals as those of the ACLU and such legislation as Senator Moynihan's bill could only be the belief that the United States is not in need of any security or intelligence. This belief, in turn, could only be based on the premise that the United States has no enemies or potential enemies. But as we see daily in our newspapers and newscasts, America has enemies, and they are prepared to take whatever aggressive actions they can get away with. This, of course, has not prevented politicians such as Senator Bradley or Senator Moynihan from offering such prescriptions anyway. They may not even suffer politically for having done so, given the limited awareness and short memory of the American people.

We should be thankful, however, that those who would thus diminish our intelligence and security capabilities are pretty clearly in the minority at the moment and that the evidence is that the great majority of Americans believe that this country does have a right to protect itself and must guard against dangers from abroad. Incumbent upon those of us who are in that majority, however, is a much more difficult decision than simply imagining that we might somehow dispense with intelligence and security in the post-Cold-War era. The challenge is finding a realistic and practical answer to the question: What is the appropriate level of commitment, in terms both of money and of the degree of control to be exercised, which the United States must make in the current international atmosphere in order to protect the sensitive material which must continue to be designated "classified" by proper government authority?

There can be little doubt that the reduction in international tensions will make it even more difficult to maintain the integrity of American secrets. Therefore we surely need to reflect on some of the following considerations:

- The argument is already being widely made that the United States now faces no dangerous enemies and therefore needs no security capability, and that all of the money currently being spent to protect our national secrets should now be reduced, or phased out, to be spent instead as a "peace dividend."
- With no Cold War adversary, government managers and operations personnel may be tempted to rationalize that there is no one interested in our secrets anymore anyway, and therefore there is no real security threat; if there is no threat, there is no need for any government security system or for strict observance of security procedures and restrictions already in place. Incidentally, as we have seen, some government managers unfortunately appear to have held this belief even while the Soviet threat loomed large and unmistakable.
- Others may conclude that, with the threat of nuclear war so greatly diminished, our secrets are now less important than they were before, and therefore less deserving of vigilance in being protected.
- Certainly potential traitors will use both of the previous arguments to excuse any betrayals they have decided upon. If there are neither any significant threats to America's interests, nor any significant secrets to be protected, what could possibly be the harm in selling whatever someone is willing to buy?
- Finally, enforcement of security rules and punishment of security violations will become more difficult if managers, military leaders, prosecutors, judges and juries, begin to question whether any serious crime has been committed by someone engaged in selling secrets to a foreign power.

These are only a few of the questions which are already very much in the air since the end of the Cold War. However, countries which have a capability to spy on the United States effectively, and to benefit from doing so, have greatly increased in number, motivation, and sophistication. As the Soviet Union has disintegrated, other powers have appeared on the scene. China, Iraq, Iran, Syria, and Russia itself are examples of countries which have an obvious interest in knowing America's military secrets. These and many other countries covet our economic secrets, including Japan, the countries of Latin America and even our historical allies. Still other countries are interested in, for example, the highly integrated and miniaturized weapons and industrial devices which have been developed in this country.

Considering the tremendous impact which decisions concerning the severity of current threats may have on America's commitment to its own security programs, it is appropriate to consider these threats in more detail.

IS THERE STILL A 'SOVIET' THREAT?

For more than forty-five years the Soviet Union and its allies and satellites constituted the greatest threat to the security of the United States. The disintegration of the Soviet satellite empire, followed by the break-up of the Soviet Union itself, and the dissolution of the Warsaw Pact, have all greatly reduced this threat. What next? Obviously, nobody can predict with any accuracy very far into the future. However, among other things, we need to reflect seriously on the following points:

- The successor republics to the old Soviet Union continue to undergo tremendous stress and change. Everything is in short supply, chaos reigns, and massive hunger is a distinct possibility in some cases.
- No leader or politician such as Boris Yeltsin, for example, can be considered to have a "lock" on power in Russia. The same thing is true in the other successor states. Moreover, most of these leaders were themselves Communists up until "yesterday," and we still have no idea how many of them—or *their* successors—might end up as authoritarian dictators, wielding arbitrary power as many of them are used to doing. Particularly in the Ukraine, for example, which suffered so much in the early days of collectivization, many of the features of the failed Communist system have been retained.
- If economic improvements do not come fairly quickly to the successor states of the Soviet Union, the pressure for "drastic" solutions may become overwhelming. If not a return to Communism, then at least there could be a return to authoritarian systems or military dictatorships which could both destabilize the region further and threaten peace and world order. The fact that Vladimir Zhirinovsky could receive nearly a quarter of the popular vote, indicates only too eloquently the state of mind of the people. A massive, violent lurch backwards is always possible.
- Russian expansionism was invented neither by the Communists nor by the Soviet Union. Over centuries Russia became an empire by conquering and annexing its neighbors. Over the long term, "Russia" has been synonymous with "aggression."
- The fact that the Russians continued to utilize the services of the traitor Aldrich Ames after the Soviet Union was dissolved and the

Cold War was supposedly "over" should make it quite plain that Russian-directed espionage will continue.

- It has been verified that thousands of tanks and other weapons, previously understood to have been destroyed under arms reduction agreements with the United States, were instead retained, once again demonstrating the kind of duplicity on the part of the Russian leaders which was par for the course in the Communist past, and which apparently is still the case today.
- Elements of the *Stasi*, the Communist East German secret police, joined the KGB after the break-up, making up for a major portion of the capability that was lost when East Germany was united with West Germany.
- At the present time, Russia's major problem is economic. It is not likely that the nation whose leaders have shown few or no scruples in appropriating the secrets of others will refrain from using one of its greatest capabilities, its intact intelligence network, to acquire whatever economic and technical information it can acquire. We surely face not only continued military and political espionage but increased economic and technical spying. Even with the best of intentions, a nation suffering protracted economic chaos will not hesitate to spy in order to survive.
- History has demonstrated that, whenever relations with Russia have begun to warm up, espionage has actually increased, in part because a period of friendly relations offers a multitude of new espionage opportunities not available during periods of tension and suspicion. Immediately after the beginning of Willy Brandt's Ostpolitik (The easing of tensions between the Soviet Union and West Germany) the KGB substantially increased its activity in West Germany, just as it had done after the Helsinki accords.
- In April, 1990, a Russian defector, Major General Alexander Karbainov, reported that in the time period following the launching of Gorbachev's reforms in 1985, up until 1990, the Russians had arrested thirty spies, and executed twenty-nine of them.
- On November 29, 1989, the CIA Director William Webster was asked at the National Press Club if the KGB and the GRU military intelligence services had slowed their efforts under Soviet President Mikhail Gorbachev. Webster replied: "We believe just the reverse is taking place . . . Around the world, our [CIA] stations are reporting more aggressive action and a more robust intelligence collection effort, more effort to recruit our embassy and intelligence personnel than we have seen for a long time." The KGB was using less confrontational spying tactics in an apparent effort to avoid embar-

rassing public disclosures, Webster added. "But the activity is there
and it's very logical that it should be."
- On April 4, 1990, FBI Director William Sessions stated before Congress that Russian intelligence operations in the United States were
on the rise, despite warmer relations. Sessions stated: "While current U.S. Soviet relations present an unprecedented climate of cooperation, the FBI has documented the reality that the Soviet intelligence operations have increased in sophistication, scope, and number . . . As a result of arms control agreements, business opportunities in both the Soviet Union and the United States, immigration
policies and numerous cultural and educational exchanges, Soviet
intelligence services have now a much greater opportunity than ever
before to exploit the United States and its citizens in an effort to
compromise our national security . . . Foreign intelligence services
routinely use visitors, emigres, students, and scholars to conduct
intelligence operations directed against the United States . . . We see
no evidence that this will decrease in the next year . . . There is no
reason to believe espionage is on the decline . . . We must not drop
our guard, especially when faced with the prevailing uncertainties."
    Mr. Sessions also said spying by agents of the Chinese intelli-
gence service is a continuing problem, and both the Soviets and
Chinese are seeking defense secrets and high-technology data that
would enhance their economies. "The number of Chinese students
and scholars in the United States increased to more than 40,000 last
year, including more than 2,600 diplomatic and commercial personnel. There are also an estimated 25,000 visiting business and government officials and 20,000 emigres from China."
- On January 21, 1991, *The Washington Times* reported on Russian
espionage and military efforts carried out during the Iraqi War:
    "The Soviet Union is intensifying efforts to spy on U.S. and allied
military operations in the Gulf conflict and is believed to be gaining
valuable information on U.S. war-fighting tactics and capabilities . . .
    "Meanwhile, CIA sources said new shipments of Soviet arma-
ments were sent recently to Yemen and Libya—both allies of Iraq—
and some analysts fear the equipment may be diverted to Baghdad.
Also, an Eastern European government still allied with Moscow
delivered a shipment of Soviet SA-16 surface-to-air missiles to
Baghdad shortly before the outbreak of hostilities . . .
    "U.S. intelligence officials said the Soviets are concentrating a
formidable array of electronic monitoring equipment in their spying
effort. The equipment includes numerous photographic satellites
and ground stations in the southern Soviet Union, Syria, and Yemen.
Several ships in the region are also supplying electronic intelli-

gence. The main objective of the Soviet spying is to intercept communications and other signals that would provide clues to U.S. military operations. For example, the Soviets might be able to learn how U.S. aircraft were able to orchestrate simultaneous air strikes. They could also learn how effective U.S. precision weapons are and how to develop defenses against them...

"There are an estimated 150 Soviet military advisers in Iraq. What role they are playing in supporting the Iraqi military is uncertain, although some analysts suspect the technicians are operating Soviet-made air defense and electronic warfare equipment.

"Earlier... allied naval forces intercepted a Soviet ship destined for the Jordanian port of Aqaba that carried an undeclared shipment of weapons and spare parts meant for Iraq. The contraband was found inside the captain's cabin and the ship was forced to go to an Egyptian port. The discovery raised questions about whether the Soviets were publicly supporting the allied coalition against Iraq, while secretly supporting a country that in the past has been a key purchaser of Soviet weapons."

- The Soviet Union did not leave Afghanistan on moral grounds; rather it was for reasons of economics, military failure and morale.
- The Eastern European nations were not unshackled for moral or political reason, but for economic ones.
- Although the Soviet Union admitted the illegality of its annexation of the Baltic states, it was obviously prepared to retain them via force and murder.
- A Readers Digest article, printed shortly before the ascendancy of Yeltsin, exposed a special KGB group, the "Special Reserve", which infiltrates Soviet Diplomatic and Commercial missions, unbeknownst even to others in the mission. The purpose is both to spy upon the other Soviets and to provide a more effective cover, fooling Western political and business representatives into believing that they are speaking to their counterparts in the Soviet Union. The KGB can then more effectively perform its espionage, as well as conveying "party line" messages that appear to be genuine thoughts from individual Soviets.

President Clinton's short-sightedness concerning Russian expansionism was demonstrated again in July, 1994, when, in exchange for a Russian promise not to veto a U. N. resolution permitting an invasion of Haiti, Clinton supported Moscow's request for U.N. endorsement of its "peace-keeping" efforts in Georgia.

As columnist Lally Weymouth stated in the July 24, 1994, *The Washington Post*:

In the past, Russia has insisted its interest in Georgia and the rest of the "near abroad" turned on a desire to protect Russians living in the republics. Now that claim no longer withstands scrutiny. There aren't many Russians in Abkhazia. Currently, Russia asserts that it desires to bring peace to embattled regions. Close study of the situation in Georgia doesn't support Moscows's claim. The Russians, after all, supported the Abkhaz separatist against Shevardnadze (the man who helped bring down the "Evil Empire").

Thanks to Clinton's eagerness to invade Haiti, Russia—with U.S. support—has been granted U.N. backing to begin to reconstitute its empire. Georgia will likely prove only the first step toward a new Russian assertiveness. Moscow is also seeking to amend the Treaty on Conventional Forces in Europe so it can move troops and armaments to its Caucasus region just across the border from Georgia.

According to well-informed experts, Russia will move next on Nagorno-Karabakh, an Armenian-populated enclave, where the government of Azerbaijan is already under pressure to permit Russian peace-keepers and/or a "separating" force. Abkhazia will probably be the model: Russia will in all likelihood freeze Armenian gains in place and then sign an agreement permitting it to establish bases.

The world is certainly paying a high price for Russian support of a Haitian invasion. What will the Administration offer Russia for support in those areas where our national interest is truly at stake?

The above examples must lead us to the conclusion that there is strong impetus for Russia to continue "business as usual" in the espionage field, and that Russian espionage is continuing, despite the wishes of such Senators as Bill Bradley and Pat Moynihan.

As late as March 1992, CIA Director Robert Gates was telling Congress that "we've seen relatively little change in the Russian intelligence service's operations in the United States." The first priority of the Russians, according to Mr. Gates, "is still the United States and . . . their first priority in that context is still the acquisition of technology and high-technology equipment." Wayne R. Gilbert, FBI Intelligence Division Chief, told the Associated Press: "More and more we see that it's a formal intelligence operation directed from Moscow. *We see no reduction.*" (Emphasis added.) If there is no longer formally a "Soviet" espionage threat, there is most certainly a Russian one "directed from

Moscow." In spite of all the changes since 1989 this is something that has remained.

Russia has been able to project a positive, benevolent, and harmless international image at the same time that it is going right on with such things as covert operations and espionage. The following story from *The Washington Times* of January 11, 1990, illustrates this:

> Perhaps the most sensitive new task assigned to the KGB is propagating the Soviet "charm offensive" in Western Europe. The double aim is to erase the image of the "Gulag state" and make friends abroad who will sympathize with Moscow's plight.
>
> Soviet agents work much less than before through Western Communist parties, which are now discredited, preferring to operate through unofficial Soviet professional groups and their Western counterparts, as well as directly through the media. During the past six months the once-reticent KGB has given some 40 interviews, mostly to Soviet media, according to a count by the U.S.-financed Radio Liberty. The interviews emphasized the KGB role in fighting organized crime and its offers of cooperation with Western security organizations in efforts to stem international terrorism.
>
> Soviet officials appear frequently on television in France, Italy, and West Germany, where they speak with remarkable frankness. Some of these officials, who frequently captivate their audiences, were subsequently identified as KGB agents.
>
> Despite the increased sophistication, Soviet affairs experts in Western Europe see the new direction as merely a change of emphasis, tactics, and approach for the KGB. According to an analyst at the Institute for International Relations in Paris, the "KGB has become essential in supporting Soviet foreign policy initiatives by portraying them as beneficial to the rest of Europe."

Another analyst, Victor Yasmann of Radio Liberty, has said that "the KGB has finished . . . in better shape than the party itself." Remember, while the Soviet Union may "come and go", rather, go and maybe come, the KGB and Russia will remain forever, and the U.S. and Russia share few basic, cultural, emotional or other ties. Their yearnings and our realities hold many antagonisms.

In a speech made to the Sarasota Tiger Bay Club in March 1990, concerning the dramatic changes that were taking place in Eastern Europe and the Soviet Union, William A. Webster, then recently retired director of the Central Intelligence Agency (and also former director of the FBI), made the following observations which still remain most pertinent:

> I am convinced that intelligence—that is, information about the plans, the intentions, and the capabilities of other nations—is critical in this period of change. And I want to tell you about our continuing counter-intelligence concerns, which I believe will take on even more importance in protecting our national security well into this decade ... The Soviet Union remains a nuclear super-power, let there be no doubt about that. Strategic forces continue to be modernized, and their military research and development programs continue to receive generous funding ... Even with the reductions, in strategic terms, they can still reach all their targets.
>
> At the same time, counter-intelligence—our need to know what other countries want and how they are going about getting it—remains critical for us. And in the 1990s, as countries focus more on economic competitiveness, what will be sought is sensitive information that will give a country a competitive edge ... Attempts to acquire sensitive technology by all nations are increasingly becoming more sophisticated. But in this new political climate, a climate where the enemy is not as clearly defined, we expect collection activities to be more selective ... I think the KGB has become less confrontational in the sense that they avoid the clumsy or blatant kinds of intimidation that would create a major press issue, but the activity is there and it will continue ... It is important to remember that espionage and counter-intelligence are widely recognized in Eastern Europe as necessary functions. The apparatus for this work is likely to remain in place. The intelligence and counter-intelligence services may be re-organized and re-subordinated to new elected masters instead of the party bosses, but the work will continue ... I don't expect military intelligence collection efforts to abate—certainly not in the near future ... The new political leadership in Eastern Europe is bringing in new oversight mechanisms. We hope oversight will reduce some hostile intelligence activity, such as passing sensitive technology to the Soviets, an activity which is incompatible with requests for U.S. loans and aid ...

William Webster's service at various times as director of both the CIA and the FBI surely afforded him a unique perspective on these matters. Nothing that has occurred since he spoke, even in the fast-moving Russian and Eastern European situations, would seem to indicate that his analysis was anything but accurate. Russian and other Eastern European intelligence systems are likely to remain in place performing some of the same espionage functions they have always performed, though hopefully under governments which will be democratically elected and thus perhaps less antithetical to the interests of the United States. Yet, this too remains uncertain.

OTHER NATIONS

The former Soviet Union was hardly the only power that ever attempted to steal secrets from the United States. Many other powers have also been involved, often successfully. Moreover, the technical details of instruments of war are not the only objects of espionage. There are many other types of information which the United States understandably desires to keep confidential in order to protect the country's vital interests. Meanwhile, other countries are equally desirous of acquiring such information and, generally, are willing to pay dearly to discover it. The following are merely examples:

- United States strategy for any of the scores of different sessions of negotiations going on in any given year.
- The American positions on NATO membership for Eastern European countries such as Poland, the Czech Republic, Slovakia, and Hungary.
- American support, open or covert, for world leaders; economic positions to be supported, country by country; political leaders versus political leaders; projects versus other projects, etc.
- Elements of government programs and budgets under development.
- Planned diplomatic initiatives.
- Strategies in a vast array of political, military, economic, and geopolitical arenas.
- Names of informants and dissidents in other countries.
- Space exploration, rocketry, telecommunications, and other scientific research; also, inventions, technological developments, etc.
- Military contingency plans for various scenarios throughout the world.
- "Game plans" on world issues including negotiating strategies, issue priorities, fall-back positions, etc.
- Knowledge necessary to develop weaponry or other technologies which the United States considers unsuitable for general dissemination, such as knowledge concerning nuclear weaponry.

Clemens von Metternich of the Austrian Empire once observed that there are no permanent friends and no permanent enemies, only permanent interests. Many different examples could serve to illustrate the point. The United States and Great Britain, for example, were antagonists in two wars in America's early history, and were wary potential rivals for most of the nineteenth century, but have been faithful allies through most of the twentieth century. In this century, the Soviet Union went from being our antagonist (1920s and 1930s) to being our ally (1940s) to being our Cold War adversary (1950s through 1980s) to the present uncertain status. Germany and Japan have gone from being our bitter, hated wartime enemies to becoming our close friends and allies and then on to becoming our economic rivals. Israel, while being dependent upon the United States economically, has nevertheless readily opposed American policies when it suited their interests. Many other countries which thirty years ago were economically underdeveloped or were even colonies of a Western power are now independent with their own interests and policies. Some are already quite capable of conducting such espionage as serves their interests. As one of the most advanced technologically, as well as the wealthiest country in the world, the United States possesses a wide array of targets for anybody making the decision to profit via espionage.

Accordingly, America faces espionage threats from a wide variety of sources of which the following are examples:

- In 1985, a CIA clerk stationed in Ghana was co-opted into turning over to Capt. Jerry Rawlings' government the names of persons known to oppose the government.
- The Israelis, although allies of ours, nevertheless pose a demonstrated and highly sophisticated espionage threat, both because of their great desire for technical information and because of their formidable espionage capability. Jonathan Jay Pollard was an agent willing to work for the Israeli Mossad against his native land. As we have seen, Pollard pleaded guilty in 1986 to conspiring to provide military secrets to Israel. The Israelis insisted that the whole affair was the work of a "rogue" Israeli agent acting on his own. Over time, however, it has been revealed that Pollard in fact dealt with a very highly placed secret espionage organization (the Israeli Defense Ministry's Science Liaison Bureau) whose mission is to increase the flow of technological and scientific knowledge to Israel. This organization exists *solely* to provide covert support (espionage) for the Israeli defense industry.
- Before and during the 1991 Gulf War with Iraq, U.S. Army special-

ist Albert Sombolay passed deployment data concerning the U.S.-led allied forces and also samples of chemical weapons protection equipment to Jordan and Iraq.

- In late 1990, *Jane's Defense Weekly* stated that it was "highly probable" that certain Iraqi planes carried a version of advanced radar stolen from the U.S. by Soviet spies.
- In the 1980s a subsidiary of Toshiba was instrumental in the illegal sale to the Soviet Union of secret submarine propeller technology, which enabled submarines to escape sonar detection. After Japan made the requisite apologies, a telling comment appeared in the Americanized (sanitized) version of *The Japan That Can Say No* by Shintaro Ishihara, a member of the Japanese parliament, and Sony founder Akio Morita. The two Japanese authors made the point that Japan could seriously compromise U.S. military superiority by the simple expedient of selling missile microprocessor chips to the Russians.
- Less than six months before the Iraqi invasion of Kuwait, American scientists issued an invitation to Iraqi scientists to attend an American conference on techniques for initiating nuclear detonations.
- In late 1993, it was reported that Chinese government agents were surreptitiously searching the hotel rooms of American diplomats visiting that country, and were copying or removing classified CIA and Department of State documents.

These examples represent only a few of the espionage threats to America coming from a variety of different countries and sources. It should be evident that vital information has been at stake in most of these cases. The fact that espionage activity is now coming from such a wide variety of different countries poses new risks to our government security system. In any event, it is beyond dispute that the threat of espionage is in no way merely a Cold War problem which we can now put behind us. It is a permanent, ongoing threat to America as the major power in a modern, high-technology world.

TECHNICAL AND ECONOMIC ESPIONAGE

Our government security system and its philosophy of security do not exist solely to protect the United States against possible military threats. Economics makes all countries our potential espionage enemies and us their target. Some countries strive mightily, and too often successfully, to acquire our knowledge and technology. China, France, Japan and many other countries, have committed formidable resources to the task.

Business and commercial espionage have always been a concern of private firms in America. Perpetrators of this kind of espionage often include foreign competitors, which may be subsidized or nationalized industries in other countries. Thus, even government participation in business or commercial espionage can be encountered, as has been the case over the centuries. For example, Venice and Genoa carried on full-scale economic, as well as military, warfare during the period of the Renaissance. Enormous intrigue was involved in the competition for the spice trade, and similar intrigue is not unknown today in various industries and markets, only it is on a far more sophisticated level.

We are entering a period, in fact, when economic espionage is likely to become even more common than it has been at any previous time. We see in the Russian economy and society, for example, an increasingly desperate need to reorganize and redevelop what was left in place after the collapse of Communism. A former KGB major who defected to the United States, Stanislaw Levchenko, has warned that the KGB's First Directorate will continue in operation as part of the Russian Republic. Levchenko has predicted an expanded espionage effort to steal high-technology secrets in order to jump-start the stalled Russian economy.

Other observers agree that economic espionage is certainly one technique the Russians will use in their attempts to modernize their society, and in view of the considerable expertise they have already acquired, the KGB and GRU (military intelligence) will no doubt be major participants in this regard.

An article, "The Soviets and Our Secrets," by Lance E. Revo and Gary Figelski, which appeared in *Security Management* in February 1989, speaks pertinently on this subject. Revo and Figelski describe some of the systems and techniques used by the Soviet Union to steal both military and civilian technology. These systems and techniques will undoubtedly be continued and expanded and made more effective in the coming years.

> Since 1982, the Soviets have made a commitment to acquiring Western technology through Soviet intelligence services and their surrogates. Both the KGB (Committee for State Security) and the GRU are primarily responsible for collecting Western military and scientific information.
>
> The VPK (Military Industrial Commission) manages the development of all Soviet weapons, military equipment, and various programs to raise the technical levels of manufacturing. The VPK is the most powerful organization in the defense-research establish-

ment . . . The VPK translates requests for Western hardware and documents into lists called collection requirements. Once approved by the VPK, requirements are selectively levied among the KGB, the GRU, and at least four other national-level collection agencies . . .

The overall program involves espionage by hostile intelligence officers, overt collection by Eastern bloc officials, acquisition by scientific exchange program participants, and illegal trade-related activity. In some cases, clandestine collection is preferred over buying or developing the technology because it is cheaper and provides the best short-term results . . .

The Soviet Academy of Sciences is another collector in the VPK program. So are the GKNT (State Committee for Science and Technology) and the GKES (State Committee for Foreign Economic Relations). These three collection agencies, especially the Academy of Sciences and the GKNT, operate in the West under the guise of scientific, academic, and business conferences. They send approximately 2,000 Soviet bloc citizens to the United States each year. Many Soviet scientific personnel have been co-opted to provide assistance to the VPK in their collection activities.

Yet another effective, but less structured, Soviet collection program is the Ministry of Foreign Trade. Along with the other industrial ministries, it operates a large network of legal and illegal foreign trade organizations, commercial offices, joint companies, and foreign procurement offices. The staffs of these operations know the hardware markets and act as ready contacts for technology traders and diverters, particularly in the areas of computers and microelectronics. They are adept at taking advantage of opportunities for diversions and obtaining controlled Western products through seemingly normal trade channels. Many of the 141 Soviets expelled from 25 countries during 1983 were assigned in some capacity to the Ministry of Foreign Trade . . .

Most people are simply unaware of the highly organized and staffed, experienced and technically competent, yet wholly unprincipled apparatus which has long existed and been utilized by the Russians to acquire technical knowledge and know-how from the West, illegally and without compensation to its inventors or owners. In reading this account by Revo and Figelski, for example, we certainly get an entirely different idea of what a "collection agency" is in Russian parlance than anything we would imagine when we use or hear the phrase! We also need to reflect for a moment on the significance of the statistic that 141 Russians were expelled from 25 countries for espionage during the course of a *single year*!

The Revo and Figelski article goes on to describe another one of the espionage cases that became public in the West during the 1980s, that of Richard Mueller:

> Richard Mueller, a West German, has assisted the Soviets with acquiring Western computers, microelectronics, and other products. His involvement with illegal technology acquisition on behalf of the Soviet Union dates back to the early 1970s. Mueller has used a network of more than 75 firms operating in Austria, France, Switzerland, the United Kingdom, the United States, South Africa, and West Germany. Between 1978 and 1983, it has been estimated that Mueller delivered to the Soviets advanced computers, peripherals, and microelectronics manufacturing equipment worth at least several tens of millions of dollars.
>
> One of Mueller's best-known operations was his 1983 attempted diversion of several large VAX computers and software to the Soviet Union. Needed for its CAD applications in microelectronics fabrication, this equipment was purchased in the United States for dummy firms in South Africa and West Germany and seized by Sweden and West Germany en route to the Soviet Union.

This case insistently raises the question of how many other successful espionage operations are going on which are never exposed. Revo and Figelski point out that Moscow has regularly acquired in the West such things as automated control systems, artificial intelligence systems, high-density disk storage systems, software development systems, stand-alone mainframe computers, supercomputers, minicomputers, computer networking systems, and command, control, communications, and intelligence software of all kinds. The list goes on and on.

In making their acquisitions, the Russians have also targeted for bribery, blackmail, and deception many thousands of employees of the U.S. government and its contractors who have access to classified and sensitive information. They are interested in every possible type and source of data. High-tech industries, commercial data bases, scientific conferences, and universities are all targets for information that can often be obtained with little or no risk. The highest ranking Soviet ever to defect to the West, Arkady Shevchenko, has stated: "No Soviet scientist is allowed to travel outside the country without being asked to collect specific information. Scientists are given one chance to come back minus the information when they travel abroad. If they come back empty-handed after the second trip, their traveling days are pretty much over."

In short, the Russians neglect nothing when organizing their espionage efforts. If they had been able to run their country and organize their economy as well as they have been able to organize and manage their espionage networks and manage their spies, they would not find themselves in the trouble that they are in today. Nor will anything change now that Russia has assumed the old "Soviet" role.

The Russians have saved billions of dollars and years of research by acquiring and making use of stolen Western technology. Just as in the case of the development of their own nuclear weapons, it was precisely the acquisition of critical U.S. technology which enabled them to produce effective and workable weapons systems which were often (thanks again to the genius of America) "state of the art." The money they thereby saved on research they channeled into the development of countermeasure techniques and other weapons. The acquisition of this Western technology enabled them to bear the financial burden of trying to keep up with the West for as long as they did. The collapse of the Soviet system might have come much sooner without their espionage successes.

This immense Soviet espionage effort has been understood by knowledgeable U.S. observers all along. In the August 12, 1985 issue of *U.S. News and World Report*, for example, the late William Casey, then director of the CIA, in an article entitled, "How Soviets Steal America's High-Tech Secrets," wrote that "gaining access to U.S. advanced technology continues to be the Soviets' top priority; it's a big effort." Casey's article reported that there were no fewer than 2,000 agents and international middle-men working for Moscow at that time.

Similarly, an article entitled "Silicon Valley: No. 1 Soviet Spying Target," printed in *U.S. News and World Report* at the same time as the Casey article, writer Steve Hawkins reported that the participants at a recent electronic trade show included at least fifty foreign agents all busily engaged in collecting a veritable wealth of information. Reportedly, foreign agents were equally busy infiltrating hundreds of high-tech firms, especially those with U.S. defense contracts. It is clear that harmful espionage against the U.S. is not confined to the theft of secrets from the government.

Revo and Figelski provide an indication of some of the harmful results for America from the success of Russian technical and industrial espionage:

As a result of past acquisitions, sophisticated laser range finders on Soviet tanks are carbon copies of U.S. devices; precision transmission gears for heavy-lift helicopters are forged on American-made machine tools; MIG-25 Foxbat jets are equipped with look-down, shoot-down radar systems comparable to those on America's sleek F-15s; and Soviet cruise missiles incorporate the same designs, and in some cases components, as their U.S. counterparts. The Atoll air-to-air missile is so closely based on blueprints of the American Sidewinder that even a single left-hand-threading screw is repeated.

Recently the Soviets completed their entire building program for manufacturing military microelectronics components by acquiring more than 2,500 pieces of major Western controlled and uncontrolled microelectronics fabrication equipment.

Soviet Acquisition provides the following summary of VPK program results from the late 1970s through the early 1980s:

- An average of 5,000 Soviet military equipment and weapon system research projects each year benefitted from Western hardware and technical documents. Over half of these projects were in the electronics, armor, and electro-optics industries.
- More than 3,500 requirements were levied annually for specific Western hardware and documents, with roughly one-third satisfied each year and the other two-thirds still targeted.
- About 60 percent of document and hardware acquisitions considered to be the most significant to the Soviets were of U.S. origin.
- About 50 percent of the 10,000 pieces of hardware and 20 percent of the 100,000 documents prepared annually are used by the Soviets in transferring Western technology into their military research projects.

We have found it necessary to dwell at this length on past Soviet capabilities and successes in the field of technological and industrial espionage in order to make the point that there is danger not only from the theft of *government* secrets as such but also, and, in these high-tech days, perhaps *especially*, the theft of this kind of technological and industrial information and know-how from American research and industrial facilities. There can be no doubt at all that this kind of espionage will go on in the future.

The new Russian Republic and its allies *must* develop economic strength in order to survive. It is both reasonable and wise for the United States to assist to the extent that its own security is not endangered. However, it is inevitable that there will be instances in which the United States will decline to impart certain information which the Russians may consider vital, and it would be naive to assume that they will not employ the capabilities they so obviously possess in order to try to acquire what they need.

Obviously, the Russians are not the only ones who covet our technical and economic secrets. Virtually every country in the world could materially benefit from access to expensive and creative American research which is currently restricted. Precisely in view of Russian high-tech espionage successes—as well as appreciation of the ease with which all too often American technology export restrictions can be overcome—it is more than probable that other countries have not only contemplated acquiring, they have perhaps even have undertaken to acquire, the American secrets from which they would derive such great benefit and profit. Japan, for example, has been willing to take extraordinary steps to ensure its economic and trade dominance, even to the point of violating free-trade agreements and evading laws and agreements intended to limit military technology transfer. What assurance have we that Japan is not just as willing to resort to espionage as the Russians in instances where Japan sees vital interests to be at stake? The evidence is clear that individual Japanese companies are conducting espionage to acquire American technology. The only question is the extent of Japanese government involvement. Other foreign corporate entities have the same desires for profit and power as their governments.

Some may nevertheless question the need to protect economic secrets as opposed to military or diplomatic secrets. Why not share our knowledge, they may ask, as we already share our wealth? The answer, of course, is that the United States already does share an immense amount of its economic, scientific, technical, and commercial knowledge with all the world, not only through direct transfer of technology but through open publication of the results of most scientific and other studies in thousands of periodicals and other organs. The United States has always been, and remains, the most open society in the world. Nevertheless our wealth, know-how, and technical and scientific genius are not limitless.

Economic realities teach us that nations do compete with each other, and our own continued strength and prosperity depend upon our

success in defending our own acquisitions and developments and inventions against systems which more commonly employ bribery, kick-
backs, extortion, market lock-outs, overt and covert subsidies, long-
term price fixing, state and private collusion in manipulating the
economy and economic and commercial espionage. In view of these
unsavory realities and practices, both American firms and the United
States government must, in planning and executing their various economic strategies, include decisions limiting which secrets will be sold
or released to specific economic or trading partners or to the world at
large—and which will have to be kept restricted or confidential in our
own interests.

A RESPONSE TO THE END OF THE COLD WAR

The Bush Administration seemed generally aware that foreign
espionage does pose a continuing threat to the United States, a stance
the Clinton Administration would be well advised to follow. Thus, there
was at least no attempt to dismantle the whole security system once the
Cold War was over, especially following the dramatic events of 1989.
One indication of this was the headline in *The Washington Times* for
October 24, 1990:

Thaw in Cold War
Bush Heats Up Counterspy Operations

This story reported that President Bush had ordered U.S. intelligence agencies to expand their counterspy programs and capabilities
despite the vast improvement that had taken place in Russian-American
relations. A senior administration official was quoted as saying that
Russia was a formidable intelligence threat despite its own problems,
and was expected to remain a formidable intelligence threat for a long
time to come. The story continued:

National Security Directive 147 was signed by Mr. Bush early
this month. It directs the CIA, the FBI, the National Security
Agency, the State, Defense, and Justice Departments, and other
security components to continue rebuilding U.S. counter-intelligence programs, a process that began during the Reagan Administration. The secret five-page directive was based on a yearlong
interagency review of U.S. security threats and vulnerabilities,
completed earlier this year.

"This administration continues to believe that counter-intelligence is a critical element of our national security," said the senior official, who spoke on condition of anonymity. "The fact of
the matter is there is a substantial threat. This document [the
directive] asserts as much and says we need to redouble our efforts to counter that threat." "The threat is complex and is coming
from many areas," a second official said. The new directive states
that countering spies is a U.S. "strategic priority." "It says there
will always be a hostile climate," the official said.

The new policy also takes into account the shift from long-
standing U.S. policy of containing Communist nations to one of
integration. "That presents new opportunities for intelligence activities against us," the official said. Spying by the KGB has not
diminished despite reforms in the Soviet Union, although the KGB
foreign operations are "in a state of flux" because of the loss of
surrogate spy services once provided by the Eastern Europeans ...

The disbanding of East Germany's vast spy apparatus has
created new uncertainties. "We don't know what the Soviets picked
up from that," the U.S. official said. "Part of our program is to
keep up with those things ... whether somebody has sold his
services to the Soviets now that his first client is out of business."

One intelligence source noted how the CIA had recently set up a
special task force under a veteran analyst, Kay Oliver, to review the files
of the *Stasi*, the former East German secret police, for clues to possible
American *Stasi* agents. At least a dozen people had reportedly come
under investigation as a result of the labors of this task force.

The Bush Administration official serving as the primary source of
this newspaper story indicated that this new National Security Directive
had become necessary because of the dramatic changes in the previous
year in the entire former Soviet bloc; some of the Eastern European
intelligence services were just "fading away," while others were continuing their activities unabated.

The new directive ordered all U.S. agencies concerned to:

- Target hostile intelligence services and actively disrupt their operations by expulsion or arrest and prosecution of their American agents.
- Step up actions against "non-adversarial" spying—espionage against
  the United States carried out by such friendly nations as Israel,
  France, and Japan. The directive indicates that this is a serious and
  growing problem.

- Direct security agencies to improve cooperation to prevent foreign spies from exploiting gaps in security caused by separate agency jurisdiction and procedures.
- Shift limited counter-intelligence resources—agents, funds, and equipment—to account for changes in the world political environment.
- Increase protection of military-related high technology, which continues to be a major target of spies, specifically the KGB's Line-X officers.
- Protect personnel, documents, hardware, computers, and technological information from spies with a number of new security programs.

The goal of this Bush Administration National Security Directive was said to be to reduce the vulnerability of secret facilities, equipment, and information to being spied upon and to prevent recruitment of those with access to secrets, with special emphasis on the so-called "volunteers" who offer to spy for cash. One interesting feature of the directive was that it did *not* call for increased use of polygraph tests for officials with access to highly secret material.

It seems that the Bush Administration did understand that the United States continues to face a serious espionage threat, in spite of the end of the Cold War. The directive they issued on the subject is likely to remain in force in the Clinton Administration. While there is no apparent incentive for the latter administration to change it, since it scarcely concerns partisan political matters, there does remain the question of the Clinton Administration's commitment to security considerations. The study of American security policies and capabilities performed in 1993 - 1994 seems to be at least as concerned with economics as with effectiveness.

Nevertheless while the Bush Administration directive did address some of the problems which we too have identified in these pages, and therefore is useful as far as it goes, there is still little indication in the provisions of this directive that the Bush administration understood *why* the United States has so often failed to protect its secrets.

Still not understood is the role of proper and effective ongoing security management, which is critical if there is to be any real expectation of identifying those employees who, for whatever reason or motivation, make the decision to engage in espionage. The fact that employees are "cleared" because of a prior security investigation cannot be relied upon. Security practitioners must recognize and cope successfully with the problem of security management, a responsibility of mammoth proportions that must constantly be restated and reenforced.

The espionage threat to America remains as great as it ever was, and it is certainly more complex than it ever was. In fact, both more sophisticated and less expensive espionage techniques, coupled with today's decline of moral restraints, could bring about a veritable explosion of espionage against us. The United States must therefore maintain at least the same level of effort and commitment to security as before, while vastly improving its effectiveness.

As we shall see in our final chapter, this can actually be done with a *substantial decrease* in cost. Considering the current pressures to divert budget dollars from defense to domestic social programs, we may *have* to operate a much more economical security system if we are going to be able to operate any security system at all.

SEVEN

Solutions

So many security failures have occurred over the past decade that they may have lost their capacity to shock. This is tragic. In this regard, they resemble all the many previous security failures over the past half century and more. It is logical to assume that, having suffered so much damage to our national security, the United States would have finally put in place a security system which would address the real problems encountered in trying to protect our vital national secrets—and which would be designed to provide for solutions to those problems.

However, we still have in place the security system that was designed over forty years ago. As we have seen, it did not work then and it does not work now.

Periodically, various commissions, task forces, and study groups have been asked to analyze the system, and, especially, its failures. Many recommendations have been offered, and, as we were once told by Mr. Thomas O'Brien, former Director of the Defense Investigative Service, "those that could be implemented without cost were implemented; those that would cost money were not."

To a very great extent what has been wrong with security, and with most of the recommendations made in the course of previous reviews of the system, has had little or nothing to do with money or the lack of it. Certainly there are individual weaknesses which could be corrected or improved with additional money. However, the basic fallacy of each of the studies that have been performed is that it has proceeded on the assumption that the current security system is basically effective and should be maintained and improved. In fact, the current system, and the basic principles and premises on which it is based, are unsound and unworkable and should be abolished and replaced.

Is it possible to do it differently and better? Can America success-fully protect our secrets and therefore our resources, and at the same time maintain due process and protect our freedom?

It can. However, the solution requires a total rethinking of our basic approach to security. The system described here is far more effective than the one we have and is capable of protecting our nation's secrets. This proposed system will also provide more significant safeguards for equity and fairness and due process. More than that, the system proposed will also result in cost savings of a considerable magnitude.

LIMIT SECURITY INVESTIGATIONS

We have described the extensive effort and exorbitant cost of per-forming thousands upon thousands of detailed full field investigations of personnel. The information gathered is then substantially ignored in an evaluation and adjudication process. This results in the granting of se-curity clearances to practically everybody for whom application is made.

Conducting full field investigations on thousands of applicants is not only unnecessary, it is both wasteful and counter-productive. It creates the illusion that the people investigated and then "cleared" will always be loyal and honest and there is therefore no present or future govern-ment security problem. It provides a false sense of security which en-ables management and staff to avoid the constant vigilance that is their obligation. This self-delusion makes even more baffling the puzzle con-cerning how any reasonable, and reasonably intelligent, person can re-ally support a system where more than 96.5% of all DoD applicants and 99% of other OPM applicants are routinely cleared! Total reliance on full field investigations is nothing but a gigantic pretense that we are somehow effectively practicing "security." "We must be if we are going to such cost and effort"—so the illusion persists.

There exists a very simple, even elegant, solution to the problem of the expensive and futile investigation: Eliminate them, except for specific defined purposes!

Again, for emphasis: the vast majority of full field investigations serve no useful purpose whatsoever and should be discontinued. At first sight, this solution may appear to be an excessively radical one. How-ever, we need to reflect carefully on the following facts:

1. The current system has proven to be ineffective.

2. Persons with a criminal background or serious mental conditions or record of drug addiction will almost certainly be identified through the routine national agency name check.
3. Financial and other important personal information is typically and readily available through consumer credit name checks and from similar sources.
4. The type of background information most frequently accumulated through the detailed field investigation, especially that related to personal morality, has always been rather subjective in nature, was frequently misused in years past, and now today is virtually ignored in the clearance process.
5. The dollar savings to be realized are enormous. They are far more than will be required to put into place the recommendations which are proposed herein. Hundreds of millions of dollars are being wasted on unproductive full field investigations. Those dollars should be re-directed to carrying out the recommendations offered to strengthen the security system, to the extent necessary, and the remaining dollars returned to the taxpayers in savings and to repay for the terrible costs visited upon them from the crimes of traitors and the failures of managers.

But is there any other way to evaluate an applicant's or an employee's character if the security investigation is eliminated? Before entering upon employment in the federal service, or in any organization with government contracts where access to classified information is required, *the applicant would have to offer proof of both suitability and trustworthiness and loyalty.*

Some agencies and organizations have been operating on a similar system all along. Nearly fifty years ago, when I prepared to join the Central Intelligence Group (later the CIA), I was required to fill out a questionnaire which went into extensive personal details of my entire life and its activities, including birth, education, employment, marriage, divorce, relatives, associations, organizations, credit history, and so on. That information was evaluated by a trained evaluator who then interviewed me in person, asked questions, analyzed and weighed my responses, and then made judgments about my veracity, integrity, suitability, and loyalty. I was also required to submit to a polygraph examination conducted by a properly trained polygraph operator.

A similar process, administered on a very large scale, would involve *less* cost and trouble than current investigations, and could be carried out much faster by far fewer security employees. This process would include the following:

1. Applicants will complete a detailed, written Personal History statement which, in addition to the normal application data, will have space for the identification and description of any problem conditions—drug use, serious marital problems, criminal convictions, previous job terminations, financial problems, etc.[6]
2. A national agency name check will be performed to identify hidden criminal activity or convictions, aliases, commitment to mental institutions or other problems.
3. Standard information sources will be used to verify employment claims and discover potential problems with respect to any of the following:
   a. Proof of citizenship.
   b. Credit history.
   c. Social Security Number verification, to confirm the person's identity and the validity of his or her Social Security Number.
   d. Driver's license records to verify a person's identity, including physical description and residence, and to discover any serious violations, such as drunken driving.
4. An intensive interview will be conducted by an adjudicator exploring all questionable or derogatory information turned up in any of the previous actions. The applicant will then be given the opportunity to explain, orally and in writing, any issues brought up in this process. To aid the adjudicator in his review, a set of suggested standard questions will be available for use in various specific situations.
5. A drug-screen urinalysis test will be used to detect the presence of illegal substances and their derivatives.
6. A polygraph examination will be conducted to ascertain, to the extent that the technique permits, the truth of the statements made by the applicants. A polygraph specialist will perform this examination, utilizing questions supplied by the adjudicator. Questions raised by the polygraph examination will be pursued, including investigation if appropriate.

This approach obviously recognizes and accepts that the applicants seeking government employment and security clearance must, as a condition of their employment, accept reasonable limits of privacy and their constitutional rights against self-incrimination. In addition, the clearance concept being urged here would eliminate the practice of periodic reinvestigation—a practice which has been an admitted failure with many

---

[6]And, where the applicant has had prior experience in other agencies, the security files of those agencies on the applicant will be utilized in the process.

years of delinquency backlogging the reinvestigation cases. Instead regular, in-depth, but random spot check investigations would be performed. Moreover, as a normal practice, employees would be given bi-annual interviews by trained interviewers, which would include polygraph examinations to determine whether their clearances should be maintained.

It might be argued that there are not enough trained polygraph operators around to make it practical to utilize this method in government. However, it would be far less expensive to train and develop the required number of polygraph operators than it currently is to perform full field investigations on every person requiring a Top Secret or above clearance.

Another major argument against the use of the polygraph test, namely, that it is unconstitutional because it forces self-incrimination on people, loses merit when we recall that the protection against self-incrimination has reference to the possibility of prosecution. If there is to be no prosecution, the argument is moot. If the only purpose of the polygraph test is to aid in the identification of any violations of the security standards and any possible falsehoods in an application for government employment, the constitutional prohibition against self-incrimination does not apply, and should not be invoked. This is a case of persons wishing to enjoy the privilege of government employment and promotion, not one in which charges might be brought against them.

Understand, also, that a major objective of the polygraph is to identify "leads," to search for possible indicators of trouble, not necessarily to "solve the case."

Are there some government agencies, or positions within agencies, that, because of their sensitivity, require more than a personal history, interview and interrogation, and polygraph test? Yes, but exceptions for them can easily be made to include additional investigations, as necessary.

Are there instances in which a government manager needs to know whether a candidate or applicant will pass the security test before the latter is contacted about an assignment? There again exceptions can easily be made on a case-by-case basis, but the normal route to clearance will be as described above.

Make no mistake. When we urge the selective use of full field investigations we are not talking about the elimination of intensive scrutiny by every means, including agents conducting rigorous investigations. We are talking about the routine expenditure of time, money, resources, an enormous expense spent on verifying over and over again elementary, high school and higher education; residences back for many years; inquiries with neighbors who invariably know nothing and, if they knew something would not know its meaning or significance; employments back to teen years, etc.

But if—as former DCI Woolsey apparently believed—there may be more moles in the CIA, then not one hour should elapse without intensive scrutiny of every person who could *possibly* be a mole, beginning with the Director himself. In these cases, every means available, surveillance, investigation, polygraph, psychological testing, etc., should be rigorously employed until either the traitors are unmasked or the concern by the Director is proved unjustified. And the DCI should willingly be the first to show that he "means business".

From the time it was recognized that we were losing our agents and other people in our network, this scrutiny should have been continued until every traitor was found, or the Director could say, "We're clean"!

SUITABILITY STANDARDS AND STANDARDIZATION

The second major failure in the process of security investigation and adjudication involves the lack of specific standards for use in determining the suitability of persons for access to secure information and the lack of appropriate qualification standards for use by the persons performing the adjudications. The current concept is that an adjudicator must look at all the information on a specific person and then make a "common-sense determination" regarding an applicant's suitability and loyalty.

This system has never worked properly. For one thing, it is too subjective. This becomes a major failing when the adjudicator is not properly qualified and trained. The system worked after a fashion in the 1940s in a very different moral climate. In the early 1950s and for about a decade thereafter, the common-sense determinations made were too often overly harsh and unfair and exhibited little respect for due process (and even then the system failed to "weed out subversives"). Today, the problem is excessive leniency. Failure to define factors that are specifically disqualifying, and to apply such standards, has caused the government to lose nearly every security judgment which has ever been appealed to the courts—a fact which only encourages further leniency in applying "common-sense judgments."

To make matters worse, the decentralization of security clearance decisions, and the use of in-house personnel to make them, subjects the whole process to pressures from the individual employing agencies and departments. Their insufficient training also makes the adjudicators more susceptible to in-house pressure.

It is time for the U.S. security profession, working with both the executive and legislative branches of government, to develop an appropriate and comprehensive set of standards that state concretely what is and what is not acceptable to qualify for a U.S. government security clearance and what we are willing to act on and defend. There is no doubt that the process for the development of such standards will stir up debate, consternation, dissent, and protest in some quarters. Disputes will arise. However, an honest debate on the subject will be salutary, and dissent and protests are going on constantly under the current system on the rare occasions when anyone is denied a security clearance. The government is usually the loser. Even if the resultant standards are less stringent than what security practitioners would prefer, it is better to have a set of usable concrete standards than a theoretical set of ideals which are never applied and enforced.

Development of a set of usable security standards would require us to come to grips with the issues of morality, integrity, honesty, etc., and the degree to which they must be required in the granting of security clearances. Similarly, we cannot go on side-stepping the question of whether a person is unsuitable for security clearance or government employment if he or she engages in adultery, homosexual acts, lying, stealing, slander, falsifying personal records, and so on. The very notion that government employment is a privilege and not a right is rejected by many today. Standards themselves are rejected. No conduct, however amoral or dishonest, would appear to be disqualifying in the eyes of some activists. All these issues must therefore be resolved. The preparation and promulgation of a set of realistic security standards will provide the means for resolving them. In fact, it is likely that a frank, open, debate on these subjects, including the miserable performance of clearance personnel in recent years, may give our elected representatives and security professionals the courage to require reasonably high standards. In any event, the standards must be specific and consistent.

Concerning the skills and qualifications of the adjudicators of clearances requests, it is necessary to develop a set of requirements and qualifications for appointment to security positions which entail making adjudications. The appropriate qualifications would be closer to those of a legal hearing officer or magistrate than to those of an investigator, since under the system being proposed, the incumbents of these positions would be obliged to assess, evaluate, and weigh the evidence against the concrete qualifying standards that are to be developed. Training programs must also be developed, with required attendance by all current and prospective investigators and adjudicators. Before being given job assignments, each attendee must be required to pass a test to demonstrate his or her understanding of the material. There must also be developed an adjudication data base, as well as the means to disseminate and consult the contents of that data base, in order to insure that consistent judgments are being made government-wide where similar facts and evidence are presented.

IMPROVE THE QUALITY OF MANAGEMENT

"The Buck Stops Here!"

President Harry Truman had his limitations as a President, without question. But one thing he knew and practiced as a politician and a bureaucrat: The CEO—be it President, cabinet officer, or agency head—was the individual at whose desk the buck stopped.

He knew also that it took guts to be the CEO and that hard judgments had to be exercised regardless of consequences and, when the vital interests of the U.S. were at stake, the CEO had to act and let the chips fall where they may. History may not treat Harry Truman kindly for his destruction of the OSS in order to vent his dislike for Major General Donovan. And it may not treat him favorably for similar feelings and actions against the other heroic figure of World Wars I and II, General Douglas MacArthur. But, in both cases, as with the attacks on Japan, Truman acted regardless of consequences, and he acted out of convictions which, he felt, were in the vital interest of his country.

The underlying cause of the failure of the Federal government's security program over the past several decades is the abysmal quality of management exercised by the Executive Branch from the President on down.

At the Presidential level, in every case of treason, right up to and including that of Aldrich Ames, the Chief Executive has failed to react with anger and outrage over the criminal negligence and the malfeasance of those charged with the responsibility and the obligation to protect both the secrets of the United States and the lives of those who risk them—both Americans and allies in the interests of the United States and of freedom from tyranny.

The day that the Ameses were arrested, every head in the CIA, which in any way had or could have had any responsibility for the Ameses should have rolled and rolled with a vengeance. Instead, not only did no heads roll, but the Director of Central Intelligence waved his powder puff over those responsible and declared: "No more promotions until we get to the bottom of this." Punishment for eight years of negligent management and neglect of responsibility: "Promotions will be delayed."

The day that the arrests were announced, every knowledgeable veteran of the espionage and treason game knew that neither of the Ameses would ever go to trial—not because of the potential damage to the security of the United States—the Soviet system, what remained of it, long since knew everything that could be revealed at trial—but because of the damage to the reputation, careers and paychecks of all those who failed to fulfill their obligations to so manage the intelligence operations as to protect the United States and those put at risk through their service to this country.

The reaction of the Clinton Administration to the revelations of the Ames case speaks volumes concerning their naiveté. Instead of calling for penalties for those whose negligence permitted the Ameses' treason to continue for so long, the Administration blamed the Russians and demanded an apology and assistance in identifying everything the Ameses had compromised. The Russians quite logically responded that, since this controversy involves the destruction of an American espionage network operating within the then-Soviet Union, if anyone should apologize, it would be the United States!

Over and over, year after year, traitor after traitor, security disaster after security disaster, the same disgraceful scenario has played out. Management neglect has permitted American traitors to betray their country for greed and ego. Ignoring even the most obvious signs, bureaucrats have refused to, first, recognize and act against the betrayers and, second, to punish those whose neglect of duty has made the treason possible.

Membership in the "Club" has long been the protective shield against identification of spies and traitors within the fold. Once an individual becomes a member, blindness ensues on the part of those charged with management of the intelligence and counter-intelligence functions. No matter the examples of the Philby-McLean-Burgess-Blunt quartet followed by repetitive examples. The blind refusal to ruthlessly scrutinize conduct and behavior with a questioning, suspicious eye is an intolerable failure which has cost America—and Britain—untold losses in money and lives of dedicated, brave and now forgotten heroes.

Unquestioning acceptance of one's subordinates and colleagues is a luxury that cannot be afforded in the security and counter-intelligence business. It was so during an era when only a few traitors performed their dirty business and then typically for ideological reasons. But today massive numbers of Americans can be corrupted by money, drugs, luxuries and power. Every single person who has access to our secrets must be viewed as a potential danger to the security of the United States, to the same extent as every person having access to the gold at Fort Knox, of the diamonds, silver and gold at the U.S. Assay Office.

Clearance to work with highly classified data, like clearance to work in the U.S. Assay Office, does not guarantee the incorruptibility of the individual. Ascendancy to the pinnacle of power in the office where secrets are available does not raise the incumbent above scrutiny.

The failure at CIA is not just that of the Office of Security. That function has limited capacity (and the potential to know, or learn, the telltale signs of corruption leading to treason). It is at the operating and management levels that the scrutiny and awareness must function. No one can be considered to be immune from possible corruption. In this regard, my mind often dwells on the absolute power—the virtual dictatorship—exercised by James Angleton during his many years of control over counter-intelligence at the agency. Angleton, was virtually a protegé and student of the British Master Spy, Kim Philby, from their days in the old M16 office in Ryder Street in London. And even as their "relationship deepened when Philby was posted to Washington as Station Chief in 1949," to quote Peter Wright, former Assistant Director of M15, and author of *Spy Catcher*, Angleton neither questioned Philby nor came under question, as he developed his reputation for obsession over possible penetration of the Agency.

Who should be above suspicion? Who is incorruptible? How many traitors must be exposed before no one is immune?

Lest this be judged a too harsh approach to protecting America, her secrets and the lives of her agents, ponder the words of former DCI Woolsey even after the Ames revelations and admissions that there are "a fair number of espionage cases"—later amended to "leads"—still in the pipeline.

Of course, this abysmal mismanagement is not limited to the CIA. It just happens to occupy the "hottest spot" because of the nature of its business and the dramatic and costly effects of its failures. Security mismanagement is as great or greater elsewhere, but under less scrutiny. In every agency and department, the most fundamental failing of the

U.S. government security system is the failure of government officials and managers in charge at every level to manage the system properly. *Every successful penetration and theft of classified documents always results from managerial failure somewhere, and each one is preventable.*

One of the most devastating indictments of government management is provided by the case of the American Embassy in Moscow, which we have also looked at more than once in these pages.

When it was learned that one or more American Marine guards had accepted payment and sexual favors and may have admitted Russian agents into the restricted areas and offices of the embassy, a great public hue and cry went up attacking the morality of the guards and deploring the inadequacy of the prior investigations conducted on these guards which failed to prevent them from being assigned to the highly sensitive Moscow post. Some thought only people of stronger character should have been assigned to such positions. Others, obviously unconcerned about the character issue, thought the government had to address the sex "needs" of its single personnel more realistically. After months of investigation, it was concluded that the Marines had "probably" not admitted the Soviets into the embassy.

But there was never a word said by anyone on the subject of the performance of the senior officials, from the ambassador on down, charged with the security management of the American Embassy in Moscow. Nothing was said about the scandal of leaving the embassy in the care of unsupervised enlisted men or giving to them, without oversight or monitoring, the capability to admit to the embassy agents of an enemy government. Nothing was said about the absence of even a rudimentary system of access control and monitoring of entries which would have served to alert the ambassador or other responsible officials of the fact that the physical security of the premises had been compromised. Nor, after the whole sorry incident came to light, *was any administrative or management official in the embassy ever called to account.*

No one at all, apparently, amidst all the sensational publicity given to the Marine guard case, thought to question the idea of a security system which could allow mere guards to admit Soviets into the building and its "secure" areas without any oversight being exercised. No one thought to question a security system based upon the assumption of the incorruptibility of "cleared" personnel.

What was chiefly at fault in this American Embassy in Moscow case was not the fact that some Marines succumbed to temptation. It was the failure of the embassy's administrative and management team to understand that they were obligated to be actively in charge of managing the embassy's security, including its physical security. The security responsibility of the ambassador and his senior staff was not discharged once a Marine guard was assigned to the front desk for the night. They had no right to assume that the Marines had everything under control; they were obligated to establish, test, and confirm the security of an area known to be a prime Soviet target and constantly watch over the Marines guarding it as well. No security system can be based on the assumption that everybody working in the system is automatically loyal and beyond the reach of temptation.

No matter how thoroughly we investigate people, and even assuming everybody is loyal at any given point, many people will nevertheless subsequently succumb to temptation, even the temptation to sell out their country. And some will sell it out when the price or the enticement is great enough. They have to be stopped. No matter what actions have been taken to assess the suitability, loyalty, and integrity of applicants or employees, the bottom line of security is still always protection of the data and operations by whatever methods and measures are necessary.

Except for the relatively few cases of moles intended to influence policy, almost every case of espionage comes down to the physical theft of data—the copying or removing of it. In this situation, effective controls must be imposed to protect the data, just as we impose such controls at Fort Knox to protect the gold, at the mint to protect the money or in a high-hazard laboratory to prevent the release of potentially harmful or lethal infectious agents. These controls must be clearly laid out, explained and put in place, enforced in *every* case, be under continual supervision (which itself must then be monitored from a higher supervisory level), and be constantly tested by challenges and in other ways to insure that they are working; then they need to be checked again after the fact. They must work. In addition, data requiring protection must be audited at unpredictable intervals in order to insure that it is *not* missing or tampered with. Moreover, every breach or penetration of the system must be thoroughly investigated and vigorously critiqued, the causes identified and corrected where necessary, and responsibility for the lapse or failure identified and appropriate penalties then meted out, *including genuine punishment for managerial failure*.

There is no excuse for managing the security of classified material in any other way. Security should be managed as if lives depended upon its effectiveness. They do, lives *are* at stake. The Israelis, for example, understand this. We need to assume the same commitment.

Nor is there anything particularly mysterious or difficult about the proposed procedures. They are essentially the same ones that, say, supermarkets use to check on the money their cashiers take in, or banks use to insure the security of their vaults and the contents of the latter; or that laboratories use to control harmful agents. No failure can be tolerated or excused.

The level of security management in departments and agencies must be improved to the extent that, even though there may be employees within the organization prepared to steal or betray, they will be unable to succeed in their attempts because of the controls in place—or else they will seriously risk detection and apprehension shortly after they do steal or betray. This means that management and operations personnel must be trained and indoctrinated to be vigilant, informed, and aware of the threat to the classified material in their charge that could come from anyone exhibiting the signs of psychological impairment, alcohol or drug dependency, or other behavior or personality disorders. Furthermore, there must be well-understood rules in place that access to classified material will be immediately withdrawn under certain specified conditions. The personality traits of Jonathan Pollard, for example, should have been noted much sooner in the course of his CIA employment and his further access to classified material cut off. Perhaps they were noticed earlier, but the system did not provide that his access be immediately denied.

In those cases where a Pollard, a Chin, or a Walker does slip through the new "security safety net" and succeed in committing an act of espionage, the damage will be limited under the system proposed here because such a spy, even if momentarily successful, will be discovered at his or her next security interview and polygraph examination. No huge investigation backlogs, but rather semi-annual personnel screenings on top of the strict managerial controls. All of these measures will also create the heightened security awareness that our present system woefully lacks. What is being proposed for our national secrets is no more than is already in effect at the U.S. Assay Offices.

The above represent the major concepts behind a workable security system. The following recommendations identify the required specific improvements which would be necessary to create the primary administrative and managerial goals, premises, attitudes, responsibilities, and approaches which are essential if such an effective security capability is to be developed at our government agencies and departments.

CONCEPT OF INFORMATION SECURITY

Many persons within and outside the government have their own concept of what security really means, how secrets are lost and stolen, and what is necessary for their protection. Some of these concepts are rather inaccurate, to put it gently. A government Security Concept document therefore needs to be developed and disseminated to all government employees and contractors. Such a document should include:

- Definition of secure information.
- Explanation of its importance.
- Description of the way in which foreign espionage agents approach U.S. government employees.
- Identification of the responsibilities at all levels and for all employees.
- Specific advice on identifying, observing, and reporting on potential problem conditions and persons.

ASSIGNMENT OF RESPONSIBILITY

It is mandatory to assign unequivocally the responsibility for the protection of classified information within the organization. Although the security officer is responsible for security audit procedures and for identifying and reporting abuses, he does not have responsibility for the success of the whole program. Many conscientious security officers find it impossible to be heard within the agency under the present set-up. Too many other priorities reign, and he is typically not high enough in rank to prevail in any disputed case. More importantly, he cannot be present within the operational spheres of the organization at every level of performance. To have a "security officer" present at every level would be economically and logistically impracticable. It follows, then, that concern for security in the organization cannot be limited to the "security officer" alone, even though his expertise is always important. Overall management and administrative responsibility for security must reside with the regular levels of supervisory management, reenforced at each successively higher level. To imagine that "security" is exclusively the responsibility of the "security officer" is one of the worst of all organizational cop-outs.

Another problem with the current practice of assigning security to the security officer, without any upper-level administrative responsibility, is that for any issue not falling within the technical purview of the security officer, security considerations come to be ignored. For example, for years during the construction of the new American Embassy in Moscow, Soviet suppliers and construction personnel were actually KGB directed, not American directed. It apparently never occurred to American management, construction or security personnel that transmitters and listening devices would be implanted in the building materials, converting the entire building into a multiple transmitter of security information. If it did occur to anyone, nothing was done about it. No one examined these materials either before, during, or after the installation process, even though the Russians had long been known for their propensity to install similar devices wherever they could, in walls, lamps, telephones, and typewriters, and even in the Great Seal of the United States given to the U.S. by Nikita S. Khrushchev, supposedly as a goodwill gesture. We all know the story: once the device was discovered in the Great Seal, of course, the whole thing was displayed before the United Nations Organization by Ambassador Henry Cabot Lodge, and one could only assume from all the hullabaloo that some kind of lesson had been learned. When it came to the construction of the new American Embassy, so many devices were included in the construction that the building could not be occupied. We blamed the Soviets instead of our own administrative and management people.

This fiasco of the construction of the Embassy in Moscow provides us with yet another example of what can result when upper management and the employees throughout the organization do not understand the vital importance of security and do not share a commitment and responsibility for carrying it out. A recent fire in the embassy similarly resulted in the admission of Russian fire-fighters into the building and their dispersal throughout the structure without proper American escort. Interspersed with the fire-fighters, of course, were KGB agents, who rifled through and stole whatever classified information they could find. We were publicly informed that the losses were not of great significance, but this was, after all, the material being processed by the embassy staff prior to the fire. It is more likely that the disclaimer was meant only to avoid further embarrassment.

Thus, it is imperative that the final responsibility for security rest with the agency or departmental head or administrator and then successively with the latter's regular line management. Concrete guidance and direction and overall attitudes must come from the organization's head, communicated through the regular organizational structure and channels. Security must be incorporated into operational and functional performance at every level. If the organizational head is knowledgeable and properly committed to security, this attitude will be communicated to the organization and his subordinate managers will quickly come to understand that maintaining effective security is one of the things on which their job performance ratings, indeed their survival as managers, will be based.

If, on the other hand, the agency head, ambassador, unit or division chief, or whoever is in charge takes the position that security is merely an onerous and unreasonable set of restrictions and that none of *his* people, for example, could ever possibly be corrupted or be working for foreign agents, and that protection of classified information is not a sufficiently important priority anyway—then these are the attitudes that will come to prevail throughout the agency. Unfortunately, these are the attitudes that do prevail throughout many government agencies today and it has a remarkable similarity to the attitudes of the reigning U.S. Ambassador at the time of the Marine guards episode in Moscow.

Government agency and departmental administrators must be *formally* assigned direct security responsibility, educated in the concept of information security, familiarized with the security systems in place, instructed to improve those systems in cooperation with security personnel and to report on their improvements, and then informed that their performance in this area will be a grading factor in their performance evaluations.

RESPONSE TO POOR PERFORMANCE

Until the minor reprimands issued after the Ames revelations, there are apparently no instances in which administrators, supervisors, or co-workers of those who turned out to be traitors were ever reprimanded or punished for their failure to prevent or even notice and report the crimes taking place in their presence. Yet the responsibilities of all these personnel have always inherently included insuring that proper security procedures are in place and followed.

The American ambassador to Russia at the time the security violations occurred at the embassy had actually made known his disdain for the security function generally and his belief that there was no great necessity for it. Neither he nor his senior staff apparently ever bothered to become aware of the forbidden fraternization that was taking place between his Marine guards and Russian women. Yet this particular ambassador, as well as his senior staff, emerged unscathed from the whole disgraceful incident, and moved on to other assignments where no doubt their low opinions of the security function continue to infect and be communicated to those who work under their supervision.

Personnel quickly perceive the degree of commitment, if any, of top management to the security function. If people are not disciplined, or otherwise penalized, for failure to perform properly, then performance will inevitably suffer. In cases where treasonous or criminal behavior is involved, this failure by administrators amounts to something little short of criminal negligence. Appropriate disciplining and penalties must follow if American secrets are to be safe and secure.

Whenever there has been a serious breach of security, whether or not any actual loss of classified data occurred, a full investigation of the relevant facts should be undertaken and appropriate; i.e., severe, disciplinary action should be taken against those, including even an agency head, whose apathy, improper actions or failure to act allowed the breach to take place or contributed to it. That report of investigation must require a finding and an action at the highest executive level.

REMOVAL OF CLEARANCES

The authority and the system must be developed in such a way as to insure swift action, in accordance with established concrete written procedures, including the removal of security clearances against those who, because of apathy, neglect, carelessness, fraud, or other wrongful or unsuitable actions, have contributed, directly or indirectly, to the loss of classified material or other serious breach of security. They have demonstrated their unreliability and should be denied further access to classified material.

ENFORCEMENT OF THE "NEED TO KNOW"

Although access to classified information is officially limited to those with a "need to know" in accordance with the required level of approved clearance, in practice classified information is shared readily among members of the "club" of cleared individuals. In fact, the same question of ego exists here as it does in other areas of life: being "on the inside" brings recognition and prestige. In groups of insiders, there is frequently an acceptance of each other with the assumption that since each person has been cleared, each is necessarily pure and incorruptible forever.

Once again, the issue is simply a failure to live by or enforce sensible regulations. However, the system has failed to reckon with the ignorance of some people regarding proper security; with the arrogance which some other people acquire when they are given some power or information not generally shared by others; with the facts of changed behavior in persons who have decided to betray; with the pressures and temptations which can assail persons with access to classified information that this country's adversaries dearly wish to have; and with the neglect, apathy, and laziness which so frequently result in lapses and failures. Given such human behavior and such situations, the security restrictions in place can never simply be considered to be for "others." The rules must apply impartially to everyone and at all times. Failure to observe them, or toleration of other kinds of abuse of the system, can only be corrected by rigorous policing by vigilant managers, by conscientious observation by all employees and prompt reporting of violations, and as a result of independent audit reviews, followed by disciplinary measures for those who either fail to observe the "need to know" restrictions, or fail to report the infractions of others.

It is critically important that weaknesses and lapses in behavior be recognized and halted at the outset. Those who reply, "No, this is Orwellian, and smacks of Hitler's Gestapo or Stalin's NKVD," must be reminded that we are not talking here about the communication of public information that ought to be available to society as a whole. The inside operations of a government agency are not the same thing as a college campus, a debating society, or a radio talk show. We are talking here about sensitive, sometimes life-and-death, information, the loss of which can do grave damage to our Republic. Besides a real need to know, the rule for government employees at all levels handling sensitive material should be: "If it is not important, don't classify it; if it has to be classified, or has been classified, protect it." Managers should manage according to these rules. There is no future for America in a manager in a sensitive or national security agency who goes on trying to be "a good guy well-liked by everybody" at the expense of proper observance of security.

REDUCTION OF CLASSIFIED MATERIAL

A method must be developed to control more effectively the ever-burgeoning classification of material. One is sometimes tempted to wish we could disinvent the copying machine which so easily generates ever greater numbers of copies of classified documents to be logged, controlled, delivered, mailed, filed, traced—and lost! A copy of an original

Top Secret document is just as vital as the original, but today the universal availability of copying machines can contribute to treating classified material with contempt. Rigorous discipline is required.

The current system permits grossly excessive classification, which in turn requires the granting of security clearances to an excessively large number of people. In addition, the classification of material for political, personal, or trivial reasons encourages both internal opponents of certain policies and the press to justify leaking and publication of such material in violation of the law.

Most classified documents will stay that way forever unless specific action is taken to declassify them. We need only think of the millions of "Cold War" documents that could now be declassified and destroyed, but probably will not be removed. Of course, declassification, like classification, must be done in accordance with strict standards and criteria, written and promulgated and made familiar to all employees handling classified material.

Whether by statute or executive order, then, regulations should be developed which severely restrict the authority to classify material and spell out concretely the necessary characteristics which permit or require classification (and declassification). While the authority to classify or declassify should be able to be delegated, specific limits should be placed on such delegation. It's power in this area should be expanded and given the responsibility to review the classification process and its results, in a manner similar to the operation of the OSHA in safety matters, with specific procedures, effective power, and the ability to enforce its rulings and discipline transgressors. As long as embarrassing cartoons can be classified, as occurred during the Gulf War, we have a long way to go. The declassification efforts and reporting of the Information Security Oversight Office described in Chapter Three, represents a credible start and should be expanded.

Reduction in the classification of documents will permit reduction in numbers of persons requiring clearance which will result in lessening the number of investigations and adjudications. Both improved security and cost savings will result.

ATTITUDE TOWARDS SECURITY

There must be a change in attitude towards security among personnel who handle, utilize, and are responsible for protecting classified information, and even among personnel who do not normally handle such materials but who are in the same work environment. One of the most difficult of all Loss Prevention management phenomena—and it applies not just to the problem of treason but also to the problem of theft in general—is the common assumption of most Americans that if an individual is "known" and one has worked with him he is automatically honest and worthy of trust. Americans dislike thinking ill of others, especially those with whom they have to work or otherwise deal with in an everyday relationship. It makes them uncomfortable. It seems to follow for many that an individual is necessarily honest and trustworthy merely if he has not stolen anything lately. In fact, even former convicted criminals are often accorded this same assumption of honesty and trustworthiness as soon as they enter a work environment. Also, Americans do not like to "tell tales," and hence they are only too likely to let even suspicious or questionable actions go by without reporting them or even reacting to them.

A corollary of this same attitude is that actions taken or procedures adopted by management to insure that employees will be honest are too often greeted with the judgment that they are both unnecessary and indeed insulting to people. Security professionals encounter this attitude in all kinds of public and private organizations. It comes with the job, and it represents an attitude that is almost impossible to change unless a specific incident occurs in a organization and then suddenly people come to see that, yes, precautions did need to be taken after all. But by then it is often too late. The circumstances will be a little different the next time and the same attitudes will reappear.

Examples abound of situations where traitors were able to accomplish their crimes simply because others around them were too ignorant, apathetic, lazy, timid, trusting, or otherwise unwilling to question what was going on under their very noses. Michael Walker, Jr., would surely not have been able to rifle his ship's burn bag if his superiors, especially his commanding officer, carried out his oversight duty and confirmed his claim that he had a top secret clearance. The chauffeur, Corporal Drummond, would not have been able to copy and sell the classified documents in his possession if his commanding officer had not entrusted these materials to his chauffeur instead of returning them himself as regulations required and maintained proper control over the unit's copying facilities. It should have been noticed that the secretary, Ruby Schuler, was requesting an unusual number of classified documents, even in the absence of her boss. Conversely, Jonathan Pollard finally *was* noticed reviewing classified information which he had no valid need to know, and this precipitated his downfall.

The problem of attitude towards security on the part of all employees in an organization must thus be addressed forthrightly if any security system is to be effective. Persons with any responsibility for the protection of classified material—which includes everyone in any organization that deals in any way with sensitive, restricted, or classified information—must understand that people may be deceitful and dishonest even when they appear friendly and open on the surface; and that even normally honest people can be sometimes enticed, coerced, or otherwise driven to commit acts not normal to them. Our threshold of resistance to temptation, especially today, is frighteningly low. The potential in human nature for dishonest and destructive behavior must be candidly brought out in all security briefing and indoctrination courses and materials. It must be established beyond question that the security procedures in force *must* be scrupulously carried out at all times and actions on the part of anybody in the organization, which seem suspicious or out of place, must be reported. It is imperative that higher managers and commanding officers be imbued with these principles and that they require them to be adhered to within their units or organizations. Neglect or rejection of these principles on the part of a manager or commanding officer should be grounds for summary removal.

TO POLYGRAPH OR NOT TO POLYGRAPH

Polygraph tests—and the fear of having to undergo one—are among the few really effective tools available to the government to deter and detect treason or prevarication.

For decades, professionals in security, intelligence and law enforcement have recognized, applied and relied upon the polygraph as a critically necessary and effective tool. Nothing has changed.

Except: people as far apart as former Director of Central Intelligence (DCI) R. James Woolsey and Aldrich Ames have given the lie detector test a bad name for their own purposes. DCI Woolsey—like former Secretary of State George Schultz—made it clear that such indignities as being tested for integrity, loyalty, etc., were not only beneath his contempt, but that he had no confidence in their effectiveness. What really is at stake for people like Woolsey and Schultz is that, given their dealings, past associations, and attitudes, they do not wish to submit to searching and penetrating scrutiny of all they have done, said and known. I know, because, I learned at a far more youthful age, like anyone who has lived and erred, that laying bare one's past is traumatic. And that is the very point: The polygraph does lay bare when in the hands of a talented, capable operator.

The problem with the polygraph is not that the tool and the technique is faulty or ineffective. Rather it is the use made of the data developed or, as in the case of Ames, the failure to use the data. Given the arrogance and narrowness of counter-intelligence bureaucrats, and the cloaking of members of the "Club" with unimpeachable qualities of loyalty and honesty, if Ames had shown up on the chart as a confidant of Stalin, the polygraph—and not Ames—would be guilty. The problem is institutional blindness and apathy. Every individual is susceptible to successful penetration by the skillful use of the polygraphs. Excuses by Woolsey, et al., who are philosophically opposed to the polygraph notwithstanding, the tests can be scheduled, administered and evaluated so as to yield valuable information—information which can provide, at the least, clues to lead to greater certainty as to the trustworthiness of the subject. Further investigation can then prove or disprove the validity of individual findings.

One justification for opposition is that, through medication, the subject can defeat the test. For those rare individuals who may, it requires that they know the date and time of the test; otherwise, presumably the individual would need to be kept on medication indefinitely. It is only sound—and simple—management technique to refrain from telling subjects weeks, or days, in advance, the time and date of the testing. Certainly, for an individual like Ames, in a critical position and with all the clues already available, it only requires setting the test without advance notice. On August 8, 1994, in an interview with Representatives Dan Glickman and Larry Combest, Aldrich Ames admitted that frequent polygraph examinations would have caused him to at least reconsider whether to spy for the Soviet Union.

People at the highest government levels, even a Secretary of State or a Director of Central Intelligence need to be polygraphed, not only on their integrity, but also on their philosophies. The polygraph is an effective tool and it is unseemly for the head of the Nation's highest intelligence agency to damn its use either out of desire to avoid being tested, or as a baseless excuse for agency failures to protect America's most vital secrets.

We need to provide the investigative process with all the tools consistent with protection of employee and citizen guarantees which are available to us. Increasingly, metropolitan police departments are utilizing voice stress analysis equipment in a manner analogous to what we have recommended for polygraphs, because of their great value in witness and suspect interrogation. This and follow-up capabilities should be utilized appropriately.

Before rejecting the use of the polygraph, decision-makers should go back over the records of its use in security and intelligence cases and in law enforcement, and talk with the many skilled operators who have used the lie detector as a tool for the past half century and more. Study the evidence and alternate techniques, rather than rely on the self-serving views of reluctant subjects.

RESPONSE TO PROBLEM CONDITIONS

Another vital area in which security management performance must be improved is the speed and effectiveness with which managers and supervisors respond to signals, statements, or other indications that a security breach or similar improper action may be occurring or have occurred, or that individuals in the organization are finding themselves in emotional, financial, or other situations which can give rise to the suspicion that there could be a real security problem. The statement of CIA employee Edward L. Howard that he was considering espionage should have triggered an immediate review of all the areas of which he had any knowledge. Surveillance should have been placed upon him; an assessment of the potential damage should have been made at once; and procedures and structures changed to minimize any such damage. To merely conclude that the man needed a psychiatrist and provide one, as the CIA did in this case, was a disastrously limited response to what could only have been either a cry for help or an open declaration of war.

Employees who come under suspicions of this kind should undergo an immediate polygraph test, as should have been done in Howard's case. The technique is not perfect but it is an effective tool which does point to possible problems. There is no constitutional "free speech" issue here. Government employees, entrusted with sensitive classified material, are obligated to protect and prevent the divulging of that which would be harmful to the United States. Their freely accorded consent to a polygraph test should be a condition of their "security clearances" and their employment.

Each security program must include written plans about appropriate responses to situations bearing upon possible security violations, for example, cases where it appears that employees are in emotional or financial trouble. Written guidance should exist concerning what measures are to be taken in regard to the people themselves and to protect the secrets which may have been available to them, especially if these secrets turn out upon investigation to have been already compromised.

EVALUATION, TRAINING AND TESTING

All personnel must be formally trained and indoctrinated in the need for and the operation of the organizational security system.

Programs must be developed to evaluate and test the capability of organizations to protect classified information, including the technical effectiveness of their security programs in place, the extent to which their security regulations are observed and enforced, the kinds of organizational responses they have planned in the event of a potential breach, and so on. These evaluation programs should not be mere "paper" plans, either. Just as "tiger" teams are used to test computer and physical installation security, so exercises should be devised that would actually test an organization's capability, or vulnerability, in advance of any actually attempted espionage by a real spy. "Fire drills" help make for effective performance when the "real thing" is at stake.

IMAGINATION AND OPENNESS

Perhaps what security management most needs today, however, is the recognition and admission that we have, in fact, not been successful, technically or managerially, in protecting America's secrets. Our U.S. government security program has been nothing less than "fifty years of failure." A sobering realization of this fact should engender a willingness to consider and develop new approaches to security. We should approach the problem not only with new technical and managerial ideas but also with open minds and a determination that there are solutions to our security problems and that these solutions are within our capabilities.

Traditionally, whenever the nation's security performance has ever been questioned, there has been a closed-minded tendency simply to "circle the wagons" and dig in, fight off the criticism, wait for the attacks to subside and the dust to settle. This defensive attitude has resulted in the same old ineffective security techniques being employed, regardless of whether they work, or could ever succeed in serving the purpose for which they were supposedly designed. For example, access control systems, both manual and electronic, have been employed in pretty much the same manner for over the past thirty years, with the only improvements being registered in the physical devices themselves and their technical specifications (improvements devised not by government but usually by entrepreneurs and industry). Government generally does not think of updating or improving these systems.

Similarly, although great strides have now been made technically with imaging systems and systems intended either to prevent unauthorized copying or identify those carrying it out, these advances rarely show up in government security systems. Government security personnel are rarely to be found on the cutting edge of engineering and technical advances.

A SINGLE CENTRAL SECURITY AGENCY

There is a bewildering variety of different government departments and agencies conducting security investigations and other activities in observance of the now fifty-plus-year-old failed E.O. 10450 security program. Some of them operate on their own authority, while others operate on the authority delegated by the Office of Personnel Management. Each department or agency is currently responsible for its own security adjudications.

The excessive fragmentation of these very similar functions creates a situation in which each investigative or adjudicative group is organizationally and operationally isolated, although each is performing what should be virtually identical duties from one agency to another. This situation has created a multitude of problem conditions:

Consider the Following:

1. The vast reduction in numbers of investigations which has been recommended will greatly reduce the overall magnitude of both investigations and adjudications; however, given the size of our federal bureaucracy, the drag on cost and efficiency of continuing this de-centralized system will still remain great.
2. Isolated from those performing similar duties in other departments

and agencies, security personnel do not receive the same level of guidance and direction that they would if they were working in a centralized unit.

3. Redundancies and duplications exist not only in personnel, but in management, office space, equipment, files, and other organizational support features, with excess costs running into hundreds of millions of dollars for such things as a) repetitive and unnecessary investigations of the same people; b) accumulation of millions of square feet of extra file space; c) "empires" built up in numerous agencies on the basis of evaluators, administrators, clerical and other support staff; d) travel and living expenses for investigators; and e) office space, furniture, equipment, vehicles, etc.

4. Ideally, when a reinvestigation is necessary because of a job change or for some other reason, the investigator is given the files resulting from any previous investigations and then he begins his field work as of the close of the most recent investigation. In actual fact, however, inter-agency rivalries, as well as the opinion of some agencies that their files and the quality of their services are more secure or sensitive than others, usually prevent complete cooperative interchange of information when needed. As persons transfer from one agency or department to another and a new investigation is made, incomplete or misleading information may be transferred, resulting in either a lower quality product or a duplicate investigation. Sources of information who are at first cooperative are continually being approached for information which they have already supplied concerning the same individuals, resulting in a degradation of the quality of the information as the witnesses become irritated, impatient, or disillusioned. Data already accumulated on file may be lost through dispersal of records. As a result, an individual may be cleared who would otherwise be rejected. Explanatory information might also be accidentally or deliberately withheld, resulting in the unfair rejection of an applicant.

5. At best, the information transferred to a requesting agency consists of the background information developed during the field investigation and that resulting from name checks. Analytical work is virtually never transferred, probably out of fear of outside criticism of the quality of the product. The requesting agency must perform its own analysis of all this data and is generally denied the thinking of the original agency.

6. Persons who should be disqualified are able to stay ahead of the investigative process by changing agencies or departments in advance of the slow-moving and often redundant investigation.

7. Each department or agency maintains its own staff of analysts and

security "experts" who pass on the loyalty of its applicants. This can result in seriously conflicting decisions by two or more agencies concerning the loyalty or suitability of the same applicants, because the adjudicators possess only part of the available information, have different standards of appraisal, have received different levels and quality of training, or have different philosophies as to what is disqualifying or even important. In general, this training is of poor quality anyway, particularly since the persons performing the analysis and passing judgment, and training others to perform this same function, are still coming from the investigative ranks rather than being qualified adjudicators in their own right. Moreover, in many cases adjudicators are not even required to attend the training.

8. Under a decentralized system, judgments may often be influenced by the pressure to fill a vacancy, familiarity or friendship with the applicant (especially at the upper levels of a department or agency), variations in political or social beliefs of the evaluators and decision-makers, and different degrees of knowledge and competency in the task of evaluation and the application of standards to the facts.

9. The existence of personal and perhaps derogatory information on people which is accessible to personnel in the same agency who may perhaps be acquainted with the individual constitutes a real potential for violation of privacy.

10. The fear that Congress, the media, or the public may learn that the U.S. government security system has failed to keep out dangerous elements sometimes results in agencies permitting persons known to be disloyal to resign or transfer in order to obtain other government employment. This also results in agency refusals to make available all the information they may have on those being investigated by other employment offices.

11. The built-in inefficiencies of the current system prevent the fulfillment of the security mission in spite of the scores of millions spent annually to do this. We need think only of the enormous backlog in the required reinvestigations of Defense Department employees. Nevertheless the system grinds on ineffectively.

12. Without a single, guiding unifying center, it is impossible to provide effective guidance and direction to government security personnel. Instead they are overly influenced by, if not totally subservient to, the bureaucracy of the agency or department where they are located. Guidance by the Office of Personnel Management of the government security personnel of the agencies under its authority is remote and ineffective. Meanwhile agencies not under its authority, such as the DoD, FBI and the CIA, go off on their own

anyway, often basing very different judgments on similar or identical data. The government is unable to benefit from the experience and know-how of an organization of trained and experienced security investigators and evaluators. Even when committees are found to study and advise on particular issues, different agencies decide for themselves whether they will or will not implement each recommendation, resulting in a failed study or a hodgepodge of procedures among agencies.

13. The potential for abuse, as well as deficient performance, is much greater in a situation in which each security office or security investigative analysis group operates as an autonomous unit loosely supervised, if at all, from outside that agency or department. A direct and uniform line of management, supervision, and control would minimize the untoward independence and power which frequently spawns abuse by security units.

14. As a smaller group within a large agency or department, the security function is typically outside the main managerial channels and without the high-level influence within the organization which is necessary to get the job done and insure compliance both with its security decisions and with the organization-wide procedures it may attempt to put in place.

15. Greater security effectiveness made in this book is substantially more difficult to implement in the present environment of dispersed and fragmented security authority. The present system almost guarantees that security will not be taken with much seriousness in agencies or departments where it has low priority, both in terms of agency budgets and prestige and in terms of agency policies and priorities.

16. A decentralized system diminishes the capacity and will of the government to establish and apply standards of conduct, character, morality, and integrity in clearance decisions. Individual agencies are more susceptible to vocal abuse and threat from the media, politicians, and the many and varied activists who agitate on this subject and individuals agencies are thereby more easily dissuaded from denying clearances or employment to persons who fail to meet the standards.

17. Standards of character, conduct, and morality are likewise diluted because of fear of attack by the media or by the activists of various causes. By contrast, a single, central, unified security authority would provide a firm, independent, and consistent application of established standards to the decisions made regarding security clearances.

The cumulative effect here is to indicate the need for a single, central government security agency to carry out the U.S. government's security function. Virtually all of these flaws could be eliminated by the creation and effective direction of such an entity.

This Central Security Agency would be responsible for performing all security investigations and for adjudicating the results. It would have government-wide responsibility for granting or withholding security clearances. It would also be responsible for developing and disseminating government-wide security policies and procedures.

Although putting in place and implementing many of these security policies and procedures would necessarily be the responsibility of the line management in the individual departments and agencies, the Central Security Agency should have inspection and oversight responsibilities and should also conduct audits to measure the effectiveness of the efforts of department and agency management in security matters and to ensure uniform compliance throughout the government. The Agency would also identify and help respond to specific security deficiencies identified within other agencies and departments. It would provide a single, unified voice before Congress and the public in connection with the U.S. Government security system generally.

The centralization of all security functions in a single Central Security Agency would also make possible the creation of a well-trained and highly motivated corps of security specialists in a position to serve the entire U.S. government. It would save many millions of dollars annually. These savings could be achieved in many ways, but specifically by consolidating all government security records and processes in a single location under a single authority. All other security activities would similarly be performed on a centralized basis: application processing, investigations, record checks, polygraph tests, security hearings, updates, adjudications, issuance of clearances or denials, and hearings and appeals. Because of the ability of a centralized agency to focus its resources, the improvements in security specialist qualifications, control, training, consistency, and other performance measurements would be immense. The reductions in the size of the work force, with attendant reductions in salary, retirement and other benefits, travel, and other costs would also be immense.

The validity of the conclusions set forth in this book are confirmed over and over again by the various commissions and committees which have examined the quality and performance of various aspects of the government's security program, frequently after a devastating and expensive act of revealed treason or espionage.

The study results uniformly recommend patching one or another of the many facets of the program, but without ever addressing the fundamental premises upon which the overall program is based.

Typically, "fix-it" nostrums are recommended, although a number of recommendations have been positive and constructive as we have noted, and certain recommendations have ascribed cost savings ranging up to the hundreds of millions of dollars.

We are deliberately refraining from putting a specific dollar amount on the savings to be realized by the adoption of a total approach to security; however, stated categorically, the sums will be massive. Dollar specifics must await the shape and outline of the program to be designed. The Single Security Agency concept, if adopted, along with the adoption of the recommendation to rely upon other measures than full field investigations for the vast number of clearances, will produce such savings over a ten-year period as to refund to the American taxpayers much of the treasure lost through the treason and treachery of the traitors who have paraded through our last half century of history.

The need for coordination and control of the security function is finally beginning to be recognized and as a result of several commissioned studies, some elementary recommendations have been proposed.

An office has been recommended that would develop and promulgate consistent policies, documents and procedures. The Information Security Oversight Office is already performing some coordination and evaluation functions although they are primarily related to declassification of information and the development of security awareness manuals. However, these actions represent only a fraction of the function and controls of a single security agency.

In early March 1992, Senator David Boren of Oklahoma, Chairman of the Senate Intelligence Committee, proposed a set of far-reaching, even sweeping reforms of the currently dispersed and fragmented U.S. intelligence and counter-intelligence functions. Senator Boren's proposal called for the creation of an overall "intelligence Czar" with control over both domestic and foreign counter-intelligence, that is, with control over activities currently divided among the CIA, FBI, NSA, DoD, and some other agencies. The director of the CIA is already by law the Director of Central Intelligence (DCI), but as a practical matter he has had control only over the CIA. The Boren proposal would finally bring together many of the activities originally envisaged when the function of Director of Central Intelligence was first set up after World War II, growing out of the old Office of Strategic Services (OSS). Although the proposal outlined here for a single Central Security Agency calls for a single, separate and distinct agency, performing *all* professional support functions, it is consistent with the Boren proposal and for many of the same reasons.

Although there are compelling arguments in favor of unifying related intelligence functions in the manner proposed, it is probably inevitable that the Department of Defense and others will immediately oppose the proposal. Their "empires" would be threatened. The interests of the country, however, almost certainly require that we go beyond the preservation of such established bureaucracies.

Similarly, opposition to the idea of a single Central Security Agency is probably to be expected from those agencies or entities whose current functions would be affected. Their responses may all be anticipated: "We're doing that already." "It won't help." "We tried that and it didn't work." "We are different." And so on.

But the real issue here, as we have been able to see at length, is that the current security system is not working. It has never worked; nor will it ever work. But a single Central Security Agency, implementing the recommendations contained in this book, can be highly effective.

DESCRIPTION AND FUNCTIONS OF A SINGLE CENTRAL SECURITY AGENCY

In order to correct the manifold deficiencies in the current U.S. government security system, and provide the United States with effective protection against those who would compromise the country's vital secrets and security, the following proposals are offered which, taken together, would amount to the creation of a single Central Security Agency for the United States.

1. A commission should be created under the Executive Office of the President, with ex officio representation from Congress, in order to develop standards for the suitability and loyalty of U.S. government employees; these standards should be framed in such a way that judgments could be made about whether or not to grant security clearances for government employment in accordance with them, recognizing that government employees are not by virtue of their employment entitled as a matter of right to access classified security data.

2. An Agency of the executive branch of the government should be created, to be headed by three commissioners, no more than two of whom could be members of the same political party. The appoint-

ments of these three commissioners would be for life, subject to the confirmation of the Senate. This Agency, to be called the Central Security Agency, should be made responsible by statute for the following governmental functions:

- Determining all situations where security investigations are required and the scope of such investigations and conducting all investigations of persons, federal employees and others, who require access to classified data by virtue of the positions they hold or will be holding.
- Developing security reference files and related information on all government employees and applicants and maintaining such files and records on a permanent basis.
- Analyzing all the information collected or acquired on the individuals investigated and making judgments about their loyalty and suitability to receive security clearances for access to classified information on the basis of standards to be developed by the commission described in item #1 above.

3. The Agency should have the authority to select and hire such individuals as it deems necessary and qualified to carry out the duties and functions assigned to it, and should develop and prescribe the qualifying standards for such employees.

4. The Agency should conduct studies, audits, and inquiries concerning the security policies and procedures of all other government departments and agencies, as well as contract companies in the private sector, which have or use classified government material for any purpose; and should specifically determine whether the physical security measures of such departments, agencies, or companies are adequate and sufficient for the protection of the classified material in the custody of these organizations, prescribing what measures are required, in accordance with standards to be established by the Agency itself.

5. The Agency should have the authority to grant or deny security clearances for U.S. government employment; to rescind the security clearance of any employee it deems unsuitable; to deny to any government agency or department or company access to or retention of classified security data if it determines that the organization has violated, or is likely to violate, the established standards for the protection of such data, or is failing to administer its program of physical security in a manner which will insure the protection of the classified material for which it is responsible.

6. The Agency should assume control and responsibility over all files, records, reports of investigation, and information pertaining to the security and suitability of all federal employees and employees in

the private sector who have been cleared for access to classified material, or on whom a case is in existence or pending.

7. The Agency should receive and maintain records of organizations and individuals in matters where loyalty, suitability, or related matters may provide pertinent data necessary in judging the suitability and security and loyalty of applicants and employees who will come within the purview of the Agency. Such records should include criminal records, although the Agency will have the right of access to such data in the possession of the FBI by requesting a search of the Bureau's records, as well as of the records of police departments throughout the country and abroad and of intelligence and security agencies.

8. The Agency should have subpoena power, as well as the power of putting people under oath, and of holding quasi-judicial hearings, and pursuing other such appropriate procedures, under law and accepted judicial practice, in order to be able to arrive at the truth of those matters that properly and legally come before it.

9. The Agency's central headquarters should be in Washington, D.C., but it should be authorized to establish such regional offices as may be required for the efficient performance of its responsibilities.

10. The Agency should receive all records pertaining to prior, or current, cases of treason, espionage, loss or theft or destruction of classified data, and all cases involving breaches of government security, including infractions and violations, whether inadvertent or deliberate. It should be authorized to require that government agencies and departments provide it with information, statistics, and records in connection with their physical security performances and their systems of document and logging control, and it should have similar authority with regard to companies in the private sector which are in possession of classified data as a result of federal government contracts.

11. The Agency should make such reports to the president and Congress as required by law, both at the outset of its activities, and on a continuing basis as necessary. The reports will include, but need not be limited to, the numbers of security investigations conducted; the results of these investigations, particularly with regard to the numbers of security clearances granted or denied; the numbers of security breaches which have occurred throughout the government and the nature of the corrective action taken with regard to them; the nature and type of such breaches, with an estimate of the harm, if any, arising from them; the number of treasonable or seditious acts discovered and the nature of the action taken with respect to them; the incidence of loss, theft, or destruction of classified docu-

ments including pertinent information on the perpetrators of such
actions; and the disciplinary actions taken for security violations
and other failures and deficiencies.

12. To the extent that it is consistent with national security, the Agency
should make public the pertinent facts contained in the reports to
be prepared in accordance with item #11 above.

ORIGIN OF THE CONCEPT OF A SINGLE
CENTRAL SECURITY AGENCY

The arguments for a single Central Security Agency are persua-
sive, while the arguments for maintaining our current futile and unworkable security system are negligible, and usually self-serving. In order for
this or any innovative idea to become a reality, however, there must be
astute leadership in its support. Its basic concepts must be embodied in
viable legislation, then survive the attacks that will no doubt be launched
against it.

It must be assumed that the idea of a single Central Security Agency
will be opposed by the present security establishment, most of whose
current members will perceive their own self-interest to reside in the
status quo of existing, unsupervised security fiefdoms in the various
departments and agencies.

The concept of one centralized agency handling the overall security needs of the U.S. government is not a recent development. Its benefits in terms of cost savings, efficiency, increased competence of security practitioners, and marked reduction in duplication of effort were
recognized by this author in 1947. Since that time, the basic concept has
been advocated more than once by different specialists or legislators,
and has even been included in House and Senate bills which the author,
working with Congressional staff, succeeded in having introduced. Unfortunately, these bills were never passed into law. Each effort to enact
the concept into law, lacking sufficient support, fell victim either to the
rivalries or perceived self-interest of existing agencies.

As an appropriate conclusion, a brief account of some of my own
experiences in designing and promoting the concept of a single Central
Security Agency may be interesting and instructive.

The Conception (1947)

In 1947, while employed at the Central Intelligence Agency, then
still known as the Central Intelligence Group (CIG), I served as Chief

of the Liaison Division in the Office of Security and Inspection. My role included responsibility for developing and implementing procedures for CIG access to the security and intelligence files of other agencies which could be used by CIG in investigating and assessing the security worthiness of its job applicants and employees.

As a result of earlier investigative experience with the Civil Service Commission, the Army Counter-Intelligence Corps, and the OSS under General Donovan at the Nuremberg trials, I came to the realization that, whereas there was an immense amount of intelligence data in existence, it was distributed among many organizations. Further, although there did exist varying degrees of cooperation among the intelligence-gathering and security entities, they mostly operated as competitive businesses, with each organization primarily concerned with its own advancement and only secondarily with the protection of the government's interests. The Office of Naval Intelligence, the Civil Service Commission, the Army MI, the House Un-American Activities Committee, the Senate Internal Affairs Committee, and later the OSI (when the Air Force became a separate arm) all tended to share the information they had with other agencies. The FBI, however, restricted its files and insisted on assembling a "prepared" product for any other agency requesting security or investigative information or data.

Numerous agencies were all engaged in their own investigations. For example, in the early days of my career as a federal employee, I was investigated by no less than five government agencies including the Civil Service Commission, the Department of State, the FBI, the Military Intelligence Division of the U.S. Army, and the CIA, each for separate, but related, jobs in the field of security and intelligence.

When it is recognized that integral to a full field investigation is a requirement to fan out across the same geographical territory where the applicant has been or lived in order to verify statements on the application concerning education, employment, police records, residences, and neighbors, and to follow up on any leads which might have arisen in the course of the investigation, it quickly becomes apparent that, because of overlap and duplication, such an investigation requires a substantial and wholly unnecessary investment in time, money, and personnel.

In my investigating days I very quickly recognized that, for example, once I had verified the high school and college records of an applicant and obtained the appropriate transcripts, it would be wasteful for another government investigator to go out subsequently looking for the same information, once, twice, or even more. Yet, when a government employee was transferred from one agency to another and needed to be cleared by the second agency, the only information shared between the two agencies was the level of clearance granted to the individual. Background information on the individual was not shared. It became apparent that what was at stake in sharing or not sharing this background information was not so much the information itself as it was the question of the judgment or evaluation of this security information made by an agency when granting or withholding a security clearance. Generally neither the background investigation nor the security appraisal was shared.

Compounding the wastefulness and inadequacy of the system was another agency practice of always retaining its own file on the individual. Thus, when employees transferred from one department or agency to another, not only was a new security clearance required, a new security investigation was required; whereas by the simple act of transferring the security file with the employee, all that would have been required would have been an update of an investigation, not a complete new investigation. However, bureaucratic arteriosclerosis would not permit logic to function.

Further adding to the wastefulness and confusion was the general refusal of agencies to accept the results of another agency's previous security judgment. This is akin to a medical doctor refusing to consider results of a the blood test, EKG, or other tests by a doctor who has recently seen the same patient. Agencies accepting transferred employees insisted on making their own judgment on an employee's suitability before granting security clearance. They would only do so after a new investigation had been conducted, verifying all the same information previously gathered regarding the applicant's birth, education, employment, residence, reputation with his neighbors, etc.

Historically, under the law, the Civil Service Commission was charged with announcing and holding examinations for positions in the federal service. The Commission rated the applicants who took the examinations and placed them on registers based upon their scores. Thereafter, agencies and departments communicated to the Commission their needs for employees and certificates of eligibles from the registers of qualified persons were sent to the agency requesters who were required to select from among those shown on the certificates. The system worked very well over the years and held to a minimum the inevitable abuses arising from efforts to favor friends and also from the nepotism which had plagued the federal service prior to the passage of the Civil Service Act.

I saw a similar opportunity: the Civil Service Commission could conduct all the security investigations, as the Commission had done back in the 1930s and the early 1940s before the magnitude of the wartime federal build-up had made it impossible to keep up with the workload. My basic idea provided for an independent Commission, not the employing agency, to conduct the background inquiries on applicants or employees and evaluate it, to examine the security, loyalty, integrity, and suitability of the candidate in the light of the requirements, and determine where a security clearance was specifically required by the nature of the position and either to issue or deny the clearance. The Commission would both evaluate the data and issue or deny clearances of the basis of applicable standards. I sketched out the outlines of the system that has been laid out earlier in this chapter.

Senator Taft and the Hoover Commission

The CIG, like the FBI, had created its own investigative staff. It made its own analysis of the data gathered, and then made its own judgments on the suitability and loyalty of the employee or applicant. I recognized that there was no way even my own agency was going to accept any infringement on its own "right" to perform all these functions. Nor would the Civil Service Commission undertake to challenge all of the other powerful departments and agencies on the issue.

At that time one of the dominant figures in Congress was Senator Robert A. Taft of Ohio, then known as "Mr. Republican." This Ohio senator was noted for many qualities. He was utterly honest, always doing the right thing as he saw it regardless of the consequences, and sometimes committing colossal blunders by saying something, even though it might be true, at the wrong or inappropriate time. I was a great admirer of Senator Taft.

I was determined to put my concept of a single Central Security Agency before him. I actually had a note sent out to Senator Taft on the floor of the Senate via a page; when the senator came off the floor in response to the note, I explained my concept. The senator was clearly interested, most gracious and encouraging. He observed that the concept seemed to him rational, economically beneficial, and administratively sound. He concluded that the proposal was one which merited the attention of the Hoover Commission which was then examining the administrative performance of the executive branch of the government. He told me to meet with the Executive Director of the Hoover Commission, a Mr. Brassor, with authorization to state that the referral included his personal request for consideration of my idea.

Mr. Brassor was a long-time employee of the Civil Service Commission, and remained one while he was directing the work of the Hoover Commission. My interview with him was far from a smashing success. He himself was an accomplished bureaucrat, and he had brought his bureaucratic skills with him to the Hoover Commission. He avoided any real action, regardless of the problem. At the same time, he was not about to deliver any negative judgment, considering Senator Taft's endorsement of the idea. He resolved this tough issue by passing it to the Civil Service Commission's congressional liaison.

In those days, the Civil Service Commission maintained its liaison with Congress through the instrumentality of Robert L. Bailey, who was a long-time veteran of the Federal Service and highly skilled in the political game. I prepared a written description of my concept in response to Bailey's request (see Appendix H), and, over the course of several years, he tried to promote the idea with the Congress. He made some progress and the idea acquired some sympathy on Capitol Hill, but Bailey's retirement from the federal service effectively meant that the whole thing was left hanging without ever getting enacted into law.

Another Lost Opportunity

As we have seen, the early 1950s was a period when it became impossible to keep the lid on the dramatic espionage successes of the Soviet Union in penetrating our government. Real security breakdowns and disasters were revealed and genuine Soviet agents were shown to have been at work for years penetrating our government at the highest levels while serving the interests of a foreign power. In the ferment and fury which resulted, the Administration and Congress completely lost sight of how abysmally our own security system had failed. With all the focus on the revelations concerning spies and other secret goings-on, no serious effort was made to look at the real reasons why it all was permitted to happen.

The questions that badly needed addressing was how our security system had failed and what needed to be done to fix it. But these questions were not addressed and hence they were not answered. An important opportunity was lost.

We also lost uncountable millions, not to speak of lives, in the protracted Cold War that followed—not to speak of the hot wars in Korea and Vietnam and numerous skirmishes in other trouble spots stirred up by the Soviet Union, Communist China, and other regimes. The most powerful nation on earth had been diminished while its most formidable opponent, the Soviet Union, built much of its strength on our security failures.

Meanwhile bitter accusations and hatreds divided America, especially at our leadership levels in the media, the churches, academia, labor, entertainment, and political life over charges of disloyalty, pro-Communism, McCarthyism and related issues. The resulting confusion helped prevent any reasoned, objective, deliberate approach to the issues of loyalty and security. As a result no sound security system emerged for the protection of our secrets and of our country.

Instead politically motivated and sensational accusations of disloyalty were made, as were declarations of intention couched in strong words. But these proved to be mostly for show, to "clean all the spies and security risks out of government." At the same time, however, since little or no real thought had been given to what the real problems were, the security system that was put in place at that time left a great deal to be desired. With security firmly under the influence of the FBI and FBI alumni by then, no fundamental institutional change or improvement had a chance.

There was, however, one change that occurred at that time that offered the opportunity to move towards a single central security agency. Under Executive Order 10450, J. Edgar's Hoover's FBI had responsibility for virtually all non-CIA security investigations. Concerned that the image of the FBI might change from that of the valiant crime-and spy-fighting organization to that of simple investigative agency, Hoover encouraged the transfer of this security investigative function to the Civil Service Commission. Once this transfer was effected, however, Mr. Kimball Johnson, chief of the CSC's Investigation Division—a fine government official and very dear friend—decided to delegate out as much of this investigative responsibility as possible because he felt he could not expand the number of CSC investigators rapidly enough to cover the needs of all the federal departments and agencies needing security investigations conducted.

Thus, the Departments of State, the Army, Navy, and the Air Force, as well as certain other sensitive agencies, were given by delegation of authority the responsibility for performing their own security investigations and adjudications using procedures approved by the CSC. The FBI and CIA continued to perform their own investigations. *All* of the departments and agencies continued to perform their own security adjudications. This act of expediency by the CSC—delegating the investigative authority—coupled with its failure to consolidate the adjudication process—ended all realistic hopes for a centralized security agency at that time.

Senator Olin Johnston

During and after the McCarthy era, I continued to make various attempts to better inform Congress about security.

One committee in Congress which had a legitimate interest in the ensurance of loyalty and suitability of government employees, the legitimate protection of their civil rights, and the quality of executive branch security programs was the old Senate Post Office and Civil Service Committee.

In a Senate then controlled by the Republicans, the ranking minority member was Senator Olin Johnston, a Democrat from South Carolina, who was considered almost a stereotype of the Southern senator of the day. He had hardly any conception of the real issues involved. Nor was it usually possible to explain things to him. However, the chief minority clerk for this Senate committee, William T. Brawley, was as competent and sophisticated as Senator Johnston was inadequate and confused. Himself politically ambitious and very astute, Brawley, who later became Deputy Postmaster General under Eisenhower, was very receptive to my proposal for a single Central Security Agency, and he was willing to try to push it. He immediately saw the relevance of the issue to the role and responsibilities of the Senate Post Office and Civil Service Committee.

Over a period of some two years, many discussions took place and numerous documents were drafted, all aimed at selling the basic concept to key Committee members. Finally, a Senate Bill (S. 2399) was drafted laying out the statutory requirements for a single Central Security Agency, and introduced into the Senate with the support of Senator Everett Dirksen of Illinois and a number of other senators. It would have eliminated all the waste, fraud, duplications, expense, abuses, and weaknesses of the U.S. government security system then in place—and still in place. A companion bill was also introduced into the House of Representatives with strong sponsorship. Unfortunately, the bills died in committee because the vested interests of the existing investigative agencies proved stronger than the bills' sponsorship.

JFK: The Morse Plan, "I want to do something on it."

During the Kennedy-Nixon presidential campaign in 1960, Vice President Nixon had the benefit of the boundless resources of the executive branch to provide him with security services and protection. Senator Kennedy, on the other hand, although his Senate office was directly across the hall in the Senate Office Building from the Vice President's, enjoyed no such luxuries. Since their presidential contest was fought in an era prior to the tragic assassination of President Kennedy himself, the nation at that time had not focused on the need for the protection of its presidential candidates, who in those days received no Secret Service protection. The vice president was thus better prepared for any possible violent actions against him, as he was better prepared against any "dirty tricks" or other intrusions; he had the whole federal government at his disposal.

Senator Kennedy, as a presidential candidate, did have a police escort assigned to him detailed from the Washington Metropolitan Police Department. A long-time close personal friend, Detective Sergeant James Roche, was the key man on that escort. A veteran of many years on the force, he was not only capable and fearless, but he had an Irish personality and humor which delighted the Senator from Massachusetts.

I received a call from Sgt. Roche near the beginning of the campaign asking me to provide certain specialized security services to Senator Kennedy, including technical assistance both at his Senate office and at his home in Georgetown. As a result of providing these security services, I came to know well Evelyn Lincoln, Kennedy's long-time loyal and competent secretary. I responded to Mrs. Lincoln's direct requests for security assistance on a number of occasions. Of course the day the Massachusetts Senator defeated Nixon and became the President-elect, the Secret Service, and other federal agencies very quickly and properly took over all functions having anything to do with his security.

Nevertheless, our friendship with Evelyn and Harold ("Abe") Lincoln grew, and, in the course of my dealings with Mrs. Lincoln, I had occasion to discuss various government operations with her on more numerous occasions. At some point in our discussions the concept of a single Central Security Agency came up and I described my ideas on this subject to her. I explained the advantages and benefits of the proposed system to her, as well as pointing out the deficiencies of the security system we had in place. Evelyn was a very able and intelligent person with extensive experience in the Federal Service and quickly recognized the merits of the proposal. She was particularly impressed by my concern that the program respect the legitimate rights of government employees while preventing and identifying subversive activity. She indicated that this particular emphasis reflected a deep personal commitment on the part of President Kennedy himself. Finally, there was the enormous cost savings to be realized.

At the request of the Personal Secretary to the President, then, I was pleased to prepare an indepth assessment of the whole concept and a description of how the system based upon it would function. I sent all this material to Mrs. Lincoln under a cover letter dated October 17, 1963. We were optimistic over the prospects of the idea.

This material was passed to the President. What ensued can best be described in the words of Evelyn Lincoln in response to my request to her to confirm the events in question:

> I have been delighted to read my diary which I wrote during that time and as a result I am submitting the following explanation to you:
>
> As was my custom, papers that needed the President's attention were placed in a file box on the left-hand corner of my desk. The President would come out to my office and read those papers some time during the day.
>
> The early part of November 1963, I placed the letter written to the President by George P. Morse recommending the establishment of an Agency and a program to handle all investigations and clearances at a central level and to eliminate the various investigative and clearance organizations which were scattered throughout the Executive Branch in that box.
>
> Each day thereafter the President would look at this letter and say, 'I will read this at a later date.'
>
> He was scheduled to go to Elkton, Maryland, to participate in the dedication of a new turnpike in Delaware and Maryland— from there to New York—and thence to Palm Beach, Tampa, and Miami, Florida. He asked me to put Mr. Morse's letter in his black brief case so that he might read it during his trip.
>
> We returned to Washington the evening of November 18. The next morning the papers he had in his brief case were delivered to my office and with them was Mr. Morse's letter, with the notation in the corner 'Remind me.' This I did and he said, 'Yes, remind me to bring this letter to the attention of the Cabinet members because I want to do something about it.'
>
> Two days later he flew off to Texas.

And so, the great tragedy of President Kennedy's death which brought the demise of many hopes and dreams, also killed the best opportunity for an effective security system for America.

Perhaps another leader of vision can revive our dream for stronger and better security for our great country.

APPENDIX A

EXECUTIVE ORDER 9835

PRESCRIBING PROCEDURES FOR THE ADMINISTRATION
OF AN EMPLOYEES LOYALTY PROGRAM IN THE
EXECUTIVE BRANCH OF THE GOVERNMENT

WHEREAS each employee of the Government of the United States is endowed with a measure of trusteeship over the democratic processes which are the heart and sinew of the United States; and

WHEREAS it is of vital importance that persons employed in the Federal service be of complete and unswerving loyalty to the United States; and

WHEREAS, although the loyalty of by far the overwhelming majority of all Government employees is beyond question, the presence within the Government service of any disloyal or subversive person constitutes a threat to our democratic processes; and

WHEREAS maximum protection must be afforded the United States against infiltration of disloyal persons into the ranks of its employees, and equal protection from unfounded accusations of disloyalty must be afforded the loyal employees of the Government:

NOW, THEREFORE, by virtue of the authority vested in me by the Constitution and statutes of the United States, including the Civil Service Act of 1883 (22 Stat. 403), as amended, and section 9A of the act approved August 2, 1939 (18 U. S. C. 61i), and as President and Chief Executive of the United States, it is hereby, in the interest of the internal management of the Government, ordered as follows:

PART I—INVESTIGATION OF APPLICANTS

1. There shall be a loyalty investigation of every person entering the civilian employment of any department or agency of the executive branch of the Federal Government.

    a. Investigations of persons entering the competitive service shall be conducted by the Civil Service Commission, except in such cases as are covered by a special agreement between the Commission and any given department or agency.

b. Investigations of persons other than those entering the competitive service shall be conducted by the employing department or agency. Departments and agencies without investigative organizations shall utilize the investigative facilities of the Civil Service Commission.

2. The investigations of persons entering the employ of the executive branch may be conducted after any such person enters upon actual employment therein, but in any such case the appointment of such person shall be conditioned upon a favorable determination with respect to his loyalty.

a. Investigations of persons entering the competitive service shall be conducted as expeditiously as possible; provided, however, that if any such investigation is not completed within 18 months from the date on which a person enters actual employment, the condition that his employment is subject to investigation shall expire, except in a case in which the Civil Service Commission has made an initial adjudication of disloyalty and the case continues to be active by reason of an appeal, and it shall then be the responsibility of the employing department or agency to conclude such investigation and make a final determination concerning the loyalty of such person.

3. An investigation shall be made of all applicants at all available pertinent sources of information and shall include reference to:

a. Federal Bureau of Investigation files.

b. Civil Service Commission files.

c. Military and Naval Intelligence files.

d. The files of any other appropriate government investigative or intelligence agency.

e. House Committee on un-American Activities files.

f. Local law-enforcement files at the place of residence and employment of the applicant, including municipal, county, and State law-enforcement files.

g. Schools and colleges attended by applicant.

h. Former employers of applicant.

i. References given by applicant.

j. Any other appropriate source.

4. Whenever derogatory information with respect to loyalty of an applicant is revealed a full field of applicants for particular positions, as may be designated by the investigation shall be conducted. A full field investigation shall also be conducted of those applicants, or head of the employing department or agency, such designations to be based on the determination by any such head of the best interests of national security.

PART II—INVESTIGATION OF EMPLOYEES

1. The head of each department and agency in the executive branch of the Government shall be personally responsible for an effective program to assure that disloyal civilian officers or employees are not retained in employment in his department or agency.

a. He shall be responsible for prescribing and supervising the loyalty determination procedures of his department or agency, in accordance with the revisions of this order, which shall be considered as providing minimum requirements.

b. The head of a department or agency which does not have an investigative organization shall utilize the investigative facilities of the Civil Service Commission.

2. The head of each department and agency shall appoint one or more loyalty boards, each composed of not less than three representatives of the department or agency concerned, for the purpose of hearing loyalty cases arising within such department or agency and making recommendations with respect to the removal of any officer or employee of such department or agency on grounds relating to loyalty, and he shall prescribe regulations for the conduct of the proceedings before such boards.

a. An officer or employee who is charged with being disloyal shall have a right to an administrative hearing before a loyalty board in the employing department or agency. He may appear before such board personally, accompanied by counsel or representative of his own choosing, and present evidence on his own behalf, through witnesses or by affidavit.

b. The officer or employee shall be served with a written notice of such hearing in sufficient time, and shall be informed therein of the nature of the charges against him in sufficient detail, so that he will be enabled to prepare his defense. The charges shall be stated as specifically and completely as, in the discretion of the employing department or agency, security considerations permit, and the officer or employee shall be informed in the notice (1) of his right to reply to such charges in writing within a specified reasonable period of time, (2) of his right to an administrative hearing on such charges before a loyalty board, and (3) of his right to appear before such board personally, to be accompanied by counsel or representative of his own choosing, and to present evidence on his behalf, through witness or by affidavit.

3. A recommendation of removal by a loyalty board shall be subject to appeal by the officer or employee affected, prior to his removal, to the

head of the employing department or agency or to such person or persons as may be designated by such head, under such regulations as may be prescribed by him, and the decision of the department or agency concerned shall be subject to appeal to the Civil Service Commission's Loyalty Review Board, hereinafter provided for, for an advisory recommendation.

4. The rights of hearing, notice thereof, and appeal therefrom shall be accorded to every officer or employee prior to his removal on grounds of disloyalty, irrespective of tenure, or of manner, method, or nature of appointment, but the head of the employing department or agency may suspend any officer or employee at any time pending a determination with respect to loyalty.

5. The loyalty boards of the various departments and agencies shall furnish to the Loyalty Review Board, hereinafter provided for, such reports as may be requested concerning the operation of the loyalty program in any such department or agency.

PART III—RESPONSIBILITIES OF CIVIL SERVICE COMMISSION

1. There shall be established in the Civil Service Commission a Loyalty Review Board of not less than three impartial persons, the members of which shall be officers or employees of the Commission.

a. The Board shall have authority to review cases involving persons recommended for dismissal on grounds relating to loyalty by the loyalty board of any department or agency and to make advisory recommendations thereon to the head of the employing department or agency. Such cases may be referred to the Board either by the employing department or agency, or by the officer or employee concerned.

b. The Board shall make rules and regulations, not inconsistent with the provisions of this order, deemed necessary to implement statutes and Executive orders relating to employee loyalty.

c. The Loyalty Review Board shall also:

(1) Advise all departments and agencies on all problems relating to employee loyalty.

(2) Disseminate information pertinent to employee loyalty programs.

(3) Coordinate the employee loyalty policies and procedures of the several departments and agencies.

(4) Make reports and submit recommendations to the Civil Service Commission for transmission to the President from time to time as may be necessary to the maintenance of the employee loyalty program.

2. There shall also be established and maintained in the Civil Service Commission a central master index covering all persons on whom loyalty investigations have been made by any department or agency since September 1, 1939. Such master index shall contain the name of each person investigated, adequate identifying information concerning each such person, and a reference to each department and agency which has conducted a loyalty investigation concerning the person involved.

a. All executive departments and agencies are directed to furnish to the Civil Service Commission all information appropriate for the establishment and maintenance of the central master index.

b. The reports and other investigative material and information developed by the investigating department or agency shall be retained by such department or agency in each case.

3. The Loyalty Review Board shall currently be furnished by the Department of Justice the name of each foreign or domestic organization, association, movement, group or combination of persons which the Attorney General, after appropriate investigation and determination, designates as totalitarian, fascist, communist or subversive, or as having adopted a policy of advocating or approving the commission of acts of force or violence to deny others their rights under the Constitution of the United States, or as seeking to alter the form of government of the United States by unconstitutional means.

a. The Loyalty Review Board shall disseminate such information to all departments and agencies.

PART IV—SECURITY MEASURES IN INVESTIGATIONS

1. At the request of the head of any department or agency of the executive branch an investigative agency shall make available to such head, personally, all investigative material and information collected by the investigative agency concerning any employee or prospective employee of the requesting department or agency, or shall make such material and information available to any officer or orders designated by such head and approved by the investigative agency.

2. Notwithstanding the foregoing requirement, however, the investigative agency may refuse to disclose the names of confidential informants, provided it furnishes sufficient information about such informants on the basis of which the requesting department or agency can make an adequate evaluation of the information furnished by them, and provided it advises the requesting department or agency in writing that

it is essential to the protection of the informants or to the investigation of other cases that the identity of the informants not be revealed. Investigative agencies shall not use this discretion to decline to reveal sources of information where such action is not essential.

3. Each department and agency of the executive branch should develop and maintain, for the collection and analysis of information relating to the loyalty of its employees and prospective employees, a staff specially trained in security techniques, and an effective security control system for protecting such information generally and for protecting confidential sources of such information particularly.

PART V—STANDARDS

1. The standard for the refusal of employment or the removal from employment in an executive department or agency on grounds relating to loyalty shall be that, on all the evidence, reasonable grounds exist for belief that the person involved is disloyal to the Government of the United States.

2. Activities and associations of an applicant or employee which may be considered in connection with the determination of disloyalty may include one or more of the following:

a. Sabotage, espionage, or attempts or preparations therefor, or knowingly associating with spies or saboteurs;

b. Treason or sedition or advocacy thereof;

c. Advocacy of revolution or force or violence to alter the constitutional form of government of the United States;

d. Intentional, unauthorized disclosure to any person, under circumstances which may indicate disloyalty to the United States, of documents or information of a confidential or non-public character obtained by the person making the disclosure as a result of his employment by the Government of the United States;

e. Performing or attempting to perform his duties, or otherwise acting, so as to serve the interests of another government in preference to the interests of the United States.

f. Membership in, affiliation with or sympathetic association with any foreign or domestic organization, association, movement, group or combination of persons, designated by the Attorney General as totalitarian, fascist, communist, or subversive, or as having adopted a policy of advocating or approving the commission of acts of force or violence to deny other persons their rights under the Constitution of the United

States, or as seeking to alter the form of government of the United States by unconstitutional means.

PART VI—MISCELLANEOUS

1. Each department and agency of the executive branch, to the extent that it has not already done so, shall submit, to the Federal Bureau of Investigation of the Department of Justice, either directly or through the Civil Service Commission, the names (and such other necessary identifying material as the Federal Bureau of Investigation may require) of all of its incumbent employees.

a. The Federal Bureau of Investigation shall check such names against its records of persons concerning whom there is substantial evidence of being within the purview of paragraph 2 of Part V hereof, and shall notify each department and agency of such information.

b. Upon receipt of the above-mentioned information from the Federal Bureau of Investigation, each department and agency shall make, or cause to be made by the Civil Service Commission, such investigation of those employees as the head of the department or agency shall deem advisable.

2. The Security Advisory Board of the State-War-Navy Coordinating Committee shall draft rules applicable to the handling and transmission of confidential documents and other documents and information which should not be publicly disclosed, and upon approval by the President such rules shall constitute the minimum standards for the handling and transmission of such documents and information, and shall be applicable to all departments and agencies of the executive branch.

3. The provisions of this order shall not be applicable to persons summarily removed under the provisions of section 3 of the act of December 17, 1942, 56 Stat. 1053, of the act of July 5, 1946, 60 Stat. 453, or of any other statute conferring the power of summary removal.

4. The Secretary of War and the Secretary of the Navy, and the Secretary of the Treasury with respect to the Coast Guard, are hereby directed to continue to enforce and maintain the highest standards of loyalty within the armed services, pursuant to the applicable statutes, the Articles of War, and the Articles for the Government of the Navy.

5. This order shall be effective immediately, but compliance with such of its provisions as require the expenditure of funds shall be deferred pending the appropriation of such funds.

6. Executive Order No. 9300 of February 5, 1943, is hereby revoked.

HARRY S. TRUMAN

THE WHITE HOUSE,
March 21, 1947.

APPENDIX B

EXECUTIVE ORDER 10450

Security Requirements for Government Employment

WHEREAS the interests of national security require that all persons privileged to be employed in the departments and agencies of the Government shall be reliable, trustworthy, of good conduct and character, and of complete and unswerving loyalty to the United States; and

WHEREAS the American tradition that all persons should receive fair, impartial, and equitable treatment at the hands of the Government requires that all persons seeking the privilege of employment or privileged to be employed in the departments and agencies of the Government be adjudged by mutually consistent and no less than minimum standards and procedures among the departments and agencies governing the employment and retention in employment of persons in the Federal service:

NOW, THEREFORE, by virtue of the authority vested in me by the Constitution and the statutes of the United States, including section 1753 of the Revised Statutes of the United States (5 U. S. C. 631); the Civil Service Act of 1883 (22 Stat. 403; 5 U. S. C. 632, *et seq.*); section 9A of the act of August 2,1939, 53 Stat. 1148 (5 U. S. C. 118 j) ; and the act of August 26, 1950, 64 Stat. 476 (5 U. S. C. 22-1, et seq.), and as President of the United States, and deeming such action necessary in the best interests of the national security, it is hereby ordered as follows:

SEC. 1. In addition to the departments and agencies specified in the said act of August 26, 1950, and Executive Order No. 10237[1] of April 26, 1951, the provisions of that act shall apply to all other departments and agencies of the Government.

SEC. 2. The head of each department and agency of the Government shall be responsible for establishing and maintaining within his department or agency an effective program to insure that the employment and retention in employment of any civilian officer or employee

---

[1]3 CFR, 1951 Supp., p. 430

307

within the department or agency is clearly consistent with the interests of the national security.

SEC. 3.   (a) The appointment of each civilian officer or employee in any department or agency of the Government shall be made subject to investigation. The scope of the investigation shall be determined in the first instance according to the degree of adverse effect the occupant of the position sought to be filled could bring about, by virtue of the nature of the position, on the national security, but in no event shall the investigation include less than a national agency check (including a check of the fingerprint files of the Federal Bureau of Investigation), and written inquiries to appropriate local law-enforcement agencies, former employers and supervisors, references, and schools attended by the person under investigation: Provided, that upon request of the head of the department or agency concerned, the Civil Service Commission may, in its discretion, authorize such less investigation as may meet the requirements of the national security with respect to per-diem, intermittent, temporary, or seasonal employees, or aliens employed outside the United States. Should there develop at any stage of investigation information indicating that the employment of any such person may not be clearly consistent with the interests of the national security, there shall be conducted with respect to such person a full field investigation, or such less investigation as shall be sufficient to enable the head of the department or agency concerned to determine whether retention of such person is clearly consistent with the interests of the national security.

(b) The head of any department or agency shall designate, or cause to be designated, any position within his department or agency the occupant of which could bring about. by virtue of the nature of the position, a material adverse effect on the national security as a sensitive position. Any position so designated shall be filled or occupied only by a person with respect to whom a full field investigation has been conducted: *Provided*, that a person occupying a sensitive position at the time it is designated as such may continue to occupy such position pending the completion of a full field investigation, subject to the other provisions of this order: *And provided further*, that in case of emergency a sensitive position may be filled for a limited period by a person with respect to whom a full field pre-appointment investigation has not been completed if the head of the department or agency concerned finds that such action is necessary in the national interest, which finding shall be made a part of the records of such department or agency.

SEC. 4. The head of each department and agency shall review, or cause to be reviewed, the cases of all civilian officers and employees with respect to whom there has been conducted a full field investigation under Executive Order No. 9835[2] of March 21, 1947, and, after such further investigation as may be appropriate, shall re-adjudicate, or cause to be re-adjudicated, in accordance with the said act of August 26, 1950, such of those cases as have not been adjudicated under a security standard commensurate with that established under this order.

SEC. 5. Whenever there is developed or received by any department or agency information indicating that the retention in employment of any officer or employee of the Government may not be clearly consistent with the interests of the national security, such information shall be forwarded to the head of the employing department or agency or his representative, who, after such investigation as may be appropriate, shall review, or cause to be reviewed, and, where necessary, re-adjudicate, or cause to be re-adjudicated, in accordance with the said act of August 26. 1950, the case of such officer or employee.

SEC. 6. Should there develop at any stage of investigation information indicating that the employment of any officer or employee of the Government may not be clearly consistent with the interests of the national security, the head of the department or agency concerned or his representative shall immediately suspend the employment of the person involved if he deems such suspension necessary in the interests of the national security and, following such investigation and review as he deems necessary, the head of the department or agency concerned shall terminate the employment of such suspended officer or employee whenever he shall determine such termination necessary or advisable in the interests of the national security, in accordance with the said act of August 26, 1950.

SEC. 7. Any person whose employment is suspended or terminated under the authority granted to heads of departments and agencies by or in accordance with the said act of August 26. 1950, or pursuant to the said Executive Order No. 9835 or any other security or loyalty program relating to officers or employees of the Government, shall not be reinstated or restored to duty or re-employed in the same department or agency and shall not be re-employed in any other department or agency, unless the head of the department or agency concerned finds that such reinstatement, restoration, or reemployment is clearly consistent with the interests of the national security, which finding shall be

---

[2] 3 CFR, 1947 Supp.

made a part of the records of such department or agency: Provided, that no person whose employment has been terminated under such authority thereafter may be employed by any other department or agency except after a determination by the Civil Service Commission that such person is eligible for such employment.

SEC. 8.   (a) The investigations conducted pursuant to this order shall be designed to develop information as to whether the employment or retention in employment in the Federal service of the person being investigated is clearly consistent with the interests of the national security. Such information shall relate, but shall not be limited, to the following:

(1) Depending on the relation of the Government employment to the national security:

(i) Any behavior, activities, or associations which tend to show that the individual is not reliable or trustworthy.

(ii) Any deliberate misrepresentations, falsifications, or omissions of material facts.

(iii) Any criminal, infamous, dishonest, immoral, or notoriously disgraceful conduct, habitual use of intoxicants to excess, drug addiction, sexual perversion, or financial irresponsibility.

(iv) An adjudication of insanity, or treatment for serious mental or neurological disorder without satisfactory evidence of cure.

(v) Any facts which furnish reason to believe that the individual may be subjected to coercion, influence, or pressure which may cause him to act contrary to the best interests of the national security.

(2) Commission of any act of sabotage, espionage, treason, or sedition, or attempts thereat or preparation therefor, or conspiring with, or aiding or abetting, another to commit or attempt to commit any act of sabotage, espionage, treason, or sedition.

(3) Establishing or continuing a sympathetic association with a saboteur, spy, traitor, seditionist, anarchist, or revolutionist, or with an espionage or other secret agent or representative of a foreign nation, or any representative of a foreign nation whose interests may be inimical to the interests of the United States, or with any person who advocates the use of force or violence to overthrow the government of the United States or the alteration of the form of government of the United States by unconstitutional means.

(4) Advocacy of use of force or violence to overthrow the government of the United States or of the alteration of the form of government of the United States by unconstitutional means.

(5) Membership in, or affiliation or sympathetic association with,

any foreign or domestic organization, association, movement, group, or combination of persons which is totalitarian, Fascist, Communist, or subversive, or which has adopted, or shows, a policy of advocating or approving the commission of acts of force or violence to deny other persons their rights under the Constitution of the United States, or which seeks to alter the form of government of the United States by unconstitutional means.

(6) Intentional, unauthorized disclosure to any person of security information, or of other information disclosure of which is prohibited by law, or willful violation or disregard of security regulations.

(7) Performing or attempting to perform his duties, or otherwise acting, so as to serve the interests of another government in preference to the interests of the United States.

(b) The investigation of persons entering or employed in the competitive service shall primarily be the responsibility of the Civil Service Commission, except in cases in which the head of a department or agency assumes that responsibility pursuant to law or by agreement with the Commission. The Commission shall furnish a full investigative report to the department or agency concerned.

(c) The investigation of persons (including consultants, however employed), entering employment of, or employed by, the Government other than in the competitive service shall primarily be the responsibility of the employing department or agency. Departments and agencies without investigative facilities may use the investigative facilities of the Civil Service Commission, and other departments and agencies may use such facilities under agreement with the Commission.

(d) There shall be referred promptly to the Federal Bureau of Investigation all investigations being conducted by any other agencies which develop information indicating that an individual may have been subjected to coercion, influence, or pressure to act contrary to the interests of the national security, or information relating to any of the matters described in subdivisions (2) through (7) of subsection (a) of this section. In cases so referred to it, the Federal Bureau of Investigation shall make a full field investigation.

SEC. 9.   (a) There shall be established and maintained in the Civil Service Commission a security-investigations index covering all persons as to whom security investigations have been conducted by any department or agency of the Government under this order. The central index established and maintained by the Commission under Executive Order No. 9835 of March 21, 1947, shall be made a part of the security-investigations index. The security-investigations index shall contain the name of each person investigated, adequate identifying information concerning each such person, and a reference to each department and agency which has conducted an investigation concerning the person involved or has suspended or terminated the employment of such person under the authority granted to heads of departments and agencies by or in accordance with the said act of August 26, 1950.

(b) The heads of all departments and agencies shall furnish promptly to the Civil Service Commission information appropriate for the establishment and maintenance of the security-investigations Index.

(c) The reports and other investigative material and information developed by investigations conducted pursuant to any statute, order, or program described in section 7 of this order shall remain the property of the investigative agencies conducting the investigations, but may, subject to considerations of the national security, be retained by the department or agency concerned. Such reports and other investigative material and information shall be maintained in confidence. and no access shall be given thereto except, with the consent of the investigative agency concerned, to other departments and agencies conducting security programs under the authority granted by or in accordance with the said act of August 26, 1950, as may be required for the efficient conduct of Government business.

SEC. 10. Nothing in this order shall be construed as eliminating or modifying in any way the requirement for any investigation or any determination as to security which may be required by law.

SEC. 11. On and after the effective date of this order the Loyalty Review Board established by Executive Order No. 9835 of March 21, 1947, shall not accept agency findings for review, upon appeal or otherwise. Appeals pending before the Loyalty Review Board on such date shall be heard to final determination in accordance with the provisions of the said Executive Order No. 9835, as amended. Agency determinations favorable to the officer or employee concerned pending before the Loyalty Review Board on such date shall be acted upon by such Board, and whenever the Board is not in agreement with such favorable determination the case shall be remanded to the department or agency concerned for determination in accordance with the standards and procedures established pursuant to this order. Cases pending before the regional loyalty boards of the Civil Service Commission on which hearings have not been initiated on such date shall be referred to the department or agency concerned. Cases being heard by regional loyalty boards on such date shall be heard to conclusion and the determination of the board shall be forwarded to the head of the department or agency concerned: *Provided*, that if no specific department or agency is involved, the case shall be dismissed without prejudice to the applicant. Investigations pending in the Federal Bureau of Investigation or the Civil Service Commission on such date shall be completed, and the reports thereon shall be made to the appropriate department or agency.

SEC. 12. Executive order No. 9835 of March 21, 1947, as amended, is hereby revoked. For the purposes described in section 11 hereof the Loyalty Review Board and the regional loyalty boards of the Civil Service Commission shall continue to exist and function for a period of one hundred and twenty days from the effective date of this order, and the Department of Justice shall continue to furnish the information described in paragraph 3 of Part III of the said Executive Order No. 9835, but directly to the head of each department and agency.

SEC. 13. The Attorney General is requested to render to the heads of departments and agencies such advice as may be requisite to enable them to establish and maintain an appropriate employee-security program.

SEC. 14. (a) The Civil Service Commission, with the continuing advice and collaboration of representatives of such departments and agencies as the National Security Council may designate, shall make a continuing study of the manner in which this order is being implemented by the departments and agencies of the Government for the purpose of determining:

(1) Deficiencies in the department and agency security programs established under this order which are inconsistent with the interests of, or directly or indirectly weaken, the national security.

(2) Tendencies in such programs to deny to individual employees fair, impartial, and equitable treatment at the hands of the Government, or rights under the Constitution and laws of the United States or this order.

Information affecting any department or agency developed or received during the course of such continuing study shall be furnished immediately to the head of the department or agency concerned. The Civil Service Commission shall report to the National Security Council, at least semiannually, on the results of such study, and shall recommend means to correct any such deficiencies or tendencies.

(b) All departments and agencies of the Government are directed to cooperate with the Civil Service Commission to facilitate the accomplishment of the responsibilities assigned to it by subsection (a).of this section.

SEC. 15. This order shall become effective thirty days after the date hereof.

DWIGHT D. EISENHOWER

THE WHITE HOUSE,
April 27, 1953.

APPENDIX C

1954 MEMORANDUM REGARDING "NUMBERS GAME" AND QUALIFICATIONS OF HEARING BOARD MEMBERS

November 30, 1954

To: Mr. Schmidt

From: George P. Morse

In accordance with your request, the following suggestions are made with a view to possible improvements in the present government security program:

I. HEARING BOARD PROCEDURES

(a) At the present time, those individuals who serve as Hearing Board members frequently do not have sufficient time to devote to study of the case which they are to hear; are not sufficiently trained and grounded in loyalty, subversive, and security matters to hear the case; and their judgments do not have any final effect on the action which will ultimately be taken since their opinions are only advisory.

It is therefore recommended that permanent panels be established, made up of board members whose sole or primary responsibility is to hear security cases. These individuals should be trained in the subject matter and their determinations, wherever possible, be final.

II. RECORD KEEPING AND STATISTICAL REPORTING

(a) For over a year, we have been recording and reporting cases in our statistics which have obviously not been security cases, nor has the action been taken by the Security Office. Such cases involve suitability matters in connection with occupants of non-sensitive positions, reductions-in-force, retirements, resignations, etc. The review of the Form 77 should go a long way to correct this practice.

It is recommended that only those cases in which the action was taken pursuant to E. O. 10450 be recorded under the sections relating to removals and adverse security actions.

(b) In cases where individuals are neither applicants nor incumbents of positions requiring security clearance or sensitive position clearance, and where there is no subversion involved, it is recommended that the termination of the individuals not be recorded in the security statistics unless action was taken under the provisions of E. O. 10450.

(c) In cases where an individual has voluntarily terminated his employment, it is recommended that there be no tabulation in our statistics which would reflect a security removal, unless there has been a determination by the Security Office that the individual's continued employment was not clearly consistent with the interests of the national security.

III. Significance From Security Standpoint of Membership in Questionable Organizations Which Have not Been Cited as Subversive by the Attorney General

(a) There has been confusion with regard to the significance that should be attached to membership and activities in organizations which have been characterized as Communist-front organizations by committees of both the Congress and the state legislatures, but which organizations have not been cited as subversive by the Attorney General. The information is ordinarily reported to us by the FBI or other investigative agency, therefore, indicating that they consider the material to be of significance from a subversive standpoint. However, in such cases as the American Labor Party (Manhattan branch), the Progressive Party, and other organizations and publications, we have refrained from pursuing the subject's activities in these organizations, or in giving serious consideration to the significance of his activities therein, because they have not been cited as subversive by the Attorney General.

It is recommended that a clear-cut policy be established, setting forth the significance, if any, of affiliation or activities in these organizations for guidance to the security offices.

IV. Training of Evaluators

(a) The responsibility for evaluating subversive and suitability information in connection with the cases of applicants and employees of the Federal Government is a grave one. Persons who have such responsibilities should be adequately prepared for these assignments by virtue of experience and training.

It is recommended that   a continuing program of training be adopted—government-wide—in order that evaluators be prepared as adequately as possible to carry out their responsibilities.

V.   There have been cases, both in this Department and in other agencies, where individuals have been recorded in our statistics as security removals who have, subsequently, either re-entered on duty with us or with another agency of the government. In other cases, adverse determinations have been made by one agency and a favorable determination by another agency on the same set of facts and, presumably, both determinations recorded in the statistical reports.

(a) It is recommended that the practice be adopted as set forth under II above in order to insure that inaccuracies and inconsistencies do not continue to occur.

APPENDIX D

EXECUTIVE ORDER 10865

SAFEGUARDING CLASSIFIED INFORMATION WITHIN INDUSTRY

WHEREAS it is mandatory that the United States protect itself against hostile or destructive activities by preventing unauthorized disclosure of classified information relating to the national defense; and

WHEREAS it is a fundamental principle of our Government to protect the interests of individuals against unreasonable or unwarranted encroachment; and

WHEREAS I find that the provisions and procedures prescribed by this order are necessary to assure the preservation of the integrity of classified defense information and to protect the national interest; and

WHEREAS I find that those provisions and procedures recognize the interests of individuals affected thereby and provide maximum possible safeguards to protect such interest:

NOW, THEREFORE, under and by virtue of the authority vested in me by the Constitution and statutes of the United States, and as President of the United States and as Commander in Chief of the armed forces of the United States, it is hereby ordered as follows:

SECTION 1.   (a) The Secretary of State, the Secretary of Defense, the Commissioners of the Atomic Energy Commission, the Administrator of the National Aeronautics and Space Administration, and the Administrator of the Federal Aviation Agency, respectively, shall, by regulation, prescribe such specific requirements, restrictions, and other safeguards as they consider necessary to protect (1) releases of classified information to or within United States industry that relate to bidding on, or the negotiation, award, performance, or termination of, contracts with their respective agencies, and (2) other releases of classified information to or within industry that such agencies have responsibility for safeguarding. So far as possible, regulations prescribed by them under this order shall be uniform and provide for full cooperation among the agencies concerned.

(b) Under agreement between the Department of Defense and any other department or agency of the United States, including, but not limited to, those referred to in subsection (c) of this section, regulations

318

prescribed by the Secretary of Defense under subsection (a) of this section may be extended to apply to protect releases (1) of classified information to or within United States industry that relate to bidding on, or the negotiation, award, performance, or termination of, contracts with such other department or agency, and (2) other releases of classified information to or within industry which such other department or agency has responsibility for safeguarding.

(c) When used in this order, the term "head of a department' means the Secretary of State, the Secretary of Defense, the Commissioners of the Atomic Energy Commission, the Administrator of the National Aeronautics and Space Administration, the Administrator of the Federal Aviation Agency, and, in sections 4 and 8, includes the Attorney General. The term "department" means the Department of State, the Department of Defense, and the Atomic Energy Commission, the National Aeronautics and Space Administration, the Federal Aviation Agency, and in sections 4 and 8, includes the Department of Justice.

SECTION 2. An authorization for access to classified information may be granted by the head of a department or his designee, including, but not limited to, those officials named in section 8 of this order, to an individual, hereinafter termed an "applicant", for a specific classification category only upon a finding that it is clearly consistent with the national interest to do so.

SECTION 3. Except as provided in section 9 of this order, an authorization for access to a specific classification category may not be finally denied or revoked by the head of a department or his designee, including, but not limited to, those officials named in section 8 of this order, unless the applicant has been given the following:

(1) A written statement of the reasons why his access authorization may be denied or revoked, which shall be as comprehensive and detailed as the national security permits.

(2) A reasonable opportunity to reply in writing under oath or affirmation to the statement of reasons.

(3) After he has filed under oath or affirmation a written reply to the statement of reasons, the form and sufficiency of which may be prescribed by regulations issued by the head of the department concerned, an opportunity to appear personally before the head of the department concerned or his designee, including, but not limited to, those officials named in section 8 of this order, for the purpose of supporting his eligibility for access authorization and to present evidence on his behalf.

(4) A reasonable time to prepare for that appearance.

(5) An opportunity to be represented by counsel.

(6) An opportunity to cross-examine persons either orally or through written interrogatories in accordance with section 4 on matters not relating to the characterization in the statement of reasons of any organization or individual other than the applicant.

(7) A written notice of the final decision in his case which, if adverse, shall specify whether the head of the department or his designee, including, but not limited to, those officials named in section 8 of this order, found for or against him with respect to each allegation in the statement of reasons.

SECTION 4.   (a) An applicant shall be afforded an opportunity to cross-examine persons who have made oral or written statements adverse to the applicant relating to a controverted issue except that any such statement may be received and considered without affording such opportunity in the circumstances described in either of the following paragraphs:

(1) The head of the department supplying the statement certifies that the person who furnished the information is a confidential informant who has been engaged in obtaining intelligence information for the Government and that disclosure of his identity would be substantially harmful to the national interest.

(2) The head of the department concerned or his special designee for that particular purpose has preliminarily determined, after considering information furnished by the investigative agency involved as to the reliability of the person and the accuracy of the statement concerned, that the statement concerned appears to be reliable and material, and the head of the department or such special designee has determined that failure to receive and consider such statement would, in view of the level of access sought, be substantially harmful to the national security and that the person who furnished the information cannot appear to testify (A) due to death, severe illness, or similar cause, in which case the identity of the person and the information to be considered shall be made available to the applicant, or (B) due to some other cause determined by the head of the department to be good and sufficient.

(b) Whenever procedures under paragraph (1) or (2) of subsection (a) of this section are used (1) the applicant shall be given a summary of the information which shall be as comprehensive and detailed as the national security permits, (2) appropriate consideration shall be accorded to the fact that the applicant did not have an opportunity to cross-examine such person or persons, and (3) a final determination adverse to the applicant shall be made only by the head of the department based upon his personal review of the case.

SECTION 5.   (a) Records compiled in the regular course of business, or other physical evidence other than investigative reports, may be received and considered subject to rebuttal without authenticating witnesses, provided that such information has been furnished to the department concerned by an investigative agency pursuant to its responsibilities in connection with assisting the head of the department concerned to safeguard classified information within industry pursuant to this order.

(b) Records compiled in the regular course of business, or other physical evidence other than investigative reports, relating to a controverted issue which, because they are classified, may not be inspected by the applicant, may be received and considered provided that: (1) the head of the department concerned or his special designee for that purpose has made a preliminary determination that such physical evidence appears to be material, (2) the head of the department concerned or such designee has made a determination that failure to receive and consider such physical evidence would, in view of the level of access sought, be substantially harmful to the national security, and (3) to the extent that the national security permits, a summary or description of such physical evidence is made available to the applicant. In every such case, information as to the authenticity and accuracy of such physical evidence furnished by the investigative agency involved shall be considered. In such instances a final determination adverse to the applicant shall be made only by the head of the department based upon his personal review of the case.

SECTION 6. Because existing law does not authorize the Department of State, the Department of Defense, or the National Aeronautics and Space Administration to subpoena witnesses, the Secretary of State, the Secretary of Defense, or the Administrator of the National Aeronautics and Space Administration, or his representative, may issue, in appropriate cases, invitations and requests to appear and testify in order that the applicant may have the opportunity to cross-examine as provided by this order. So far as the national security permits, the head of the investigative agency involved shall cooperate with the Secretary or the Administrator, as the case may be, in identifying persons who have made statements adverse to the applicant and in assisting him in making them available for cross-examination. If a person so invited is an officer or employee of the executive branch of the Government or a member of the armed forces of the United States, the head of the department or agency concerned shall cooperate in making that person available for cross-examination.

SECTION 7. Any determination under this order adverse to an applicant shall be a determination in terms of the national interest and shall in no sense be a determination as to the loyalty of the applicant concerned.

SECTION 8. Except as otherwise specified in the preceding provisions of this order, any authority vested in the head of a department by this order may be delegated to the

(1) Under Secretary of State or a Deputy Under Secretary of State, in the case of authority vested in the Secretary of State;

(2) Deputy Secretary of Defense or an Assistant Secretary of Defense, in the case of authority vested in the Secretary of Defense;

(3) General Manager of the Atomic Energy Commission, in the case of authority vested in the Commissioners of the Atomic Energy Commission;

(4) Deputy Administrator of the National Aeronautics and Space Administration, in the case of authority vested in the Administrator of the National Aeronautics and Space Administration;

(5) Deputy Administrator of the Federal Aviation Agency, in the case of authority vested in the Administrator of the Federal Aviation Agency; or

(6) Deputy Attorney General or an Assistant Attorney General, in the case of authority vested in the Attorney General.

SECTION 9. Nothing contained in this order shall be deemed to limit or affect the responsibility and powers of the head of a department to deny or revoke access to a specific classification category if the security of the nation so requires. Such authority may not be delegated and may be exercised only when the head of a department determines that the procedures prescribed in sections 3, 4, and 5 cannot be invoked consistently with the national security and such determination shall be conclusive.

DWIGHT D. EISENHOWER

THE WHITE HOUSE
February 20, 1960

APPENDIX E

EXECUTIVE ORDER 10909

AMENDMENT OF EXECUTIVE ORDER NO. 10865, SAFEGUARDING CLASSIFIED INFORMATION WITHIN INDUSTRY

By virtue of the authority vested in me by the Constitution and statutes of the United States, and as President of the United States, and as Commander in Chief of the armed forces of the United States, Executive Order No. 10865 of February 20, 1960 (25 F.R. 1583), is hereby amended as follows:

Section 1. Section l(c) is amended to read as follows:

"(c) When used in this order, the term 'head of a department' means the Secretary of State, the Secretary of Defense, the Commissioners of the Atomic Energy Commission, the Administrator of the National Aeronautics and Space Administration, the Administrator of the Federal Aviation Agency, the head of any other department or agency of the United States with which the Department of Defense makes an agreement under subsection (b) of this section, and in sections 4 and 8, includes the Attorney General. The term 'department' means the Department of State, the Department of Defense, the Atomic Energy Commission, the National Aeronautics and Space Administration, the Federal Aviation Agency, any other department or agency of the United States with which the Department of Defense makes an agreement under subsection (b) of this section, and, in sections 4 and 8, includes the Department of Justice.

Section 2. Section 6 is amended to read as follows:

"Section 6. The Secretary of State, the Secretary of Defense, the Administrator of the National Aeronautics and Space Administration, the Administrator of the Federal Aviation Agency, or his representative, or the head of any other department or agency of the United States with which the Department of Defense makes an agreement under section l(b), or his representative, may issue, in appropriate cases, invitations and requests to appear and testify in order that the applicant may have the opportunity to cross-examine as provided by this order. Whenever a witness is so invited or requested to appear and testify at a proceeding and the witness is an officer or employee of the executive branch of the Government or a member of the armed forces of the United States, and the proceeding involves the activity in connection with which the witness is employed, travel expenses and per diem are authorized as provided by the Standard Government Travel Regulations or the Joint Travel Regulations, as appropriate. In all other cases (including non-Government employees as well as officers or employees of the executive branch of the Government or members of the armed forces of the United States not covered by the foregoing sentence), transportation in kind and reimbursement for actual expenses are authorized in an amount not to exceed the amount payable under Standardized Government Travel Regulations. An Officer or employee of the executive branch of the Government or a member of the armed forces of the United States who is invited or requested to appear pursuant to this paragraph shall be deemed to be in the performance of his official duties. So far as the national security permits, the head of the investigative agency involved shall cooperate with the Secretary, the Administrator, or the head of the other department or agency, as the case may be, in identifying persons who have made statements adverse to the applicant and in assisting him in making them available for cross-examination. If a person so invited is an officer or employee of the executive branch of the Government or a member of the armed forces of the United States, the head of the department or agency concerned shall cooperate in making that person available for cross-examination.

Sec. 3. Section 8 is amended by striking out the word "or" at the end of clause (5), by striking out the "period" at the end of clause (6) and inserting "; or," in place thereof, and by adding the following new clause at the end thereof:

"(7) the deputy of that department, or the principal assistant to the head of that department, as the case may be, in the case of authority vested in the head of a department or agency of the United States with which the Department of Defense makes an agreement under section l(b).

DWIGHT D. EISENHOWER

THE WHITE HOUSE
January 17, 1961

APPENDIX F

EXECUTIVE ORDER 12356

National Security Information

This Order prescribes a uniform system for classifying, declassifying, and safeguarding national security information. It recognizes that it is essential that the public be informed concerning the activities of its Government, but that the interests of the United States and its citizens require that certain information concerning the national defense and foreign relations be protected against unauthorized disclosure. Information may not be classified under this Order unless its disclosure reasonably could be expected to cause damage to the national security.

Now, by the authority vested in me as President by the Constitution and laws of the United States of America, it is hereby ordered as follows:

Part 1

Original Classification

Section 1.1 *Classification Levels.*

(a) National security information (hereinafter "classified information) shall be classified at one of the following three levels:

(1) "Top Secret" shall be applied to information, the unauthorized disclosure of which reasonably could be expected to cause exceptionally grave damage to the national security.

(2) "Secret" shall be applied to information, the unauthorized disclosure of which reasonably could be expected to cause serious damage to the national security.

(3) "Confidential" shall be applied to information, the unauthorized disclosure of which reasonably could be expected to cause damage to the national security.

(b) Except as otherwise provided by statute, no other terms shall be used to identify classified information.

(c) If there is reasonable doubt about the need to classify information, it shall be safeguarded as if it were classified pending a determination by an original classification authority, who shall make this determination within thirty (30) days. If there is reasonable doubt about the appropriate level of classification, it shall be safeguarded at the higher level of classification pending a determination by an original classification authority, who shall make this determination within thirty (30) days.

Sec. 1.2 *Classification Authority.*

(a) *Top Secret.* The authority to classify information originally as Top Secret may be exercised only by:

(1) the President;

(2) agency heads and officials designated by the President in the **Federal Register**; and

(3) officials delegated this authority pursuant to Section 1.2(d).

(b) *Secret.* The authority to classify information originally as Secret may be exercised only by:

(1) agency heads and officials designated by the President in the **Federal Register**;

(2) officials with original Top Secret classification authority; and

(3) officials delegated such authority pursuant to Section 1.2(d).

(c) *Confidential.* The authority to classify information originally as confidential may be exercised only by:

(1) agency heads and officials designated by the President in the **Federal Register**;

(2) officials with original Top Secret or Secret classification authority; and

(3) officials delegated such authority pursuant to Section 1.2(d).

(d) *Delegation of Original Classification Authority.*

(1) Delegations of original classification authority shall be limited to the minimum required to administer this Order. Agency heads are responsible for ensuring that designated subordinate officials have a demonstrable and continuing need to exercise this authority.

(2) Original Top Secret classification authority may be delegated only by the President; an agency head or official designated pursuant to Section 1.2(a)(2); and the senior official designated under Section 5.3(a)(1), provided that official has been delegated original Top Secret classification authority by the agency head.

(3) Original Secret classification authority may be delegated only by the President; an agency head or official designated pursuant to Sections 1.2(a)(2) and 1.2(b)(1); an official with original Top Secret classification authority; and the senior official designated under Section 5.3(a)(1), provided that official has been delegated original Secret classification authority by the agency head.

(4) Original Confidential classification authority may be delegated

only by the President; an agency head or official designated pursuant to Sections 1.2(a)(2), 1.2(b)(1) and 1.2(c)(1); an official with original Top Secret classification authority; and the senior official designated under section 5.3(a)(1), provided that official has been delegated original classification authority by the agency head.

(5) Each delegation of original classification authority shall be in writing and the authority shall not be redelegated except as provided in this Order. It shall identify the official delegated the authority by name or position title. Delegated classification authority includes the authority to classify information at the level granted and lower levels of classification.

(e) *Exceptional Cases.* When an employee, contractor, licensee, or grantee of an agency that does not have original classification authority originates information believed by that person to require classification, the information shall be protected in a manner consistent with this Order and its implementing directives. The information shall be transmitted promptly as provided under this Order or its implementing directives to the agency that has appropriate subject matter interest and classification authority with respect to this information. That agency shall decide within thirty (30) days whether to classify this information. If it is not clear which agency has classification responsibility for this information, it shall be sent to the Director of the Information Security Oversight Office. The Director shall determine the agency having primary subject matter interest and forward the information, with appropriate recommendations, to that agency for a classification determination.

Sec. 1.3 *Classification Categories.*

(a) Information shall be considered for classification if it concerns:

(1) military plans, weapons, or operations;

(2) the vulnerabilities or capabilities of systems, installations, projects, or plans relating to the national security;

(3) foreign government information;

(4) intelligence activities (including special activities), or intelligence sources or methods;

(5) foreign relations or foreign activities of the United States;

(6) scientific, technological, or economic matters relating to the national security;

(7) United States Government programs for safeguarding nuclear materials or facilities;

(8) cryptology;

(9) a confidential source; or

(10) other categories of information that are related to the national security and that require protection against unauthorized disclosure as determined by the President or by agency heads or other officials who have been delegated original classification authority by the President. Any determination made under this subsection shall be reported promptly to the Director of the Information Security Oversight Office.

(b) Information that is determined to concern one or more of the categories in Section 1.3(a) shall be classified when an original classification authority also determines that its unauthorized disclosure, either by itself or in the context of other information, reasonably could be expected to cause damage to the national security.

(c) Unauthorized disclosure of foreign government information, the identity of a confidential foreign source, or intelligence sources or methods is presumed to cause damage to the national security.

(d) Information classified in accordance with Section 1.3 shall not be declassified automatically as a result of any unofficial publication or inadvertent or unauthorized disclosure in the United States or abroad of identical or similar information.

Sec. 1.4 *Duration of Classification.*

(a) Information shall be classified as long as required by national security considerations. When it can be determined, a specific date or event for declassification shall be set by the original classification authority at the time the information is originally classified.

(b) Automatic declassification determinations under predecessor orders shall remain valid unless the classification is extended by an authorized official of the originating agency. These extensions may be by individual documents or categories of information. The agency shall be responsible for notifying holders of the information of such extensions.

(c) Information classified under predecessor orders and marked for declassification review shall remain classified until reviewed for declassification under the provisions of this Order.

Sec. 1.5 *Identification and Markings.*

(a) At the time of original classification, the following information shall be shown on the face of all classified documents, or clearly associated with other forms of classified information in a manner appropriate to the medium involved, unless this information itself would reveal a confidential source or relationship not otherwise evident in the document or information:

(1) one of the three classification levels defined in Section 1.1;

(2) the identity of the original classification authority if other than the person whose name appears as the approving or signing official;

(3) the agency and office of origin; and

(4) the date or event for declassification, or the notation "Originating Agency's Determination Required."

(b) Each classified document shall, by marking or other means, indicate which portions are classified, with the applicable classification level, and which portions are not classified. Agency heads may, for good cause, grant and revoke waivers of this requirement for specified classes of documents or information. The Director of the Information Security Oversight Office shall be notified of any waivers.

(c) Marking designations implementing the provisions of this Order, including abbreviations, shall conform to the standards prescribed in implementing directives issued by the Information Security Oversight Office.

(d) Foreign government information shall either retain its original classification or be assigned a United States classification that shall ensure a degree of protection at least equivalent to that required by the entity that furnished the information.

(e) Information assigned a level of classification under predecessor orders shall be considered as classified at that level of classification despite the omission of other required markings. Omitted markings may be inserted on a document by the officials specified in Section 3.1(b).

Sec. 1.6 *Limitations on Classification.*

(a) In no case shall information be classified in order to conceal violations of law, inefficiency, or administrative error; to prevent embarrassment to a person, organization, or agency; to restrain competition; or to prevent or delay the release of information that does not require protection in the interest of national security.

(b) Basic scientific research information not clearly related to the national security may not be classified.

(c) The President or an agency head or official designated under Sections 1.2(a)(2), 1.2(b)(1), or 1.2(c)(1) may reclassify information previously declassified and disclosed if it is determined in writing that (1) the information requires protection in the interest of national security; and (2) the information may reasonably be recovered. These reclassification actions shall be reported promptly to the Director of the Information Security Oversight Office.

(d) Information may be classified or reclassified after an agency has received a request for it under the Freedom of Information Act (5 U.S.C. 552) or the Privacy Act of 1974 (5 U.S.C. 552a), or the mandatory review provisions of this Order (Section 3.4) if such classification meets the requirements of this Order and is accomplished personally and on a document-by-document basis by the agency head, the deputy agency head, the senior agency official designated under Section 5.3(a)(1), or an official with original Top Secret classification authority.

Part 2

Derivative Classification

Sec. 2.1   *Use of Derivative Classification.*

(a) Derivative classification is (1) the determination that information is in substance the same as information currently classified, and (2) the application of the same classification markings. Persons who only reproduce, extract, or summarize classified information, or who only apply classification markings derived from source material or as directed by a classification guide, need not possess original classification authority.

(b) Persons who apply derivative classification markings shall:

(1) observe and respect original classification decisions; and

(2) carry forward to any newly created documents any assigned authorized markings. The declassification date or event that provides the longest period of classification shall be used for documents classified on the basis of multiple sources.

Sec. 2.2   *Classification Guides.*

(a) Agencies with original classification authority shall prepare classification guides to facilitate the proper and uniform derivative classification of information.

(b) Each guide shall be approved personally and in writing by an official who:

(1) has program or supervisory responsibility over the information or is the senior agency official designated under Section 5.3(a)(1); and

(2) is authorized to classify information originally at the highest level of classification prescribed in the guide.

(c) Agency heads may, for good cause, grant and revoke waivers of the requirement to prepare classification guides for specified classes of documents or information. The Director of the Information Security Oversight Office shall be notified of any waivers.

Part 3

Declassification and Downgrading

Sec. 3.1 *Declassification Authority.*

(a) Information shall be declassified or downgraded as soon as national security considerations permit. Agencies shall coordinate their review of classified information with other agencies that have a direct interest in the subject matter. Information that continues to meet the classification requirements prescribed by Section 1.3 despite the passage of time will continue to be protected in accordance with this Order.

(b) Information shall be declassified or downgraded by the official who authorized the original classification, if that official is still serving in the same position; the originator's successor; a supervisory official of either; or officials delegated such authority in writing by the agency head or the senior agency official designated pursuant to Section 5.3(a)(1),

(c) If the Director of the Information Security Oversight Office determines that information is classified in violation of this Order, the Director may require the information to be declassified by the agency that originated the classification. Any such decision by the Director may be appealed to the National Security Council. The information shall remain classified, pending a prompt decision on the appeal.

(d) The provisions of this Section shall also apply to agencies that, under the terms of this Order, do not have original classification authority, but that had such authority under predecessor orders.

Sect. 3.2 *Transferred Information*

(a) In the case of classified information transferred in conjunction with a transfer of functions, and not merely for storage purposes, the receiving agency shall be deemed to be the originating agency for purposes of this Order.

(b) In the case of classified information that is not officially transferred as described in Section 3.2(a), but that originated in an agency that has ceased to exist and for which there is no successor agency, each agency in possession of such information shall be deemed to be the originating agency for purposes of this Order. Such information may be declassified or downgraded by the agency in possession after consultation with any other agency that has an interest in the subject matter of the information.

(c) Classified information accessioned into the National Archives of the United States shall be declassified or downgraded by the Archivist of the United States in accordance with this Order, the directives of the Information Security Oversight Office, and agency guidelines.

Sec. 3.3   *Systematic Review for Declassification.*

(a) The Archivist of the United States shall, in accordance with procedures and timeframes prescribed in the Information Security Oversight Office's directives implementing this Order, systematically review for declassification or downgrading (1) classified records accessioned into the National Archives of the United States, and (2) classified presidential papers or records under the Archivist's control. Such information shall be reviewed by the Archivist for declassification or downgrading in accordance with systematic review guidelines that shall be provided by the head of the agency that originated the information, or in the case of foreign government information, by the Director of the Information Security Oversight Office in consultation with interested agency heads.

(b) Agency heads may conduct internal systematic review programs for classified information originated by their agencies contained in records determined by the Archivist to be permanently valuable but that have not been accessioned into the National Archives of the United States.

(c) After consultation with affected agencies, the Secretary of Defense may establish special procedures for systematic review for declassification of classified cryptologic information, and the Director of Central Intelligence may establish special procedures for systematic review for declassification of classified information pertaining to intelligence activities (including special activities), or intelligence sources or methods.

Sec. 3.4   *Mandatory Review for Declassification.*

(a) Except as provided in Section 3.4(b), all information classified under this Order or predecessor orders shall be subject to a review for declassification by the originating agency, if:

(1) the request is made by a United States citizen or permanent resident alien, a federal agency, or a State or local government; and

(2) the request describes the document or material containing the information with sufficient specificity to enable the agency to locate it with a reasonable amount of effort.

(b) Information originated by a President, the White House Staff, by committees, commissions, or boards appointed by the President, or others specifically providing advice and counsel to a President or acting on behalf of a President is exempted from the provisions of Section 3.4(a). The Archivist of the United States shall have the authority to review, downgrade and declassify information under the control of the Administrator of General Services or the Archivist pursuant to sections 2107, 2107 note, or 2203 of title 44, United States Code. Review procedures developed by the Archivist shall provide for consultation with agencies having primary subject matter interest and shall be consistent with the provisions of applicable laws or lawful agreements that pertain to the respective presidential papers or records. Any decision by the Archivist may be appealed to the Director of the Information Security Oversight Office. Agencies with primary subject matter interest shall be notified promptly of the Director's decision on such appeals and may further appeal to the National Security Council. The information shall remain classified pending a prompt decision on the appeal.

(c) Agencies conducting a mandatory review for declassification shall declassify information no longer requiring protection under this Order. They shall release this information unless withholding is otherwise authorized under applicable law.

(d) Agency heads shall develop procedures to process requests for the mandatory review of classified information. These procedures shall apply to information classified under this or predecessor orders. They shall also provide a means for administratively appealing a denial of a mandatory review request.

(e) The Secretary of Defense shall develop special procedures for the review of cryptologic information, and the Director of Central Intelligence shall develop special procedures for the review of information pertaining to intelligence activities (including special activities), or intelligence sources or methods, after consultation with affected agencies. The Archivist shall develop special procedures for the review of information accessioned into the National Archives of the United States.

(f) In response to a request for information under the Freedom of Information Act, the Privacy Act of 1974, or the mandatory review provisions of this Order:

(1) An agency shall refuse to confirm or deny the existence or non-existence of requested information whenever the fact of its existence or non-existence is itself classifiable under this Order.

(2) When an agency receives any request for documents in its custody that were classified by another agency, it shall refer copies of the request and the requested documents to the originating agency for processing, and may, after consultation with the originating agency, inform the requester of the referral. In cases in which the originating agency determines in

writing that a response under Section 3.4(f)(l) is required, the referring agency shall respond to the requester in accordance with that Section.

Part 4

Safeguarding

Sec. 4.1   *General Restrictions on Access.*

(a) A person is eligible for access to classified information provided that a determination of trustworthiness has been made by agency heads or designated officials and provided that such access is essential to the accomplishment of lawful and authorized Government purposes.

(b) Controls shall be established by each agency to ensure that classified information is used, processed, stored, reproduced, transmitted, and destroyed only under conditions that will provide adequate protection and prevent access by unauthorized persons.

(c) Classified information shall not be disseminated outside the executive branch except under conditions that ensure that the information will be given protection equivalent to that afforded within the executive branch.

(d) Except as provided by directives issued by the President through the National Security Council, classified information originating in one agency may not be disseminated outside any other agency to which it has been made available without the consent of the originating agency. For purposes of this Section, the Department of Defense shall be considered one agency.

Sec. 4.2   *Special Access Programs.*

(a) Agency heads designated pursuant to Section 1.2(a) may create special access programs to control access, distribution, and protection of particularly sensitive information classified pursuant to this Order or predecessor orders. Such programs may be created or continued only at the written direction of these agency heads. For special access programs pertaining to intelligence activities (including special activities but not including military, operational, strategic and tactical programs), or intelligence sources or methods, this function will be exercised by the Director of Central Intelligence.

(b) Each agency head shall establish and maintain a system of accounting for special access programs. The Director of the Information Security Oversight Office, consistent with the provisions of Section 5.2(b)(4), shall have nondelegable access to all such accountings.

Sec. 4.3 *Access by Historical Researchers and Former Presidential Appointees.*

(a) The requirement in Section 4.1(a) that access to classified information may be granted only as is essential to the accomplishment of authorized and lawful Government purposes may be waived as provided in Section 4.3(b) for persons who:

(1) are engaged in historical research projects, or

(2) previously have occupied policy-making positions to which they were appointed by the President.

(b) Waivers under Section 4.3(a) may be granted only if the originating agency:

(1) determines in writing that access is consistent with the interest of national security;

(2) takes appropriate steps to protect classified information from unauthorized disclosure or compromise, and ensures that the information is safeguarded in a manner consistent with this Order; and

(3) limits the access granted to former presidential appointees to items that the person originated. reviewed, signed, or received while serving as a presidential appointee.

Part 5

Implementation and Review

Sec. 5.1 *Policy Direction.*

(a) The National Security Council shall provide overall policy direction for the information security program.

(b) The Administrator of General Services shall be responsible for implementing and monitoring the program established pursuant to this Order. The Administrator shall delegate the implementation and monitorship functions of this program to the Director of the Information Security Oversight Office.

Sec. 5.2 *Information Security Oversight Office.*

(a) The Information Security Oversight Office shall have a full-time Director appointed by the Administrator of General Services subject to approval by the President. The Director shall have the authority to appoint a staff for the Office.

(b) The Director shall:

(1) develop, in consultation with the agencies, and promulgate, subject to the approval of the National Security Council, directives for

the implementation of this Order, which shall be binding on the agencies;

(2) oversee agency actions to ensure compliance with this Order and implementing directives;

(3) review all agency implementing regulations and agency guidelines for systematic declassification review. The Director shall require any regulation or guideline to be changed if it is not consistent with this Order or implementing directives. Any such decision by the Director may be appealed to the National Security Council. The agency regulation or guideline shall remain in effect pending a prompt decision on the appeal;

(4) have the authority to conduct on-site reviews of the information security program of each agency that generates or handles classified information and to require of each agency those reports, information, and other cooperation that may be necessary to fulfill the Director's responsibilities. If these reports, inspections, or access to specific categories of classified information would pose an exceptional national security risk, the affected agency head or the senior official designated under Section 5.3(a)(1) may deny access. The Director may appeal denials to the National Security Council. The denial of access shall remain in effect pending a prompt decision on the appeal;

(5) review requests for original classification authority from agencies or officials not granted original classification authority and, if deemed appropriate, recommend presidential approval;

(6) consider and take action on complaints and suggestions from persons within or outside the Government with respect to the administration of the information security program;

(7) have the authority to prescribe, after consultation with affected agencies, standard forms that will promote the implementation of the information security program;

(8) report at least annually to the President through the National Security Council on the implementation of this Order; and

(9) have the authority to convene and chair interagency meetings to discuss matters pertaining to the information security program.

Sec. 5.3 *General Responsibilities.*

Agencies that originate or handle classified information shall:

(a) designate a senior agency official to direct and administer its information security program, which shall include an active oversight and security education program to ensure effective implementation of this Order;

(b) promulgate implementing regulations. Any unclassified regulations that establish agency information security policy shall be published in the **Federal Register** to the extent that these regulations affect members of the public;

(c) establish procedures to prevent unnecessary access to classified information, including procedures that (i) require that a demonstrable need for access to classified information is established before initiating administrative clearance procedures, and (ii) ensure that the number of persons granted access to classified information is limited to the minimum consistent with operational and security requirements and needs; and

(d) develop special contingency plans for the protection of classified information used in or near hostile or potentially hostile areas.

Sec. 5.4 *Sanctions.*

(a) If the Director of the Information Security Oversight Office finds that a violation of this Order or its implementing directives may have occurred, the Director shall make a report to the head of the agency or to the senior official designated under Section 5.3(a)(1) so that corrective steps, if appropriate, may be taken.

(b) Officers and employees of the United States Government, and its contractors, licensees, and grantees shall be subject to appropriate sanctions if they:

(1) knowingly, willfully, or negligently disclose to unauthorized persons information properly classified under this Order or predecessor orders;

(2) knowingly and willfully classify or continue the classification of information in violation of this Order or any implementing directive; or

(3) knowingly and willfully violate any other provision of this Order or implementing directive.

(c) Sanctions may include reprimand, suspension without pay, removal, termination of classification authority, loss or denial of access to classified information, or other sanctions in accordance with applicable law and agency regulation.

(d) Each agency head or the senior official designated under Section 5.3(a)(1) shall ensure that appropriate and prompt corrective action is taken whenever a violation under Section 5.4(b) occurs. Either shall ensure that the Director of the Information Security Oversight Office is promptly notified whenever a violation under Section 5.4(b) (1) or (2) occurs.

Part 6

General Provisions

Sec. 6.1 *Definitions.*

(a) "Agency" has the meaning provided at 5 U.S.C. 552(e).

(b) "Information" means any information or material, regardless of its physical form or characteristics, that is owned by, produced by or for, or is under the control of the United States Government.

(c) "National security information" means information that has been determined pursuant to this Order or any predecessor order to require protection against unauthorized disclosure and that is so designated.

(d) "Foreign government information" means:

(1) information provided by a foreign government or governments, an international organization of governments, or any element thereof with the expectation, expressed or implied, that the information, the source of the information, or both, are to be held in confidence; or

(2) information produced by the United States pursuant to or as a result of a joint arrangement with a foreign government or governments or an international organization of governments, or any element thereof, requiring that the information, the arrangement, or both, are to be held in confidence.

(e) "National security" means the national defense or foreign relations of the United States.

(f) "Confidential source" means any individual or organization that has provided, or that may reasonably be expected to provide, information to the United States on matters pertaining to the national security with the expectation, expressed or implied, that the information or relationship, or both, be held in confidence.

(g) "Original classification" means an initial determination that information requires, in the interest of national security, protection against unauthorized disclosure, together with a classification designation signifying the level of protection required.

Sec. 6.2 *General.*

(a) Nothing in this Order shall supersede any requirement made by or under the Atomic Energy Act of 1954, as amended. "Restricted Data" and "Formerly Restricted Data" shall be handled. protected, classified, downgraded, and declassified in conformity with the provisions of the Atomic Energy Act of 1954, as amended, and regulations issued under that Act.

(b) The Attorney General, upon request by the head of an agency or the Director of the Information Security Oversight Office, shall render an interpretation of this Order with respect to any question arising in the course of its administration.

(c) Nothing in this Order limits the protection afforded any information by other provisions of law.

(d) Executive Order No. 12065 of June 28, 1978, as amended, is revoked as of the effective date of this Order.

(e) This Order shall become effective on August 1, 1982.

RONALD REAGAN

THE WHITE HOUSE
April 2, 1982.

APPENDIX G

EXECUTIVE ORDER 12829

NATIONAL INDUSTRIAL SECURITY PROGRAM

This order establishes a National Industrial Security Program to safeguard Federal Government classified information that is release to contractors, licensees, and grantees of the United States Government. To promote our national interests, the United States Government issues contracts, licenses, and grants to nongovernment organizations. When these arrangements require access to classified information, the national security requires that this information be safeguarded in a manner equivalent to its protection within the executive branch of Government. The national security also requires that our industrial security program promote the economic and technological interests of the United States. Redundant, overlapping, or unnecessary requirements impede those interests. Therefore, the National Industrial Security Program shall serve as a single, integrated, cohesive industrial security program to protect classified information and to preserve our Nation's economic and technological interests.

Therefore, by the authority vested in me as President by the Constitution and the laws of the United States of America, including the Atomic Energy Act of 1954, as amended (42 U.S.C. 2011-2286), the National Security Act of 1947, as amended (codified as amended in scattered sections of the United States Code), and the Federal Advisory Committee Act, as amended (5 U.S.C. App. 2), it is hereby ordered as follows:

Part 1. Establishment and policy

Section 101. *Establishment.*

(a) There is established a National Industrial Security Program. The purpose of this program is to safeguard classified information that may be released or has been released to current, prospective, or former contractors, licensees, or grantees of United States agencies. For the purposes of this order, the terms "contractor, licensee, or grantee means current, prospective, or former contractors, licensees, or grantees of United

States agencies. The National Industrial Security Program shall be applicable to all executive branch departments and agencies.

(b) The National Industrial Security Program shall provide for the protection of information classified pursuant to Executive Order No. 12356 of April 2, 1982, or its successor, and the Atomic Energy Act of 1954, as amended.

(c) For the purposes of this order, the term "contractor" does not include individuals engaged under personal services contracts.

Sec. 102. *Policy Direction.*

(a) The National Security Council shall provide overall policy direction for the National Industrial Security Program.

(b) The Director of the Information Security Oversight Office, established under Executive Order No. 12356 of April 2, 1982, shall be responsible for implementing and monitoring the National Industrial Security Program and shall:

(1) develop, in consultation with the agencies, and promulgate subject to the approval of the National Security Council, directives for the implementation of this order, which shall be binding on the agencies;

(2) oversee agency, contractor, licensee, and grantee actions to ensure compliance with this order and implementing directives;

(3) review all agency implementing regulations, internal rules, or guidelines. The Director shall require any regulation, rule, or guideline to be changed if it is not consistent with this order or implementing directives. Any such decision by the Director may be appealed to the National Security Council. The agency regulation, rule, or guideline shall remain in effect pending a prompt decision on the appeal;

(4) have the authority, pursuant to terms of applicable contracts, licenses, grants, or regulations, to conduct on-site reviews of the implementation of the National Industrial Security Program by each agency, contractor, licensee, and grantee that has access to or stores classified information and to require of each agency, contractor, licensee, and grantee those reports, information, and other cooperation that may be necessary to fulfill the Director's responsibilities. If these reports, inspections, or access to specific classified information, or other forms of cooperation, would pose an exceptional national security risk, the affected agency head or the senior official designated under section 203(a) of this order may request the National Security Council to deny access to the Director. The Director shall not have access pending a prompt decision by the National Security Council;

(5) report any violations of this order or its implementing directives to the head of the agency or to the senior official designated under section 203(a) of this order so that corrective action, if appropriate, may be taken. Any such report pertaining to the implementation of the National Industrial Security Program by a contractor, licensee, or grantee shall be directed to the agency that is exercising operational oversight over the contractor, licensee, or grantee under section 202 of this order;

(6) consider and take action on complaints and suggestions from persons within or outside the Government with respect to the administration of the National Industrial Security Program;

(7) consider, in consultation with the advisory committee established by this order, affected agencies, contractors, licensees, and grantees, and recommend to the President through the National Security Council changes to this order; and

(8) report at least annually to the President through the National Security Council on the implementation of the National Industrial Security Program.

(c) Nothing in this order shall be construed to supersede the authority of the Secretary of Energy or the Nuclear Regulatory Commission under the Atomic Energy Act of 1954, as amended, or the authority of the Director of Central Intelligence under the National Security Act of 1947, as amended, or Executive Order No. 12333 of December 8, 1981.

Sec. 103. *National Industrial Security Program Policy Advisory Committee.*

(a) *Establishment.* There is established the National Industrial Security Program Policy Advisory Committee ("Committee"). The Director of the Information Security Oversight Office shall serve as Chairman of the Committee and appoint the members of the Committee. The members of the Committee shall be the representatives of those departments and agencies most affected by the National Industrial Security Program and nongovernment representatives of contractors, licensees, or grantees involved with classified contracts, licenses, or grants, as determined by the Chairman.

(b) *Functions.*

(1) The Committee members shall advise the Chairman of the Committee on all matters concerning the policies of the National Industrial Security Program, including recommended changes to those policies as reflected in this order, its implementing directives, or the oper-

ating manual established under this order, and serve as a forum to discuss policy issues in dispute.

(2) The Committee shall meet at the request of the Chairman, but at least twice during the calendar year.

(c) *Administration.*

(1) Members of the Committee shall serve without compensation for their work on the Committee. However, nongovernment members may be allowed travel expenses, including per diem in lieu of subsistence, as authorized by law for persons serving intermittently in the Government service (5 U.S.C. 5701—5707).

(2) To the extent permitted by law and subject to the availability of funds, the Administrator of General Services shall provide the Committee with administrative services, facilities, staff, and other support services necessary for the performance of its functions.

(d) *General.* Notwithstanding any other Executive order, the functions of the President under the Federal Advisory Committee Act, as amended, except that of reporting to the Congress, which are applicable to the Committee, shall be performed by the Administrator of General Services in accordance with the guidelines and procedures established by the General Services Administration.

Part 2. Operations

Sec. 201. *National Industrial Security Program Operating Manual.*

(a) The Secretary of Defense, in consultation with all affected agencies and with the concurrence of the Secretary of Energy, the Nuclear Regulatory Commission, and the Director of Central Intelligence, shall issue and maintain a National Industrial Security Program Operating Manual ("Manual"). The Secretary of Energy and the Nuclear Regulatory Commission shall prescribe and issue that portion of the Manual that pertains to information classified under the Atomic Energy Act of 1954, as amended. The Director of Central Intelligence shall prescribe and issue that portion of the Manual that pertains to intelligence sources and methods, including Sensitive Compartmented Information.

(b) The Manual shall prescribe specific requirements, restrictions, and other safeguards that are necessary to preclude unauthorized disclosure and control authorized disclosure of classified information to contractors, licensees, or grantees. The Manual shall apply to the release of classified information during all phases of the contracting process including bidding, negotiation, award, performance, and termination of contracts, the licensing process, or the grant process, with or under the control of departments or agencies.

(c) The Manual shall also prescribe requirements, restrictions, and other safeguards that are necessary to protect special classes of classified information, including Restricted Data, Formerly Restricted Data, intelligence sources and methods information, Sensitive Compartmented Information, and Special Access Program information.

(d) In establishing particular requirements, restrictions, and other safeguards within the Manual, the Secretary of Defense, the Secretary of Energy, the Nuclear Regulatory Commission, and the Director of Central Intelligence shall take into account these factors: (i) the damage to the national security that reasonably could be expected to result from an unauthorized disclosure; (ii) the existing or anticipated threat to the disclosure of information; and (iii) the short- and long-term costs of the requirements, restrictions, and other safeguards.

(e) To the extent that is practicable and reasonable, the requirements, restrictions, and safeguards that the Manual establishes for the protection of classified information by contractors, licensees, and grantees shall be consistent with the requirements, restrictions, and safeguards that directives implementing Executive Order No. 12356 of April 2, 1982, or the Atomic Energy Act of 1954, as amended, establish for the protection of classified information by agencies. Upon request by the Chairman of the Committee, the Secretary of Defense shall provide an explanation and justification for any requirement, restriction, or safeguard that results in a standard for the protection of classified information by contractors, licensees, and grantees that differs from the standard that applies to agencies.

(f) The Manual shall be issued no later than 1 year from the issuance of this order.

Sec. 202. *Operational Oversight.*

(a) The Secretary of Defense shall serve as Executive Agent for inspecting and monitoring the contractors, licensees, and grantees who require or will require access to, or who store or will store classified information; and for determining the eligibility for access to classified information of contractors, licensees, and grantees and their respective employees. The heads of agencies shall enter into agreements with the Secretary of Defense that establish the terms of the Secretary's responsibilities on behalf of these agency heads.

(b) The Director of Central Intelligence retains authority over access to intelligence sources and methods, including Sensitive Compartmented Information. The Director of Central Intelligence may inspect and monitor contractor, licensee, and grantee programs and facilities that involve access to such information or may enter into written agreements with the Secretary of Defense, as Executive Agent, to inspect and monitor these programs or facilities, in whole or in part, on the Director's behalf.

(c) The Secretary of Energy and the Nuclear Regulatory Commission retain authority over access to information under their respective programs classified under the Atomic Energy Act of 1954, as amended. The Secretary or the Commission may inspect and monitor contractor, licensee, and grantee programs and facilities that involve access to such information or may enter into written agreements with the Secretary of Defense, as Executive Agent, to inspect and monitor these programs or facilities, in whole or in part, on behalf of the Secretary or the Commission, respectively.

(d) The Executive Agent shall have the authority to issue, after consultation with affected agencies, standard forms or other standardization that will promote the implementation of the National Industrial Security Program.

Sec. 203. *Implementation.*

(a) The head of each agency that enters into classified contracts, licenses, or grants shall designate a senior agency official to direct and administer the agency's implementation and compliance with the National Industrial Security Program.

(b) Agency implementing regulations, internal rules, or guidelines shall be consistent with this order, its implementing directives, and the Manual. Agencies shall issue these regulations, rules, or guidelines no later than 180 days from the issuance of the Manual. They may incorporate all or portions of the Manual by reference.

(c) Each agency head or the senior official designated under paragraph (a) above shall take appropriate and prompt corrective action whenever a violation of this order, its implementing directives, or the Manual occurs.

(d) The senior agency official designated under paragraph (a) above shall account each year for the costs within the agency associated with the implementation of the National Industrial Security Program. These costs shall be reported to the Director of the Information Security Oversight Office, who shall include them in the reports to the President prescribed by this order.

(e) The Secretary of Defense, with the concurrence of the Administrator of General Services, the Administrator of the National Aeronautics and Space Administration, and such other agency heads or officials who may be responsible, shall amend the Federal Acquisition Regulation to be consistent with the implementation of the National Industrial Security Program.

(f) All contracts, licenses, or grants that involve access to classified information and that are advertised or proposed following the issuance of agency regulations, rules, or guidelines described in paragraph (b) above shall comply with the Industrial Security Program. To the extent that is feasible, economical, and permitted by law, agencies shall amend, modify, or convert preexisting contracts, licenses, or grants, or previously advertised or proposed contracts, licenses, or grants, that involve access to classified information for operation under the National Industrial Security Program. Any direct inspection or monitoring of contractors, licensees, or grantees specified by this order shall be carried out pursuant to the terms of a contract, license, grant, or regulation.

(g) Executive Order No. 10865 of February 20, 1960, as amended by Executive Order No. 10909 of January 17, 1961, and Executive Order No. 11382 of November 27, 1967, is hereby amended as follows:

(1) Section. 1(a) and (b) are revoked as of the effective date of this order.

(2) Section 1(c) is renumbered as Section 1 and is amended to read as follows:

"**Section 1.** When used in this order, the term 'head of a department' means the Secretary of State, the Secretary of Defense, the Secretary of Transportation, the Secretary of Energy, the Nuclear Regulatory Commission, the Administrator of the National Aeronautics and Space Administration, and, in section 4, the Attorney General. The term 'head of a department' also means the head of any department or agency, including but not limited to those referenced above with whom the Department of Defense makes an agreement to extend regulations prescribed by the Secretary of Defense concerning authorizations for access to classified information pursuant to Executive Order No. 12829."

(3) Section 2 is amended by inserting the words "pursuant to Executive Order No. 12829" after the word "information.

(4) Section 3 is amended by inserting the words "pursuant to Executive Order No. 12829" between the words "revoked" and "by" in the second clause of that section.

(5) Section 6 is amended by striking out the words "The Secretary of State, the Secretary of Defense, the Administrator of the National Aeronautics and Space Administration, the Secretary of Transportation, or his representative, or the head of any other department or agency of the United States with which the Department of Defense makes an agreement under section (1)(b)," at the beginning of the first sentence, and inserting in their place "The head of a department of the United States . . . ."

(6) Section 8 is amended by striking out paragraphs (1) through (7) and inserting in their place ". . . the deputy of that department, or the principal assistant to the head of that department, as the case may be."

(h) All delegations, rules, regulations, orders, directives, agreements, contracts, licenses, and grants issued under preexisting authorities, including section 1(a) and (b) of Executive Order No. 10865 of February 20, 1960, as amended, by Executive Order No. 10909 of January 17, 1961, and Executive Order No. 11382 of November 27, 1967, shall remain in full force and effect until amended, modified, or terminated pursuant to authority of this order.

(i) This order shall be effective immediately.

GEORGE BUSH

THE WHITE HOUSE,
January 6, 1993.

APPENDIX H

January 5, 1949

Mr. Robert L. Bailey
Civil Service Commission
Congressional Contact Representative
House Office Building
Washington, D.C.

Dear Mr. Bailey:

There is set forth below a brief statement of the proposal for the integration of government investigative functions which I verbally outlined to you during our conversation. I will be glad to prepare a much more detailed analysis whenever you desire.

Proposal:

To consolidate in one office or agency all investigative functions concerned with the investigation and clearance of Federal personnel.

Problem:

1. At the present time, there are approximately twenty different governmental offices conducting investigations and handling the security clearances of Federal employees. The result is that scores of thousands of Federal agents are constantly travelling about the country investigating employees and applicants for the Federal government, many of whom have been investigated up to six or seven times; mountainous investigative files are being compiled and maintained by thousands of stenographers, typists, file clerks, administrative and other personnel in millions of feet of space in government buildings; many thousands of dollars are unnecessarily spent in salaries, traveling expenses, per diem, building rents, supplies and equipment, accounting procedures, and personnel operations; and the same witnesses are constantly approached for information previously supplied by them on the same individuals.

2. The present procedure of "Investigation by Confusion and Overlapping" results in a serious security danger because it has repeatedly permitted disloyal and dangerous persons to move from one sensitive and strategic position to another, despite the fact that a previously

employing office was in possession of information sufficient to bar employment or raise serious questions regarding the individual.

3. Each office maintains its own staff of analysts and security "experts" who pass on the loyalty of its applicants. This results frequently in entirely conflicting decisions by two or more agencies on the question of the loyalty or suitability of the same applicants, because they possess only a part of the available information, or have different standards of appraisal. This, too, is a real security danger.

4. The fear of having Congress, the press, or the public learn that their security system has failed to keep out dangerous elements repeatedly results in: 1) Agencies seeking to justify their actions by permitting known disloyal persons to resign and thus obtain other government employment, or 2) Refusal to make available all of the information in their possession to another employing office.

Solution:

Just as the Civil Service Commission is the personnel agency for the entire government, so should there be established an office, either within the Civil Service Commission or an independent agency, to pass on the suitability and loyalty of all personnel and applicants. *One* agency, *one* staff of investigators, analysts, and clerical personnel, *one* set of investigative files, and *one* determination on the basis of *all* available information to establish an individual's right and suitability to work for his government. This office would also pass on the individual's subsequent transfer to another agency and, if necessary, conduct the brief investigation necessary to bring his file up-to-date, but *not* go back to prove birth, education and other information already on file in three, four or seven other government offices. *All* investigative files with *all* the pertinent information in one office, which interprets the data according to *one* set of standards.

The resultant savings in money, time, confusion, personnel, and irritation will total countless millions of dollars, *but above all*, it will plug up the serious loopholes which have permitted persons such as GEORGE SHAW WHEELER, formerly of NLRB, Labor Department, War Production Board, Foreign Economic Administration, and the War Department, to move from one sensitive position to another, even after a thorough investigation had proved beyond a reasonable doubt that his loyalty to the United States was questionable. Incidentally, Mr. Wheeler is now teaching in a University in Prague, Czechoslovakia, under Soviet approval, after having been terminated from his position with the De-

partment of the Army as U.S. representative in the four-power conferences, by the action of a U.S. Congressman.

It should be pointed out that, inasmuch as the Federal Bureau of
Investigation is concerned with the criminal aspects of investigation and
law enforcement, and the above functions are purely applicant investigations, there would be no conflict of functions with the proposed office, and the FBI would be free to carry on its excellent work in the
criminal and law enforcement field.

Thank you very much for your consideration,

Sincerely,

GEORGE P. MORSE

APPENDIX I

Agency Cost Estimates for
Personnel Security Investigations

Executive agency/office	In-house cost	Reimbursement cost[a]	Contract cost	Total
Council of Economic Advisers[b]				
Department of Commerce	$89,500[c]	$964,550	$567,111	$1,621,161[c]
Arms Control and Disarmament Agency	2,699	159,300		161,999
Agency for International Development	686,441	30,957[c]	644,154[c]	1,361,552[c]
Board for International Broadcasting	17,082[c]	2,375		19,457[c]
Central Intelligence Agency[d]				
Department of Defense	180,565,374	9,957,050	2,120,000	192,642,424
Department of Energy	5,116,000	57,289,000	6,663,000	69,068,000
Department of Education		5,000		5,000
Export-Import Bank of the U.S.		87,108		87,108
Farm Credit Administration	8,420[c]	35,925		44,345[c]
Department of Transportation	646,000	1,025,627		1,671,627
Environmental Protection Agency	320,000[c]	677,623		997,623[c]

Executive agency/office	In-house cost	Reimbursement cost[a]	Contract cost	Total
Federal Communications Commission	30,000[c]	16,000		46,000[c]
Federal Emergency Management Agency		382,000		382,000
Federal Reserve System		103,790		103,790
Department of Health and Human Services	53,000	347,700		400,700
Interstate Commerce Commission		44,469		44,469
Department of Interior		2,343[c]		2,343[c]
Department of Labor[b]				
Federal Maritime Commission	125	150		275
General Services Administration	249,069[c]	306,827[c]		555,896[c]
Department of Housing and Urban Development	168,364	675,378		843,742
International Trade Commission		23,000		23,000
Department of Justice	11,349,288[c]	23,142,230[c]	3,986,704[c]	38,478,222[c]
Marine Mammal Commission	17,082[c]	1,350		18,432[c]
Merit Systems Protection Board	629[c]	5,800		6,429[c]
National Aeronautics and Space Administration	785,000	969,050	625,000	2,379,050
Nuclear Regulatory Commission	213,543	526,008	26,889	766,440
National Security Council[b]				
Office of Administration	82,500			82,500

Executive agency/office	In-house cost	Reimbursement cost[a]	Contract cost	Total
Office of Personnel Management	4,725			4,725
National Archives and Records Administration	125,000	262,000		387,000
National Science Foundation		35,000		35,000
Office of Management and Budget	1,000[c]			1,000[c]
Overseas Private Investment Corporation[e]				
Office of the Vice President[b]				
President's Foreign Intelligence Advisory Board[d]				
Small Business Administration		68,775		68,775
Securities and Exchange Commission		24,175		24,175
Department of State	2,055,336	151,000	4,190,000	6,396,336
Tennessee Valley Authority	1,000[c]	6,300		7,300[c]
Office of Science and Technology Policy[b]				
Peace Corps of the U.S.	48,186	14,404	127,513	190,103
President's Intelligence Oversight Board[d]				
Selective Service System	142[c]	186		328[c]
Department of Treasury	472,958[c]	398,412[c]	781,223[c]	1,652,593[c]
Department of Agriculture	177,000	1,561,973		1,738,973
Department of Veterans Affairs		308,500		308,500

Executive agency/office	In-house cost	Reimbursement cost[a]	Contract cost	Total
U.S. Trade Representative		7,825		7,825
U.S. Postal Service	76,510	3,168		79,678
U.S. Information Agency	1,205,017	156,600	465,093	1,826,710
Total	**$204,566,990[c]**	**$99,778,928[c]**	**$20,196,687[c]**	**$324,542,605[c]**

[a]Reimbursement cost to other federal agencies

[b]Agency/office reported zero cost for personnel security investigations.

[c]Figures are estimates submitted by agencies/offices for cost associated with personnel security investigations.

[d]Agency/office did not submit cost figures for personnel security investigations.

[e]Figures were included in the Agency for International Development's totals.

Source: GAO Executive agencies' responses to Personnel Security Investigation and Clearance Questionnaire.

DoD Security Clearance Applications
Most Recent Fiscal Year 1993 Clearance Action

Agency	COLLATERAL CLEARANCES					SCI ACTIONS	
	Top Secret	Secret	Confi-dential	Total	Unfav-orable	Issued	Denied/Revoked
Army	29,382	106,324	4,230	139,936	8,267	27,584	233/305
Navy	24,617	44,753	10,272	79,542	3,144	11,505	45/50
Air Force	46,236	68,639	0	114,875	3,119	27,246	73/15
DIA	3,428	0	0	3,428	4	3,428	0/0
DLA	680	2,011	0	2,671	67	0	0/0
DMA	269	112	0	381	32	0	0/0
DISA	251	215	4	470	1	0	0/0
DNA	95	35	0	130	4	0	0/0
DCAA	34	150	14	198	2	0	0/0
JCS	14	0	0	14	0	0	0/0

Agency	COLLATERAL CLEARANCES					SCI ACTIONS	
	Top Secret	Secret	Confi-dential	Total	Unfav-orable	Issued	Denied/Revoked
OSD (WHS)	895	374	0	1,270	9	0	0/0
DODIG	239	82	0	321	1	0	0/0
DIS	389	60	0	449	15	0	0/0
OSIA	19	32	0	51	1	2	0/0
DFAS	36	224	0	260	9	0	0/0
AAFES	0	2	0	2	0	0	0/0
DISP	23,130	80,804	8,016	111,950	2,128	0	0/0
NSA	0	0	0	0	0	628	160/0
Total	129,595	303,817	22,536	455,948	16,803	70,393	511/370

Source: DoD

Index

357

Biographical Note

George P. (Pat) Morse embarked upon his career in security when he came to Washington from Milwaukee in 1940 as part of President Roosevelt's "War-Preparedness" program.

Early in 1942 he was appointed by the U.S. Civil Service Commission to be the government's youngest security investigator. Persons suspected of Communist affiliations and activities soon became his major field of expertise. His successful investigation of the members of Ware Group of pro-Communists in the government, and particularly of George Shaw Wheeler, who subsequently proved his disloyalty by defecting were of particular note. He also headed the government's program of investigations of persons of Japanese ancestry under the War Relocation Program.

He volunteered for the Army during World War II and was assigned to the Office of Strategic Services (OSS). He served in the War Crimes Section of the OSS in anticipation of the eventual prosecution of Nazi war criminals. He was appointed the aide to OSS Director General William ("Wild Bill") Donovan, who, at the end of the war in Europe, was made deputy prosecutor at Nuremberg, along with Prosecutor Supreme Court Justice Robert H. Jackson, for the trial of the major Nazi war criminals, and Morse was sent to Nuremberg to set up Donovan's office.

After Donovan's departure from Nuremberg, Mr. Morse served as assistant to Rev. Edmund Walsh, S.J., Vice President of Georgetown University, who was charged with preparation of the briefs on Expropriation of the Christian Churches. On completion of their brief, he was appointed executive officer of Section VI of the Legal Staff Trial Organization, Office of U.S. Chief of Counsel, charged with the preparation of the briefs on the Nazi Criminal Organizations (Reich Cabinet, SA, SS, Gestapo, etc.) at the trial of the 24 Major War Criminals before the International Military Tribunal.

After Nuremberg, and while still in the army, Morse served as chief of investigations for the 116th Detachment of the Counter-Intelligence Corps. When the Central Intelligence Group was formed from the SSU (the OSS having been wiped out by President Truman when he removed General Donovan), he joined the fledgling intelligence agency in the Office of Security and Inspections. As chief of the Contact Division, he was responsible for setting up liaison with other intelligence agencies to facilitate access to and exchange of security information. He later headed the covert Operations Control Desk.

In 1951, Mr. Morse was appointed Director of Security for the U.S. Public Health Service and Deputy Director for the Federal Security Agency and later Chief of the Personnel Security Division, Department of Health, Education, and Welfare (HEW), then the government's largest, most complex, and diverse civilian agency, as is its successor agency, the Department of Health and Human Services (HHS) today.

Appointed Director of Protection and Safety Management for the burgeoning National Institutes of Health in 1955, he served there until his retirement from the federal service in 1970, receiving on that occasion a commendation for meritorious service from President Richard M. Nixon.

Mr. Morse is an attorney and a member of the U.S. Supreme Court, the U.S. Circuit Court of Appeals for the District of Columbia, the U.S. District Court of the District of Columbia, the Maryland Supreme Court, and the courts of the District of Columbia. He served as chairman of the American Bar Association's and the District of Columbia Bar Association's Civil Service Law Committees and coordinated the responses of both associations to concerns over the actions of Senator Joseph R. McCarthy of Wisconsin and the abuses which had emerged during the Eisenhower Administration's security program concerning infringements of basic rights and denial of due process.

In the broader area of loss prevention, Mr. Morse has devoted himself to teaching, writing, and consulting on all forms of loss—security, safety, fire prevention, waste, neglect, fraud, abuse, etc.; and to improving managerial and operational performance in both government and the private sector. He is the author of *Protecting the Health Care Institution: A System of Loss Prevention Management Effective for All Industry*, (Williams & Wilkins Co., Baltimore, 1974). Morse continues to direct George P. Morse & Associates, a loss prevention management consulting firm established in 1970.

With his wife, Margaret, he lives in Maryland. Devoted to their Church and faith, Mr. and Mrs. Morse have, for the past ten years, headed an Apostolate, *Catholics Committed To Support The Pope,* which is engaged in the preparation and publication, distributed worldwide, of an eleven-volume series of *Precis of Official Catholic Teaching*, a service which Pope John Paul II has recognized by appointing him a Knight Grand Cross of the order of St. Gregory, the highest honor in the Order, and bestowing upon Margaret the high Papal honor of *Pro Ecclesia et Pontifice.*